Governing the New Europe

Governing the New Europe

Edited by

Jack Hayward and Edward C. Page

Polity Press

First published in 1995 by Polity Press
in association with Blackwell Publishers.

Editorial office:
Polity Press
65 Bridge Street
Cambridge CB2 1UR, UK

Marketing and production:
Blackwell Publishers, the publishing imprint of Basil Blackwell Ltd
108 Cowley Road
Oxford OX4 1JF, UK

ISBN 0 7456 1219 9
ISBN 0 7456 1220 2 (pbk)

A CIP catalogue record for this book is available from the British Library.

Typeset in 10 on 12 pt Bembo
by Best-set Typesetter Ltd., Hong Kong
Printed in Great Britain by Hartnolls Ltd, Bodmin, Cornwall

This book is printed on acid-free paper.

Contents

List of Contributors

Jack Hayward is Professor of Politics, Fellow of St Antony's College and the Director of the Institute of European Studies, University of Oxford.

Jolyon Howorth is Professor of French Civilization at the University of Bath.

Herbert Kitschelt is Professor of Political Science at Duke University.

Marie Lavigne is Professor of Economics at the University of Pau.

Tom Mackie is Senior Lecturer in Government at the University of Strathclyde.

Michael L. Mezey is Professor of Political Science at DePaul University.

Edward C. Page is Professor of Politics at the University of Hull.

Richard Parry is Lecturer in Social Policy at the University of Edinburgh.

Richard Rose is Professor of Politics and Director of the Centre for the Study of Public Policy, University of Strathclyde.

Anthony Smith is Professor of Sociology at the London School of Economics and Political Science.

Alec Stone is Professor of Political Science at the University of California, Irvine.

Introduction
A Plural Europe: Undivided and Unbounded

Jack Hayward and Edward C. Page

Between 1947 and 1989 European politics was dominated by an East–West divide that was geographically identified with a split between the areas dominated by the Soviet Union and the United States superpowers, and ideologically identified with the split between capitalist democracy and communist autocracy. Within each part of Europe there developed separate alliances of states dependent upon each of the superpowers for their security, and closely linked to them economically and culturally. The nature of the dependence was more or less voluntary in the West and compulsory in the East, but for practical purposes communist autocracy was almost as unthinkable in the West as was a capitalist democracy in the East. The economic revival of the West European states was promoted by a benign USA, which actively assisted in the early stages of the forty-year process of integration that led from the European Coal and Steel Community via the European Economic Community and Euratom to the Single Market and the European Union.[1] This was intended both to integrate the Western part of a defeated and divided Germany and to use its reviving strength as a bulwark against the threat of expansion by the Soviet bloc. There, a counteracting and repellant form of integration took place under the malign influence of the USSR, with almost identical political and economic institutions being imposed throughout East-Central Europe in the name of a totalitarian ideology.

Since 1989, the destabilization and then demise of a postwar division of Europe that split a Germany which had attempted to conquer the whole of Europe have detonated the fundamental assumption underlying past analyses of European politics. The implosion and disintegration of the former Soviet superpower, as well as the weakening capacity and will of the USA to assert its position of surviving superpower, have thrown the initiative back to Europe in a way that is unfamiliar to anyone whose political life has been lived entirely in the postwar world. However, it is less strange to those with even an elementary grasp of the last thousand years of European history. Nevertheless, it would be a grave mistake to conceive the new European politics primarily as a return to past delights and poisons. While it is possible that we have not learnt enough from, and forgotten too much about, our recent past, we are still much closer to a shared view about what constitutes the best basis for social, economic and political activity. While this book will be concerned to explore the important and enduring variants from the dominant type of new European politics, it takes as its point of departure the presupposition that the plurality of European states can be treated as aspiring to conform to a common type of political, economic and social system. While a range of options are available within liberal democracy, the regulated market economy and the welfare state, the tendency has been towards convergence rather than divergence owing to objective demographic and technological pressures, the propensity to accept competitive constraints and the attraction of institutional imitation.

To extrapolate from the present, especially in the complex endeavour of cross-national comparison, is to cross a *pons asinorum* with a pretentiousness that vies for folly with its naivety. Accepting that their provisional analyses are based upon a reappraisal of an unpredictable because rapidly shifting subject matter, the authors of this book responded to the exciting challenge to make interim judgements on what is necessarily patchy information. The interplay between re-emerging historical diversities reasserting purported or genuine national interests and the deep-seated countervailing trends towards increased international uniformity create an inescapably confusing, complex picture which we have endeavoured not to oversimplify while being conscious of the need to remain comprehensible. Some of the changes that have occurred cut across all the countries of Europe and are sometimes the causes and sometimes the consequences of the emergence of a single desirable model of a political, economic and social system. They are often the manifestations of near universal tendencies, thereby making Europe itself less specific within the global system. Other changes are particular to the countries of East-Central Europe, as they aspire to become part of a European Union that has a vocation to be continent-wide. The speeds may be different, but the general direction is common. The European Union of which they each seek to become a part is itself struggling to grasp the implications of such enlargement for its institutions, policies and sense of identity, prior to attempting to achieve agreement on the necessary practical actions to be taken. Germany's partners are anxiously wondering how far Thomas Mann's early postwar preference for a European Germany over a German Europe can be successfully sustained in the wake of a reunification that places her once again at the geo-political centre of the continent (Garton Ash 1993, Epilogue).

'What belongs together grows together' was the optimistic saying of Willy Brandt after the fall of the Berlin Wall. Here he was referring to two parts of the same nation which had previously lived for three-quarters of a century within the same state. The two parts of Europe that had been separated by a bigger iron curtain had never been so closely related. To some extent the political systems of most of the parts of Europe which were under Soviet domination for 45 years after the Second World War had always been different from those of many in the West. They had for the first decades of the twentieth century a history of weak economic development; they were states whose borders were defined mainly by military defeat and occupation, which contained a larger or smaller number of more or less mutually antagonistic ethnic groups; and, with the exception of Czechoslovakia, they had no lengthy experience of stable parliamentary self-government.

While the countries of East-Central Europe are currently democratic regimes within a mixed economy, the outcome of social, economic and political reform cannot be predicted, and continued progress towards an established liberal democracy cannot be taken for granted. In some respects the states within this region resemble those of the southern peripheries such as Greece, Portugal and Spain. Both regions had relatively lengthy experience of slow economic development and authoritarian forms of government. In Southern Europe the transition to democracy in the 1970s was both swift and smooth. The East-Central region in the 1990s faces somewhat more severe problems, including ethnic diversity and the wide-scale replacement of state-owned means of production, distribution and exchange by private enterprises.

It is quite possible that East and West Europe might continue to grow together in the sense that their economic, social and political systems will become more similar. They have most certainly grown together in another sense. The component countries of Europe have become more directly interdependent than before in culture, trade and investment as well as in politics. Political interdependence results not only from the prospect of the nations of East-Central Europe belonging to major international organizations such as the European Union and NATO. The collapse of communism also meant changed priorities for Western political systems. One of the clearest examples of this can be seen in the fears among German and French politicians, among others, voiced not only at the time of German unification but also during the debate over the Maastricht Treaty, that open borders with the former communist countries would mean a gradual change in German foreign and trade policy, drawing the most powerful member of the European Union eastwards.

In the study of politics the growing together of Europe after the fall of communism means that it is becoming increasingly less fruitful to look at Western Europe on its own when we come to use comparisons to illustrate, understand and explain the nature and performance of political systems. The East–West split in terms of academic interests was, for the crucial years after the Second World War when political science in Europe and America was expanding, one of the major fault lines in the discipline. East and West specialists were themselves virtually separated by an intellectual iron curtain. The gap was probably smaller in the United States, where the term 'comparative politics' was generally understood to mean comparing all types of political system, whether of developed, developing or communist countries. But it was still there. Even those who subscribed to the most internationalist of theories, Marxism, generally made statements about the condition of 'capitalist' society, such as its impending legitimacy crisis, without bothering to see whether the features they determined as specific to that form of economic system could be found in non-capitalist societies.

Growing closer together does not mean East-Central Europe developing towards a static Western European model. For one thing, as the chapters in this book make clear, there is no one model of West European politics, whether one takes, for example, the parliament, the judiciary, the political parties or the structure of belief systems. Just as important, Western European nations themselves have experienced enormous changes in their political systems over the past few decades. We have gone through massive changes in the structuring of opinions about the political system, and we can list a few of them here. Whether or not one agrees that this has taken the form of a 'silent revolution' (see Chapter 5), the evidence that something has been going on can be seen in the decline in class and religious cohesion in voting patterns. Parties themselves are appearing to become increasingly remote from their electorates. Moreover, basic structures of government are changing. Not only does the development of closer integration within the European Union mean a progressively weaker role for the nation-state, many of the nation-state's institutions are changing largely unprompted by the European Union. For example, courts have grown in importance since the 1970s and the past two or three decades have witnessed a large increase in the number of interest groups regularly consulted by government and in the influence they have been able to exert.

The purpose of this book is not to predict the shape of the new Europe but to offer an outline of the major contours of politics and government within it five years after a turning-point in its development. Most of our contributors have written extensively on Western nations. We asked them to develop their ideas within the context of the rejection of communism and invited them, where appropriate, to see how the countries of East-Central Europe fitted in with, or had to be modified to change, approaches to understanding government and politics which had been developed in the West. The book is divided into three parts. The first, A Constellation of Sovereign States, focuses on the political, economic and cultural development of nation-states within Europe. The second, The Political System at Work, looks at contemporary political behaviour and institutions. The third part, From Leader to Follower, examines trends in the three broad areas that go to make up the priorities of the modern state – 'defining' (foreign and defence policy), 'resource mobilization' (economic and industrial policy) and social policy (Rose 1976).

A wholly satisfactory general comparison of the governments of European states should be able to rely upon the reader's ability to refer to good up-to-date studies of the politics of each of the specific countries. Unfortunately, this is not yet the case for many of the states, particularly but not exclusively of East Europe, and *Governing the New Europe* clearly cannot claim to be a substitute for them. However, in this comprehensive comparison we have drawn upon such information as is currently available in conjunction with the research that our authors have undertaken within their specialist fields. While each of the chapters can be read independently by those wishing to obtain a cross-national perspective combined with some national vignettes on specific aspects of government, they collectively constitute an assessment of both the common and the contrasting predicaments with which contemporary European governments are confronted.

The boundaries of 'Europe' are not specified because they are the shifting subject of dispute – as they have been perennially – lacking any natural confines in the Eurasian East such as the Atlantic Ocean has provided in the West. The countries to which we have usually referred are those that can plausibly lay claim to becoming members of the European Union before the twenty-first century gets well into its stride. While respecting the enduring legacies of the past, *Governing the New Europe* looks forward to the Europe of the future, in which its constituent states will combine the preservation of their plurality with the need to cooperate and integrate their activities when desirable or unavoidable. They will doubtless do so by an untidy amalgam of compromise and coercion, resignation and enthusiasm, as they have so often done in the past, frequently devising the new in reassuringly familiar ways. Europe in the making will be a discontinuous creation, its impetus and direction being determined by the piecemeal conflict and comprehensive complementarities dictated by the interaction between its simultaneously plural and unitary characteristics. It is within this interdependent and unpredictable context that our several attempts to understand the specific problems of government in an unstable Europe should be placed. It is for those directly engaged in political action to grapple with the implications of what Jean Monnet and his associates, those masters of generic innovation in conflict resolution *par le haut*, called 'dynamic disequilibrium'. In the history of the movement from sectoral communities to European Union, that dynamic has been marked by three features: 'Any failure of Community tends to bring back to the surface problems it was designed to settle . . . every move to Europe has tended to create vested interests . . . adequate to prevent movement back . . . what cannot fall back presumably at some point has good chances of moving forward' (Duchêne 1994: 351–2). Although Europe's trajectory is uncertain and has no agreed ultimate destination, it contains an inbuilt if discreet dynamic that will in time overcome the obstinate forces of inertia.

Notes

1 Throughout this book the term 'European Community' (EC) will be used to designate the European Coal and Steel Community established by the 1951 Paris Treaty, as well as the European Economic Community and Euratom established by the 1957 Rome Treaties, whose institutions were partially merged in 1967 creating, above all, a common Commission and Council of Ministers. The institutions of the European Union (EU) established by the 1992 Maastricht Treaty, cover, in addition to the policy areas dealt with by the EC, monetary union, foreign and security policy and law and order.

Bibliography

Duchêne, F. (1994). *Jean Monnet: the first statesman of interdependence*. London and New York: W. W. Norton.

Garton Ash, T. (1993). *In Europe's Name: Germany and the divided continent*. London: Jonathan Cape.

Rose, R. (1976). 'On the priorities of government: a developmental analysis of public policies'. *European Journal of Political Research* 4 (2): 247–89.

Part I

A Constellation of Sovereign States

1

Patterns and Diversity in European State Development

Edward C. Page

Introduction

If you look at the diversity of political systems operating within Europe you might be hard pressed to talk about a European model. The European continent and its islands contain monarchies, republics, federations, unitary systems and systems with forms of decentralization that defy unambiguous categorization, unicameral and bicameral parliaments, figurehead and executive presidents, dominant party, two-party and multi-party systems, states with constitutional courts and states without them. European countries tend to have developed industrial economies and comprehensive welfare provision. Yet on the face of it, to say that a country is in Europe is to say little about its political system. Not only are there diverse institutional arrangements within Europe, but also countries throughout the world borrow and adapt ideas about institutional forms from one another: parliaments, cabinets, civil services, local government structures and constitutional courts among many others have been exported to and imported from other parts of the world. In this environment what is specifically European and what is not are hard to determine.

Why, then, look at Europe? One practical reason for looking at Europe is that growing political integration through expansion of European Community membership and deepening of political and legal ties among members require that we have some understanding of the backgrounds and traditions of policy-makers within present and future EC member states. Important though this reason may be, there is another which helps explain why so many historians, sociologists and political scientists since the early origins of their respective disciplines have given European political institutions an identity of their own: common experiences of political development.

One striking feature of the state within Europe is that many of the most important features shaping this development were widespread. While there exists a variety of different forms of feudal system, the influence of feudalism in social, economic and political organization extended throughout the entire continent, from Spain to the Nordic countries, from Russia to the British Isles; the influence of Roman law in the development of legal systems was variable in impact but nevertheless universal (Vinogradoff 1909); the development of key institutions throughout Europe, such as the separation of royal authority and administration from the household or the emergence of ministerial structures, show common patterns if not identical timing.

Why this commonality should exist is of course a function of physical proximity, geographical position, from which a number of other factors flow: linkages of trade and competition, military rivalry as well as common religious affiliation, and family connections between the rulers of different European territories as well as conscious emulation of countries perceived to be in a similar position.

However, if the process is so similar why do institutions vary so much? The process of state building was not uniform. There were significant differences in timing and the nature of the way in which developments within Europe affected individual territories. Guizot discusses the basic difference between England and continental Europe in the context of the absence of an 'exclusive principle' of political organization in England in contrast with continental European experience. Broadly he suggests that, while on the continent transitions from one form of government to another sweep away the older form entirely, in England much of the older forms is retained. Consequently, 'never has any element completely perished, any new element wholly triumphed or any special principle attained an exclusive preponderance. There has always been a simultaneous development of different forces, a compromise between their pretensions and their interests' (Guizot 1851: 249). Even when royalty triumphed in England under Elizabeth, as in France under Louis XIV, 'the monarchical principle was introduced in England never so completely, so exclusively as upon the continent; the conqueror has always been compelled to tolerate the presence of his rivals, and to allow each his share' (Guizot 1851: 250). This fundamental distinction exists despite the fact that 'the path and goal of development' of England and the continent have been identical. 'Considered in their entirety the Continent and England have traversed the same grand phases of civilization; events have, in either, followed the same course, and the same causes have led to the same effects' (Guizot 1851: 252).

Yet a model that pits England against the rest of Europe is quite limiting (see, for example, Dunleavy 1989). There is a modest but well developed literature which seeks to explain differences in patterns of political development within Europe and puts any apparent English (or French, German, Spanish and so on) exceptionalism within a broader framework. Such frameworks indicate that any features that distinguished one country from another could be found to have been present to a greater or lesser degree in yet other countries and had similar effects there too. Four major theories spring to mind here. The first is Barrington Moore's (1967) *Social Origins of Dictatorship and Democracy*, the second is found in the later work of Stein Rokkan (see the review by Allardt and Valen 1981), the third in Tilly's (1990) *Coercion, Capital and European States*, and the fourth in the writings of Otto Hintze (for a review, see Page 1990). Let us look at each of these in turn.

Theories of European State Development

Barrington Moore's study distinguishes between three 'routes to modern society'. First there was a 'bourgeois-capitalist' path of modernization, a 'democratic route', which 'combined capitalism and democracy after a series of revolutions: the Puritan Revolution, the French Revolution and the American Civil War', and was found above all in England, France and the United States (Moore 1967: 413). Second there was the 'conservative revolution' approach to modernity, above all experienced in Germany, in which a coercive state was the major force for modernization, and modernity was achieved through a 'revolution from above' in the form of a repressive state apparatus. It ended with the development of Fascism. Third there was a path to modernity created through peasant revolutions, of which the major European example is Russia, leading to the development of communism. These models differ above all in the role of the bourgeoisie, the landed aristocracy and peasants in political development – a powerful bourgeoisie is associated with a capitalist route to modernity and thus democracy, a weaker bourgeoisie and powerful landed aristocracy with conservative revolution, and an even weaker bourgeoisie with peasant revolution. Although Moore is rather brief on this question, he suggests that through a process of diffusion and emulation these models shaped institutions in other countries, although he regards the 'spread and reception of institutions that have been hammered out elsewhere' as a rather peripheral concern of his work (Moore 1967: x).

Stein Rokkan's 'conceptual map' of Europe builds on what he identifies as the 'underlying dimension' of Moore's analysis (Rokkan 1973). There are two axes of this map. The East–West axis differentiates between political systems built on surpluses from a 'highly monetized economy' in the West, to those based upon 'surpluses from agricultural labour in the East' (Rokkan 1973: 80). The North–South axis distinguishes between those countries in which the cultural conditions for the development of national identities were more favourable: the dominance of a supra-national church in the Catholic South versus the Protestant North. The North–South axis is central to the process of nation building, that is to say in defining processes of allegiance to or identification with national political organizations. The East–West axis is crucial to the understanding of state formation – the creation of institutions of political authority. At the core of Europe (in the territories which now form northern Italy, west Germany, the Benelux countries and Switzerland) was 'city-state Europe', the heartland of the Western Roman Empire, in which the wealth and strength of cities prevented the emergence of large territorial systems. Instead, states developed on the periphery of this central belt. The 'earliest successes in . . . efforts of system-building at the edges of the old Empire came in the west and in the north, in France and in England, later also in Spain. . . . The second wave . . . took place on the landward side: . . . Austria, the eastern march of the German Empire; next the Swedes; and finally . . . the Prussians'. It was not until the nineteenth century that national states developed in the European heartland in Germany and Italy (Rokkan 1973: 80). Rokkan uses his East–West dimension to produce a typology of different state-building forms; seaward peripheries (Iceland, Norway, Scotland, Wales, Ireland and Brittany), two types of seaward empire-nations (Denmark, England, France, Spain and Portugal), three types of city-states (including the Netherlands, Switzerland, the Rhineland, the Hanseatic towns and Belgium), two types of landward empire-nations (Prussia, Bavaria, Austria and Sweden) and landward buffers (Finland, Bohemia, the Baltic states, Poland and Hungary). The North–South axis produces four categories (Protestant State Church, National Catholic, Counter-Reformation and mixed territories) which, combined with the East–West axis, create a typology with 36 separate cells (Rokkan 1973: 82).[1]

Tilly (1990) develops this model further, and builds on the role of the bourgeoisie and cities in European development, to some degree left up in the air by Rokkan. Like Barrington Moore, Tilly emphasizes the strength of a bourgeoisie in differentiating the development of state organization in Europe. He suggests that there are three broad 'trajectories' of state development which capture much of the variation in the development of European states: coercive, capitalist, and capitalized coercion. Capitalist trajectories of development can be found where there was sufficient economic development to sustain an active bourgeoisie, which could be enlisted by state-building elites in the process of building up an army and generating state revenues. Under this form of state, 'commercial oligarchies promoted the development of states organized around the protection and expansion of commercial enterprise', the institutions of municipal government, which were the organizations used for promoting the interests of the urban bourgeoisie, became primary state organizations, and 'the availability of capital and capitalists permitted these states to borrow, tax, purchase, and wage war effectively without creating bulky, durable, national administrations'. Such a course of development characterized above all northern Italy and the Low Countries. Coercive trajectories can be found where such bourgeois classes were weak and there was no concentration of capital. State formation thus consisted of setting up an administrative organization that could extract resources for the maintenance of the state and its armies. These states 'grew up starved for capital, bartered state-guaranteed privilege for armed force, and relied heavily on coercion to assure compliance with royal demands' (Tilly 1990: 143). Examples of such states would include Poland, Hungary, Russia and Brandenburg-Prussia as well as southern Italy, Spain and Sweden. In between these two extremes countries such as France and Britain used a mixture of both coercion and capital to develop *national* states. Eventually, a mixture of coercion and capital proved to be the most effective as a means of mobilizing resources for military purposes, and this 'military competition eventually drove [coercive and capitalist trajectories] . . . in the same general direction. It underlay both the creation and the ultimate predominance of the national state' (Tilly 1990: 191).

Such theories place a very heavy emphasis upon class and class conflict as the motor force propelling state development. Moore, Rokkan and Tilly have at the heart of their analyses the relationship between the bourgeoisie, large landowners and a state-building elite. It is understandable that, since Moore is also concerned with countries outside of Western Europe such as China and Japan, the peasantry occupies a more central position in his work than in that of Tilly and Rokkan. Otto Hintze explicitly sought to present a counterbalance to the dominance of socio-economic classes in explanations of state formation. Hintze argued that the crucial factor in explaining state formation was the relationship between states – a point also stressed by Tilly in his *Coercion, Capital and European States*. Although the origins of bureaucratic state organization can be found in the high Middle Ages, the military struggle for power in Europe after the sixteenth century produced an impetus towards bureaucratic military organization requiring a concentration of authority in order to extract resources to maintain and supply a large army. This 'intensivization' of state activity, produced by international military competition, was experienced by territories with very different initial conditions. Throughout much of his work Hintze emphasizes the division between the heartland of Europe – the area of the Empire of the Franks including territories now covered by France, western Germany, Austria, northern Italy, the northernmost part of Spain and the Benelux countries – and the peripheral territories. In the Empire of the Franks feudalism had a disintegrative effect which had an impact upon political development right up until the end of the eighteenth century. Political disintegration at the core of Europe made the continent's heartland the focus of military competition and rendered it

Table 1.1　*Classification of patterns of state development in Moore, Tilly, Rokkan and Hintze*

Territory	Moore	Tilly	Rokkan	Hintze
Austria	Landowners	Coercive	East/Catholic	Core
Belgium	Bourgeoisie	Capitalistic	West/Catholic	Core
Bohemia	Landowners	Coercive	East/mixed	Periphery
Denmark	Bourgeoisie	Coercive	West/Protestant	Periphery
England	Bourgeoisie	Capitalist-coercive	West/Protestant	Periphery
France	Bourgeoisie	Capitalist-coercive	West/Catholic	Core
Germany (East)	Landowners	Coercive	East/Protestant	Periphery
Germany (West)	Bourgeoisie	Capitalist-coercive	West/mixed	Core
Hungary	Landowners	Coercive	East/Catholic	Periphery
Italy (North)	Bourgeoisie	Capitalistic	Central/Catholic	Core
Italy (South)	Landowners	Coercive	Central/Catholic	Periphery
Netherlands	Bourgeoisie	Capitalistic	Central/mixed	Core
Norway	Bourgeoisie	Coercive	West/Protestant	Periphery
Poland	Landowners	Coercive	East/Catholic	Periphery
Portugal	Landowners	Coercive	West/Catholic	Periphery
Spain	Landowners	Coercive	West/Catholic	Periphery
Sweden	Bourgeoisie	Coercive	East/Protestant	Periphery

particularly likely to develop bureaucratic-absolutist forms of government (Page 1990).

One must not overemphasize the differences between these models. Hintze does not deny the role of class; in fact he emphasizes the role of large landowners in the creation of centralized states (Hintze 1962a). Moore argues that feudalism had a crucial impact on state building. Tilly's concern with capital and class combines with a concern for war as explanations for patterns of state formation. There are some striking similarities between Tilly, Rokkan and Hintze in their treatment of the central core of Europe, and both Tilly and Hintze argue that trajectories of state formation began to converge (although Hintze places the beginning of the process of convergence some-what after Tilly). However, this is not the place to put forward detailed discussion of theories of political development. Each of these theories offers somewhat different categorizations of countries according to the trajectories of state development.

One can give a rough summary of the major distinctions outlined as they affect different territories of Europe (see table 1.1). Table 1.1 is not intended as a summary of the more complex works of these four authors; rather it groups together those countries each author suggests, implicitly or explicitly, should have similar experiences of state formation. Of course there are problems fitting historical territories into contemporary or largely contemporary boundaries. Moreover, since Moore explicitly eschewed broader comparative analysis of nations other than those included in his study (for our purposes this means Germany, France and England), the second column of table 1.1 gives an assessment of whether a state-building elite tended to ally with an urban bourgeoisie or with a class of large landowners. This assessment is based upon Lipset and Rokkan's (1967) analysis, with Bohemia, Poland and Hungary (excluded from the Lipset and Rokkan typology) all classed as having allied with large landowners. Tilly's categorizations, column three of table 1.1, are found in the text of his *Coercion, Capital and European States*, while column four gives a simplified version of Rokkan's 'conceptual map' of Europe. These have been reduced from the much larger number of possible categories, while retaining his basic East–West and North–South (or Protestant–Catholic) division in order to avoid many countries being unique examples. Column five simply divides Europe between the territory of Charlemagne's empire (Hintze's understanding of the 'core') and the areas outside (the 'periphery').

Some indication of how well these models explain variations in the path of state development within Europe can be gained from seeing whether the categorizations of countries coincide with major variations in state-formation experiences. In order to assess them systematically one must first set out the dependent variable: variations in state development. One possibility would be to come up with a typology of contemporary states with, say, long-established democracies in one category, Southern European ex-dictatorships in another, ex-communist East European countries in another, and so on, and then see whether the countries in each category had the sorts of trajectories one would expect. However, grouping countries together into distinctive categories on such general criteria as state forms and state development is a hazardous exercise, since there is unlikely to be agreement on which are the important characteristics, even within the common-sense Mediterranean category (see Lijphart et al. 1988) and any categories derived are likely to appear arbitrary. Moreover, as the transformation of state structures in Germany since 1945, Southern Europe since the 1970s and East-Central Europe in the 1990s has shown, attempting to read back the past on the basis of the present is hazardous, not least since the present cannot be assumed to be the terminus of political development.

In this chapter I look at the ability of these models to explain differences in experiences of state formation with specific reference to state institutions. Over a period of around one thousand years, Europe has been transformed from a collection of tribes into a series of modern states covering large geographical areas, with national systems of law, administration and the provision of public benefits in which public participation through electoral choice and interest group pluralism has flourished. While periodizations of the major steps towards the development of the modern European state vary, we may point to six main phases in this transformation of Europe that feature in many accounts and see how far they fit the models discussed above. The next part of this chapter outlines generally the importance of each phase in the state-building process. This is then followed by an extended discussion of how these grand phases of transition were experienced in different parts of Europe.

The Grand Phases

Feudalism

Basic to the notion of feudalism is the fief, a piece of land that could be given to an individual in return for particular services. The fief was heritable and could in principle be reclaimed if the services were not provided. The origins of feudalism in Europe have been traced by Ganshof (1952) to practices found developing after the fifth century, but its full development as a political system is associated with the Empire of the Franks, which under Charlemagne (768–814) covered the territories of modern France, Germany to the Elbe, Switzerland, Austria, the Benelux countries and the northernmost parts of Spain. Strayer describes feudalism as 'a type of government in which political power was treated as a private possession and was divided among a large number of lords' (Strayer 1971: 63). Hintze has portrayed feudalism as a natural form of organizing large territories in a technologically primitive society with limited communications. Certainly, feudalism is not unique to Europe: variants can be found throughout the world, yet only Japanese forms of feudalism are generally regarded as close to the European model but ultimately readily distinguishable from it (see Hintze 1962b).

Under the Franks imperial officials – dukes, margraves, counts, abbots and bishops – were vassals. They held fiefs from the emperor and were expected to take on administrative and legal duties. In turn these territorial lords would themselves build up their own support by creating their own vassals. Under Charlemagne the duties of vassalage became progressively concerned with military service. The territorial officials became increasingly powerful in their own right: Ganshof discusses how originally vassals owed allegiance to their lord only if the latter was on imperial service, yet it became practice after the time of Louis the Pious (814–70) for lords to call on their vassals for their own purposes and even to rebel against the emperor. Even before the death of Charlemagne 'it had become apparent that the bonds which united a vassal to his lord, bonds which were direct and immediately appreciable by the senses, were stronger by far than those which bound the subject to the king' (Ganshof

1952: 52). Not only the land but also the offices that went with it were heritable and became increasingly remote from imperial authority. The fact that imperial authority always remained indirect under feudalism, and that this authority rested upon the creation of territorial centres of power, meant that feudalism was ultimately disintegrative.

The legal revolution

The 'legal revolution' of the eleventh and twelfth centuries was crucial for the formation of the European state. The revolution refers to the separation of the system of law from religion. The folklaws of Europe after the decline of the Roman Empire did not distinguish between law, religion and morality; law had no identity of its own, it was indistinguishable from general norms and customs, and as such was not subject to scrutiny or change by any secular authority. 'In the late eleventh, twelfth and early thirteenth centuries a fundamental change took place in Western Europe in the very nature of law both as a political institution and as an intellectual concept' (Berman 1983: 86). One of the important origins of this revolution can be sought in the Cluniac reforms following the founding of the Cluniac monasteries in southern France in 910 by William, Duke of Aquitaine. Unlike other monasteries, which were headed by an abbot under a local bishop, and usually with a local patron, the Cluny monasteries formed a network under the rule of the Abbot of Cluny. William of Aquitaine had relinquished his rights over the monastery to the Church of Rome. The Abbot of Cluny had extensive powers over the monasteries within the order, including the appointment of abbots and priors and the sending of visitors to them. Centralization was further ensured by the insistence that all full members of the order had to visit Cluny Abbey (see Watson 1949: 550–1). This network embraced probably over one thousand monasteries by the early eleventh century.

As Berman argues, in order to achieve the objective of emancipation from the dominance of local economic and political forces, the Church enlisted the support of emperors and kings, on whom they thus remained dependent. This gave kings power over the Church, which was above all exemplified by the power to appoint senior clergy. Later in the eleventh century the revolution turned on royal authority when Pope Gregory VII proclaimed the supremacy of the Pope over all Christians; the clergy was to be appointed by the pope and subject to his authority. This claim was published in the Papal Manifesto of 1075 which brought a short-lived victory for Gregory over Emperor Henry IV. However, the issue of church and secular authority, in this case in the question of the investiture of bishops and senior clergy, reflected wider questions of royal authority in the Church. This led to the Wars of Investiture which were resolved by the Concordat of Worms in 1122 (although in

England this was settled fifteen years earlier). It gave the Church the right to elect and invest bishops and abbots while according the Emperor the authority to be present at the election and intervene under some circumstances in the process (Berman 1983: 98–9).

The impact of these developments was immense. Berman (1983: 526) summarizes:

> The first of the great revolutions of Western history was the revolution against domination of the clergy by emperors, kings and lords and for the establishment of the Church of Rome as an independent, corporate, political and legal entity, under the papacy. . . . This was, however, only one side of the Papal Revolution. Another side of it was the enactment of the secular political and legal authority of emperors, kings and lords as well as the creation of thousands of autonomous, self-governing cities. Still another side of it was the enormous expansion of economic activity, especially in agriculture, commerce and crafts. Still another was the founding of the universities, and the development of the new sciences of theology and law. . . . The Papal Revolution had, in short, the character of a total change.

The legal 'revolution' itself did not immediately bring about strong cohesive states. In fact its first impact was to create a stronger and cohesive Church. However, it did represent the first step towards a separation of Church from state authority from which secular legal systems could develop. It also prepared the way for an autonomous civil society, operating independently of both Church and state.

The estates system in Europe

The development of legal authority over a territory in the medieval period after the twelfth century was bought at a price. Groups such as the clergy, the nobility or the burgesses or bourgeoisie of the towns – the three main 'estates' – sought to extract exemptions and benefits from princes through collective action and organization. Such benefits included above all the right to be consulted by the king or prince and the ability to veto plans to tax. The estates from at the latest the fourteenth century onwards had established a right to representation throughout Europe.

Such forms of representation were important for much of Europe between the thirteenth and the late eighteenth century, and it is common to describe the organizing principle of European states of the period as that of the *Ständestaat*, with the original German term most often used in preference to the literal English translation 'estates-state'. That such estates were not identical throughout Europe and shared different fates in different parts of Europe will be discussed below. However, the estates were universally a limitation to the centralizing aspirations of kings and princes, which were overcome with varying degrees of success. Their importance lies above all in their contribution to the 'prototype of the modern constitutional system [which is] . . . spread throughout the world. It was not a general human discovery, but was an indigenous product of the Christian West' (Hintze 1962c: 185).

The growth of absolutism

Max Weber argued that a bureaucracy in which authority is vested in an impersonal office rather than the person of the holder, which recruits personnel according to impersonal (usually technical) criteria rather than patronage, which has a strict hierarchy with defined spheres of competence and activity for each level within it, and in which all subordinates obey the orders of their superiors is a distinguishing feature of a modern state. Other non-European regions certainly developed bureaucratic organizations many hundreds of years ago. Perhaps the most extensive comparative study of such early non-bureaucratic states can be found in Wittfogel's (1957) *Oriental Despotism*, which shows how arid and semi-arid regions of the world, including India, the Middle East, China and Central and Southern America, developed governmental organizations that could plan and build irrigation schemes. Technically advanced though such oriental despotic systems may have been, however, they differed from rational bureaucratic systems since the characteristic feature of oriental despotism was the fusion of temporal and spiritual authority in the ruler.

The development of rational-legal bureaucracy in the heartland of Europe (Britain was an especially late developer in this respect) is closely associated with the struggle for the assertion of royal authority above all in the face of the estates. This assertion of authority throughout the realm has been described as a 'rationalization' or 'intensivization' of the act of government reaching a particular high point. In some countries during the period of 'absolutism', frequently described as beginning in 1660 and ending in 1789, this power was concentrated in the hands of a monarch with relatively few limitations on the exercise of such authority. The term 'absolutism' has been the subject of some debate, above all because the technology and in most cases the capacity to rule 'absolutely' were simply absent. The term is closely linked to notions in Roman law that the right and power to make and execute law rest solely and absolutely with the prince. The period is one where a significant increase in the administrative and political capacity of monarchs to govern can be detected. This increase in the power of monarchs is generally associated with the military needs of the emerging nation-states of Europe.

Two broad empirical trends are associated with the growth of absolutism: the use of territorial commissioners and the 'rational' organization of national ministries. The typical royal agents associated with absolutist states of the seventeenth and eighteenth centuries are the *intendants, corregidores* or *amtmand*. These were *commissary* agents who were appointed with specific purposes and were far more dependent upon the monarch than the *office* holders they replaced. *Offices* were often created simply to raise extra revenue for the exchequer and could be sold, the venality of office being especially marked in the seventeenth century. *Commissions* in principle were designed for specific purposes and involved a more direct responsibility to the monarch. The analytical distinction between office and commission was set out by Bodin (1583: 372–92) in his *Les six livres de la république*. Such commissary officials could be found in the high Middle Ages, as for example in the institution of the *bailli* in France (Fesler 1962), yet they played a continuous and decisive role in the whole push towards bureaucratic organization after the sixteenth century (Hintze 1962d). These commissary officials typically originated as organizers of localities where troops were stationed. In this sense military necessity within a system of rivalry between European states was a major impetus towards bureaucratization. As Brandenburg's Great Elector Frederick William (1640–88) argued, the Thirty Years War was the 'great school' which convinced him that a reform of the state centred on the creation of a standing army with a War Commissary which subordinated the older provincial governments (Hintze 1915: 202). The French *intendants* (developed in fact somewhat earlier, in the sixteenth century) were originally given the title of military governors. None of this is to suggest that centralization was always effective in the hands of the commissary officials of the absolutist period, but the tendency to strengthen direct control over the whole of the territory through more responsive territorial agents was one of the characteristic features of the period for most of Europe with the major exceptions of Hungary, Poland, Britain, Holland and parts of Italy.

The second characteristic feature is the early development of ministerial organization. The ministry was not the creation of the absolutist period; however, at this time we see a substantial tendency towards the separation of specialist executive organizations. French administrative specialization began well before the period of absolutism. The title of secretary of state became prominent in France after the middle of the sixteenth century, and by the reign of Louis XV there had developed posts for four secretaries of state (foreign, war, navies and colonies and *maison du roi*, largely equivalent to the interior). In Sweden central government was organized in boards beginning from the seventeenth century. What developed in the *Ancien Régime* was not a modern specialized ministry – the French Revolution gave the major impetus to forms of bureaucratic specialization (see Hintze 1962e) – but rather 'all countries in the eighteenth century saw steps taken towards more efficient methods of administration and towards a greater degree of specialisation whether in colleges, ministries, boards or departments' (Rudé 1972: 113).

The development of nationality

The French Revolution was subversive of the dynastic absolutist state. This was not simply because it spread ideas about liberalism and democracy, which had been current in English thought and American practice before the French Revolution. However, the French Revolution was clearly a turning-point in the development of European states. While it is frequently regarded as a 'democratic' revolution, its impact on the establishment of democracy, in the sense of the creation of constitutions which gave power to elected assemblies and of the extension of suffrage, was hardly revolutionary. One century after the Revolution much of Europe, including the lands of the Habsburg Empire and the German Reich, Italy, and the Iberian Peninsula, could be described as undemocratic if that meant there were limited opportunities for citizens to influence the complexion of the government through free elections. Moreover, in France itself there had been prolonged inconclusive experiments through a restored monarchy, a republic and an empire. 1789 was no overnight democratic revolution.

Perhaps a more accurate description of the impact of the French Revolution on the government systems of Europe is through the development of nationalism. The notion that the French Revolution was the originator of modern nationalism has been challenged on a variety of grounds: that the political mobilization of 'national consciousness' can be found earlier, in the medieval period even, or that it was not until the Spanish Revolution of 1802 that the true potential of national movements came to be realized (see Seeley 1878; Reynolds 1984).

In some countries nationality and statehood posed particular problems either because there were multi-state nations (Poland, Italy and Germany) or because they were multi-national states (the Austro-Hungarian Empire, the United Kingdom and Sweden-Norway). In these countries nationalism is associated with the growth of unification or secessionist movements. More widely, nationalism in the nineteenth and early twentieth centuries is associated with two main developments. First, it meant that the state apparatus was a property of the nation, not of a ruling dynasty. In principle, the development of nationalism meant the curtailment of the extensive powers of the monarch. The monarch may serve as a focus of national unity, but not as its dominator. Second, it developed mechanisms for representation of wider groups within the state. To say that it brought democracy as such would be misleading, since those represented, until the expansion of the franchise generally later in the nineteenth and early twentieth centuries, largely excluded the working class. Hence it is often termed the bourgeois-national state of the nineteenth century. In some countries, such as Sweden or the Netherlands, there were existing, functioning parliaments from the old estates. Alternatively, countries such as Belgium and Britain offered models of democratic parliaments which could be copied.

These two features of nationalism are associated with the development of liberal constitutions in the early nineteenth century: the 1830 constitutions of Belgium and France and the British Reform Act of 1832 were landmarks in this constitutional development. 'The two decades stretching from the British Reform Act of 1832 to the proclamation of the Second Empire in 1852 constituted a period of rapid advance in the development of democracy as defined by Tocqueville's *Democracy in America*, John Stuart Mill's *Representative Government*, of the whole nineteenth century. During the six months preceding June 1848 its progress seemed irresistible and its complete achievement everywhere only a matter of time' (Haywood 1960: 186). The diverse forms of government embodied in French constitutions of the nineteenth century and the reversal of the liberal trends after the 1848 revolutions show that the progress of liberal constitutionalism was not simply linear.

The era of mass mobilization

The development of the national state implied the consent of the nation. The mechanism by which this consent could be expressed was through elections and a wide basis of suffrage. This was even in many nominally liberal constitutional systems a long time in coming. While variations in timing will be discussed below, by the end of the First World War most men of voting age were eligible to vote in almost all countries. The immediate causes of the extension of the franchise included the discrediting of monarchies with limited and indirect suffrage in the wake of military defeat and elite recognition of the partisan advantages to be gained from suffrage extension as well as citizen pressure. Nevertheless, the extension of the franchise had two major consequences that will be discussed here: the mobilization of the citizenry in mass parties and the mobilization of the state above all in the development of public welfare programmes.

Parties and factions, 'cadre parties', formed in parliaments with modest extra-parliamentary organizations for electoral purposes, and Otto Kirchheimer (1966) discusses this mass mobilization of the citizenry through political parties in the West as going through two broad phases; the antebellum mass party and the postwar 'catch-all' party. The mass party of the interwar era was generally part of a wider subculture, whether it was religious or socio-economic. Members of the subculture, say socialist or Catholic, would also be members of the socialist or Catholic union, insurance society and social club. The party 'represented' its membership by being closely tied to the subculture of its members. While Roberto Michels (1915), in his critique of European socialist parties at the turn of the century, pointed out the oligarchic trends in the internal organization of parties which profess the most radical democratic sentiments, the tendency for the leadership to pursue electoral success rather than the representation of a subculture is most clearly seen after the Second World War in the development of the catch-all party. This form of party, characterized by the German and Italian Christian Democrats, sought to maximize electoral success by expanding the freedom of manoeuvre of the leadership, in part by internal constitutional change and in part by dropping much of the 'ideological baggage' of the antebellum mass party.

The involvement of a mobilized electorate in the massive expansion of state services, particularly welfare services, varied in intensity throughout the growth of the welfare state in the twentieth century. In the early development of the welfare state a number of authors have suggested that countries such as Germany pursued social insurance legislation in order to buy off potential working-class discontent (see Flora and Alber 1981). In later years the direct competition for votes, with each party offering to do more while not retreating from the bulk of inherited programmes, was one of the main motor forces of the 'juggernaut of incrementalism' (Rose and Peters 1978) which saw public employment in Western nations rise from an average of 14 per cent of the workforce in 1951 to 30 per cent by the early 1980s (Rose et al. 1985).

Assessments of the consequences of these forms of mobilization for the shape of the modern state have been highly diverse. One interpretation, especially popular in the interwar years but similar to Kornhauser's (1960) famous critique of 'mass society', sees the development of a 'corporate state' in which large-scale organizations were integrated into the state apparatus as they were in the Soviet Union, Fascist Italy or Nazi Germany (see Hintze 1962f). This leads to an extreme concentration of power in the hands of a state which faces an atomized and alienated citizenry. More recently, in the literature on 'ungovernability' in liberal democracies, commentators have pointed to a tendency for government growth to spiral out of control, placing high fiscal demands on the citizen and leading to public distrust and apathy towards politics (see Crozier et al. 1975).

One of the most significant consequences for the organization of the state has been the erosion of the traditional state organization that has accompanied the development of welfare services. While the focus of the activity of the state was in what Rose calls its 'defining' services – law and order, taxation and defence – the state was not only relatively small; it also had a distinctive set of purposes that required a hierarchical organization mirroring the military organization at its core (see Rose 1976). With the growth of 'resource mobilization' (largely economic) and social welfare functions, the distinctiveness of public organizations began to disappear. Newly developing state functions were carried out through a host of different agencies – local authorities, boards and institutions, as well as new national agencies and ministries. The state, which had once been a relatively small organization with distinctive purposes and a distinctive set of conditions of work for its employees, had now become a business where the distinctions became blurred.

The last two developments, nationalism and citizen mobilization, are not distinctively European. In the evolution of the nationality principle, as well as the growth of constitutionalism and mass political parties, the experience of the United States played a pioneering role to such an extent that Tocqueville's ([1835] 1945) masterpiece *Democracy in America* was based upon the premise that America in the 1830s offered a clear vision of the future development of Europe.

Variations in State Development

The feudal core of Europe

While these developments of feudalism, the development of Roman law, parliamentary estates, absolutism and nationalism and the creation of mass states, were experienced in some form throughout most of Europe, the patterns they formed and their intensity varied enormously. This can be seen especially clearly in the experience of feudalism in different parts of Europe.

In the Frankish Empire, feudalism was a form of political association which limited the power of a central monarch. After the ninth century the Frankish Empire was divided into several kingdoms, and even within these the powers of the feudal lords made it difficult to talk of any state system involving the exercise of authority over any extensive territory. When a Holy Roman Empire was created after 962 with the crowing of Otto I, it consisted primarily of the old Frankish Empire, with the major exception of much of the territory that became France and subsequently came under the nominal rule of the Capetian dynasty (987–1328). This fragmentation within the heartland of Europe was not effectively countered in France until the thirteenth century, with the expansion of a relatively small feudal territory of the Ile de France under Philip Augustus. Germany and Italy had to wait until the nineteenth century for their unification.

Feudalism outside of this core did not have such a disintegrative effect. In England, where the system of *thegnage* bore some superficial resemblances to the feudal system, it was not until the Norman Conquest that feudal institutions were introduced. They were introduced in order to 'minister to the needs of the Crown' (Ganshof 1952: 149). Fealty was sworn directly to the Crown. Similarly, it was the creation of the Norman kingdom in Southern Italy that brought the formal institutions of feudalism to Naples and Sicily as a means of strengthening the monarchy. In Spain, feudalism never became a system of government, even in Catalonia, the part of the Iberian Peninsula which appeared to have institutions most closely resembling those of Carolingian feudalism (Glick 1979: 213). In Norway, Sweden and Denmark to the north and Bohemia, Poland and Hungary to the east, similar observations can be made: feudalism never developed as the means of uniting disparate territories within one political system (Koht 1929).

In fact, the striking feature of Europe in the tenth and early eleventh centuries is the creation of states in these peripheral portions outside the Carolingian heartland: not only in England but also in Castile (under Fernan Gonzales, 930–70), Denmark (Gorm the Old, who died circa 936), Norway (Harald Fairhair, 860–930), Sweden (Olof Skötkonung, 980–1021), Bohemia (Boleslaw I, 929–67), Hungary (St Stephen, 997–1038) and Poland (Miesko I, 965–92). The patterns of state formation in Central Europe were subsequently altered radically. Poland did not remain united for long, yet disintegration was not due to feudalism. The division of Poland under Boleslaw III (1102–38) was a response to the problem of dynastic strife over the succession to the Crown. Moreover, while a fiefdom of the Carolingian state, Bohemia was not dependent upon officials owing allegiance ultimately to the emperor, but directly to the Duke of Bohemia. In both the disintegrating core of Europe as well as the more coherent monarchies of the peripheries, the development of a secular system of law was crucial to the development of the modern European state. The legacies of the past help us to understand the differences that have since emerged.

Common law and Roman law

The development of a system of law presided over by royal authority was most marked and most rapid in England. Like the continent of Europe, England was subject to a diversity of customary law and, especially after the Norman Conquest, feudal law. Yet before the Norman Conquest the Anglo-Saxons had established a court system presided over by the royal reeve. While feudalism on the continent of Europe generally had a disintegrative effect, the blending of the relatively centralized system with continental feudalism after 1066 brought about a greater degree of centralization in England. Under the brand of feudalism brought with the Normans, William established that all land was held from the king, and thus his authority extended across the whole kingdom and not primarily, as in France, in his own domains.

Moreover, the king's court was superior to manorial courts. But the most remarkable development both in judicial organization and in the emergence of a common law came in the reign of Henry II, when royal judicial officials were sent out as itinerant judges, from which developed the system of circuit courts. Under the Assizes of Northampton and Windsor in 1176 and 1179 the jury system started to become a firm feature of the English legal system. Its functional importance lay in the pressures that it created for systematization and standardization of substantive law: '. . . the jury in twelfth and thirteenth century England led to an emphasis on the techniques of pleading and also to a growth in the substantive law' (Robinson, Fergus and Gordon 1985: 228).

Spain and Southern Italy are further examples of an early consolidation of law and the legal system. In Castile between the seventh and tenth centuries the *Liber Iudiciorum* of the Visigoths was in force – *Fuero Juzgo* in Castilian – even under the Moorish occupation after the eighth century (van Kleffens 1968: 95). This law was also applied to the areas of Spain as they were reconquered by the Christians – a process that lasted from the eleventh century and was for the most part over by the middle of the thirteenth (it was not, however, until the late fifteenth century that Granada was reconquered). Over time, towns and villages were excepted from this law to become subject to local law, or *fueros*. These *fueros* were not complete local laws in the way of customs of, say, Germany or France, but 'only such regulations as concerned the status of the inhabitants of the foral district, exemption from tributes and services, the local government and certain details of police and justice' (Altamira 1912: 112). Even here the potential for diversity was greatly reduced by the practice of model *fueros*; the laws that were given to one town or district were in many cases identical to those given in another. In the other territories of Spain where the *Fuero Juzgo* remained in force, there was a greater tendency towards fragmentation through the granting of more diverse local *fueros* and other exceptions to the law. This was especially pronounced in the feudal territories, such as northern parts of Catalonia and Navarre. Over time, and especially in the thirteenth century, the fragmentation introduced by the *fueros* increased and the status of the *Fuero Juzgo* itself decreased.

In Castile these disintegrative tendencies in the law were countered by a programme of unification of law started under Fernando III (the Saint)(1199–1252) and continued by Alfonso X (the Learned)(1221–84), and culminating in the publication of the *Setenario* (circa 1253), the *Fuero Real* (1255) and the *Siete Partidas* (circa 1265). Van Kleffens (1968: 237) points out that a similar pattern of standardization of law could be found in other parts of Spain, but not as marked as in Castile.

Germany represents a direct contrast with the relative centralization of the administration of law and the creation of a common law. The process of systematizing law prior to the late fifteenth century was later and less extensive than in England. In Germany the lasting influence of the feudal system was that law remained highly fragmented. Courts were predominantly *Schöffen* courts, consisting of a presiding judge, usually a feudal lord and a panel of appointees, the *Schöffen*, who interpreted and applied the law. 'In this patch-work of localized and diverse bodies of custom, uncoordinated by any judicial hierarchy, the court of each community developed and applied its own customary usages, without any concern for a broader systematic whole' (Robinson, Fergus and Gordon 1985: 313).

The major change in Germany came with the 'reception' of Roman law, usually designated as occurring between the mid-fifteenth and the mid-seventeenth centuries. (For a discussion of the moves towards codification of the law in Germany before the 'reception', such as the development of town law and the influence of the *Sachsenspiegel*, see Brunner (1901) and Kroeschell (1983).) Probably the most important single impetus to the reception was the institution of the imperial *Reichskammergericht* (Imperial Court) in 1495. Be-cause of the weakness of the empire, this court had only limited direct powers, yet it had a powerful effect on the pattern of legal development in the territories of Germany for four main reasons. First, it elevated the status of lawyers, already heavily influenced by Roman law, since the statute instituting the court specified that eight of its sixteen members were 'learned in the law'. Second, it used written procedure. These two factors contrasted with the customary law practices of courts in most parts of Germany. Third, its influence was exerted through the process of appeal from lower territorial courts. Fourth, this was the time princes were consolidating their power and could use imperial court procedures as a model for centralization within a more limited territory.

The feudal system of Germany created powerful barriers not only to political unity, but also to the early development of a national legal system until the wide-scale reception of Roman law. In the Netherlands feudalism had a similar disintegrative effect. Attempts to create provincial and (in the fifteenth century) central courts had 'a result the opposite of that intended. The towns managed to become famous as the cradles of a municipal auton-omy, and even sovereignty. And the courts ended by growing into independ-ent bodies, desirous on their part to protect local privileges and immunities' (van Hamel 1912: 459). In France, on the other hand, feudalism's political and legal impacts were not so marked. Under the Capetian kings, most notably Philip Augustus from 1165 to 1223, the Ile de France expanded to include the great fiefdoms of the former Frankish Empire, including Normandy in 1204. They had, as Mitteis (1974: 376) suggests, exploited the feudal system to strengthen their own power. Philip Augustus, like the English kings, sought to make himself the pinnacle of a feudal hierarchy in which the territorial lords swore loyalty directly to the Crown. The Capetian kings had, as will be discussed below, created administrative structures which were impressive probably more because of the contrast with the feudal past and France's feudal neighbour Germany than in comparison with the more centralized states in England and Sicily.

Yet the legal system itself remained remarkably fragmented. The area south of the Loire, where Roman law had been influential since the pre-Merovingian era (i.e., before the mid-fifth century), above all in the Visigothic compilation, became characterized as the *pays de droit écrit* (lands of written law), and the north the *pays de droit coutumier* or lands of customary law. The influence of Roman law, even in the *pays de droit écrit*, remained a subsidiary source to be referred to where custom was unclear, and it was possible to identify at least three hundred different custom law areas within Provence in the twelfth century (Robinson, Fergus and Gordon 1985: 191).

In a development similar to that of the growth of the *curia regis* in England, the royal court developed nationwide judicial functions in its progression to the *Parlement* of Paris. As Hintze's discussion (1962e: 275–7) shows, the king's court in many European countries tended to divide between a full court, called at irregular intervals and on feast and holy days, and a more regular court which offered advice to the king on matters that included legal judgements. In France this division between close counsellors and the remainder of the liege men came especially around the end of the eleventh century, towards the end of the reign of Philip I (1060–1108)(Brissaud 1915: 433). It heard appeals from lower feudal courts. From it developed the *Parlement* of Paris, serving an advisory, administrative and judicial function, probably under Philip the Fair (1285–1314) at the beginning of the fourteenth century (see Shennan 1968). In its judicial functions the *Parlement*, operating through its different courts (the *chambre des enquêtes*, the *chambre des requêtes*, the *tournelle* or criminal chamber), served to bring about some standardization in the *pays de coutumes*. This fragmentation persisted right up until the Revolution, although its degree was reduced after the fifteenth century with the progressive institution of provincial *Parlements*, beginning with Toulouse in 1443; Nancy was the last one, designated in 1775. The customs of Paris gained influence through the pre-eminence of the Paris *Parlement* in this system of provincial *Parlements*. While some customs were contained in (unofficial) written compilations well before the sixteenth century, it was only then that the customs were systematically written down, so that

> By the end of the sixteenth century the process of codification in the *pays de coutumes* was complete in the sense that all officially recognised customs had been reduced to writing and carried the royal authority. On the other hand, uniformity was still a long way off. On the eve of the revolution of 1789 it is easily possible to count more than three hundred customary jurisdictions. However, the compilation of settled written texts meant that for the first time the

material existed for a thorough juristic treatment of the customary law. The sixteenth and earlier seventeenth centuries saw a wealth of commentary on the customs that in effect, created a French national law, which in due course was to become fully codified. (Robinson, Fergus and Gordon 1985: 339–40)

If the developments following the 'legal revolution' were in Britain to consolidate and strengthen central royal authority, and in Germany to increase the level of political disintegration, in France the picture was more mixed, as we shall see.

In Scandinavia centralization in the courts system developed relatively early. In Denmark the provincial *Landthings* remained important, yet in the thirteenth century a king's court, the *Danehof*, was established, and after the beginning of the fourteenth a royal appointee presided over the provincial courts. In Norway a common legal code for all provinces was proclaimed in 1267 and, 'on the whole, these Norsemen, at the time of the extinction of their ancient race of kings in the year 1319, were presumably the best situated nation in Europe with respect to legal organization and obedience to law' (Hertzberg 1912: 552). The development of a more uniform legal system was somewhat later in Sweden. The Land Law of the mid-fourteenth century began to create a national system of law, and the old provincial *Things* were placed below royal courts, *Räfstethings*, under Erik of Pomerania in 1413.

In the Eastern territories of Poland, Hungary and Bohemia, the system of castle administration provided a relatively higher degree of integration than could be found under feudalism; since the tenth century in all three kingdoms the castellans (in Poland the *starosta*, in Bohemia the *zupan* and in Hungary the *foíspan*) exercised judicial functions. In Poland, even after the division among his sons of the kingdom following the death of Boleslaw III in 1138, and despite the tribal traditions and provincial diversity which exacerbated this (or, arguably, made the division unavoidable (Reddaway 1950: 50)), there remained a sense of community among the princes and nobility of Poland quite in contrast to the feudal divisions of the German Empire (see Reynolds 1984). Boleslaw III himself increased the sense of commonality by presiding over the defeat of the German Emperor Henry V, leaving him 'free to enjoy a prestige as a national leader . . . for the rest of his life' (Reddaway 1950: 46). Even at the end of the twelfth century, a period characterized by general political disintegration, royal authority within the legal system persisted. However, it was not until the reunion of Poland after the fourteenth century that a unification of custom law was seriously started. Casimir the Great's famous 1347 Statutes, prepared by jurists from his court under his supervision, drew on foreign experience, above all that learned from Italian and church law, but applied it to traditional custom law of the area on which the Statutes were ultimately based (Reddaway 1950: 58).

The decline of estates and the rise of absolutism

Not all estates were the same. Otto Hintze's magisteral essay (1962g) makes a distinction between the two forms of estate representation. The first, found in the European heartland – the former territories of the Carolingian Empire (plus Naples-Sicily, which forms an exception) – is termed a tricameral system. The bicameral system is found in England and the peripheries of the Carolingian Empire. These are 'ideal types', but the distinction is important for three reasons. First the bicameral system is older than the tricameral system of estate representation. Second, the bicameral system is associated with the development of institutions of local self-government (see Page 1991). Third, and most important, 'absolutist or parliamentary forms of government as they developed before the nineteenth century essentially followed the difference between the tricameral and the bicameral types of estate representation' (Hintze 1962g: 125), with the tricameral tending towards absolutism and the bicameral towards parliamentarianism.

The upper house of the bicameral system is composed of the higher nobility (often but not invariably those who under feudal law were immediate vassals of the king, such as the barons in England or the *voivodes* and castellans in Poland). The lower house was a representative of the territory. This could take on a variety of forms: the petty nobility of England and Poland, the towns in Castile and Hungary (at least initially before it was taken over by the nobility after the fifteenth century). The three estates, clergy, nobility and bourgeoisie, were represented in France and the parts of Germany to the East of the Elbe.

The outcomes of these two different types of estates were also different. In the peripheries of Europe they frequently remained as limitations to a centralizing state power. In France the Estates-General were dismissed in 1615 and did not meet again until 1789, although the provincial estates continued to administer public services in parts of the kingdom – the *pays d'état* – and remained important political powers in peripheral parts of the country, above all in Brittany and Languedoc. In the German Empire the Reichstag continued to meet. In Bavaria and Austria the support for the Reformation among the estates meant that Catholic princes could target estates and gained the upper hand after the Thirty Years War. When the Prince of Württemberg converted to Catholicism in the early eighteenth century it seemed as if the Protestant estates would be similarly suppressed, but they survived there in part due to support from the emperor as well as from Britain, Prussia and Denmark. In Brandenburg the military reforms of the Great Elector were financed initially with taxes approved by the estates, but created a state which was powerful enough to raise further taxes without their consent. Estates nevertheless remained important in parts of Prussia, notably Cleves and Mark, as they did in Mecklenburg. The Imperial Diet continued to meet from 1663 until the dissolution of the empire in 1806, although its decisions carried little weight since the empire had long ceased to be an effective political unit. 'Even if it is true that many assemblies of estates survived in Germany to the French Revolution and beyond, it was absolute monarchy which enjoyed prestige in the seventeenth and eighteenth centuries' (Myers 1975: 110).

In most of Italy, assemblies of estates had fallen into disuse by the early eighteenth century. In Portugal the estates continued to have theoretical power to approve new taxes, but the income from Brazil meant the monarchy could govern without them in the seventeenth and eighteenth centuries. In Spain the Cortes of Castile suffered a decline in importance in the sixteenth century, and a revival in the early seventeenth and an effective transfer of the powers of the Cortes to the provinces (Thompson 1990: 82). The estates of Aragon, Catalonia and Valencia also experienced a revival in the seventeenth century, as the Spanish monarchy found its dwindling revenues from South American colonies insufficient to finance its participation in the Thirty Years War. A Catalan republic was recognized and supported by France in 1640, and it returned to Spain only after guarantees that the privileges of the estates would be respected. After the War of the Spanish Succession the Spanish monarchy effectively abolished the Cortes of Aragon, Valencia and Catalonia, which had sided with Austria, England and Holland. 'Henceforth the Spanish monarchy legislated by decree, and the Cortes was reduced to an assembly of subservient flatterers' (Myers 1975: 100).

In Denmark the Rigsdag did not meet after 1660, its influence blamed by King Frederick III for the defeat at the hands of the Swedes in the First Northern War (1654–60). The 1660 coup was bloodless and supported by the clergy and the commons, even though it paved the way for 'the most absolute monarchy in Europe' (Reddaway 1908: 559). In Sweden, however, the power of the estates, which had been severely curtailed in the period of absolutism between 1680 and 1720, revived thereafter in the *Frihetstiden* (age of liberty) until Gustavus III's 1772 coup cut them back once more. Nevertheless, the influence of the estates persisted and developed to form the basis of the modern parliament.

In Bohemia the Protestant estates were effectively crushed by the Habsburg monarchy after the Thirty Years War. However, elsewhere in East-Central Europe the estates survived as effective political forces. In Poland the traditional 'dualism' of estates and monarchy had become grossly imbalanced in favour of the estates, which themselves had become dominated by the nobility to the virtual exclusion of the towns. Since 1573 the nobility had the right to elect the king. The rules of the Diet, above all the requirement that decisions be unanimous, made it ineffectual and obstructive. For over one hundred years up until 1764, 53 diets had met without passing any laws, leading contemporary commentators to describe the government of Poland as 'perpetual anarchy' making the country 'defenceless and weak' (Myers 1975: 124; Lindsay 1957: 160). In Hungary the estates, especially in the country diets, remained a powerful counter-balance to the Habsburg monarchy. They had 'a degree of power over their own affairs and their nation's greater than any possessed by any equivalent class on the continent at that time [mid-18th century] except Sweden' (MacCartney 1957: 403).

The demise in the power of the estates coincided with the growth of administrative centralization in many of the German states, Denmark and France. In some countries, notably the Netherlands, Switzerland, Britain, Sweden, Hungary and Poland, the estates persisted, although in many of these countries they became increasingly dominated by landed interests, with a concomitant decline in the role of the urban bourgeoisie. In a third group of countries the power of estates was effectively ended and absolutist institutions were introduced, but although strengthening the role of the monarchy these failed to eliminate the power of provincial and local elites, who exploited the networks of venality, patronage and clientelism into which the absolutist officials became integrated. In Spain one of the characteristic weaknesses of royal authority despite the trappings of absolutism (*corregidores* were territorial governors borrowed from the French institution of the *intendant*) was the weak linkage between central and local government (Thompson 1990: 92); what *corregidores* were expected to do was 'very fine . . . but about as far from reality as the dreams of Plato or of Sir Thomas More' (Lindsay 1957: 155). Portugal remained administratively inefficient until the dramatic reforms of Pombal in the 27 years he served as Secretary of State after 1750. In Italy the development of absolutism had been 'superimposed upon and had not replaced the existing structures', although in Piedmont the reforms of Victor Amadeus II (1675–1713) made 'the sub-Alpine kingdom the most efficiently organized, bureaucratic-militaristic state in Italy', a strong contrast with Naples in the south, which appeared to be impervious to such reforms (Woolf 1979: 63).

Variations on the road to democracy

Goldstein argues that it was only after 1870 that the major patterns of differentiation in the response to demands for liberal constitutional reforms became apparent. In the period from 1815 until then, 'most European countries tended to go through phases of repression and relative toleration at about the same time' – repression in immediate response to uprisings, as in 1820, 1830 and 1848, easing off as the memory of these uprisings faded (Goldstein 1983: 240). After 1870 the development of liberal constitutionalism in Europe differed in three major zones: Northwestern Europe (including France,

Switzerland, the Low Countries, Scandinavia and Britain), which engaged in the development of liberal reforms, the poorer Southern and Eastern European peripheries (Spain, Portugal, Hungary), which pursued strategies predominantly of repression, and the 'in-between countries' of Central Europe (Germany, Austria, Bohemia, non-Russian Poland and Italy), which 'responded to dissent with a mixture of reform and repression' (Goldstein 1983: 247).

The Southern and Eastern European peripheries maintained repressive stances after the First World War. In Hungary elections were forced on the government in 1920 by the Allies (free elections were agreed to in order to secure the removal of Romanian troops from Budapest) and thereafter restrictions were placed on voting. In Spain and Portugal elections were managed at first by agreements between parties to alternate in office and share its spoils – in Spain the *turno pacifico* and in Portugal *rotavism*. When these systems disintegrated after the 1890s, the response by the political elite was to carry on 'as before, pausing only to apply increasing force and chicanery to rig elections in rural areas (it became increasingly difficult to fake elections in the politicized cities) and growing more disconnected from social realities' (Goldstein 1983: 291). In Hungary a similar form of electoral management was created by the Liberal Party under the leadership of Tisza (1875–90), where 'the Liberal Party and bureaucracy were welded into a single powerful machine in which the bureaucracy was charged with making the elections and perpetuating the liberal majority while parliament and the party would lend an aura of legitimacy to bureaucratic policies and provide a forum for the articulation of bureaucratic interests' (Janos 1982: 97). Political dissent had therefore to be repressed, and each of these systems maintained authoritarian forms of government through the leadership of Horthy, Bethlen and Gömbös in Hungary, the de Rivera and Franco regimes in Spain and the Pais Carmona and Salazar regimes of Portugal.

In four of Goldstein's Central European group, the outcome of developments in the interwar era was also authoritarian dictatorship. In Poland the assumption of power of Pilsudski in 1926, and his consequent consolidation of his authority through constitutional changes in 1926 and 1935, was only partially reversed after his death in 1935. In Italy it was Mussolini's coup in 1922 that created a Fascist dictatorship. In Austria and Germany reformed parliamentary constitutions and electoral laws after 1918 and the fragmentation of the party system created the conditions of pluralistic stagnation in which a 'disloyal opposition' could survive, provoke repressive measures from the government and ultimately triumph. Here the progression was from liberal parliamentary democracy through government by emergency decree (under Brüning in Germany in 1930 and Dolfuss in Austria after 1934) to National Socialist dictatorship in Germany in 1933 and in Austria in 1938, following the German invasion and *Anschluss* (union with Germany). The exception in this central group was Czechoslovakia, which maintained its democratic constitution until the German invasion. Despite indigenous Fascist movements in the former Austrian territory of Czechoslovakia, the collapse of democratic institutions in 1939 was clearly the result of exogenous forces.

Mass mobilization of the electorate within a democratic system in these Southern, Central and Eastern portions of Europe came in two waves: immediately after the Second World War for Germany, Austria and Italy and in the 1970s for Spain and Portugal. For the East European countries that progressed from Nazi to Soviet domination, the prospects for a more durable democratic system since the collapse of communism look favourable but cannot be taken for granted in the light of, among other things, the extraordinarily severe economic problems they face as well as the fragmentation of political parties.

The development of welfare states

One of the major consequences of the development of electoral competition for government office was the development of public welfare services. As Rose (1976) has shown, there is a clear similarity among European states in terms of the development of public services. The first public services were 'defining' services of tax collection, law and order and defence. In the nineteenth century, states pursued 'resource mobilization' policies, such as public works, aimed at economic development. After the late nineteenth century, once states had defined their borders and authority and become involved in generating economic prosperity, they could move on to develop social welfare functions. As Flora argues, 'The modern welfare state is a European invention . . . it was born as an answer to problems created by capitalist industrialization; it was driven by the democratic class struggle' (Flora 1986: xii).

The question of the causes of growth of government, above all the massive growth since the Second World War, has been hotly debated. The major contributory factors examined have included industrialization, economic growth, political parties, the changing expectations of the electorate, interest groups (including provider groups) and budget-maximizing bureaucrats (Flora 1986: xvi–xxi). Heclo's (1981) analysis, which suggests four broad overlapping stages of welfare state development, indicates that the broader social, economic, political and cultural factors shaping welfare state development are likely to have been different at each period. In the phase of experimentation (between the 1870s and the 1920s) the major political events were the development of workers' movements, suffrage extensions and the growth of mass parties. In the phase of consolidation (1930s to 1940s) the notion of state intervention in welfare became less contentious. In the period of postwar expansion (1950s to 1960s) there was a rate of economic growth sufficiently high to allow both state revenues as well as the personal income of citizens to rise; consequently public revenue could increase 'painlessly' and parties bidded against one another to raise public spending. After the 1970s came a period of 'reformulation' characterized by recession, inflation and increasing attacks on government as a welfare provider. (The subsequent development of the welfare state is discussed in chapter 13 by Richard Parry.)

As Flora (1986) argued, the rate and nature of early welfare state growth varied. Many of these variations are set out in Flora and Heidenheimer's (1981) *The Development of Welfare States in Europe and America*. If we look at contemporary welfare states there is some general agreement about the way in which they differ from one another. Perhaps the most famous categorization is provided by Richard Titmuss (1974), who distinguishes between a 'residual' welfare model (where the state operates only when the market and the family fails to meet social needs), an 'industrial achievement' model (in which needs are met on the basis of merit and differences in social status are preserved) and an 'institutional redistributive' model (in which the state provides universalistic services on the basis of need).

More recently Esping-Andersen (1990) has developed a categorization which has much in common with that of Titmuss both in theory as well as in the countries which fall into the different groups. A 'liberal' welfare state, as found in Britain and the Anglo-American democracies, is dominated by low-value means-tested benefits and thus 'erects an order of [social] stratification that is a blend of relative equality of poverty among state-welfare recipients, market-differentiated welfare among the majorities and a class-political dualism between the two' (Esping-Andersen 1990: 27). A 'corporatist' welfare state exists where the state plays a large role in providing benefits, but fails to adopt a redistributive role, with benefits closely related to status and earnings while in work. This form of welfare state places particular emphasis upon the family as the provider of welfare of first instance. Welfare states which fall into this category include Austria, France, Germany and Italy. A third form of welfare state is the social-democratic, in which the state redistributes income to 'promote an equality of the highest standards, not an equality of minimal needs as was pursued elsewhere' (Esping-Andersen 1990: 27).

These three types of welfare state were shaped by different historical patterns of development. Particularly important, the paternalistic-conservative tradition saw the welfare state as a means of preserving existing power structures against the onslaught of liberalism and democracy. This tradition was at the origin of welfare states throughout Europe, but in Scandinavia and Britain this became overlaid with a liberal principle that state intervention in welfare should be limited to redressing the problems of market failure. In postwar Scandinavia as well as the Netherlands universalistic approaches to welfare developed as socialism became less concerned with benefits for the working class, but for the 'masses of rural and urban "little people" . . . Universalism . . . became a guiding principle because it equalized the status, benefits and responsibilities of citizenship, and because it helped to build political coalitions' (Esping-Andersen 1990: 68).

Our knowledge of the growth and development of welfare states in Eastern Europe is less detailed than that of the West. However, the initial stages of the welfare state in East-Central Europe, despite the economic weakness of the region in the early twentieth century, appear to be broadly similar to those of the West. In Poland state unemployment and sickness insurance schemes were introduced in 1919 and even continued through the conservative and authoritarian Pilsudski regime after 1926 (Polonsky 1972). In Hungary the right-wing radical governments of the 1930s sought to buy off potential discontent by extending the social legislation that had developed in the 1920s, above all in the 1927 Social Security Act, although it must be added that the levels and standards of provision remained far below those found in the West. In Czechoslovakia an unemployment insurance scheme was introduced in 1918, and state provision of welfare developed so that 'by 1929 all the regular labour force was covered by various forms of insurance, dealing with sickness, injury, disability and old age. Behind this lay a complex of modern hospitals, sanatoria and rest homes. There were flaws, some bureaucratic, most financial. Levels of payment were not really high enough. Czechoslovakia lacked the money, but its performance was at least the equal of many in Europe' (Wallace 1976: 172). In the postwar period the East-Central European states followed a Soviet pattern of development very different from those of the West, with correspondingly low comparative performance scores (see Rose 1992).

Weighing up the Theories

Table 1.2 summarizes the argument so far about the experiences of different parts of Europe in these key aspects of state formation. The information in this table can be compared with the major characterizations of trajectories of development set out in table 1.1 to determine in how many cases historical experience, as interpreted in this paper, is consistent with the theoretical expectations of Hintze, Tilly, Rokkan and Moore. It has to be remembered that in so doing I will be subjecting these theories to tests for which they were not specifically designed: Moore, for example, did not seek to 'explain' feudalism by his model, but rather the origins of dictatorship and democracy. The purpose of this rather rough and ready combination of theory with

Table 1.2   *Summary of major differences in experiences at key stages of state formation*

Country	Feudal political organiz- ation	Establish- ment of national legal system	Estates	Liberal- ization in 19th century	Welfare states
Austria	Strong	Later	Declined	Mixed	Corporatist
Belgium	Strong	Later	Declined	Liberal	Corporatist
Bohemia	Weak	Earlier	Declined	Mixed	Eastern
Denmark	Weak	Earlier	Declined	Liberal	Social Democratic
England	Weak	Earlier	Persisted	Liberal	Liberal
France	Strong	Later	Declined	Liberal	Corporatist
Germany (East)	Weak	Later	Declined	Mixed	Corporatist
Germany (West)	Strong	Later	Declined	Mixed	Corporatist
Hungary	Weak	Earlier	Persisted	Repressive	Eastern
Italy (North)	Strong	Later	Declined	Mixed	Corporatist
Italy (South)	Weak	Earlier	Declined	Mixed	Corporatist
Netherlands	Strong	Later	Persisted	Liberal	Corporatist
Norway	Weak	Earlier	Declined	Liberal	Social Democratic
Poland	Weak	Earlier	Persisted	Mixed	Eastern
Portugal	Weak	Earlier	Declined	Repressive	Corporatist
Spain	Weak	Earlier	Declined	Repressive	Corporatist
Sweden	Weak	Earlier	Persisted	Liberal	Social Democratic

experience is simply to see whether the distinctions between different paths of development highlighted by these authors point out fundamental differences throughout the process of state formation.

On a simple head count (see table 1.3), Tilly comes out on top, with a total of 70 out of 85 consistent answers. The ambiguity of his capitalist–coercion trajectory of development puts him ahead of Hintze (66 out of 85), whose count is inflated by the fact that his theoretical expectations are derived from the experience of one of the phases (feudalism). Moore and Rokkan fare somewhat worse, but still in the large majority of cases the theoretical explanations fit the historical experiences.

More striking than a simple adding up of the numbers is the observation that some of the authors score far higher on the aspects of development closest to the core of their theoretical interests: every country is consistent with Moore's expectations when it comes to the development of democratic forms of government in the nineteenth century; Rokkan's approach, which orig-inated in a quest for explanations of different party systems, scores best on the welfare state – as was discussed above, the development of welfare states was closely tied to the development of mass democratic political organizations; and

Table 1.3   *Comparing historical experiences of state formation with major theories*

Phases	Hintze		Tilly		Moore		Rokkan	
	C	I	C	I	C	I	C	I
Feudalism	17	0	16	1	12	5	12	5
Law	16	1	15	2	11	6	11	6
Estates	9	8	12	5	9	8	10	7
Liberalism	11	6	14	3	17	0	13	4
Welfare	13	4	13	4	12	5	16	1
Total	66	19	70	15	61	24	62	23

C = *number of territories consistent with theory at each stage; I = number of territories inconsistent with theory at each stage. 'Mixed' categories (e.g., capitalist-coercive regimes in Tilly's theory or states which used a mixture of coercion or repression in the nineteenth century) are counted automatically as consistent.*

Hintze's division of Europe into core and periphery works best in accounting for the late development of legal systems in the core of Europe.

Conclusions

Much of what is assumed to be the mark of modernity in political develop-ment derives from specifically European conditions. The growth of the secular state, where political and religious authority are separated, developed in the form in which it was exported to much of Europe. In addition, the European development of representative government reflected a long process of change, of which one striking feature was the near ubiquity of estate-based represen-tation from the fourteenth century. Certainly one might be able to detect some precursors of these European developments among the ancient Greeks and Romans, as one may point to the importance of *Roman* law in the growth of the European state. However, as a number of authors point out, '"Greece" and "Rome" became spiritual ancestors of the West not primarily by a process of survival or succession but primarily by a process of adoption: the West adopted them as ancestors' (Berman 1983: 3; see also Vinogradoff 1909; Hintze 1962c). Such precedents were adopted and adapted to fit European conditions.

The model of the European secular state, with representative democratic institutions and a rational-legal bureaucracy, finds its purest form in a system of parliamentary democracy where the executive is selected by the representa-tive legislature but thereafter the former dominates the latter. This model has powerful implications for other institutions of government; the linkage between the executive and the legislative branches of government requires the development of relatively strong party cohesion to organize government majorities in the legislature (Harmel and Janda 1982). Interest group activity becomes focused on the executive branch of government. Although the French *Conseil Constitutionnel* as well as the German *Bundesverfassungsgericht* have annulled important government legislation, judicial authorities, even when empowered to challenge the executive, tend to exercise restraint when controversial political issues are at stake. The parliamentary form of government is at the heart of the ministerial form of political leadership. In each of these respects European experience contrasts strongly with that of the United States, where the separation of powers between the legislature, executive and judiciary has produced looser party organization, a highly activist judiciary, 'issue networks' that are focused as much on the legislative as the executive branch and a fragmentation of executive authority among a plethora of executive boards and agencies.

The state-building experiences which led to this form of government and administration were common to many European nations but had different impacts and outcomes at the time. It is not, however, possible to place these experiences together and state with confidence that there is a series of defined and distinct paths to the modern European state down which different countries have progressed. Different factors distinguish developments in the various parts of Europe at different times. Broadly the four sets of authors who have been examined either suggest one (Hintze) or give some combination (Tilly, Rokkan and Moore) of three main types of division of Europe: a heartland periphery division (a feudal core versus a non-feudal or weakly feudal periphery), an East–West division (a relatively developed commercial and industrial West versus an agrarian East) and a North–South division (Protestant versus Catholic). At different stages in the state-formation process differing divisions of Europe appeared important. In the early stages of consolidating royal administrative and legal power, the heartland–periphery distinction was the most important. Moving on to the institution of liberal political systems in the nineteenth century, the East–West axis appeared important. Leaving aside the enormous distinction between the former communist states of East-Central Europe and those of the West, the North–South or Protestant–Catholic division has emerged as the most significant in explaining recent patterns of state development.

Notes

1   The number of distinct categories of states in Rokkan's model does, however, vary. Peter Flora (1983) presents a slightly different typology with 35 cells.

Bibliography

Allardt, E. and Valen, H. (1981). 'Stein Rokkan: an intellectual profile', in Per Tosvik (ed.), *Mobilization, Center-Periphery Structures and Nation-Building: a volume in commemoration of Stein Rokkan*. Bergen: Universitetsforlaget.

Altamira, R. (1912). 'Spain', in J. H. Wigmore (ed.), *A General Survey of Events, Sources, Persons and Movements in Continental Legal History*. London: John Murray.

Berman, H. J. (1983). *Law and Revolution: the formation of the Western legal tradition*. Cambridge, MA: Harvard University Press.

Bodin, J. (1583). *Les six livres de la république*. Paris: DuPuis [repr. in 1961 by Scientia Aalen].

Brissaud, J. (1915). *A History of French Public Law*. London: John Murray.

Brunner, H. (1901). *Grundzüge der deutschen Rechtsgeschichte*. Leipzig: Duncker & Humblot.

Crozier, M. et al. (1975). *The Crisis of Democracy*. New York: New York University Press.

Dunleavy, P. J. (1989). 'United Kingdom: paradox of an ungrounded statism', in F. G. Castles (ed.), *The Comparative History of Public Policy*. Cambridge: Polity Press.

Esping-Andersen, G. (1990). *The Three Worlds of Welfare Capitalism*. Princeton, NJ: Princeton University Press.

Fesler, J. W. (1962). 'French field administration: the beginnings'. *Comparative Studies of Society and History* 5 (1): 76–111.

Flora, P. (1983). 'Introduction: Stein Rokkan's macro-model of Europe', in Peter Flora (ed.), *State, Economy and Society in Western Europe, 1815–1975*, Vol. 1: *Growth of Mass Democracies and Welfare States*. Frankfurt am Main: Campus Verlag.

—— (1986). 'Introduction', in Peter Flora (ed.), *Growth to Limits: the Western European welfare states since World War II*. Berlin: Walter de Gruyter.

Flora, P. and Alber, J. (1981). 'Modernization, democratization and the development of welfare states in Western Europe', in Peter Flora and Arnold J. Heidenheimer (eds), *The Development of Welfare States in Europe and America*. New Brunswick, NJ: Transaction Books.

Flora, P. and Heidenheimer, A. J. (1981). (eds), *The Development of Welfare States in Europe and America*. New Brunswick, NJ: Transaction Books.

Ganshof, F. L. (1952). *Feudalism*. London: Longmans, Green.

Glick, T. F. (1979). *Islamic and Christian Spain in the Early Middle Ages*. Princeton, NJ: Princeton University Press.

Goldstein, R. J. (1983). *Political Repression in Nineteenth Century Europe*. London: Croom Helm.

Guizot, F. (1851). *The History of Civilization from the Fall of the Roman Empire to the French Revolution*, Vol. 1 (trans. William Hazlitt). London: David Bogue.

Harmel, R. and Janda, K. (1982). *Parties and their Environments: limits to reform*. New York: Longman.

Haywood, J. A. (1960). 'Liberalism and constitutional development', in *New Cambridge Modern History of Europe*. Cambridge: Cambridge University Press.

Heclo, H. (1981). 'Toward a new welfare state?', in Peter Flora and Arnold J. Heidenheimer (eds), *The Development of Welfare States in Europe and America*. New Brunswick, NJ: Transaction Books.

Hertzberg, E. (1912). 'Scandinavia', in J. H. Wigmore (ed.), *A General Survey of Events, Sources, Persons and Movements in Continental Legal History*. London: John Murray.

Hintze, O. (1915). *Die Hohenzollern und ihr Werk, 1415–1915*. Berlin: Paul Parey.

—— (1962a). 'Staatenbildung und Kommunalverwaltung', in Otto Hintze, *Staat und Verfassung: gesammelte Abhandlungen zur allgemeinen Verfassungsgeschichte*. Göttingen: Vandenhoeck & Ruprecht.

—— (1962b). 'Wesen und Verbreitung des Feudalismus', in Otto Hintze, *Staat und Verfassung: gesammelte Abhandlungen zur allgemeinen Verfassungsgeschichte*. Göttingen: Vandenhoeck & Ruprecht.

—— (1962c). 'Weltgeschichtliche Bedingungen der Repräsentativverfassung', in Otto Hintze, *Staat und Verfassung: gesammelte Abhandlungen zur allgemeinen Verfassungsgeschichte*. Göttingen: Vandenhoeck & Ruprecht.

—— (1962d). 'Der Commissarius und seine Bedeutung in der allgemeinen Verwaltungsgeschichte', in Otto Hintze, *Staat und Verfassung: gesammelte Abhandlungen zur allgemeinen Verfassungsgeschichte*. Göttingen: Vandenhoeck & Ruprecht.

—— (1962e). 'Die Entstehung der modernen Staatsministerien', in Otto Hintze, *Staat und Verfassung: gesammelte Abhandlungen zur allgemeinen Verfassungsgeschichte*. Göttingen: Vandenhoeck & Ruprecht.

—— (1962f). 'Wesen und Wandlung des modernen Staates', in Otto Hintze, *Staat und Verfassung: gesammelte Abhandlungen zur allgemeinen Verfassungsgeschichte*. Göttingen: Vandenhoeck & Ruprecht.

—— (1962g). 'Typologie der ständischen Verfassungen des Abendlandes', in Otto Hintze, *Staat und Verfassung: gesammelte Abhandlungen zur allgemeinen Verfassungsgeschichte*. Göttingen: Vandenhoeck & Ruprecht.

Janos, A. C. (1982). *The Politics of Backwardness in Hungary, 1825–1945*. Princeton, NJ: Princeton University Press.

Kirchheimer, O. (1966). 'The transformation of West European party systems', in Joseph LaPalombara and Myron Weiner (eds), *Political Parties and Political Development*. Princeton, NJ: Princeton University Press.

Koht, H. (1929). 'The Scandinavian kingdoms until the end of the thirteenth century', in *Cambridge Medieval History*, Vol. VI. Cambridge: Cambridge University Press.

Kornhauser, W. (1960). *The Politics of Mass Society*. London: Routledge & Kegan Paul.

Kroeschell, K. (1983). *Deutsche Rechtsgeschichte 2 (1250–1650)*. Opladen: Westdeutscher Verlag.

Lijphart, A. et al. (1988). 'A Mediterranean model of democracy? The Southern European democracies in comparative perspective'. *West European Politics* 11 (1): 7–25.

Lindsay, J. O. (1957). 'Monarchy and administration', in *Cambridge Modern History of Europe*, Vol. VII: *The Ancien Régime*. Cambridge: Cambridge University Press.

Lipset, S. M. and Rokkan, S. (1967). 'Cleavage structures, party systems and voter alignments: an introduction', in Seymour M. Lipset and Stein Rokkan (eds), *Party Systems and Voter Alignments*. New York: Free Press.

MacCartney, C. A. (1957). 'The Habsburg dominions', in *Cambridge Modern History of Europe*, Vol. VII: *The Ancien Régime*. Cambridge: Cambridge University Press.

Michels, R. (1915). *Political Parties: a sociological study of the oligarchical tendencies of modern democracy*. Glencoe, IL: Free Press.

Mitteis, H. (1974). *Der Staat des hohen Mittelalters: Grundlinien einer vergleichenden Verfassungsgeschichte des Lehnszeitalters*. Cologne: Bohlau.

Moore, B. (1967). *Social Origins of Dictatorship and Democracy: lord and peasant in the making of the modern world*. Harmondsworth: Penguin.

Myers, A. R. (1975). *Parliaments and Estates in Europe to 1789*. London: Thames & Hudson.

Page, E. C. (1990). 'The political origins of bureaucracy and self-government: Otto Hintze's conceptual map of Europe'. *Political Studies* 31 (1): 39–55.

—— (1991). *Localism and Centralism in Europe: the political and legal base of local self-government in Europe*. Oxford: Oxford University Press.

Polonsky, A. (1972). *Politics in Independent Poland, 1921–1939*. Oxford: Clarendon Press.

Reddaway, W. F. (1908). 'The Scandinavian kingdoms', in *The Cambridge Modern History*. Cambridge: Cambridge University Press.

Reddaway, W. F. et al. (1950). *The Cambridge History of Poland: from the origins to Sobielski (to 1696)*. Cambridge: Cambridge University Press.

Reynolds, S. (1984). *Kingdoms and Communities in Western Europe, 900–1300*. Oxford: Clarendon Press.

Robinson, O. F. et al. (1985). *An Introduction to European Legal History*. Abingdon: Professional Books.

Rokkan, S. (1973). 'Cities, states and nations: a dimensional model for the study of contrasts in development', in S. N. Eisenstadt and Stein Rokkan (eds), *Building States and Nations: models and data resources*. London and Beverly Hills: Sage.

Rose, R. (1976). 'On the priorities of government: a developmental analysis of public policies'. *European Journal of Political Research* 4 (2): 247–89.

—— (1992). *Making Progress and Catching Up: a time-space analysis of social welfare across Europe*. Glasgow: University of Strathclyde Studies in Public Policy No. 208.

Rose, R. and Peters, B. G. (1978). *Can Government Go Bankrupt?* London: Macmillan.

Rose, R. et al. (1985). *Public Employment in Western Nations*. Cambridge: Cambridge University Press.

Rudé, G. (1972). *Europe in the Eighteenth Century: aristocracy and the bourgeois challenge*. London: Weidenfeld & Nicolson.

Seeley, J. R. (1878). *Life and Times of Stein, or Germany and Prussia in the Napoleonic Age* (3 vols). Cambridge: Cambridge University Press.

Shennan, J. H. (1968). *The Parlement of Paris*. London: Eyre & Spottiswoode.

Strayer, J. (1971). *Medieval Statecraft and the Perspectives of History*. Princeton, NJ: Princeton University Press.

Thompson, I. A. A. (1990). 'Castile', in J. Miller (ed.), *Absolutism in Seventeenth Century Europe*. London: Macmillan.

Tilly, C. (1990). *Coercion, Capital and European States, 990–1990*. Oxford: Blackwell.

Titmuss, R. M. (1974). *Social Policy*. London: Allen & Unwin.

de Tocqueville, A. ([1835] 1945). *Democracy in America* (2 vols). New York: Knopf.

van Hamel, J. A. (1912). 'Netherlands', in J. H. Wigmore (ed.), *A General Survey of Events, Sources, Persons and Movements in Continental Legal History*. London: John Murray.

van Kleffens, E. N. (1968). *Hispanic Law until the End of the Middle Ages*. Edinburgh: Edinburgh University Press.

Vinogradoff, P. (1909). *Roman Law in Medieval Europe*. London: Harper.

Wallace, W. V. (1976). *Czechoslovakia*. London: Benn.

Watson, E. W. (1949). 'The development of ecclesiastical organization and its financial basis', in *The Cambridge Medieval History*. Cambridge: Cambridge University Press.

Wittfogel, K. (1957). *Oriental Despotism: a comparative study of total power*. New Haven, CT: Yale University Press.

Woolf, S. (1979). *A History of Italy, 1700–1860*. London: Methuen.

2

The Nations of Europe
after the Cold War

Anthony Smith

Nationalism has suddenly become a 'problem' again on the agenda of the international community. After some decades when it appeared to have been erased, at least in Europe, from the popular consciousness, it began to re-emerge among the minority 'peripheral' ethnic communities, and today has become a major concern, especially in Eastern Europe and the former Soviet Union. In the minds of many, nationalism is linked to the increase in terrorism (the IRA, the ETA, neo-Nazism in Germany, Bosnia) as well as to the outbreak of ethnic wars in the former Yugoslavia, Abkhazia and Nagorno-Karabakh.

Despite all this, it is remarkable how little attention has been given by students of European integration to the problem of nationalism. Ranging over the various spheres of European concern from finance, economics and agriculture to industry, politics and education, studies of European trends utilize a form of 'methodological nationalism' that takes the national state as its operating unit for data collection and analysis, but allows no influence for national identities and differences or for nationalist sentiments and ideologies. But, in the light of current events in Europe and the wider world, such a stance is myopic and self-defeating. If we cannot confront the major issue of our times, what hope is there for containment and accommodation of ethnic and national forces, let alone for the construction of a genuinely 'European identity'?

In fact, it is impossible to disregard the issue of nationalism in Europe, whether our concerns are academic or practical. In this respect, little has changed in two centuries. Ever since the patriots of the French Revolution inscribed *fraternité* on their banner, the nation and nationalism have been central issues of European history and politics, if only because societies and polities have been increasingly organized around the dimensions and features of 'national states', while what we call 'international' relations takes the 'national state' form for granted as its norm, both in theory and political practice. Nowhere is the centrality of the 'national state' so much in evidence as in Europe today, despite the dual challenge of ethnic nationalism 'from below' and supra-nationalism 'from above'. Indeed, these challenges only serve to reinforce the power of nationalism and the centrality of the nation in the hearts and minds of most people in Europe. The elusive concept of the 'nation' has played a key role in the formation of the European system of states and, as I shall argue, will continue to do so, even in the attempts to 'create Europe' which are the subject of so much heated debate.

The Nations of Europe

Let me start with some definitions and then apply them in the European context. From classical antiquity on, the concept of the 'nation' has always referred to a human community of shared culture and territory. At first, the term *natio* was used by the Romans to refer to distant, often barbaric peoples, as opposed to the Roman *populus*. But in the course of the middle ages, *natio* came to signify the geo-cultural segments of universities and Church councils: the English, German, French contingents. After the Renaissance, the term came to stand for the populations of the European states themselves, insofar as they were felt to form ethnic communities as well as polities; and by the eighteenth century our modern idea of the nation as both a mass cultural and a political community had taken shape, to inspire the French patriots with their belief in a free nation of co-cultural citizens inhabiting a historically defined territory and obeying common laws (Zernatto 1944; Tonkin, McDonald and Chapman 1989, Introduction).

Culture, territory, political community: these are the basic elements of our modern concept of the nation. They imply, first and foremost, that the nation, unlike the state, is a social group, a historical community of shared culture. Like the state, however, the nation is also a territorial unit. Hence the frequent tendency to elide the two concepts (particularly in the English language) and speak of the 'nation-state'. But, as Walker Connor and others have demonstrated, 90 per cent of states are 'plural': they contain within their borders more than one ethnic community (Belgium, Switzerland and Romania) and often more than one nation (Britain and Spain). This is certainly the case in Europe. So much so, indeed, that we may well ask whether the concept of the 'nation' serves any useful purpose (Connor 1972; Wiberg 1983).

Within what we conventionally designate as the boundaries of 'Europe', two different concepts of the nation have taken root and on occasion clashed. The first stems from the West European experience of the dynastic state as the matrix of the nation; we may call this the *territorial* nation. Examples include France, England (then Britain), Spain, Sweden and Denmark. The second emerged, mainly in Eastern and Southern Europe, in opposition to imperial expansion by Habsburgs, Ottomans and Romanovs, and was forged 'from below' largely by intelligentsias claiming to speak on behalf of 'the people' and their vernacular cultures; this we may term the *ethnic* nation. Bulgaria, Serbia, Poland, as well as Czechs and Slovaks, are examples of ethnic nations.

The first kind of nation – France, for example – is a community of citizens defined by common laws, territory and culture; its primary elements are historic territory, shared public culture (usually language), citizenship and a common set of laws and unified legal system. The second, or ethnic, type of nation (Poles, Greeks) is a community of citizens defined by genealogical ties, vernacular culture, mass mobilization and native history. Hans Kohn, who originally proposed a dichotomy of European nationalisms along these lines, felt that the territorial type was characteristic of Western Europe, while the ethnic kind was to be found east of the Rhine; and that the explanation for this divergence was the relative failure of communities east of the Rhine to evolve a strong bourgeoisie to push for a 'rational' political community. There is some truth in his thesis, though it needs to be modified and shorn of its ideological moorings: these two kinds of nationalism, *civic-territorial* and *ethnic-genealogical*, have operated and continue to operate in the European continent, and their conflict forms the basic grid of many European political developments to this day (Kohn 1967, ch. 7; Plamenatz 1976).

Given this bifurcation, can we salvage the idea of the 'nation' as a unitary concept? I think we can, if we bear in mind the assumptions common to the territorial and ethnic versions. These are:

1   a shared culture for all the citizens
2   a shared history (myths and memories)
3   a historically delimited territory or 'homeland'
4   common laws (rights and duties) for citizens (or nationals).

The last two assumptions, while not explicit in the ethnic version of the nation, are clearly present, since it too seeks to create nations of citizens with common rights and duties and limited boundaries defined by shared 'ethno-history'.

We can accordingly propose the following unitary definition:

> A nation is a territorial community of shared history and mass culture, a unified economy and common rights and duties for all members.

The only addition here is a reference to a 'unified economy', but this seems again to be implicit in all the formulations of territorial and ethnic nationalists everywhere; for without a single division of labour, the nation could have neither unity nor autonomy.

What of our other key concept, 'nationalism'? Here I think we can take our cue from the goals of self-declared nationalist movements themselves.

Beneath the undergrowth of nationalist rhetoric, we can discern three basic recurrent demands and aspirations: for national identity, national unity and national autonomy. Without an identity, there can be no distinctive community and without a community, there can be no claim to constitute a nation. Without unity, the nation falters. Its claims can be belittled, it lacks moral weight and its identity fragments. Without autonomy, the nation cannot 'be itself'. It cannot be 'true to itself'. That is to say, it can no longer determine its course, listen to its inner voice, express its authentic culture. Hence, it must obey first and last its 'own law', *autos nomos*; otherwise, it remains unfree.

Nationalism, then, is a summons for freedom – social, cultural and political. But not the freedom of individuals, only of culture communities. The freedom for national communities to determine their own fate. So:

> Nationalism is an ideological movement to attain and maintain autonomy, unity and identity for a human population some of whose members believe it to constitute an actual or potential nation.

In the European context, these concepts have translated themselves in varying ways in different periods and areas. In the west and north of Europe, as we saw, the growth of powerful states in England, France, Spain and Sweden helped to forge the idea of territorial nations, whose dominant ethnic communities what the French term *ethnies* (a term I shall use here) – formed the basis of the subsequent civic nation. But, even in the West, this dominance and its legitimating concept has been repeatedly challenged by ethnic nationalisms – notably by the Irish, Norwegians and Finns in the last century, and by Catalans, Basques, Bretons, Corsicans, Welsh and Scots in this century. To the surprise of many observers, the 'ethnic revival' of the 1960s and 1970s called into question the common evolutionary belief in the ascending scale of human association and the obsolescence of smaller, more localized units, while simultaneously undermining the powers and scope of existing national states.

In the more open south and east of Europe, on the other hand, ethnic nationalisms emerged from the early nineteenth-century to challenge and undermine the existing polyethnic Habsburg, Ottoman and Romanov empires. Though the civic ideals of the French Revolution inspired some intellectuals from these areas, the states that emerged after the demise of these empires owed more to the pre-existing social forms of a mainly agrarian economy, as well as to the surviving political and ethnic memories of their intertwined peoples. Given the much greater ethnic heterogeneity and intermingling in these eastern and southern states, in Poland, Hungary, Romania and the Balkans, ethnic nationalism, with its calls for mobilizing the people on the basis of genealogical ties and vernacular culture, was bound to result in much greater conflict and confusion than in the more territorially separated and ethnically stable western and northern areas of the continent (Kedourie 1960, chs 6–7; Argyle 1976).

The result is a continent of extraordinary ethnic diversity and kaleidoscopic national variety. Though other continents can boast a much greater number of ethnic categories and ethnic communities (Africa has some six thousand ethnolinguistic categories), the range of ethnic and national attachments in the relatively small area of Europe is unparalleled. Krejci and Velimsky conducted a survey of 73 ethnic communities in Europe west of the Urals in the late 1970s, to discover that the majority (60) was defined in linguistic terms and another large group (59) in territorial-political terms, i.e., as basing their claims on compact territory and memories of a previous polity, like the Poles, Hungarians, Czechs, Croats, Catalans and Scots. The size and power of these communities also varied greatly, from small declining language groups (Sorbs, Faroese – with fewer than 100,000) to powerful large nations like the French and Germans dominating their respective 'national states' (Krejci and Velimsky 1981).

These differences, which need always to be borne in mind when attempting to generalize about the elusive field of European nations and nationalisms, attest to the global phenomenon of 'national incongruence', which is responsible for so many of the world's major conflicts today. This is the failure of ethnic and political boundaries to coincide, with the result that many ethnic communities are either incorporated in wider territorial-political units or straddle them, like the Kurds or Ewe. In Europe, incorporation of *ethnies* into 'alien' national states is now more common than their fragmentation across different states; but Europe has had its share of irredenta – of Italians in Austrian lands, of Germans in Eastern Europe, of Greeks in Anatolia and Thrace – with all the ensuing conflicts.

National incongruence in Europe has meant a fairly high incidence of ethnic and national conflict. Here I am thinking not only of the national dimension of the two World Wars, but of the many ethnic revolts and nationally influenced wars of the last two centuries, beginning with the Revolutionary and Napoleonic Wars. The fact is that ethnic incorporation and fragmentation have contributed to the instability of the continent on a number of occasions; one has only to think of the Peninsular War, the 'Spring of the Peoples' and the Hungarian War of 1848–9, the Italian wars of the Risorgimento, the Franco-Prussian War, the Balkan Wars, the Polish-Russian War of 1920, and, more recently, the wars in the Baltic states and Yugoslavia. Add the ethnic struggles in places such as Ulster, Euzkadi and Transylvania, and the list of ethnic instabilities due to lack of fit between ethnic and territorial borders is much greater (Kohn 1955; Seton-Watson 1977, chs 2–4).

The European State System

Perhaps the most potent factor in the formation of European nations has been the system of states that has emerged on the continent since the fifteenth century. There is little doubt that repeated failure to unite the landmass of Europe, on the model of the Roman Empire, together with the ethnic diversity of its population, provided the framework for the subsequent formation of European nations. The economic and political competition of European dynastic states, their trade rivalries, colonial ventures and territorial wars, has meant that political pluralism has been enshrined in both the traditions and the organization of the European states. This pluralism was most forcibly and vividly expressed in the principle of territorial sovereignty, whereby the state, as a set of public, autonomous institutions differentiated from other social institutions, and exercising a monopoly of coercion and extraction in a given territory, became supreme both internally *vis-à-vis* its subjects and externally in relation to other sovereign states. By the eighteenth century, political competition and territorial sovereignty were enshrined in the doctrine of a 'balance of power' between the European states, and later in the ideal of a European 'concert of nations'. All of which suggest the priority, temporal as well as logical, of the state and the system of states to the formation of European nations and the rise of nationalism (Tilly 1975; Tivey 1980; Gellner 1983).

But the idea that in Europe the state has been the matrix and agent of the nation needs to be qualified in two ways. In the first place, it applied historically more in the western and northern parts of the continent than in the south and east. Here strong rulers helped to forge powerful, expansionist states which succeeded in attracting by their economic and political success the loyalties of most (though not all) of their populations. In England, France, Spain, Denmark and Sweden, absolutist monarchs were able to harness the loyalties of their dominant ethnic communities and bind them to the new political community being fashioned through the agencies of the state. To the east and south, however, the large polyethnic empires were unable to command the loyalty of many of their subjects, whose primary attachments to their religious and ethnic communities proved a major obstacle to the kind of state building that absolutist monarchs such as Joseph II aimed to promote. Here, then, the state proved to be a target of the nationalists, to be over-thrown and removed, before the task of nation building could commence on the basis of the ethno-religious or ethno-linguistic community (Stavrianos 1961; Sugar and Lederer 1969).

The second qualification concerns the core population of the new states and nations. Even in the west and north of Europe, a dominant or core ethnic population formed the basis of both state and nation. In other words, from the start the state which became the matrix and agent of the nation was built on the foundations of a prior *ethnie*, that is, on the basis of a core cultural population – for example, the English, French, Castilians, Danes and Swedes. Nevertheless, it was the incorporating bureaucratic state that turned a much older ethnic community into a nation. Later (from the fifteenth century) the centralizing state began to forge (though quite unintentionally) out of this core population and neighbouring ones which it annexed what Seton-Watson has called the 'old, continuous nations' of Europe, as opposed to the much later 'nations of design' (after 1815), those that were deliberately created by rulers and nationalists as a result of the various treaties which concluded successive rounds of European warfare. Even in these cases, then, states did not form nations single-handed; they had the basic building-block of a definite *ethnie* around which to ground the subsequent nation (Seton-Watson 1977, ch. 2; Orridge 1982).

This suggests a further glimpse into the European past as a way of under-standing the complexities of the present. As Tilly has shown, the sheltered nature of the western part of the European landmass allowed for the settle-ment and political conquest of distinct areas relatively unmolested, after the end of the 'barbarian irruptions'. As successive waves of barbarian *ethnies* moved into a western half of the continent protected by the Atlantic and North seas, they each soon found a territorial niche and succeeded in building it up and protecting it with a *regnum*, a discrete kingdom based on the customs, languages and descent myths of particular ethnic communities. But in the eastern and southern parts of Europe, no such ethnic stabilization occurred. On the contrary, even after the Avar and Magyar invasions, there were continual ethnic migrations and disturbances well into the medieval era, up to the time of the Mongol and Turkish invasions. The result was a much greater ethnic intermingling, and a complete lack of subsequent national congruence between states and ethnic populations – a failure which is a root cause of many of the recent conflicts afflicting the Balkans and Eastern Europe (Tilly 1975, Introduction; Jelavich 1983, vol. I; Reynolds 1984, ch. 8).

Perhaps this was also the cause of the economic and political predominance of the western half of the continent through the centuries. Whether it was because of Roman settlement and government or as a result of natural resources and greater political stability, already by the time of the Holy Roman Empire and the later Burgundian realm, the wealth, power and demographic preponderance of the western half were all too evident, and its position was greatly strengthened by the rise of absolutist states, colonial discoveries and ultimately the industrial revolution. These factors encouraged the dynastic, and later the national, state to harness unprecedented technologi-cal, scientific and cultural powers, and attract a highly skilled and ambitious intelligentsia to its service. In the West, the territorialized 'scientific state' increasingly usurped the powers of God and a universal Church, as well as other more local powers, to instil in the minds and hearts of its citizens the virtues and values of a civic nationalism. In this crisis of authority, the Western state became the model and standard for other parts of Europe, and later the world, secular politicians and professionals took the place of clergy and aristocrats as the fount of wisdom and value, and reason and history replaced divine revelation as the source of authority (A. D. Smith 1971, ch. 10; Poggi 1978; Wallace 1990, ch. 4).

The main instruments of the national state, so clearly exemplified in the Third Republic in France, were compulsory military training in the citizen army, a unified system of public, mass education, and growing state control over the press and communications and, in a later age, radio and television. Crucial to the success of the national state was the formulation and dissemination of a single canon of national history, literature and the arts. Through the standardization of history textbooks, and the elaboration of a national literary and artistic heritage, the civic-territorial nationalism of the political community of the national state took root among the mass of the population, turning them into politically conscious and participant citizens. In a later era, this nationalism permeated other cultural media and products purveyed under the aegis of the state – film, radio, television, telecommunications, and satellite and information technology (see Weber 1977; Citron 1988).

Europe in a Wider World

The upshot of the analysis so far is to underline the historical priority and power of the national state, first in Western and later in Eastern Europe. This has meant that the ideal form of the nation is civic and territorial, the type canonized by the secular nationalism of the French patriots in the Revolution. At the same time, this headstart and preponderance has been gradually eroded by the inroads of the ethnic, genealogical nationalisms which flourished in Eastern and Southern Europe. Even in the West, ethnic nationalism has surfaced periodically – in Ireland, in Norway, in France during the Dreyfus Affair, and, more recently, in the many minority communities within the major Western European states – among Basques, Catalans, Corsicans, Bretons, Flemish, Scots and Welsh. Why should we be witnessing this extension and proliferation of ethnic nationalisms in Western Europe today? And what is its relationship to the revival of ethnic nationalisms in the eastern and southern parts of the continent?

Part of the answer to the first question lies in the changed global position of Europe and its major political actors. To begin with, the twentieth century witnessed the emergence of the two nuclear superpowers to the West and East, as well as serious trade and political rivals in the Far East. This meant that the old imperial powers of Europe were each reduced to second-class political and economic status, and that, insofar as one could speak of a united 'Europe', it has become one of several power centres in a multi-polar world, perhaps one with less political force than the other centres (see Barraclough 1967).

In the second place, the previous protection offered by the western coastline of Europe became increasingly irrelevant in a world of missiles, computerized technology and multi-national corporations. Naval power, on which the Atlantic seaboard states had depended, became less important in an era of nuclear weaponry and air power. This was understood already in the 1950s by the Benelux countries, and was slowly but clearly grasped by British governments and people after Suez and especially with the increases in oil prices in the 1970s, producing a reluctant but definite reorientation away from the old idea of Britain as a sea-power tied to a maritime commonwealth, to that of an offshore island bound increasingly to the continental European trading, industrial and political networks. This led to the reapplication in 1973 for British membership of the European Economic Community. Only by becoming part of a wider European union, it was felt by many, could the loss of military protection for the seaboard states be offset and a new, political and economic security be assured. The impact of this reorientation towards Europe on a continuing sense of British national identity has been ambiguous and conflictual, polarizing political opinion in both major parties and sharpening the different visions of a British identity (Tilly 1975, Introduction; Camps 1965).

Third, this development was hastened by the heritage and demise of empire. The preponderance of Western European states was intimately bound up with their global status, as imperial powers with often vast overseas colonies. The resulting 'traditions of empire' have been an important legacy for the leading European powers to this day, and the factual demise of their empires has left a powerful sense of past grandeur, evident in the monumental and artistic heritage of so many European capitals. The 'great museum' of Europe built up through this imperial heritage of conquest and its mission of 'rescuing' the monuments of other great civilizations for European posterity was closely associated with the rise of civic and ethnic nationalisms in Europe. In some ways, it was a powerful expression of the rivalry produced by those nationalisms (see Horne 1984).

Finally, the sense of European distinctiveness in an increasingly interdependent globe has been accentuated by the pioneering role the West has played in the diffusion of capitalist democracy, or, more accurately, the combination of bourgeois capitalism with varying degrees of social democracy. This has left a strong sense of Europe as an oasis of affluent liberal democracy amidst a desert of military dictatorship and authoritarian party rule. Of course, many Europeans are all too aware of the precarious nature of both affluence and democracy; the vivid memory of Fascism and Nazism, and the ongoing struggles to achieve a measure of civil and political rights in many Southern and Eastern European countries, dramatize the benefits and threats to the democratic tradition across the continent, giving each of the European states a political stake in the stability and civic order of the others. Yet one 'test' of what we increasingly mean by the concept of 'Europe' is the ability to share in the liberal capitalist experiment, with affluent democracies and rights of citizenship for members of the civic nation.

The sense of threat to a fragile democratic balance composed out of many conflicting interests, as well as to national identities within Europe, has been augmented by the tides of immigration into the central and southern parts of Europe, and, more recently, by the spectre of a widening Balkan war and the human misery it has brought within the continent itself. (It is not uncommon to hear the Bosnian tragedy referred to as taking place 'on the doorstep of Europe'. One wonders how and where the boundaries of 'Europe' are being drawn.) The demise of communism in Eastern Europe and the former Soviet Union, and the gradual lifting of barriers to mobility across state borders, have posed a particularly acute problem for a reunited Germany, which is seen as the 'front-line' national state of the affluent, democratic Europe, i.e., of Western Europe, and which till recently tried to maintain a liberal immigration policy, albeit one that distinguishes radically between German citizens and foreign residents and *Gastarbeiter*. This has come hard on the heels of the historians' debate about 'revisionism', i.e., the revising of views about the Nazi regime and the Holocaust, initiated by Nolte in 1985, which has once again posed the question of whether and what kind of national identity might legitimately be held by Germans who have emerged from the shadows of the Nazi memory.

Other Western national states, notably France, Holland and Italy, have felt their affluent democracies and national identities to be under pressure from large influxes of foreign migrants – from Algeria and Morocco, Turkey, Albania and elsewhere. The threat of massive immigration from the republics of the former Soviet Union and Eastern Europe has led to growing restrictions on entry, to fears of cultural 'swamping' and to a sharpened sense of the *Western* orientation of 'Europe' which, coupled with the rigorous tests of economic parity and market transformation, will make it increasingly difficult for Eastern European national states to 'join Europe' on any but Western European terms. There is the further danger that the civic model of national identity characteristic of the Western states will give way in France, Germany and Italy, perhaps even in Britain, to a more pronounced ethnic model (see Husbands 1991; Miles and Singer-Kerel 1991).

Globalization and Ethnic Revival

The changed position of Europe in an increasingly interdependent world also reflects a broader process of 'globalization'. The latter is perceived as a process in which space and time are diminished or 'compressed' in the consciousness of groups and individuals. This is largely a function of the exponential growth of mass communications and computerized information technology, and of the increasingly rapid pace of technological and social change. Through radio, television, videos and satellites, individuals all over the world are immediately apprised of events and persons in far-off areas, of which they previously had little or no knowledge, and messages that formerly took days to send can now be flashed instantaneously to their recipients. More important, perhaps, is the acceleration of 'time': the sense of the succession of simultaneous events is becoming far denser and the events themselves are perceived as more urgent and immediate. The multitude of these events and developments 'fills out' the sensation of an 'empty, homogenous' chronological time along which we move; individuals are fed with far more and more diverse information than in previous eras, and they become aware of events and processes that bear only indirectly on their own situation (see Anderson 1983, ch. 2; Featherstone 1990).

Given the developed state of European mass communications and information technology and the resulting vigorous flow of messages among the states of Europe, these global pressures on individual and group perception are particularly acute in Europe. But, as elsewhere, the results have been paradoxical. They have produced not the 'global culture' and cosmopolitan outlook that are so often predicted, except among a tiny minority, but a vague sense of 'Europe' and 'European culture', sharply and often discordantly punctuated by a series of protests, revolts and social movements, which we may broadly term 'the ethnic revival'.

Let me start with this 'revival' and then deal with the broader issue of European culture. From the late 1950s to the 1970s, most of the states of Western Europe experienced protests, revolts and social movements in the name of ethnic minorities who had for ages resided within the borders of these states, having been long ago incorporated by the monarchs and elites of the 'core' *ethnie*. Among Basques, Catalans, Corsicans, Occitanians, Bretons, Flemish, Scots and Welsh, to mention only the most prominent cases, there were mass protests and movements of varying scope and degree for a far greater measure of cultural, economic and political autonomy, if not outright independence. Most of these movements, including the Scots, Welsh, Bretons and Flemish, have to date been satisfied with greater 'regional' autonomy, and the 1980s witnessed a downturn in the support and demands of these movements, except among Basques and Catalans. It would be a mistake to assume, however, that the 'ethnic revival' has spent itself. Rather, it has entered a new phase, one in which the opening to Europe, with its slogan *L'Europe des ethnies*, has become an important, if elusive, factor in the self-presentation and appeal of ethnic movements like the Scottish National Party (Esman 1977; A. D. Smith 1981).

There are a number of observations about this 'ethnic revival' which bear on the shape of Europe and its nations. First, we may be misled by the term 'ethnic revival' if we imagine that these movements surfaced again in the 1960s after a long period (going back to the late Middle Ages?) when the *ethnie* in question was 'unaware' of itself and its members had no collective aspirations. In fact, the origins of many of the modern ethnic movements go back a long way: culturally to the late eighteenth or nineteenth centuries in the case of Welsh, Scots, Catalans, Occitanians and Bretons, politically to the late nineteenth century for Scots, Welsh, Catalans, Basques and Flemish, and after 1918 for others. The Welsh cultural revival, for example, goes back to the reinstitution of the Eisteddfod in 1789, the Catalan cultural revival to the Jocs Floral in 1859; the Welsh and Scots Home Rule movements emerged in the 1880s and 1890s, along with the first ideological statements of Catalan and Basque nationalism by Almirall and Arana. Hence we may speak as much of ethnic survival as of revival. What was new in the 1960s was a broadening of middle-class support, witnessed in the Hamilton and other by-elections in Britain, a sharpening of political demands by the ethnic parties and a greater emphasis on economic issues than before (Mayo 1974; Beer 1977; Webb 1977; Reece 1979).

Second, these ethnic movements were closely associated with the more general Western rebellion of the 1960s against the prevailing order. They formed part of the more general neo-romantic revolt of subjectivist authenticity against bureaucratic rationality and elite standards. The civil rights movement in America, the feminist and gay critiques of heterosexual patriarchy, the protests of university students against 'bourgeois knowledge' and bureaucratic rationality, the larger movement of anti-colonial liberation provided the later ethnic movements with many of their themes and cultural models. As the influence of these other models and movements waned, the ethnic movements too began to falter, except in Spain (A. D. Smith 1979, chs 6–7; Melucci 1989).

Third, several of these movements achieved at least some of their goals. In varying degrees, governments in Belgium, France, Spain and Britain took greater cognizance of and interest in the situation of their ethnic 'peripheries', as the French did in Brittany and the British with the Devolution Bill; they grasped the need to placate and appease a sense of ethnic neglect and grievance on the part of these *ethnies*, even where they had no real intention of handing back powers to local bodies. In certain realms, notably those of culture, ethnic movements won some concessions (for example, indigenous-language schooling and TV channels), though not enough to satisfy them or dampen their aspirations for greater autonomy.

Finally, the broader ethnic movement was one that was confined to the Western half of the continent, and had more in common with the analogous revolt in Quebec than with the contemporary or later movements in Eastern Europe – with the possible exception of the Slovene and Croat movements. The 'Western' ethnic revival was fuelled by the parallel histories and common economic and political experiences of 'the West' (including the United States, where there was a neo-romantic 'ethnic revival' in the 1970s among white *ethnies*). Hence it was played out separately from developments in the then communist-dominated Eastern half of the continent (see Glazer and Moynihan 1975; Hechter and Levi 1979).

Of course, we may never know if this separate development was a function of the very different economies and polities of Western and Eastern Europe in the 1960s and 1970s. It is possible that, had perestroika in the East occurred earlier, the 'ethnic revival' there would have been contemporaneous with that in the West. But could we infer similar causes for both sets of ethnic revivals? Clearly not, in any detail. The historical origins of the Western and Eastern ethnic revivals are quite dissimilar. The recent liberation of Eastern Europe, the movement to recognize ethnic republics in the former Soviet Union, and the consequent inter-ethnic conflicts belong to an entirely different historical trajectory, in which the Eastern European and former Soviet *ethnies* could look back to longer or shorter periods of independence. In the Baltic republics and in much of Eastern Europe, many of these *ethnies* formed nations with states of their own or dominated polyethnic states, as in Poland or Yugoslavia. In the area of the former Soviet Union, many *ethnies* secured a temporary independence after the fall of the Romanov Empire in 1917, until their short-lived republics such as those of the Ukraine or Georgia were crushed and swallowed by the advancing Bolshevik armies (Pipes, 1970).

These relatively recent historical memories, together with the experience of communist takeover and oppression, have combined with much longer and deeper ethnic ties and memories in the East, often going back to the medieval era and celebrated in chronicle, epic and song, to undergird the present movements for ethnic autonomy or independence. In fact, today's ethnic revival in the East represents a 'second attempt' by these *ethnies* to secede from imperial states and form nations pursuing an independent national existence, in the geo-ethnic space between Germans and Russians. It is as if history invited them to have a second start in the process of nation formation and political development, which had been temporarily aborted by communism.

In short, the present national and ethnic movements in Eastern Europe and the Commonwealth of Independent States owe little to the influences that shaped the ethnic revival in the West. They also owe little to movements of decolonization in the Third World, to the black civil rights movement or to feminist or gay critiques. They do, however, have links with some Western experiences, notably with movements for civil and political rights (Charter 77, etc.) and with the ecology movement, especially after the disaster at Chernobyl. Yet it is possible to argue that, however important in themselves, these influences were only secondary, and that the primary sources of ethno-nationalism in the East are to be found in the ethnic composition and historical memories of these areas (G. E. Smith 1985; Goble 1989).

These sources, while they exhibit important regional variations, conform to a wider overall pattern of 'vernacular mobilization'. In this pattern, indigenous intelligentsias attempt to mobilize 'their' chosen populations for political activity on the basis of the latters' customs, symbols, languages and traditions. That, at any rate, is the theory. In practice, matters are more complicated. The intelligentsias are often forced to choose between different versions, or strands, of custom, myth and tradition and select particular dialects and ethno-histories as the 'authentic' ethnic heritage and tradition. They may on occasion even have to forge a new language (for example, the Greek *katharevousa* language) or resurrect and modernize an ancient language (Hebrew, Norse). The point, however, remains the overriding need for the intelligentsia of couching any political appeals in the language and culture of 'the people', as Nairn so graphically describes. No other form of political mobilization is conceivable (Nairn 1977 ch. 2; A. D. Smith 1989).

Crucial to the re-emergence of ethnic nationalism in Eastern Europe and Russia has been the presence of distinctive 'ethnic cores', though often intermixed with 'peripheral' ethnic communities (such as German and Russian settlers, Jews and Gypsies), with often profound historical memories of former glory and/or statehood in the particular area. Such memories are cherished by Hungarians, Czechs, Serbs, Bulgarians, Poles, Georgians and Armenians, whose communities can point to well-defined ethnic states in the ancient and/or medieval epochs. While it is by no means always the case that modern ethnic conflicts in Eastern Europe and Russia are the product of so-called ancient ethnic antagonisms, the presence of historical memories of former statehood or autonomy, coloured by sentiments of pride in a 'glorious past' of heroes and sages, is a vital ingredient both in the preservation of ethnic ties into the modern period, and in the intensification and justification of recent conflicts between adjacent *ethnies*, even where the causes are mainly social and political. Thus the conflicts over Transylvania and Nagorno-Karabakh may have more recent political and socio-economic causes, but they are greatly amplified and embittered by sentiments of pride consequent on the dissemination of historical memories of former greatness of the community (Krejci 1978; Krejci and Velimsky 1981; Sugar 1980).

Whatever the deeper roots of these conflicts, the present scene is one of increasing post-Cold War disorder and the emergence of a multi-polar inter-state order, particularly in Eastern Europe and the area of the former Soviet Union. The post-communist drive towards market economies and multi-party democracy in several states has undoubtedly permitted and stimulated the expression of ethnic and national sentiments. This is not to endorse the common theory of 'underlying ethnic sentiments' awaiting to explode once the totalitarian lid was lifted. That may have been true of Poland and Hungary, where they did in fact erupt despite the presence of totalitarian oppression, or in the Baltic states, where memories of former statehood were kept alive as much by Western refusal to recognize Soviet annexation as from internal causes. Other cases like the movements in Belorussia and Ukraine were dependent less on internal historic causes than on immediate ecological (Chernobyl) and political factors.

In this fluid and uncertain era, changes in the general climate of inter-state relations, the demonstration effect of ethnic separatisms in other parts of the world and an increasingly mobile, immigrant population have generated more opportunities and stimuli for ethnic nationalisms and have made the attainment of a territorial, civic nation more difficult. This has also led to more violent xenophobic reactions and a marked increase in anti-Semitism in Eastern Europe and Russia. Such unwelcome manifestations have in turn forced European governments to take stronger measures and cooperate more closely on 'law and order', citizenship and immigration issues. We are therefore likely to see more violent tensions between the territorialized political order and the ethnically fragmented social order, with greater possibilities for conflict and even warfare, as has occurred in the former Yugoslavia. The evident unwillingness of European and world powers to intervene in Bosnia, despite well-founded fears of the conflict spreading, suggests the limits of state power in the area of ethnicity and nationalism (Glenny 1991).

Towards a Unified Europe?

It is against this background that we must evaluate the current moves to greater European unification. The Croatian and Bosnian (as well as the earlier Kuwaiti) crises underlined a vital dimension of the pan-European argument: namely, the urgent need for a single source of political authority in Europe to counteract the centuries-long ethnic antagonisms and national conflicts that have wracked and debilitated the continent and caused such disastrous world wars. In its updated form, pan-Europeanism envisages a federal Europe which protects its 'regions', a term often used to denote separate *ethnies* which inhabit ethno-historically defined territories – like the Bretons in Brittany or the Basques in Euzkadi – even where that territory may be host to other *ethnies* or parts thereof, or to immigrants. So a single centralized political authority in Brussels, accountable to a single European Parliament in Strasbourg, presiding over a single European economy and financial system, would represent and protect the interests of Europe's smaller and peripheral *ethnies*, through the Regional Fund, as well as constitutionally. The modern formulation of pan-Europeanism, therefore, emphasizes this regional dimension in the ideal of *l'Europe des ethnies* (see Heraud 1963; Nairn 1977, ch. 9).

This federal vision is in marked contrast to the more conservative and limited ideal of *l'Europe des patries* envisaged by de Gaulle and most British governments. The debates in Britain over the history curriculum emphasizing the differences in rival conceptions of British national identity, some of them more inward-turning towards an insular English 'national past', others more multi-cultural and ready to embrace a European vision, highlight this scepticism. The difficulties over the ratification of the Maastricht Treaty also illustrate these contrasting visions and tendencies; sufficient numbers of the French, Danish and British populations appear to be so hostile to the Treaty because they are only prepared to accept the Gaullist vision of economic cooperation between national states which in all other respects jealously guard their national identities and political sovereignties – a vision that allows each national state to interpret and, if powerful enough, to fashion 'Europe' in its own image, and thereby lead and dominate the new European superpower. This, of course, is also the danger espied by the Euro-sceptics, who suspect that France and Germany are vying for supremacy of a federated Europe and are seeking to impose their (rather different) nationally derived conceptions of Europe onto the other states and ethnic populations (de Rougemont 1965; Galtung 1973; Gardiner 1990).

In contrast to these traditional visions of 'Europe' stand other less extreme and clearcut formulations. One is the idea of a European pooling of sovereignties, or aspects of sovereignties. The idea here is that, in a global economy, the state has become more porous and interdependent in the contemporary world, and that one manifestation of this trend is the growth of regional networks to fulfil certain functions which states can no longer perform on their own. The European network is a particularly good example of a functional organization in which the principle of 'subsidiarity' – of problems and activities finding their appropriate organizational/political level – is being embodied. The traditional state on this view is handing over some of its functions and powers, upward, to a federal authority, and devolving others, downward, to more local (and ethnic or regional) units, according to the nature of the problem and activity involved (see Deutsch 1957; Haas 1964; Wallace 1990, ch. 4).

This is a largely organizational and political formulation. It ignores the cultural dimensions of Europe. It is also rather a 'top-down', institutional conception, one which focuses on the elite, as opposed to the popular, level. It needs to be complemented by a conception that addresses the social and cultural dimensions at the popular as well as the elite level. One possibility is the idea of a European 'family of cultures' (*not* 'family of nations', as the official rhetoric claims). The cultures in question are transnational heritages, movements, traditions and styles, such as Roman law, Judeo-Christian ethics, democracy and revolution, the Renaissance, the Enlightenment, Romanticism and Realism, Art Deco and Pop – traditions and movements which swept the continent in varying degrees, and which together have brought the nations and states of Europe into a 'family of cultures'. Though none of these cultures and traditions have affected *all* the European states and areas, and most of them have been uneven in their effects, they have spread and formed overlapping circles which have tied different groups of European nations and states together in various ways, like an intricate set of ornamental patterns in a tapestry or Persian carpet (A. D. Smith 1990).

Althought their 'high culture' manifestations at the elite level are most familiar, many of these cultural and political traditions affected the middle and lower classes and gave them a transnational 'European' currency. Here we must exercise caution. Even the most transnational traditions and heritages – Roman law, Christianity, Renaissance and Romanticism – also had localized expressions based on ethnic and national differences at the popular as well as the elite level. Thus we speak of Greek Orthodoxy, the Italian Renaissance and German Romanticism, where the adjective is something more than just a geographical or linguistic expression, signifying also the inclusion of a popular way of life and ethnic expression. So today, too, we should not overlook the continuing importance of the national form and expression of wider European currents like social democracy, post-modernism and pop art, at the popular as well as the elite level (see Porter and Teich 1988).

This focus on the *popular* level is necessary to counteract the frequent tendency to think of European unification mainly in terms of elite sentiments and activities. Considerable differences remain in many European states between elite aspirations and cultures and those of the mass of the population. Though public education, the mass media and mass tourism in Europe are opening new vistas for many lower-middle-class members, considerable differences persist in taste and outlook between the European middle and lower classes in many states. Traditionally, pan-Europeanism and the creation of the common European market have catered to the needs and aspirations of business and administrative elites, supported by professional groups like journalists, broadcasters and many academics. The lower classes, urban and rural, have proved to be less attracted to the European ideal; their horizons, where they are not regional, are tied to the national state framework and the national culture.

This weakness of the European project, which was revealed in the Maastricht ratification process, is bound up with another problem: the tenuous and abstract nature of the European ideal in comparison with national identities and aspirations. While we should not fall into the trap of thinking that the relationship between a 'European identity' and a 'national identity' is a zero-sum relationship, since individuals frequently possess multiple collective identities and move fairly easily between them, there is little doubt that the ideal of the nation is not only more familiar and widely accepted, but also much more accessible, vivid and tangible than the idea of an all-embracing 'European identity'. For many people, there remains something nebulous, pale and uncertain about the concept of a European identity. More to the point, if the boundaries of 'Europe' remain unclear, so does the 'centre' – not just the territorial or political centre, but the symbolic and spiritual centre. Where, one might ask, are the sacred shrines of 'Europe', which are the European sites of pilgrimage or learning, and where are the heroic places of European collective remembrance (A. D. Smith 1992)?

The answer is all too clear, and it sounds the death-knell of all that pan-Europeanism represents. The sacred and heroic places are the shrines of Europe's warring religions, the battlefields of its rival nations and the grim fields of a continent-wide European slaughter, recounted by each of the European *ethnies*, nations and religions in their own national history textbooks and liturgies, and revisited today in the fields and on the mountains of Bosnia. Without a heritage of binding symbolism, mythology and ritual, the European ideal lacks the ability to present itself to 'the people', to impress itself on their hearts and minds with its feasts and ceremonies. Even the great festivals of the arts held in Europe (at Edinburgh, Spoleto, Cannes, Venice, Warsaw) are either national or international in scope and not specifically European (Doob 1964; Breuilly 1982, ch. 16).

It is this deficiency in the vital realm of myth, symbolism and communications that has held back the growth of an overarching pan-European identity and community. There is, however, a further dilemma. If this deficiency could somehow be made good, if cultural and institutional means could be found to evoke, through appropriate symbols, myths, rituals and memories, a fervent attachment to a distinctive European identity in the populace at large, would that not amount to the creation of yet another form of nationalism, this time a wider 'pan' nationalism of a European 'supernation'? This was certainly the vision of Coudenhove-Kalergi before the war; but with the association of nationalism with Fascism and Nazism, the attractions of 'pan' nationalisms waned, and other models were sought for the new European identity. But can there realistically be other models? Must not the new Europe come to resemble one of the larger nations and national states, with its own parallel, pan-European nationalism? Given the fact that most national states are polyethnic, will not the new European national state simply reflect and express this familiar ethnic and national diversity on a larger canvas (Galtung 1973)?

We are back with *l'Europe des ethnies*. The problem is that, where it is not simply a slogan designed to legitimate the minority *ethnies* and their ethnic nationalisms, a Europe of that degree of cultural diversity would have difficulty in holding together. One has only to consider questions of law, language and history, and the vast differences in the legal systems, languages and historical memories of the various European *ethnies* and national states, to grasp the complexity and difficulty of 'putting Europe together' in a comprehensible and binding manner. Without the benefit of a centralizing monarchy, or wars of conquest and annexation – the instruments of national formation for many European national states in the past – it is difficult to see how the European ideal can emerge clear and powerful from the 'cauldron of ethnicity' and the national rivalries of which Europe is composed.

The Revitalized Nations of Europe

What all this suggests is the continuing relevance of ethnic ties and the conceptual indispensability of the nation in contemporary Europe. In this, Europe is no exception to the long-term global trend to political and cultural pluralism. What we have been witnessing since the sixteenth century, if not earlier, is the break-up of empires and the formation of national states in a competitive inter-state order whose seal of legitimacy is membership in the comity of nations and parity in a plurality of sovereigns. Since at least the eighteenth century this political pluralism has been underpinned and extended by a social and cultural pluralism, which bases the legitimacy of the sovereign nation on the increasing homogeneity of the society and historic culture of its dominant or 'core' ethnic population. A world of cultural plurals explains and legitimizes the division of the globe into a plurality of political sovereigns. In this sense, of a global division of populations into historic culture communities, the nation has become the cornerstone of any inter-state order. Embodying the ideal, and often the reality, of the popular will, the nation has become the sole basis for political mobilization and state-making in the modern world. This remains true for contemporary Europe, despite current uncertain attempts to transfer that basis to the continental level. Europe, the source of political and cultural pluralism, remains firmly tied to a world order based on those premisses.

The reasons for this state of affairs are as much historical as contemporary and global. The nation in general (and the European nations in particular) constitutes one of the most historically embedded social formations. It is tied to a particular, modern, period of history, but also has its roots in much earlier cultural formations. It is therefore both historically and sociologically determined. Historically, as we saw, many of Europe's nations have been built around dominant ethnic cores within a given polity, or have been constructed on the basis of a minority or peripheral *ethnie*, which has succeeded in separating itself off from a large empire or a medium-sized polyethnic national state. In all these cases, the pre-modern ethnic roots of many of Europe's present-day nations are evident, and these have endowed the subsequent nations with much of their distinctive character and durability (Armstrong 1982; A. D. Smith 1986).

Sociologically, the centrality of national identity for most people today is a consequence of the many functions it performs for the individual and the community, and of the social and political processes of which it forms an integral part. Here I have in mind not so much the functions of the nation for industrial society *per se*, as its role in making possible the cohesion and collective self-awareness of large numbers of anonymized individuals. This it achieves through the political symbolism and collective 'rehearsal of rites' that Durkheim saw as indispensable to even the smallest tribal community, and which he compared with the ritual and symbolism during the French Revolution. Nationalism's rites and symbols are familiar enough: the flag, the anthem, the passport, the coinage, the oath of allegiance, the military parade, the history textbook, the monument to the fallen heroes, the museum of folklore, the processions and hymns in commemoration of past events, the emulation of past heroes, the celebration of the nation and its leaders (Durkheim 1915).

Europe has had its fill of all of these national rites and ceremonies. It continues to hear their echo, even in affluent, stable democracies. The 'invention of traditions' which, according to Eric Hobsbawm, was itself an invention of nineteenth-century Europe, is still with us. The flag is unfurled, and the anthem sung, in Slovenia, Croatia and Slovakia, in Lithuania, Latvia and Estonia, in Belorussia, Ukraine and Georgia; while in Spain, France and Britain, ethnic minorities aspire to advance the cause of regional autonomy in their own language, with their own TV channel and their own school textbooks (Hobsbawm and Ranger 1983, chs 1, 7).

This is where the role of mass, public education is so critical. Despite ERASMUS and the Council of Europe's history textbook project, systems of education in Europe remain firmly national to this day. There are signs of a greater openness to 'Europe', a greater interest in countries and peoples outside national boundaries, both in the mass media and in the teaching of humanities and social sciences, but these are to date secondary components of essentially national systems for the transmission of national values and cultures in predominantly national languages. There is only very partial equivalence even in the structures of these national education systems – in types of schooling, in examinations and grading, in teacher training, in curricula, teaching methods and the like – let alone in the more profound, but elusive, areas of myth, memory, symbol and value, encoded in the national interpretations of history, literature and the arts.

But symbols, myths, memories and values are the central elements of ethnicity itself, the cultural and affective components that lie at the heart of even the most polyethnic of modern nations. These elements define both the contents of a national culture and the boundary markers of the nation. In Europe, those boundaries have been the product of centuries of inter-state warfare, alliances and historic compromises, which have intermittently but increasingly mobilized the different peoples of Europe into a sense of their autonomous political status. But they are also the product of symbolic clusters of iterative rituals, traditions, shared memories and political mythologies. Today national mobilization adapts the values, myths, memories and symbols of each nation to the changed circumstances of a fluid post-communist world, without loss of their separate identity and authenticity. The contents (the values, myths, memories and symbols) of being French, German or Italian may subtly change as we move into the twenty-first century, but they are still closely linked to earlier national contents and continue to define the cultural boundaries of each historic nation. If this is true even in Russia, despite revolutions and seventy years of communism, how much more has it remained the case in the more stable Western and Central European national states, where the rapidity of technological and economic change has not abolished many central institutions, traditions, memories and values derived from earlier generations of the same culture-community.

What we are witnessing today in Europe is the attempt to provide a new continental container for the old wines of national diversity and identity, not any supersession of the old order of national states and ethnic minorities which has characterized the continent for over four centuries. The fires of nationalism in Europe may, after periodic outbursts, become less threatening and easier to contain and channel, but their underlying basis, the ethnic culture values that underpin nations, are unlikely to disappear, even when they take new forms or change direction. Each generation of the nation redefines its understanding of those culture values, of the national heritage it has received, in the light of changed economic, social and political conditions, including perceived threats and opportunities outside its borders. But that redefinition is likely to strengthen rather than erode those core memories and values and sustain that national heritage. The modern history of Europe suggests that we should be prepared to accept such processes of national self-strengthening and build upon them, if we wish to secure a peace that gives reassurance to all of the peoples of Europe.

Bibliography

Anderson, B. (1983). *Imagined Communities: reflections on the origin and spread of nationalism*. London: Verso.

Argyle, W. (1976). 'Size and scale as factors in the development of nationalist movements', in A. D. Smith (ed.), *Nationalist Movements*. London: Macmillan.

Armstrong, J. (1982). *Nations before Nationalism*. Chapel Hill: University of North Carolina Press.

Barraclough, G. (1967). *An Introduction to Contemporary History*. Harmondsworth: Penguin.

Beer, W. (1977). 'The social class of ethnic activists in contemporary Europe', in M. Esman (ed.), *Ethnic Conflict in the Western World*. London: Allen & Unwin; Ithaca, NY: Cornell University Press.

Breuilly, J. (1982). *Nationalism and the State*. Manchester: Manchester University Press.

Camps, M. (1965). *What Kind of Europe? The community since de Gaulle's veto*. London:

Oxford University Press.

Citron, S. (1988). *Le mythe national*. Paris: Presses Ouvriers.

Connor, W. (1972). 'Nation-building or nation-destroying?' *World Politics*, 24, 319–55.

Deutsch, K. (1957). *Political Community and the North Atlantic Area*. Princeton: Princeton University Press.

Doob, L. (1964). *Patriotism and Nationalism: their psychological foundations*. New Haven: Yale University Press.

Durkheim, E. (1915). *The Elementary Forms of Religious Life*. New York: Free Press.

Esman, M. (ed.) (1977). *Ethnic Conflict in the Western World*. London: Allen & Unwin; Ithaca, NY: Cornell University Press.

Featherstone, M. (ed.) (1990). *Global Culture: nationalism, globalisation and modernisation*. London: Sage.

Galtung, J. (1973). *The European Community: a superpower in the making*. London: Allen & Unwin.

Gardiner, J. (ed.) (1990). *The History Debate*. London: Collins & Brown.

Gellner, E. (1983). *Nations and Nationalism*. Oxford: Blackwell.

Glazer, N. and Moynihan, D. (eds) (1975). *Ethnicity, Theory and Experience*. Cambridge, MA: Harvard University Press.

Glenny, M. (1991). *The Return to History*. Harmondsworth: Penguin.

Goble, P. (1989). 'Ethnic politics in the USSR'. *Problems of Communism*, 38 (July–August): 1–4.

Haas, E. (1964). *Beyond the Nation State*. Stanford: Stanford University Press.

Hechter, M. and Levi, M. (1979). 'The comparative analysis of ethno-regional movements'. *Ethnic and Racial Studies* 2 (3): 260–74.

Heraud, G. (1963). *L'Europe des ethnies*. Paris: Presses d'Europe.

Hobsbawm, E. and Ranger, T. (eds) (1983). *The Invention of Tradition*. Cambridge: Cambridge University Press.

Horne, D. (1984). *The Great Museum*. London: Pluto Press.

Husbands, C. (1991). 'The mainstream right and the politics of immigration in France: developments in the 1980s'. *Ethnic and Racial Studies* 14 (2): 170–98.

Jelavich, B. (1983). *History of the Balkans: eighteenth and nineteenth centuries*. Cambridge: Cambridge University Press.

Kedourie, E. (1960). *Nationalism*. London: Hutchinson.

Kohn, H. (1955). *Nationalism: its meaning and history*. London: Van Nostrand.

—— (1967). *The Idea of Nationalism*. New York: Macmillan.

Krejci, J. (1978). 'Ethnic problems in contemporary Europe', in S. Giner and M. S. Archer (eds), *Contemporary Europe: social structures and cultural patterns*. London: Routledge & Kegan Paul.

Krejci, J. and Velimsky, V. (1981). *Ethnic and Political Nations in Europe*. London: Croom Helm.

Mayo, P. (1974). *The Roots of Identity: three national movements in contemporary politics*. London: Allen Lane.

Melucci, A. (1989). *Nomads of the Present: social movements and individual needs in contemporary society*. London: Hutchinson Radius.

Miles, R. and Singer-Kerel, J. (1991). 'Introduction to migration and migrants in France'. *Ethnic and Racial Studies* 14 (3): 265–78.

Nairn, T. (1977). *The Break-up of Britain*. London: Verso.

Nolte, E. (1985). 'Between myth and revisionism? The Third Reich in the perspective of the 1980s', in H. W. Koch (ed.), *Aspects of the Third Reich*. London: Macmillan.

Orridge, A. (1982). 'Separatists and autonomist nationalisms: the structure of regionalist loyalties in the modern state', in C. Williams (ed.), *National Separatism*. Cardiff: University of Wales Press.

Pipes, R. (1970). *The Formation of the Soviet Union: communism and nationalism*. Cambridge, MA: Harvard University Press.

Plamenatz, J. (1976). 'Two types of nationalism', in E. Kamenka (ed.), *Nationalism: the nature and evolution of an idea*. London: Arnold.

Poggi, G. (1978). *The Development of the Modern State*. London: Hutchinson.

Porter, R. and Teich, M. (eds) (1988). *Romanticism in National Context*. Cambridge: Cambridge University Press.

Reece, J. (1979). 'Internal colonialism: the case of Brittany'. *Ethnic and Racial Studies* 2 (3): 275–92.

Reynolds, S. (1984). *Kingdoms and Communities in Western Europe, 900–1300*. Oxford: Clarendon Press.

de Rougemont, D. (1965). *The Meaning of Europe*. London: Sidgwick & Jackson.

Seton-Watson, H. (1977). *Nations and States*. London: Methuen.

Smith, A. D. (1971). *Theories of Nationalism*. London: Duckworth.

—— (1979). *Nationalism in the Twentieth Century*. Oxford: Martin Robertson.

—— (1981). *The Ethnic Revival in the Modern World*. Cambridge: Cambridge University Press.

—— (1986). *The Ethnic Origins of Nations*. Oxford: Blackwell.

—— (1989). 'The origins of nations'. *Ethnic and Racial Studies* 12 (3): 340–67.

—— (1990). 'Towards a global culture?'. *Theory, Culture and Society* 7: 171–91.

—— (1992). 'National identity and the idea of European unity'. *International Affairs* 58 (1): 55–76.

Smith, G. E. (1985). 'Ethnic nationalism in the Soviet Union: territory, cleavage and control'. *Environment and Planning. C: Government and Policy* 3: 49–73.

Stavrianos, L. (1961). *The Balkans since 1453*. New York: Holt, Rinehart & Winston.

Sugar P. (ed.) (1980). *Ethnic Diversity and Conflict in Eastern Europe*. Santa Barbara: ABC-Clio.

Sugar, P. and Lederer, I. (eds) (1969). *Nationalism in Eastern Europe*. Seattle: University of Washington Press.

Tilly, C. (ed.) (1975). *The Formation of National States in Western Europe*. Princeton: Princeton University Press.

Tivey, L. (ed.) (1980). *The Nation-State*. Oxford: Martin Robertson.

Tonkin, E., McDonald, M. and Chapman, M. (eds) (1989). *History and Ethnicity*. London: Routledge.

Wallace, W. (1990). *The Transformation of Western Europe*. London: Pinter.

Webb, K. (1977). *The Growth of Nationalism in Scotland*. Harmondsworth: Penguin.

Weber, E. (1977). *Peasants into Frenchmen: the modernization of rural France, 1870–1914*. London: Chatto & Windus.

Wiberg, H. (1983). 'Self-determination as an international issue', in I. Lewis (ed.), *Nationalism and Self-Determination in the Horn of Africa*. London: Ithaca Press.

Zernatto, G. (1944). 'Nation: the history of a word'. *Review of Politics*, 6 (3): 351–66.

3

Dynamics of Democratic Regimes

Richard Rose

The history of the modern state in Europe is not about democracy; it is first of all about authority. In twentieth-century Europe a central issue has been whether or in what circumstances a modern state has become a democratic state (see Rose forthcoming, pt I). To view history as if it were the story of democracy expanding is to read history backwards, inferring purposes and goals from the unintended as well as intended consequences of wars and domestic events. The end of the Second World War was a watershed in European politics, for victorious allies concluded that peace and democracy were indivisible, thus compelling the establishment of democratic regimes in the defeated Axis powers of Germany, Italy and Austria. Yet the post-1945 period also saw the division of Europe geographically into a group of democratic states in Western Europe and Soviet-style regimes imposed by troops in Eastern Europe. The year 1989 was another watershed, for Soviet authority unexpectedly collapsed, allowing new democracies to arise there.

The dynamics of democracy in Europe involve changes in two dimensions: time and space. Within a given territory, we need to examine political developments for a century or more to see whether democracy has developed through an evolutionary process or abruptly. Reviewing a century of history also shows whether the first try at introducing democracy was successful or an error. Across space, we find big differences in the initiation, timing and tempo of democratization between the states of Northwest Europe, the first to evolve stable democratic regimes; Central European states such as Germany, which were not democratized successfully until after 1945; Mediterranean states that established their current democratic regimes only in the 1970s; and Eastern European states that have only been free to begin democratization since 1989.

Because the problems of governing are endless, the adoption of democratic institutions is not the 'end' of history; democracy does not ensure economic growth, full employment and the absence of crime. Democracy provides a set of institutions through which the mass of people can elect representatives to decide who governs. Politics by definition concerns the expression of competing ideas about what the government of the day ought to do, and conflicting standards for evaluating whether measures are successful or not. Democracy thus enables people to learn what does and does not work through the feedback of information in an open society (Deutsch 1963). It gives the mass of people the opportunity to reward or punish the government of the day by casting their votes in free competitive elections.

The argument for maintaining democracy is not that it is perfect but that it is preferable to the alternatives. Democracy has spread across Europe in the face of competition with undemocratic regimes. In this century, European countries have tried many alternatives; failures have been costly in human life and dignity. As Winston Churchill told the House of Commons shortly after the end of the Second World War:

> Many forms of democracy have been tried, and will be tried in this world of sin and woe. No one pretends that democracy is perfect or all wise. Indeed, it has been said that democracy is the worst form of government, except all those other forms that have been tried from time to time. (*Hansard*, 11 November 1947, col. 206)

What Democracy Is – and Is Not

The starting-point for the exercise of political authority is the existence of a state. The *modern state* is a permanent institution, consisting of organizations responsible for internal order (the police and courts); protection against foreign threats (the military); establishing laws of property and the supply of money, conditions for a modern market economy; and a civil administration with officials collecting taxes and carrying out these functions (see Rose 1976). The authority of the state 'often carries the implication of superior force as well as of legal competence' (Dyson 1980, 20). Since most modern states were formed without granting subjects the right to vote or speech free of censorship, their legitimacy was less certain than their claim to a monopoly of force (M. Weber 1972, 822).

A state claims the right to order subjects within its territory to obey its laws, pay taxes, and risk their lives in military service. Since modern states were created prior to the rise of nationalism, the Austro-Hungarian Empire could rule over peoples speaking more than half a dozen languages, and the United Kingdom remains a multi-national state of English, Welsh, Scots and Northern Irish peoples. Much of the politics of Europe from 1815 onwards has been about the creation of new states with boundaries more or less coterminous with a particular nationality. A modern state can create a unifying loyalty through 'nation building', as in France (cf. E. Weber 1977) and even more strikingly in Switzerland, with a population speaking four languages and dividing into three religious groups. In Germany and Italy, the formation of a state and a nation occurred simultaneously. New states such as Norway, Finland and Ireland were created by nationalist groups seceding from multinational states.

The *regime* of a state, that is, its constitution, chief political institutions and operating procedures, can take a variety of forms; democracy is only one (cf. Easton 1965). A regime does not change when a general election results in the change of the government of the day. The election of a new parliament and a change in party government is a politically significant event in a democracy; nonetheless, it does not change the regime. As the British saying puts it, the Queen's government is carried on.

The creation of a modern state normally produced a regime that was in form an absolute monarchy. Between the two world wars European regimes included military dictatorships, personalized populist regimes and totalitarian regimes. A few regimes were established by charismatic leaders such as Hitler and Mussolini, who used personal appeals to overturn a constitutional order, but their regimes did not outlast their lifetimes (Gerth and Mills 1948, 245ff). France illustrates the importance of the distinction between the state and the regime, for since the French Revolution the state has been in continuous existence but governed by many regimes, including five republics, two constitutional monarchies and empires under two Napoleons (Hayward 1983, 3ff).

The first governors of modern European states did not seek to promote democracy but authority. The first modern states are best described as *authoritarian*, involving rule by a leader or small group exercising power in predictable ways within ill-defined limits; denying extensive rights to individuals but not compelling them to accept a distinctive ideology; and recognizing the right of a limited number of institutions to organize independently of the state. An authoritarian regime is not a democracy but it is also not an arbitrary dictatorship subjecting everyone to the momentary whim of a ruler. An authoritarian regime is also not a totalitarian regime, such as Nazi Germany or Stalin's Soviet Union (Linz 1975, 264). A *totalitarian* regime claims total control of the institutions of society. It seeks to mobilize its subjects to conform to its commands and ideology, relying upon coercion and propaganda through a single party, the media and schools. A totalitarian regime also rejects conventional European ideas of law in favour of the Nazi doctrine of rule by will or Soviet doctrines of 'socialist legality'.

When an authoritarian regime accepts limitations on its powers, it is a *Rechtsstaat*, that is, a regime based on the rule of law and characterized by 'order, certainty, predictability, equality before the judge and the tax collector'. It is a regime in which right rather than might prevails, for it 'avoids capriciousness, arbitrariness and unreliability in political rule' (Freddi 1986, 158). Because a *Rechtsstaat* is not totalitarian, some civil institutions exist independently of the state, such as business enterprises, churches or intellectual and cultural bodies. The rule of law does not have to be popular rule, for laws can restrict the right to vote and authorize censorship.

A democracy is one type of *Rechtsstaat*, for it too depends on the rule of law. Yet the term *Rechtsstaat* was introduced to describe regimes in existence before democracy. History does not stand still. Changes in the political environment of Europe in the past century produced demands to liberalize the *Rechtsstaat* by granting greater freedom of speech, extending the right to vote and so forth. At this juncture, the ruling powers had the choice of trying to conserve the status quo, which ran the risk of becoming increasingly out of touch with a changing society, or following a policy of liberalization, which put their power in jeopardy. The oldest European democracies slowly evolved from regimes that had already come to respect the rule of law.

Today, democracy is both a pervasive presence and a valued symbol in European politics; it is also a term used in many different ways. Literally, democracy means rule by the people, but in a populous modern state representative institutions are essential to give effect to popular preferences. The classic realist definition of democracy is that of Joseph Schumpeter's (1952, 271): 'free competition for a free vote'. Competition between parties distinguishes democracy from government by an enlightened monarch or by a totalitarian party in a one-party state. Choosing the government through free elections, a second defining attribute of democracies, distinguishes them from regimes in which individuals and groups intrigue for a monarch's or a dictator's favour or elites form alliances in parliament without regard to popular preferences.

One condition of democracy is that the law grants freedom of association, so that organizations of business, trade unions, churches, farmers, environmentalists and so forth can freely combine to form political parties or pressure groups. The right to vote in the absence of nationwide parties can result, as in nineteenth-century France, in electors being able to choose a representative for a single constituency without this choice representing a verdict on the government of the day. In corporatist political systems, business and labour organizations have a privileged position in bargaining with government and they use government's authority to strengthen themselves (Schmitter and Lehmbruch 1980). In consociational regimes, some functions of government, such as education, can be delegated to organizations that represent different groups within society; in the Netherlands there have been separately organized Catholic, Protestant and secular school systems as well as political parties (Lijphart 1975). In Anglo-American democracies interest groups usually do not have a formal position within government, and in American presidential elections political parties can simply be vehicles for individual candidates rather than representing established social institutions.

A second condition is that elections should grant all adults the right to vote. Free competitive elections were held long before the franchise was granted to everyone. In nineteenth-century Britain, the right to vote was limited to a small minority of males with property, educational qualifications or a hereditary claim to the franchise. The Victorian electorate that chose between a government under Disraeli or Gladstone was not a mass electorate. This was the period in which the British regime was slowly evolving from a non-democratic *Rechtsstaat* with the institutions of civil society into a democracy in the twentieth-century sense.

Thirdly, votes must decide who governs; only in this way will the government of the day be accountable to the electorate. Just because people elect members of parliament, it does not follow that government is accountable. In the nineteenth century the heads of executive departments of government, including the prime minister, were often officials appointed by the monarch and responsible to the Crown and not to parliament. For example, in the Kaiser's Germany between 1870 and 1918, elections were free and competitive and a Marxist-oriented socialist party became the largest party in the *Reichstag* (parliament), but the government of Germany was accountable to the Kaiser, not the people's representatives.

Finally, a freely elected government should not be subservient to control by external forces. In an interdependent world every country is vulnerable to some influence from events in other countries, but vulnerability is not the same as subservience. In postwar Europe subservience was the fate of East European communist governments, which were compelled to follow the dictates of Moscow by the use or threat of military force. In a civil society a government may be influenced by partisan opponents and pressure groups, but if such groups consistently dictate what it does, it loses its claim to be a representative democracy.

Many important institutions of a democratic regime vary from one country to another. Control of government can be determined by electing a parliament, the normal European mode, or a president, as in the United States. Representatives can be elected by proportional representation, as happens almost everywhere in continental Europe, or by a first-past-the-post ballot, which is normal in Anglo-American democracies. One party may win a majority or government can be in the hands of a coalition of parties.

Even though democracies are usually the most economically developed countries in the United Nations, this is not a necessary condition for the creation of a democratic regime (Weiner and Ozbudun 1987). India has a longer consecutive history of free elections than at least three members of the

European Community. Even if a democracy is wealthy, it does not have to be a welfare state; in the United States and Japan the dominant political mood is against the provision of state welfare (see Rose 1991a). Nor is a welfare state necessarily democratic; Bismarck led the Kaiser's Germany to offer social welfare benefits to the mass of the population as a substitute for democracy (Flora and Alber 1981).

Nor does a democracy necessarily require every citizen to hold democratic values. Surveys in the United States and Europe show that a substantial minority of the population consistently endorses anti-democratic views. The conduct of free elections presupposes the right of people to vote for any party of their choice. The proof of democratic stability is given when anti-democratic parties contest elections and receive only a derisory share of the vote.

Alternative Paths to Democracy

To understand the uneven development of democracy in Europe we need to ask: under what circumstances have today's democratic regimes originated? As Bagehot (1867) emphasized in his mid-Victorian study of the English Constitution, the steps critical in creating democracy are different from what is required to maintain a democratic regime. By definition, the starting-point is a regime that is not democratic. In many European countries it has been the vacuum left by military defeat or the collapse of an authoritarian or totalitarian regime.

Elite bargains are important in encouraging the evolutionary change of oligarchic regimes into democracies, as happened in Britain, ruled by Whigs and Tories, and in Sweden, a conservative pre-democratic *Rechtsstaat* (Almond et al. 1973). Bargaining has also been important in the swift conversion of some authoritarian regimes into democracies, for example in Spain, involving agreement between politicians who served Franco and opponents of that regime. No hard and fast rules can be laid down about what is and is not necessary to create a democracy; as Linz and Stepan emphasize, the artful 'crafting' of an agreement is the essence of bargaining (quoted in di Palma 1990, 8).

The compromises and deals that lead to a democratic bargain involve a mixture of motives among participants (Bogdanor 1988). Some idealists are committed to democratic goals, others want to save as much as they realistically can from the old regime, and personal concerns and ambitions are evident in all camps. After a military defeat or the collapse of a police state, fear of returning to the past is a negative incentive to agree. This motivation was palpably evident in Central Europe after 1945, since defeat was followed by military occupation. It is also evident in post-communist states of

Eastern Europe today. Rustow (1970, 357) describes the 'democratic deal' as being a 'second best' solution that does not reflect agreement on fundamentals but about rules and procedures for reconciling differences of interests and values.

The creation of a democratic regime is conventionally recognized by the adoption of a constitution. Formally, a constitution is a legal document consisting of 'codes of rules which aspire to regulate the allocation of functions, powers and duties among the various agencies and offices of government, and define the relationships between these and the public' (Finer 1979, 15). If a democracy has evolved through generations, the constitution is operated according to an accumulation of values and informal understandings taken for granted by politicians and citizens socialized into a pre-existing democratic political culture. However, fewer than half of all European states have been democratic long enough for their political leaders to have been socialized when young into an established democratic culture.

The importance of bargaining between pro-democratic and pre- or anti-democratic groups makes it difficult to draw a line between reform and revolution in the initiation of a democracy (O'Donnell and Schmitter 1986; Linz 1990, 150ff). Representatives of the old order cannot be ignored because they are usually in control of such important institutions of the state as the military, police, courts, central bank and higher civil service. To dismiss all their officials would disrupt the everyday institutions on which the state relies for revenue and public order and make political enemies of people whose expertise and experience is necessary for a successful transition to democracy. The position of representatives of the old order is an ambiguous asset, however, for their own shortcomings have created the situation in which their opponents can effectively demand a democratic regime. The representatives of the old order must extricate themselves from ties with a less and less viable regime, since cooperation with democrats is a necessary condition of maintaining their place in the new regime (di Palma 1990, 37ff). Once a new democracy is established, former opponents may then become converted to democracy during a process of consolidation of the new regime (Pridham 1990; von Beyme 1993, 412ff).

The majority of European states have constitutions that have had to be written quickly in order to replace a regime that has collapsed or been discredited. Germany, Austria and Italy have drafted constitutions in the wake of military defeat and under the tutelage of occupation armies. France, Spain, Portugal and Greece have had to write new constitutions following the collapse of their old regime. East Europeans have responded to the collapse of the one-party state by hurriedly writing or amending their constitutions, while concurrently seeking to deal with pressing problems of economic transformation.

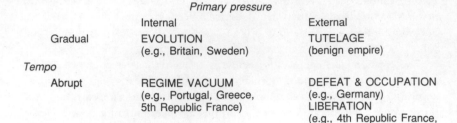

Figure 3.1   *Alternative paths to democracy*

To bring order to understanding the many forms of democratic transition (Stepan 1986; Fishman 1990, 435), we can classify movement on two dimensions, the first reflecting the *tempo* of change: the old regime can collapse almost overnight or change can reflect a gradual evolutionary process over decades or generations, as in Scandinavia. The second dimension is the source of *pressure* for change, pressure from within or external pressure.

Four very different alternative paths to democracy are illustrated in figure 3.1. The 'textbook' path to democracy is through gradual evolution, the experience of Britain and Scandinavian countries such as Sweden. However, this alternative is not possible in countries where a regime has suddenly collapsed. Many different kinds of domestic pressure can result in a regime terminating: the death of a dictator, as in the case of Franco's Spain, or a colonels' coup, as in the case of Portugal. The common factor is that a vacuum is abruptly created due to domestic political circumstances – and a democratic regime is a way of extricating those involved from a state of anarchy or an unwanted authoritarian regime.

In a Europe where small states outnumber great powers, external pressures are often of prime importance. In 1945 the defeat and occupation of Germany, Austria and Italy led to these countries becoming democracies. The liberation of France from German occupation led to the replacement of a puppet Vichy regime with the Fourth French Republic. The experience of East European states was the opposite of Central and Western Europe: Soviet occupation led to the imposition of alien totalitarian regimes there. In 1989, when Moscow showed it would no longer use Soviet power to support the communist regimes of Eastern Europe and Estonia, Latvia and Lithuania, national independence was regained, and each country was able to install a new pluralistic regime of its own devising. The fourth category, the gradual development of democracy under external tutelage, was the ideal of benign imperialists in India. Since it is not relevant within contemporary Europe, it is not discussed as an alternative in the pages that follow.

Evolution

The creation of a regime that exercised authority through the rule of law, recognizing restraints upon its own actions, was the starting-point for the creation of democracy in Britain, Scandinavia, the Benelux countries and Switzerland. The actions of the regime's leaders were scrutinized by an assembly representing some (but not all) interests in society. Such assemblies, whether called a parliament, estates of the realm or some other name, were not representative of the population generally but of functional groups such as ecclesiastical authorities, major landowners or a hereditary nobility. The politics was that

> of careful adjustment, of shared responsibility, of due respect for ancient privi-
> leges. Attempts at absolute kingship eventually broke on the concerted strength
> of particularist interests, whether corporative, regional or social. As the political
> order was in a very real sense built upon parts, the idea that men could
> reasonably be partisans found ready recognition . . . Intra-elite competition made
> it easier to weather the crisis of participation. (Daalder 1966, 47f)

To describe such institutions as undemocratic is to make an anachronistic judgement, projecting contemporary values backwards in time. The institutions are best described as *pre*-democratic. They could evolve into democratic institutions because they already constituted a check on absolutist rule and accepted competition between elites for political influence. In turn, elites could mobilize groups outside the ranks of the ruling strata in support of demands for liberalizing an authoritarian regime (Lipset and Rokkan 1967).

A rule of law regime was capable of gradual and peaceful liberalization through the enactment of statutes granting more rights to individuals and to institutions of civil society (Marshall 1950). The move from liberalization to democratization required three additional elements. Restrictive franchise rights had to be abolished and the right to vote expanded until universal suffrage was achieved. In Britain, the right to vote was not granted to all men and women until 1928. Secondly, this right required the freedom of speech and association, the right of political parties and interest groups to organize (Bendix and Rokkan 1964). The third critical step was the election of representatives who could determine the direction of government; this meant the surrender of traditional powers in the hands of servants of the Crown and hereditary estates in the House of Lords.

Sweden is an example of a very old kingdom evolving into a democracy in the course of centuries. An assembly representing four estates – nobles, clergy, burghers from the cities, and freehold farmers – first met in 1435. The Constitution of 1809 ended royal absolutism and gave a significant role to the assembly, which had evolved into the *Riksdag*, a parliament. This began a century-long struggle between adherents of royal as against parliamentary authority, and between representatives of traditional privileges and urban interests. Industrialization brought demands for the right to vote from industrial workers, who had no traditional place in parliament. Because conflicting interests were represented in the old regime, they bargained with each other and brought in new interests as they coincided with their own. The motives were mixed: traditionalists reckoned that gradual reform was better than the risk of revolution, and reformers took what they could get when they could get it. By 1907 the right to vote was granted to all adult males, and Sweden was well advanced towards being a democracy in the modern sense (Rustow 1955).

The early development of representative institutions made it possible to meet later difficulties by negotiation rather than by all-out conflict between leaders of the regime and those who were excluded from participating in governance. For example, Sweden responded to the interwar world depression with an innovative economic programme hailed as a 'middle way' between *laissez-faire* and state socialism. In Britain the same problem was met by a cross-party bargain, the formation of a coalition government under Ramsay MacDonald, which secured the biggest electoral majority in British history in 1931 (Kavanagh 1973). The early institutionalization of democratic government enabled regimes to survive military defeat and occupation. Following the German conquest of Norway, the government went into exile. The attempt of occupation forces to promote a new regime under a Norwegian, Vidkun Quisling, failed in its intent; it simply gave the world a new word for traitor.

Evolution requires freedom from immediate external or internal upheavals. However, the majority of countries in Europe have not enjoyed sufficient isolation from war or sufficient domestic harmony to maintain a regime without interruption. The typical story of a European country is not the gradual evolution of democracy through many generations but the abrupt alternation between authoritarian regimes and regimes that are democratic in aspiration or achievement.

Defeat and occupation: getting rid of tangible evils

Writing after the First World War, James Bryce (1921, II: 602) described the road to democracy as often 'the wish to be rid of tangible evils'. In the twentieth century, the state itself has been capable of producing great evils domestically and internationally. After the Second World War, Britons could view with pride a system that had stood successfully against Hitler, while Germans were left with 'the burden of German history'. The Third Reich had been not only undemocratic, a common enough phenomenon in interwar Europe, but also repressively totalitarian in governing Germans, genocidal in its treatment of Jews and murderous in its attacks on non-German peoples. The legacy posed two related problems: how could Germans be trusted to govern themselves thereafter, and how could the victors be convinced to trust Germans?

The Soviet Union had little hesitancy in treating the territory of Germany which it occupied as it was treating Eastern Europe: it imposed a Soviet-style communist regime, the German Democratic Republic. In West Germany the military governments acted differently. The first step was to remove Nazi influence from public offices. The idea that denazification meant the removal of all former members of the Nazi Party from office was soon abandoned because the Nazi Party, as a mass membership party, had formally enrolled millions. Many nominal Nazis were not ideologically committed – especially in the wake of defeat. For the Allies, coming to terms with the past meant recognizing that people who were once members of the National Socialist Party would not necessarily remain Nazis for the rest of their lives.

Although details differed between the British, French and American zones of occupation, the pattern was similar; each occupying force identified Germans to take responsibility for rebuilding their economy, society and political system (see Loewenberg 1968 for a well documented summary). This reduced the administrative burden of the occupying powers, encouraged Germans to accept new institutions, promoted the rebuilding of a major industrial economy and encouraged democratic political activities.

Since the Hitler regime had lasted only twelve years, there were millions of Germans familiar with other regimes. For example, the first Christian Democratic chancellor, Konrad Adenauer, had gone into local government under the Kaiser, and the first Social Democratic chancellor, Willy Brandt, had entered politics in the days of the democratic (but failed) Weimar Republic. Any German above the age of 42 when the war ended had been an adult for longer in a democratic regime than in Hitler's Third Reich. Even though democratic political parties had been dissolved by the Nazis, many people continued to identify with them and some had remained active in exile or in concentration camps. By the end of 1945 the Allied occupying forces were beginning to license as political parties groups that met democratic criteria. In 1946 elections were held at the local level, leading to the election of regional (*Land*) governments. The first steps towards democratization were thus taken while food was strictly rationed and malnutrition or worse was widespread.

The decision to write a new German Constitution was made by Allied powers at the 1948 London conference (Golay 1958; Merkl 1963). Because of Soviet barriers to German unity, West Germans were hesitant to institutionalize the division of the old state into two countries. *Länder* governments agreed to send delegates to a council representative of all regions and parties in West Germany. The council then prepared a Basic Law (*Grundgesetz*), which took into account preferences of German representatives, Allied occupying powers, and problems arising from a separate Soviet-occupied German territory. The draft was completed in May 1949 and quickly approved by the Allies with few amendments. It remains the constitution of Germany today.

The history of Austria is more complex but equally reflects foreign dominance. Austria became a nation-state as a consequence of defeat in the First World War. The multi-national Habsburg Empire collapsed, leaving Vienna the capital of only one of its parts. The First Austrian Republic had parties that were 'too competitive'; conflict between them sometimes erupted into street battles between armed groups. In 1934 Parliament was suspended and an authoritarian regime introduced. This ended in 1938 when Hitler annexed Austria as a part of Nazi Germany. In 1945 the occupation forces constituted the Second Austrian Republic. Prewar parties – socialists purged of illusions about Marxism and Catholics purged of illusions about authoritarianism – re-emerged to form a provisional government. The experience of living under Hitler and Allied occupation convinced them that they were better off cooperating with each other than continuing to fight (Engelmann 1966). Given Soviet occupation of eastern Austria and Vienna, no new constitution could be prepared; the constitution of the First Republic was instead amended. In 1955 the four occupying powers agreed that Austria could become a sovereign state on condition that it remained militarily neutral outside both the NATO and the Soviet bloc.

Italy had weaker democratic institutions before turning Fascist in 1922 after Mussolini seized power by a march on Rome. It was an original partner in the Axis. The Allied invasion of southern Italy in 1943 was followed by the king dismissing Mussolini and the new Italian government surrendering to the Anglo-American armies; the Soviet Union had no troops on the Italian front. Italian politicians were thus much freer to adopt a new constitution than Germans or Austrians, although they had fewer effective indigenous institutions to build on, and a large communist and a small neo-Fascist party in Parliament (Pasquino 1986). The left feared an authoritarian takeover from the right, and the right feared a communist takeover. Hence, the negotiation of a new constitution was driven by a demand from each side for protection against its worst fears through the elaboration of a series of rules protecting any party that found itself in opposition as the consequence of losing a democratic election (di Palma 1990, 46ff). A new democratic constitution for the Republic of Italy was adopted in 1948. Since then, the regime has survived attempted subversion and coups from both right and left and scandals arising from widespread corruption.

Germany, Austria and Italy have become democracies the hard way, embracing an authoritarian or totalitarian regime, going to war, and then suffering military defeat. Allied conquerors, exercising their rights under terms of unconditional surrender, treated the introduction of new institutions of government based on the rule of law and the democratic choice of governors as a matter of urgency. Given the cost in human suffering, no one would recommend as desirable the German, Austrian or Italian path to democracy through defeat in world war.

Regime vacuum: domestic trial and error

A third group of European states – France, Spain, Portugal and Greece – demonstrate that avoiding war is not sufficient to guarantee a state an uninterrupted evolution to democracy. Furthermore, they show that the experience of one authoritarian regime is insufficient to make politicians embrace democracy. In each country political change has been a process of trial and error in alternating between democratic and authoritarian regimes, a pattern that is also familiar in Latin America (O'Donnell et al. 1986). In each case big changes to and from democracy have occurred as the result of domestic upheavals.

France is the extreme example of alternations between regimes. The Gaullist Constitution of the Fifth Republic, produced when the threat of civil war loomed in 1958, is democratic in form and in practice, for control of the state has alternated between right and left. Thus, France can today claim to be a stable democracy. But it has taken more than a century of disagreements among French people – democrats in favour of the republic, reactionaries wanting an authoritarian regime, populists clamouring for a strong man and leftists enamoured of communism – before such stability could be achieved.

Mediterranean countries have histories in which democracy has been the exception rather than the rule. Spain can claim to be as old a state as France. In 1815 it became nominally a constitutional monarchy. However, this was often a facade, for the military intervened intermittently. Elections were introduced, but between 1881 and 1923 the result was normally a victory for the government, if only because its adversaries carried opposition to the extreme, for example by espousing nationalist and anarcho-syndicalist causes, and disagreed with each other about the alternative to the existing regime. From 1923 to 1931 Spain was governed by a dictatorship under General Primo de Rivera. A republic was proclaimed in 1931 and free competitive elections introduced. In 1936 civil war broke out and the country was a deadly battleground for three years; the war ended in 1939 with a victory for the authoritarian forces of General Franco.

The problem facing Franco's heirs after 1975 was how to extricate themselves from a situation in which the source of personality legitimacy was gone and there was no agreement among themselves or in the country about what was to happen next. The problem of the left was how to prevent the continuation of authoritarian rule and introduce a democracy in which the left might someday win power (Share 1985). Both sides shared a desire to avoid a return to the bloodshed of a lengthy civil war. Past errors taught Spaniards of different political outlooks that democracy was preferable to the alternatives of uncivil repression or civil war (Gunther et al. 1988). Diverse groups agreed to the establishment of a constitutional monarchy with free elections. Spain has since shown commitment to democracy through the alternation in office of conservative and social democratic administrations, and the failure of an attempted military coup in 1981. The turnaround has been as abrupt as in Germany and Austria, and without the same external pressure.

Greece has had a history similar to Spain, albeit its civil war occurred at the end of the Second World War, when anti-communist forces triumphed with Anglo-American assistance. The postwar era, like the prewar era, has experienced an alternation between dictatorship and democracy. A critical period was military rule from 1967 to 1974. This caused the military to be less happy with responsibility for civil authority in a country historically difficult to govern and it made the majority of Greeks prefer a civil government chosen by free elections. For two decades since, control of government has alternated between different governing parties (Diamandouros 1986; Featherstone and Katsoudas 1987).

Portugal too has lacked a democratic tradition. The abolition of the monarchy in 1910 was followed by more than half a century of authoritarian rule under a succession of civil and military authorities, of which the longest was the dictatorship of a civilian, Antonio Salazar. Elections were intermittently held but they were 'managed' by government rather than free. In 1974 a military coup established a new regime, but instead of seeking to rule in a traditional authoritarian way it introduced free competitive elections, and these have been held regularly since for both parliament and a president (Gallagher 1983; Corkill 1993).

Spain, Portugal and Greece were described a decade after the most recent introduction of free elections as 'uncertain democracies' (O'Donnell and Schmitter 1986), a term reflecting the lack of historical precedents for the maintenance of democratic regimes there. The same label might have been pinned on Germany, Austria and Italy a decade after the end of the Second World War. In all these countries one feature is consistently present: a variety of domestic forces not wanting to fill the political vacuum resulting from the collapse of the old regime by returning to an authoritarian past, thus supporting the Churchill hypothesis that an uncertain and imperfect democracy can be preferred to something worse.

In view of claims that democratic institutions require a long period of incubation of a democratic political culture, where democratic regimes have been introduced to fill a domestic political vacuum, institutions have become effective *before* there was time for a change in established cultural norms. Changes in norms of political culture have followed rather than preceded the introduction of democratic regimes. A lengthy time series of German public opinion data shows that only one-third of Germans indicated support for democracy in 1950, a year after the Federal Republic's constitution was introduced. Within five years a majority registered support and by 1964 two-thirds did so. Since the mid-1970s, five-sixths or more of Germans endorse democracy. In Spain, where it was introduced much later, the evidence shows an even quicker rise in public support for democracy (figure 3.2). The reversal of attitudes occurred with great speed, for the incentives were great to avoid the recurrence of tangible evils (see Weil 1989; Rustow 1970).

Double default of imposed Soviet-style regimes

For four decades after the Second World War, East-Central Europeans were forced to live under an alien regime that took advantage of national traditions of a hard, authoritarian state. Until 1918 these territories were normally part of the multi-national empire of the Russian Czar, the Prussian Kaiser or the Habsburgs. Between the two world wars each country usually had only a brief experience of free elections; governing authorities were not usually accountable to Parliament. Only Czechoslovakia sustained a democratic regime before the outbreak of the Second World War. Concurrently, communists under Stalin were crafting a new form of totalitarian regime in the Soviet Union.

During the Second World War, East-Central European states divided: Hungary, Romania, Bulgaria, Slovakia and Croatia were on the Axis side and the other countries on the Allied side. They were invaded by Nazi troops and then Soviet troops. Some countries, such as Poland, the Baltic states of Estonia, Latvia and Lithuania, and Finland, were invaded by Soviet troops before the Nazi conquest of their territories and reinvaded by Soviet forces towards the end of the war. During the war a multiplicity of armed underground partisans were formed to fight invaders on behalf of conflicting national causes.

Communist political commissars, some of whom were East-Central Europeans who had spent the war years in Russia, arrived with Soviet troops. By the end of the 1940s one-party communist regimes were installed almost

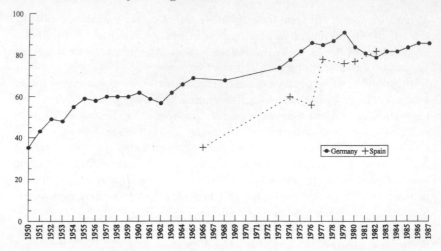

Figure 3.2 Consolidation of Popular Support for Democracy (% supporting democracy)

Source: Abstracted from Weil (1989), table 1.

everywhere in East-Central Europe, but not by popular vote. Each regime differed in its political history during the next four decades. Although all held elections, the communists always won (Furtak 1990). Soviet control was exercised by national communists acting as agents of the Communist Party of the Soviet Union. It was reinforced through the presence of Soviet troops defending the communist regime, sometimes with force, as in Czechoslovakia, Hungary and Poland. Economic control of non-market command economies was coordinated through COMECON, the Soviet-led Council for Mutual Economic Assistance. The Soviet-style regimes were instruments of social and political revolution; totalitarian powers gave a major impetus to the 'modernization' of society by purging traditional institutions and leaders and much of the old middle class.

Soviet political will to maintain these regimes was undermined by Mikhail Gorbachev's efforts to reform communism within the Soviet Union and improve relations with the United States. The openness and pluralism promoted in Russia could not be denied East-Central Europeans. Nor could Soviet forces be used to crush protests while Moscow was simultaneously seeking to negotiate with Washington an end to the Cold War. In 1989 East-Central Europeans began to test whether Soviet forces would again gaol or shoot protesters. Regime leaders and dissidents, sensing the decline in Soviet political will, began to press for greater and greater changes. The symbolic turning-point in 1989 was the fall of the Berlin Wall, which had been a physical manifestation of the separation of Eastern from Western Europe. In

1990 competitive elections free of Soviet influence were held across East-Central Europe (White 1990).

Although external events have been important both in Eastern and Central Europe after 1945, the context has been very different. In 1945 occupation by Western Allies led promptly to democracy; in East-Central Europe it led to regimes with a totalitarian bent. The introduction of new regimes in East-Central Europe came about only after the liberation of these states from Soviet influence through the default of Moscow. East-Central Europeans face a unique problem of simultaneity, the need to introduce democratic institutions *and* to create institutions of a market economy. The role of such financial institutions as the International Monetary Fund and the World Bank is limited to marginal assistance with short-term financing. Their capabilities are far too limited to play the role in East-Central Europe that Allied occupation powers played in West Germany and Austria after 1945. Nor are East-Central European countries defeated nations. Even Russia, which has lost territory and influence, is capable of rejecting foreign advice, as its December 1993 election showed.

The leaders of new East-Central European regimes have invariably been successful in tasks of 'deconstruction', removing Soviet influence and dismantling authoritarian political institutions such as the secret police, censors and border guards ready to shoot to kill to stop people leaving the country. However, sometimes deconstruction has led to the break-up or disappearance of a state held together by communists. The former Soviet Union disintegrated into states based on the territory of the republics that were formerly its constituent parts. In the former Yugoslavia, an authoritarian multi-ethnic state outside the Soviet sphere of influence, fighting has persisted about conflicting claims to territory. Czechoslovakia split non-violently into two independent states, the Czech Republic and Slovakia. A state created by Soviet force, the German Democratic Republic, was reunified with the Federal Republic of Germany.

Constructive constitution-making requires national elites to agree on a new set of rules. This happened by the beginning of 1994 everywhere in East-Central Europe except Poland. The frequency with which constitutional documents are amended shows that the new institutions have yet to become established. The circumstances in which the new Russian constitution was adopted in December 1993 emphasize that a formal constitution is not a sufficient guarantee of agreement about what constitutes the laws and practices of a *Rechtsstaat*. Of necessity, the institutionalization of democracy takes a decade or more.

However, regime transformation is occurring in societies in which distrust of the state is great. A leading Hungarian sociologist, Elemer Hankiss (1990, 7), describes ordinary people as having become anti-political under communism in order to protect themselves from the demands of an intrusive regime, cultivating the 'ironic freedom' of 'not identifying themselves with the system; the freedom of looking at it, of being able to judge it from outside'. An alien regime made it a moral virtue to hold uncivil attitudes and circumvent the commands of the party (Shlapentokh 1989; Clark and Wildavsky 1990). A democratic regime requires learning civic virtues.

> The new political class, and society as a whole, have to learn how to build up and run a democratic system. This will be a new experience and a long learning process. People will have to realize that the fight for a free and prosperous society is a much more difficult and complex task than they had imagined in the years and decades of despair and servitude. The golden age of innocence and simplicity has passed. (Hankiss 1990, 265)

Since the great majority of East Europeans have lived nearly all their lives under undemocratic regimes, one cannot expect unanimous popular support for new pluralistic regimes that at best are fledgling democracies, and some have yet to show whether they are undergoing democratization or returning to authoritarianism in a new guise. The evaluation that East Europeans make is not of democracy in the abstract but, as Churchill emphasized, between the current pluralistic regime and the old communist regime. To measure mass reaction to political transformation, the multi-national New Democracy Barometer survey of the Paul Lazarsfeld Society, Vienna, asks people their evaluation of both past and present regimes (for details see Rose and Haerpfer 1994). In 1992 an average of 43 per cent gave a positive rating to the old communist regime, and 53 per cent gave a positive rating to their new regime. Excluding two former states of the Soviet Union included in the survey, Ukraine and Belorussia, 59 per cent are positive about the new regime and 40 per cent about the old regime.

Aggregated reports of public opinion obscure differences between individuals in a society (Rose and Mishler 1994). On the basis of their evaluations of the old and new regimes, each individual can be classified into one of four groups (table 3.1). Democrats (reject the old regime, approve new) are the largest bloc in the typical East-Central European society, almost one-third of the total. They provide the hard core of support for new regimes. Sceptics (reject both regimes, but more negative about the old regime) are the second largest group, constituting a quarter of East-Central Europeans. They have doubts about the new regime, but prefer it to the old. If communists sought a return to the status quo ante they would oppose this as a step backwards, and they are most likely to evolve into supporters. The Compliant (approve of both old and new regimes) are one-fifth of the population. They are fearful of saying anything against the powers that be, the powers that have been, or such powers as may come in future. Because they are indifferent, they are not disposed to mount a positive challenge to the new regime. Reactionaries

Table 3.1　*Reactions to regime change*

	Democrats	Pro Sceptics (% in each group)	Compliant	Anti Reactionary	Pro[1] minus anti
Bulgaria	39	20	16	25	18
Croatia	35	52	7	6	74
Czech Republic	53	19	17	11	44
Slovak Republic	33	20	27	20	6
Hungary	15	16	27	42	−38
Poland	34	23	22	20	15
Romania	45	19	23	13	28
Belorussia	11	29	23	37	−20
Ukraine	16	28	9	46	−11
Mean	32	26	19	24	+15

Notes: [1] Democrats and sceptics minus compliant and reactionary.
Democrats: Disapprove of old regime and approve of current regime.
Sceptics: Disapprove of current regime less than old regime.
Compliant: Approve of both old and new regime.
Reactionary: Approve of old regime and disapprove of current regime.

Source: New Democracy Barometer Survey II of the Paul Lazarsfeld Society, Vienna; fieldwork, autumn 1992. Total number of interviews: 10,518. For full details, see Rose and Haerpfer (1994).

(approve old regime, reject new) constitute under a quarter of the total. This is the core of opposition to pluralism, but, because Soviet communist power is no more, they must seek an alternative form of authoritarianism or become either apathetic or committed democrats (Rose 1994).

In the light of the foregoing experience, how many countries of Europe can today be regarded as established democracies? Britain, the Fifth French Republic, and the Scandinavian and Benelux nations are indubitably in this category, and after half a century Germany and Austria qualify too. Even though the Italian regime has had major difficulties, democracy has survived in the face of greater challenges than in Northern Europe. The regimes of Spain, Portugal and Greece are entering their third decade of continuous operation, and in each there has been a democratic alternation in the control of government. In East-Central Europe, because of communism's suppression of the rule of law and of institutions of civil society that are concomitants of democracy, democracy has not yet had time to become established in soil even more inhospitable than that of Mediterranean Europe. The removal of repressive institutions and the introduction of free elections has been a big step forward. The prompt and positive growth in democratic opinion in Germany and Spain after the introduction of democracy is a positive sign for East-Central Europe in the years ahead (see figure 3.2).

Unfinished Business

Every newly established democratic regime is likely to face threats to democracy, which does *not* guarantee effective government. The American Founding Fathers devised an elaborate set of checks and balances intended to make it difficult for the president to act effectively and in order to guard against dictatorship. Democracy presupposes that the government of the day will sometimes fail, giving voters the right to show their dissatisfaction by turning it out of office and allowing the opposition to try its hand at government. The popular 'crisis of confidence' that threatens many administrations half-way through their term of office should not be confused with a crisis of confidence in the regime. Nor should the occasional excesses of democratic authorities be confused with the systematic suppression of democracy that was common in Eastern Europe under communist regimes.

Established democracies: changes within regimes

A government cannot treat national concerns as minor, even if they appear relatively small by comparison with those of post-communist societies. If there is the prospect of a new party entering the party system or an old one collapsing, this directly or indirectly affects all the parties in the system. Yet such a change is only a change *within* a regime. Britain will remain a democracy if proportional representation is adopted or if the first-past-the-post system remains in effect. No one suggests that there will be a military takeover in the Netherlands as a consequence of its confessional party system breaking down.

Established democracies benefit from being path dependent, since what was done in the past influences what happens in the present and the future (David 1985; Arthur 1988; Rose and Davies 1994). We can even describe such regimes as 'fool proof', for it would be difficult to think of anything that could be done to destroy democracy in long-established regimes. All the established democracies of Europe face major economic problems in the 1990s, but these regimes are established *because* they have successfully dealt with depressions and major structural changes in the economy. It is rare for an established regime to face a challenge that it has not overcome before, such as the incorporation of East Germans into the Federal Republic or the challenge of purging the Italian regime of endemic corruption.

Institutionalizing a change between regimes: East-Central Europe

In post-communist systems, there is no need to speculate about the future, for the inheritance from the past offers plenty of challenges here and now. Moreover, problems such as creating a market economy amidst the wreckage of a non-market command economy or introducing democratic institutions where none had existed for half a century cannot be solved overnight.

Institutionalization takes time, a decade or more, to demonstrate a regime's commitment to the rule of law and to changing control of government in response to changes in electoral favour. East-Central European countries cannot emulate the gradualism of Britain or Scandinavia. Nor are there the economic resources to generate an economic boom in hopes of 'buying' legitimacy. Given past alienation from the state, there is also no reservoir of trust in politicians, parties, members of parliament, or leaders of other major institutions in society (Plasser and Ulram 1993, table 4).

It would be foolish to expect all post-communist countries to follow the same political path in the years ahead. A review of states that have proceeded by trial and error offers both encouraging and discouraging examples (Rose 1992, 386ff). An audience can even be gained in East-Central Europe by citing Chile as an example, because it suspended democracy temporarily with the intent of carrying out major changes in the economy, and then reintroduced free elections. Although the pre-Soviet history of East-Central Europe is discouraging, more recent events demonstrate that undemocratic regimes find it difficult to govern indefinitely by 'sitting on bayonets'.

When the New Democracies Barometer asks East Europeans what they expect of the future, the replies tend to be optimistic. An average of 72 per cent are positive about the political regime in the future and 65 per cent are positive about the economic system. If Belorussia and Ukraine are excluded, 79 per cent are optimistic about the political regime and 71 per cent optimistic about the future of the economic system, as the current costs of transition from a non-market economy produce future benefits (Rose and Haerpfer 1994).

Given the novelty of stable representative institutions, the New Democracies Barometer also asked people whether Parliament could be suspended and parties suppressed. Across the countries of East-Central Europe an average of two-thirds thought there was no risk and one-third thought suspension possible. People were then asked whether they would approve or disapprove the suspension of Parliament. Combining answers to both questions produces four groups (table 3.2). Confident democrats (54%) do not think Parliament might be suspended and would disapprove if it happened. Anxious democrats

Table 3.2   *Confident and fearful democrats*

| | Democrats | | Authoritarians | |
	Confident	Anxious (% each group)	Hopeful	Dejected
Bulgaria	54	17	16	13
Croatia	65	29	4	1
Czech Republic	51	27	16	6
Slovak Republic	60	21	12	7
Hungary	64	11	13	12
Poland	33	24	35	8
Romania	66	15	12	7
Belorussia	45	23	19	13
Ukraine	49	11	25	14
Mean	54	21	16	9

Notes: Confident democrats: Would dislike suspension of Parliament and think it will not happen.
Anxious democrats: Would dislike suspension of Parliament but think it could happen.
Hopeful authoritarians: Would approve suspension of Parliament and think it could happen.
Dejected authoritarians: Would approve suspension of Parliament but think it unlikely to happen.
Source: New Democracy Barometer Survey II of the Paul Lazarsfeld Society, Vienna; fieldwork, autumn 1992. Total number of interviews: 10,518. For full details, see Rose and Haerpfer (1994).

(21%) think Parliament might be suspended but would disapprove if it happened. The fact that one-fifth see a potential risk of suspension is particularly significant, for it means that there is an attentive group that can readily be mobilized to defend democratic institutions. Dejected authoritarians (9%) do not think Parliament might be suspended but would approve if it happened. Hopeful authoritarians (6%) think Parliament might be suspended and would approve it happening. Together, confident and anxious democrats constitute three-quarters of East-Central Europeans, sufficient to create strong opposition to any political group that might seek to seize power without regard to democratic procedures.

Changes between states: the implications of interdependence

The logic of comparison analyses independent states in parallel (Rose 1991b). Arraying states in parallel implies that they never meet. However, contemporary European politics emphasizes interdependence, for states are constantly interacting, sometimes by accident, as when economic policies clash, sometimes by intent, as in informal consultations, and sometimes because of treaty obligations, as with member states of the European Community. The literature of international relations describes any pattern of interaction as a 'regime' (Keohane 1984), but this usage is confusing, for in Europe interdependence usually occurs in contexts in which no one state can command obedience from the others (Keohane and Nye 1977).

Today, the European Community (optimistically restyled the European Union) is the most significant example of interdependence; collectively, the member states contain most of the population and wealth of Europe. The Union is not a community in the sense of its national populations sharing a common identity. There is diversity in population between large states and diversity in individual income too. The greater the geographical expansion across Europe, the less there is a community in the sense of people sharing common experiences and traditions of governance. If a sense of community is defined by the limits of sharing tax revenues, then the national state's boundaries remain pre-eminent, for very little national tax revenue is transferred to Brussels. If a community is defined as a collectivity for which people are prepared to fight and die, national armies remain pre-eminent and NATO (the North Atlantic Treaty Organization) has a greater claim to be a defence community than does the European Union.

To speak of the European Community having a 'democratic deficit' because the Brussels Commission is not accountable to the popularly elected European Parliament is to assume that it is a regime like any other. However, it is not a regime in the conventional sense. The important actions of the Union require the approval of the Council of Ministers, which represents the national governments of each member state. National governments argue that their accountability to their national electorate justifies this arrangement.

The biggest challenges to democracy in Europe involve changes between regimes. East–Central European countries are the front-line nations in drawing the line between past and future, as they seek to replace authoritarian regimes of the past with new democratic regimes. Their success in doing so is extending the boundaries of democratic Europe further south and further east, creating a Europe that will be very different in the year 2000 than it was in 1950.

Bibliography

Almond, G. A., Flanagan, S. C. and Mundt, R. J. (eds) (1973). *Crisis, Choice and Change*. Boston: Little, Brown.

Arthur, W. B. (1988). 'Self-reinforcing mechanisms in economics', in P. W. Anderson, K. J. Arrow and D. Pines (eds), *The Economy as an Evolving Complex System*. Santa Fe, NM: Santa Fe Institute Studies in the Sciences of Complexity/Addison-Wesley, Vol. V, 9–32.

Bagehot, W. (1867). *The English Constitution*. Numerous reprints.

Bendix, R. and Rokkan, S. (1964). 'The extension of national citizenship to the lower classes', in R. Bendix (ed.), *Nation-Building and Citizenship*. New York: John Wiley, 74–100.

Beyme, K. von (1993). 'Regime transition and recruitment of elites in Eastern Europe'. *Governance* 6 (3): 409–25.

Bogdanor, V. (ed.) (1988). *Constitutions in Democratic Politics*. Aldershot: Gower.

Bryce, J. A. (1921). *Modern Democracies*. London: Macmillan, 2 vols.

Clark, J. and Wildavsky, A. (1990). *The Moral Collapse of Communism: Poland as a cautionary tale*. San Francisco: ICS Press.

Corkill, D. (1993). 'The political system and the consolidation of democracy in Portugal'. *Parliamentary Affairs* 46 (4): 516–33.

Daalder, H. (1966). 'Parties, elites and political developments in Western Europe', in J. LaPalombara and M. Weiner (eds), *Political Parties and Political Development*. Princeton: Princeton University Press, 43–78.

David, P. A. (1985). 'Clio and the economics of QWERTY'. *American Economic Review* 75 (1): 332–7.

Deutsch, K. W. (1963). *The Nerves of Government*. New York: Free Press.

Diamandouros, P. N. (1986). 'Regime change and the prospects for democracy in Greece: 1974–1983', in G. O'Donnell et al. (eds), *Transitions to Democracy: Southern Europe*. Baltimore: Johns Hopkins University Press, 138–64.

Dyson, K. H. F. (1980). *The State Tradition in Western Europe*. Oxford: Martin Robertson.

Easton, D. (1965). *A Systems Analysis of Political Life*. New York: John Wiley.

Engelmann, F. C. (1966). 'Austria: the pooling of oppositions', in R. A. Dahl (ed.), *Political Oppositions in Western Democracies*. New Haven: Yale University Press, 260–83.

Featherstone, K. and Katsoudas, D. (1987). *Political Change in Greece Before and After the Colonels*. London: Croom Helm.

Finer, S. E. (ed.) (1979). *Five Constitutions*. Harmondsworth: Penguin.

Fishman, R. M. (1990). 'Rethinking state and regime: Southern Europe's transition to democracy'. *World Politics* 42 (3): 422–40.

Flora, P. and Alber, J. (1981). 'Modernization, democratization and the development of welfare states in Western Europe', in P. Flora and A. J. Heidenheimer (eds), *The Development of Welfare States in Europe and America*. New Brunswick, NJ: Transaction Books, 37–80.

Freddi, G. (1986). 'Bureaucratic rationalities and the prospect for party government', in F. G. Castles and R. Wildenmann (eds), *Visions and Realities of Party Government*. Berlin: Walter de Gruyter, 143–78.

Furtak, R. K. (ed.) (1990). *Elections in Socialist States*. London: Harvester Wheatsheaf.

Gallagher, T. (1983). *Portugal: a twentieth century interpretation*. Manchester: Manchester University Press.

Gerth, H. H. and Mills, C. W. (1948). *From Max Weber: essays in sociology*. London: Routledge & Kegan Paul.

Golay, J. F. (1958). *The Founding of the Federal Republic of Germany*. Chicago: University of Chicago Press.

Gunther, R., Sani, G. and Shabad, G. (1988). *Spain after Franco: the making of a competitive party system*, rev. edn. Berkeley: University of California Press.

Hankiss, E. (1990). *East European Alternatives*. Oxford: Clarendon Press.

Hayward, J. E. S. (1983). *Governing France: the one and indivisible republic*. London: Weidenfeld & Nicolson.

Kavanagh, D. A. (1973). 'Crisis management and incremental adaptation in British politics: the 1931 crisis of the British party system', in G. A. Almond, S. C. Flanagan and R. J. Mundt (eds), *Crisis, Choice and Change*. Boston: Little, Brown, 152–223.

Keohane, R. O. (1984). *After Hegemony: cooperation and discord in the world political economy*. Princeton: Princeton University Press.

Keohane, R. O. and Nye, J. (1977). *Power and Interdependence*. Boston: Little, Brown.

Lijphart, A. (1975). *The Politics of Accommodation: pluralism and democracy in the Netherlands*, 2nd edn. Berkeley: University of California Press.

Linz, J. J. (1975). 'Totalitarian and authoritarian regimes', in F. Greenstein and N. Polsby (eds), *Handbook of Political Science*, Vol. 3, 175–412. Reading, MA: Addison-Wesley.

—— (1990). 'Transitions to democracy'. *Washington Quarterly* summer: 143–64.

Lipset, S. M. and Rokkan, S. (1967). 'Introduction', in Lipset and Rokkan (eds), *Party Systems and Voter Alignments*. New York: Free Press.

Loewenberg, G. (1968). 'The remaking of the German party system'. *Polity* 1 (1): 87–113.

Marshall, T. H. (1950). *Citizenship and Social Class*. Cambridge: Cambridge University Press.

Merkl, P. (1963). *The Origin of the West German Republic*. New York: Oxford University Press.

O'Donnell, G. and Schmitter, P. C. (1986). *Transitions from Authoritarian Rule: tentative conclusions about uncertain democracies*. Baltimore: Johns Hopkins University Press.

O'Donnell, G., Schmitter, P. C. and Whitehead, L. (eds) (1986). *Transitions from Authoritarian Rule: Latin America*. Baltimore: Johns Hopkins University Press.

Palma, G. di (1990). *To Craft Democracies: an essay on democratic transitions*. Berkeley: University of California Press.

Pasquino, G. (1986). 'The demise of the first Fascist regime and Italy's transition to democracy: 1943–1948', in G. O'Donnell et al. (eds), *Transitions to Democracy: Southern Europe*. Baltimore: Johns Hopkins University Press, 45–70.

Plasser, F. and Ulram, P. (1993). 'Zum Stand der Demokratisierung in Ost-Mitteleuropa'. *Transformation oder Stagnation?* Vienna: Zentrum für Angewandte Politikforschung.

Pridham, G. (1990). 'Political actors, linkages and interactions: democratic consolidation in Southern Europe'. *West European Politics* 13 (4): 103–17.

Rose, R. (1976). 'On the priorities of government'. *European Journal of Political Research* 4 (3): 247–89.

—— (1991a). 'Is American public policy exceptional?', in Byron Shafer (ed.), *Is America Different?* New York: Oxford University Press, 187–221.

—— (1991b). 'Comparing forms of comparative analysis'. *Political Studies* 39 (3): 446–62.

—— (1992). 'Escaping absolute dissatisfaction: a trial and error model of change in Eastern Europe'. *Journal of Theoretical Politics* 4 (4): 371–93.

—— (1994). *What Chance for Democracy in Eastern Europe? Testing the Churchill hypothesis.* Glasgow: University of Strathclyde Studies in Public Policy No. 236.

—— (forthcoming). *What is Europe?* New York and London: Harper Collins.

Rose, R. and Davies, P. (1994). *Inheritance in Public Policy: change without choice in Britain.* New Haven and London: Yale University Press.

Rose, R. and Haerpfer, C. (1994). 'Mass response to transformation in post-communist societies'. *Europe-Asia Studies* [formerly *Soviet Studies*], 46 (1): 3–28.

Rose, R. and Mishler, W. T. E. (1994). 'Mass reaction to regime change in Eastern Europe: polarization or leaders and laggards?'. *British Journal of Political Science* 24 (2): 159–82.

Rustow, D. A. (1955). *The Politics of Compromise: a study of parties and cabinet government in Sweden.* Princeton: Princeton University Press.

—— (1970). 'Transitions to democracy'. *Comparative Politics* 2: 337–63.

Schmitter, P. C. and Lehmbruch, G. (eds) (1980). *Trends toward Corporatist Intermediation.* London: Sage Publications.

Schumpeter, J. A. (1952). *Capitalism, Socialism and Democracy*, 4th edn. London: Allen & Unwin.

Share, D. (1985). 'Two transitions: democratization and the evolution of the Spanish socialist left'. *West European Politics* 8 (1): 82–103.

Shlapentokh, V. (1989). *Public and Private Life of the Soviet People: changing values in post-Stalin Russia.* New York: Oxford University Press.

Stepan, A. (1986). 'Paths toward redemocratization', in G. O'Donnell et al. (eds), *Transitions from Authoritarian Rule: comparative perspectives.* Baltimore: Johns Hopkins University Press, 64–84.

Weber, E. (1977). *Peasants into Frenchmen: the modernization of rural France, 1870–1914.* London: Chatto & Windus.

Weber, M. (1972). *Wirtschaft und Gesellschaft*, 5th edn. Tübingen: J. C. B. Mohr.

Weil, Frederick D. (1989). 'The sources and structure of legitimation in Western democracies'. *American Sociological Review* 54: 682–706.

Weiner, M. and Ozbudun, E. (eds) (1987). *Competitive Elections in Developing Countries.* Durham, NC: Duke University Press.

White, S. (ed.) (1990). 'Elections in Eastern Europe'. *Electoral Studies* 9 (4): 277–366.

4

Market Economies as Project and Practice

Marie Lavigne

There is no such reality as *the* market economy, understood as an economy where coordination would be ensured only through the market, that is, through sets of interacting individual decisions. There are many market economies, with various combinations of command (state) and market coordination. These combinations vary according to specific features of countries, to development level, to history and political culture. When we speak of *a* market economy, we mean that the main coordination mechanism is the market as opposed to the state.

The 1980s in Europe launched the catch phrase of going back to the market – back from excessive state intervention and away from Keynesian-type policies that had exhausted themselves. Following Thatcher-type deregulation, other governments, even social-democratic ones, moved away from what remained of planning, central regulation and state ownership. A new impetus was added to this movement when the collapse of communism sent another group of countries on the road to a market economy, through a much more radical transition from a command economy to the neo-classical model of capitalism.

Was there a project and what is the practice? Both in Western and in East-Central Europe, the project was mainly to discard something: in one case the excesses of 'big government', in the other case a whole political regime. While the negative side of the project is more or less easy to conceive, the positive side is not. The free market in Western Europe is an abstraction. Even here, it is wrong to look at the process as a move 'back' to an earlier stage. The new market economy in East-Central Europe is still more blurred. The post-communist governments want to project themselves into capitalism, but of which type?

The practice of the market is a process in the making, in terms of economic policies and structural reforms. Postwar evolution may be analysed as an apparent convergence process, twice repeated. In the early 1960s, Jan Tinbergen (1961) asked whether the market and centrally planned economies showed a convergence pattern; indeed it then seemed that both systems were evolving towards a mixed economy, each importing some features of the other. Twenty years later the pattern looked quite different. The market economies began to shed the state's involvement in the regulation of the economy and the ownership of economic assets, while the centrally planned economies seemed unable to let the market mechanisms play a significant role in economic processes. But since the beginning of the transition from communism the convergence movement has seemingly resumed, with apparent similarities in the use of deregulation and privatization. Again, the similarities veil substantial differences.

The first section of this chapter looks at the Western European market economy as it emerged following postwar reconstruction. It identifies the reasons for which that model of a regulated market economy had to change and to adjust to a new environment: the end of postwar growth, which cast doubt on the Keynesian economic policy techniques, the emergence of a global market, which created new constraints and opportunities for government intervention, and the growing precedence of the financial over the real sphere, which boosted deregulation but compelled the state to concern itself with risk and security. During the same period the centrally planned economies were increasingly conscious of the need to 'improve' the planning mechanism and to integrate themselves into the world economy, but they failed to achieve radical system change.

The second section explores the meaning of the *deregulation* process as it developed in the 1980s in Western Europe so as to identify what was abandoned by the state (and to whom), what still remained in its hands, and finally the no man's land where there is both market failure and 'state desertion'. Does this process provide meaningful lessons for the *liberalization* in East-Central Europe in transition? To create a market is not tantamount to restoring it. The only obvious similarity lies in the belief that free market forces do exist and should be allowed free play.

The third section is devoted to *privatization*. Here too the similarity is only too tempting. Apart from the fact that to privatize 10 or 15 per cent of the economy's assets is different from having to privatize 70 or 80 per cent, the aims, methods, backgrounds and outcomes are different. There is, however, a similarity, although not an obvious one: privatization as such leaves things largely unchanged. To privatize state-owned companies in a market environment and when these companies were already operating under the pressure of competition does not fundamentally change the way these firms are managed; the most obvious outcome is to provide revenue for the state. Conversely, to distribute state assets to the public in the former planned economies does not automatically bring about capitalist methods of management. So what does privatization change and how can management methods be improved? Does private ownership matter?

What kind of economic system emerges from these changes? Is the market economy tantamount to capitalism? Are there different capitalisms? The conclusion discusses the *project*. Due to the role and impact of the major international organizations, a single model of economic macro-policy is now dominant. The operation of this model (which for the sake of brevity may be called the International Monetary Fund model of structural adjustment) is based upon a free market micro-structure. Does this imply a unified micro-structure? In Europe several projects may be identified: the national projects in Western Europe, based on historical experiences and influenced by present political developments; the theoretical model of European Union; the yet unfulfilled dreams of efficient destatized markets in East–Central Europe.[1] These models are diverse. At the same time, due to financial and industrial globalization, a world market economy already exists. However, the 'global project' is yet to be defined and cannot be specified solely in economic terms.

The Postwar Market Economy in the Making: Competition and Convergence among Systems

From the end of the Second World War to the early 1970s the Western European economy developed as a mixed economy, with extensive involvement of the state as an owner of productive assets and a regulator in economic and social affairs. This regulated capitalism coincided with the postwar period of growth which extended over 25 years, and which is called in France the 'Thirty Glorious Years' after the title of the best-selling book by Jean Fourastié.[2] Was this system the cause of the buoyant development of the economy? In any case it floundered in the years following the first oil shock in 1973 and proved unable either to stabilize economies or to launch a fresh start.

The other major feature of the postwar period was the division of Europe into two rival systems. Before 1939, the Soviet Union was an exception; after the Yalta Conference (1945) and the launching of the Marshall Plan (June 1947), which was eventually rejected by the Soviet bloc countries, the socialist economic system established itself as the challenger to the capitalist model. Under central planning, East–Central Europe also experienced high rates of growth in the 1950s, which were explicitly attributed to the superiority of central planning. However, deceleration in growth rates occurred as soon as the early 1960s, which triggered a wave of economic reforms meant to combine central planning with the use of market instruments.

A converging pattern?

It then seemed obvious that capitalism had borrowed planning techniques from socialism, while socialism supplemented the centralized direction of economic life with some self-regulating market mechanisms. One could then think of a hybrid socio-economic system. Here is how Tinbergen featured in 1961 the changes that made capitalism and socialism converge:

Changes within capitalism:
1   Extension of the public sector, covering key branches such as power, transport, sometimes iron and steel, and banking. This had been achieved by postwar nationalization effected by governments of the left and not rescinded by later conservative governments. Management by the state of a large part of the nation's assets thus seemed irreversible;
2   The growing importance of the budget in the national product (from one-quarter to one-third), which gave the state considerable financial means of intervention in social and economic affairs;
3   Limitations on competition among firms, for economic reasons (such as increasing returns to scale). These limitations provided a rationale for state regulation of such market failures, for instance by anti-trust legislation;
4   The use of planning techniques by large firms and by governments, especially in France, Great Britain, the Netherlands;
5   Macro-economic regulation, anti-inflation policies through wage and price control;
6   Market stabilization policies, for instance in agriculture;
7   Regional development policies overriding considerations of short-term profitability, in an effort to raise standards in underdeveloped areas (Italy, France);
8   Extension of free or semi-free services in the field of education and health.

Changes within socialism:
1   Insistence on growing professionalism of enterprise management, instead of a reliance on their political qualifications, leading to the creation of a class of specialized managers;
2   Following a policy of wage levelling, introduction of pay differentials based on labour productivity;
3   Use of 'monetary-market categories', so as to increase the efficiency of planning;
4   Rehabilitation of capital costs (interest) as a component of production costs and of the value of goods produced;

5 Re-establishment of effective consumer choice;
6 The use of mathematical methods in planning;
7 Recognition of the positive impact of international trade on growth, which meant the implicit abandonment of self-sufficiency.

Ultimately the two systems differed essentially in the matter of ownership. In capitalist economies, private ownership was the rule and public ownership an exception that could be justified only by market failure or the existence of special duties of the state. In socialist economies, collective ownership remained the rule even when limited forms of private activity were allowed (in agriculture, craft and retail trade activities). Was this the major divide? A few years later Galbraith (1967) contended that the capitalist class in the Marxian sense did not exist any more. There had been a transfer of power within the large firm from owners to managers or techno-structure made up of those participating in group decisions. The technological revolution had overtaken both capitalism and socialism and was creating 'a new industrial state' beyond systems; differences based on ownership were no longer relevant.

It would be only too easy to stress the flaws in these conceptions. What the observers of the communist economies had failed to perceive was that one could not really separate the economic regime from the political and ideological foundations of the system. Planning and management methods were not just technical ways of allocating the use of resources; they were totally subordinated to the political and economic monopoly of the Party, which was the ultimate owner of the means of production. Much later, after the collapse of communism, the Hungarian economist János Kornai (1992) presented a theory of this specific 'political economy of communism'. He explained why the early reforms meant to 'improve' the system were by no means a sign of 'convergence'. On the contrary, these reforms were not compatible with the system, as the Party's monopoly remained intact and hence the market signals introduced in the system could not trigger the proper response from the enterprises. Thus, while the 'classical', unreformed central planning system was viable though inefficient in the long run, the reformed system could never be viable, which has since been confirmed. But the 'mixed market economy' that emerged from the Second World War was not irreversible either.

A transitional pattern: the regulated market economy

Most Western European postwar governments were deeply committed to an organized market economy, which went along with the values of democracy and freedom. In Britain, the Beveridge Report on *Social Insurance and Allied Services* (1942) set out the principles of the welfare state, later developed in *Full Employment in a Free Society* (1944), suggesting the blend between free market values and social concerns that required direct state control. In France, the National Council of the *Résistance* committed itself in 1944, before the end the war, to promote an 'organized market economy' with a *dirigiste* state, and hence restraints on the rights of the owners, as well as the equalization of opportunities which would justify active economic policies in the fields of employment, social security, housing, health, education and culture. These ideas were embodied in the preamble of the French Constitution of 1946. Later, the Federal Republic of Germany implemented a slightly different version, with a government strongly dedicated to a 'neo-liberal' market, to private ownership and to free enterprise, but with a commitment to basic social policies (*Sozialmarktwirtschaft*). Ludwig Erhard, the German minister of Economic Affairs between 1949 and 1963 and the author of the 'German miracle', embodied this approach, one of the two modern versions of capitalism, the 'Rhine model' (Albert 1991), the other being the 'neo-American' one, later emulated by France and Britain.

The components of the 'regulated market economy' (with a distribution that varied among countries) were: nationalization of 'key' industries, indicative planning and welfare policies.

Nationalization and the extension of public ownership

In most Western European postwar governments, the main economic rationale for expanding the public sector was to control the public utilities or 'natural monopolies' (post, telephone, water, railways, electricity and gas distribution, coal, sometimes steel, air transport). Some of these activities were already under state control before the war. Nationalization was also part of the political doctrine which inspired left-wing or coalition governments. Political ideology was the stimulus for the second wave of French nationalizations in 1981–2, when the socialists came to power. The political argument also explains why in France the assets of collaborationist capitalists were nationalized just after the war, as in the case of the automobile company Renault. Finally 'competitive activities' were also added to the public sector for various reasons, such as the desire to control most of the banking sector or to maintain employment. Whatever the reasons, the public sector accounted for up to 25 per cent of investment and employment in many Western European countries by the end of the 1950s. An exception was Germany, where the public sector was confined mainly to the basic utilities.

Indicative planning

France was the most systematic advocate of indicative planning, though this was also attempted in Britain and more successfully in the Netherlands. While nationalizations were clearly a part of leftist, anti-free market orientation, this cannot be said of planning. In France, the inspirer of this form of state involvement and first Planning Commissioner, Jean Monnet, was a private businessman and banker deeply committed to the market. His main concern was to restore and modernize French productive capacity destroyed by the war. It is usually assumed that the Marshall 'plan' contributed to the development of indicative planning as an instrument for managing Marshall Plan funds domestically and for developing coordination within the Organization for European Economic Cooperation (OEEC, the fore-runner of the OECD, which was set up in 1948 to ensure a dialogue with the US European Cooperation Agency which distributed the funds). It should be remembered, however, that the US administration was hostile to the idea of government involvement in the economy (Eichengreen and Uzan 1992).

It is not clear why planning has survived in France, although the Eleventh Plan (1993–7) was prepared in 1992 in a mood of great scepticism. The official functions of French planning are information gathering, dialogue between the 'social partners' (i.e., representatives of the government, of the employers' associations and of the trade unions), and the formulation of a consistent economic and social programme (Cazes 1990). In fact all three functions had already withered away in the 1960s. What remained was the intellectual exercise of building sophisticated macro-economic forecasting models, coupled with institutional inertia preventing a government agency from being wound up.

Welfare policies

Budgetary expenditure for social and welfare policies increased in all the countries of Western Europe after the war, but the welfare state is mostly associated with the *Swedish model*. It combined exceptionally generous social insurance and pension benefits, free health care and free education, and a centralized system of wage bargaining aiming at a 'solidaristic' wage policy and ensuring near-to-full employment (Delsen and van Veen 1992). While in all Western European countries social expenditure steadily rose in the 1960s, it reached its peak (over 30 per cent of the GDP) in the Nordic countries, the Netherlands and West Germany. What is typical of the 'welfare state' model is not just the high level of social expenditure but also a high degree of social consensus based on industrial democracy and employee power-sharing. This is the essence of the *German model* of co-determination or co-responsibility (*Mitbestimmung*).

The German model has its intellectual roots in a 'neo-liberalism' hostile to state intervention and planning. The state is supposed to set the rules of the game (*Ordnungspolitik*) and to ensure that the conditions of fair competition are met. However, the state should intervene in the social sphere, which is thus largely non-market, to guarantee generous coverage of the basic social needs as well as equality in the interpersonal and interregional distribution of income.

Deregulation and Liberalization

The role of the state was questioned in Western European economies in the 1970s, when Keynesian-type economic policy instruments proved unable to stop inflation and to fight unemployment following the first oil shock (1973). But deregulation proper developed only in the 1980s, either accompanying a privatization process (Britain) or largely independently (France, Italy, Spain, for instance). A decade later, the first countries in transition from communism launched their move towards the market by liberalizing economic activities, formerly tightly controlled by the state administration. Can one speak of a parallelism in these trends?

Regulation, 'régulation' and deregulation

In a broad sense, regulation would encompass all kinds of economic policy conducted by the state. In a narrow sense, the field of regulation is micro-economic and concerned with the activities of firms.

State regulation stems from the concern to have smoothly operating markets. Markets may fail when there are *information* failures, a situation which may be corrected by making private incentives consistent with societal goals, based on a consensus or a partnership established between business and the government (as in the German model). Otherwise the government may try to compensate for inadequate information by enforcing rules that compel, for instance, suppliers to give information to the consumers, or by disclosing the information itself (through special agencies). A second reason for market failures may be the *market power* of monopolies or oligopolies. This is the basis for anti-trust type legislation, or for the setting of price ceilings. State regulation here may be harmful in two ways. First, as George Stigler (1971) has shown and as has been confirmed later by many examples, the regulators themselves are captured by the regulation process and instead of fighting anti-market behaviour end up serving the interests of the given industry. Second, while government intervention should in this case pursue the aim of making the markets increasingly contestable by lowering entry and exit costs for potential new entrants, some state regulations, on the contrary, increase exit costs, such as labour laws, or enact red-tape requirements for entering an activity. To this one has to add a more general consideration, put forward by the Public Choice school: the government itself is a monopoly, so how can a monopoly power police other monopolies? Finally there is the case where *markets do not exist*, instances of which are all kinds of externalities. Regulating environmental pollution, ensuring industrial safety through setting up standards, or using taxes and subsidies may be considered as a better way of reducing social costs than creating a 'market' for these costs (Coase 1960).

In this sense then, *deregulation* means eliminating all direct intervention that impedes competition. When some intervention is needed for the above reasons, deregulation implies that the desired outcomes are reached through other methods, such as partnership between business and government. Germany offers an example of such partnership: rules and norms are enforced within the professions in a kind of neo-corporatism. In Germany, one of the most powerful state agencies is the *Bundeskartellamt*, which conducts the anti-trust policies. Fighting restrictive practices and collusion goes with facilitating the activities of small and medium enterprises through tax incentives.

In countries where, unlike Germany, the public sector was itself a source of monopolistic practices, deregulation had to be coupled with privatization; Britain and France offer examples of alternative policies. After 1979 the British government embarked on a large-scale privatization programme of which deregulation was a component and an instrument. Private sector deregulation was also resorted to, through ending monopolies of private professions guaranteed by the state (such as the monopoly of qualified opticians in the sale of spectacles). In France, while deregulation was also on the agenda in the 1980s, it proceeded along with the nationalizations effected by the socialist government in 1981–2, but was greatly expanded when a right-wing government came back to power in 1986–8 and almost immediately abolished all remaining price controls, along with the laws restricting redundancies, even before launching its reprivatization programme.

Deregulation policies are thus based on the tenet that state intervention should be avoided or replaced by other methods if a free market cannot operate without some kinds of rules. But can the state be dealt with so easily? The French school of *régulation* argues that there is a variety of institutions that matter in addition to 'the market' and 'the state'. The market cannot be seen as a self-regulating servo-mechanism; it requires a whole set of institutions that do not emerge spontaneously. The state cannot be described either as the 'good' arbiter ensuring that the conditions for free commercial exchanges are met, or the 'bad' interfering authority. There is a whole continuum of types of intervention. In addition there is a set of other institutions between the market and the state, such as alliances, private hierarchies, communities and networks (Boyer 1986 and 1987). This has to be remembered when analysing the 'liberalization process' in the countries in transition from communism.

Liberalization in East-Central Europe

Deregulation is a market economy concept, where economic activities are basically coordinated through the market and where the state intervenes only indirectly and marginally to correct market failures or dysfunctions. When state agencies have directly managed the economy, one has to create the market as well as to let it function freely.

In the countries of Central Europe which initiated the transition process, Poland, Hungary and Czechoslovakia, there was not a clear understanding of what 'a market' meant. Poland (in January 1990) and Czechoslovakia (in January 1991) both embarked on a 'shock therapy' stabilization programme of which liberalization was an obvious component. To liberalize prices and trade could apparently be done overnight by abolishing administrative interference. This policy presupposed that economic agents would immediately adjust to new conditions . The case of Hungary was different, as during the communist regime a large degree of decentralization had already been introduced in the economy. Prices were largely free by 1990. In the field of foreign trade, most of the (state) companies could trade on their own and buy foreign currency from the National Bank for their import needs. Liberalization was to be completed, not introduced.

In fact, even in Hungary, there was no market in the 'capitalist' sense. This explains why the liberalizing of prices could not have the short-term impact expected, that is, a sudden burst of inflation followed by a decline in prices as the supply adjusted to a reduced level of demand. True, decision-makers suspected that such a quick adjustment would be difficult. The first reason for concern was that most of the producers and retailers were large state enterprises, which would behave as monopolies and tend to increase prices to the highest level allowed by the market. Second, common knowledge about the socialist economies suggested that there was a very high 'monetary overhang' due to repressed inflation and shortages, and that all this excess demand would be released as soon as prices were freed. Thus there was some argument over the issue of demonopolizing first, before freeing prices, and eliminating the overhang first as well. Both debates soon faded away, as it became obvious that demonopolizing could only go hand in hand with privatizing and that the monetary overhang was eliminated much more quickly than anticipated through price rises.

The second issue was foreign trade liberalization. The standard package implied the opening up of the domestic market, along with a big devaluation of the domestic currency and a current account convertibility. In this way, price liberalization would be automatically coupled with competition from abroad, which would prevent the domestic monopolies from increasing their prices too sharply. At the same time, the distorted price structure inherited from the past would be corrected by an 'imported' price structure reflecting relative world prices. The simultaneity of trade and price liberalization has been questioned on the grounds that excessive devaluation and rapid opening up of the economy exaggerated the initial price shock (Nuti and Portes 1993) and that too early an exposure to external competition could devastate the domestic economy (McKinnon 1992). In addition, competition from abroad was initially limited by the overdevaluation of the domestic currencies that made imports very expensive.

Demonopolization thus emerges as a very complex issue. On the one hand, the huge state monopolies of the past must be dismantled, and in some countries (Hungary and Poland) the process had begun, rather unsuccessfully, even before the transition. On the other hand, the Western developed world is one of big companies. If the transition countries want to restore a small-scale capitalism, this will hinder their competition with the West and prevent modernization. The obvious but by no means easy solution would be to re-create big companies after the former monopolies have been dismantled. The countries in transition are doing just the reverse: introducing anti-trust legislation on the Western model, without as yet having 'trusts' in the Western sense! Such 'trusts' will emerge (and are emerging) in the sectors controlled by foreign investment. It might be dangerous to tend towards a dual industrial structure, with foreign-owned big corporations and a domestic sector made of medium-sized firms resulting from a forcible split of the former state monopolies. However, this risk is small in the short term. Demonopolizing proves difficult, not just because privatization and/or splitting up take time but also because of the behaviour of the 'post-socialist' coalitions among managers of state-owned or privatizing companies. These coalitions develop defensive strategies based on 'mutual protection' (of which, for instance, evading bankruptcies through inter-enterprise indebtedness is a component) rather than conflict or cooperation strategies proper to a market environment.

Creating a market environment also means having a modern financial and tax system. Reforms in this direction are underway but by no means completed. Financial markets are emerging and still very narrow. Finally the new welfare system that should cushion the impact both of stabilization and of structural transformation through building a new social security network is yet to be introduced, while the old state social security system is collapsing.

The overall debate on the state's role in these emerging markets has erupted over the question of industrial policy. Because of budget constraints, the issue of industrial policy was quite controversial from the outset. The problem is not only that there is no money to finance it, but also that national governments are very much against it because it strongly reminds them of central planning. There are no schemes for organizing the decline of whole sectors, for promoting small and medium enterprises, for encouraging R&D

or modernization, for 'picking winners' for future growth. The only substitute for industrial policy is to be found in the foreign sector. Initial devaluations have acted as an incentive for exports and a protection against imports. Tariffs were increased in 1992, after their dramatic lowering in all countries in 1991, so as to protect 'infant industries' or, on the contrary, 'ageing industries' that could provide export earnings. However, this amounts to little in terms of an active industrial policy (Fath 1992).

In fact, most of industrial policy has been involuntary. As van Brabant (1993) states, privatization was a surrogate for industrial policy, as many state-owned enterprises have been kept afloat through subsidies or through deferred bankruptcies. The need to reorient exports to the West has also acted as a substitute for an explicit industrial policy, with the result that the less competitive sectors have been supported (Hughes and Hare 1992).

Thus the laborious progress of East-Central Europe is by no means similar to the deregulation process in the West, although the avowed aim looks identical: to get rid of excessive government interference. These countries proceed towards 'liberalization' with great difficulty not only because they suffer from the legacies of their past and lack a whole set of market institutions, but also because they are only beginning to be integrated in the 'global economy'. They have reached the stage of internationalization and successfully redirected their foreign trade to the West, away from a dominant 'bloc' trade within the Comecon system. But they are not yet part of the global industrial, technological and financial system.

Global constraints to deregulation

Looking at the experience of the Eastern European countries in transition sheds additional light on the process of deregulation in the West. In Western European countries, globalization has put added constraints upon deregulation, to the extent of removing much of its substance.

Globalization can be defined in an industrial and a financial sense. Industrial globalization may be understood as the new level reached by the integration of industrial activities across countries, whereby transnational companies 'transform themselves into "placeless" networks of economic power, shifting financial and intellectual capital across the triad of major economic regions and drawing increasingly on the labour pools of the developing countries' (Howells and Wood 1993, p. 4). Financial globalization is the linking of the financial markets on a world scale, facilitated, like industrial globalization, by the technological progress in telecommunications and expressed in the development of numerous new financial instruments for raising funds or accumulating wealth.

Both developments have profoundly altered the deregulation process in Western Europe. They have accelerated it as traditional regulation by the state was becoming obsolete. Because of the interconnection of production, technology and service activities on the one hand and capital mobility on the other, the deregulation of the financial markets had to be achieved along with industrial deregulation in the 1980s. Exchange and capital controls were lifted in the UK in 1979, in France in 1990, in Southern Europe by the end of 1992; lending restrictions have been suppressed; the securities markets were freed slightly later (starting with the London 'Big Bang' in 1986); restrictions on the ability of foreign financial institutions to operate on the countries' domestic market have been eased.

At the same time, globalization blurs the very meaning of deregulation. Within Western Europe, the establishment of the Single European Market means the dismantling of national regulations, along with the imposition of European directives which may be seen as a 're-regulation' in various fields. Is regulation on the European level justified by the same kind of reasons which support national regulation? If yes, should it be challenged with the same arguments? Is it basically enforced to protect the European Union from outside competitors (an issue which was at stake in the Uruguay Round negotiations, successfully concluded in 1993) or from too hasty an enlargement (as is claimed by prospective future members from the European Free Trade Area or Central Europe)? It is increasingly difficult to determine what to regulate. Is the ultimate purpose to maintain the competitive advantage of nations or groupings? If so, the difficulty lies in identifying this advantage on global markets with global actors: promoting 'national' or 'European' champions in a global context is tricky when the interests of the 'global companies' are so interconnected. Moreover, the volatility of financial and information flows makes it easy to side-step the controls. Should one deregulate still further? Assuming that deregulation increases risk and uncertainty, how can its impact be estimated, and how can the resulting instability of financial and services markets be avoided, the latter being still the most regulated? These are unanswered questions at the end of a process leading from extended government involvement to a deregulated market.

Privatization

In a narrow sense privatization may be defined as a legal transfer of property rights from the state to private agents. This is the definition used here. A broader concept would include the creation of a private sector *ex nihilo* (as in the countries in transition). It would also refer to all measures contributing to the destatization of economic activity, including deregulation or subcontracting part of state activities. In this sense privatization may be consistent with a large state-owned sector, provided state enterprises are managed according to market rules and exposed to competition. Most of the remaining state sector in developed economies, with the exception of public utilities, would by this standard qualify as already 'privatized'. 'Marketization' or 'commercialization' of state-owned enterprises in the East would thus mean privatization, and indeed have been the first stage of the process in most countries in transition to capitalism.

The movement towards privatization is global: in 1992, public enterprises have been transferred to the private sector in fifty countries in the world, for nearly seventy billion dollars.[3] In Europe, all the countries in transition are embarked on privatization programmes. Britain pioneered the movement in Western Europe in 1979, though Italy launched its programme only in 1993. In almost all Western European countries privatization is underway. The second French programme launched in 1993 is especially ambitious.

A very special case is offered by privatization in East Germany. Following the 1990 reunification of Germany the aim was to create a new private sector from 8,000 state-owned enterprises existing in the GDR, so as to integrate the five new *Länder* into the German economy. The powerful *Treuhandanstalt*, the state agency set up to conduct privatization case by case, achieved this task in four years. It demonopolized, restructured, looked for domestic (West German) and foreign partners, liquidated and sold the state-owned companies. The sales yielded 65 billion DM but the net proceeds were negative as the *Treuhand* had taken over the debts of the East German enterprises and spent large amounts of money in restructuring firms and subsidizing jobs. This is a very sweeping transformation indeed; many issues were still unresolved when the *Treuhand* wound up in December 1994 with debts of 270 billion DM. The German experience cannot be compared with either Western European or Eastern European approaches: the urgency, the resolve, the means involved, make it a case of a huge takeover by an aggressive corporate management rather than a standard example of privatization in any other setting.

Is it possible to find similarities, in Europe, between privatization as conducted in market economies and the process bearing the same name in the East? Obviously the scope is different. In market economies, privatization affects ownership rights on a limited part of the national assets. In formerly planned economies, the bulk of the national assets is concerned, in an environment deprived until then of any significant private sector. Hence motives and methods, but also outcomes, differ.

In developed Western Europe, the move towards privatization emerged as a political reaction against welfare state policies unable to deal with the recession of the 1970s, and as an economic remedy to the inefficiency of the state-owned sector. It was also meant to raise revenues for the state budget. Privatization was conducted mainly through stock exchange institutions, in the context of well-developed capital markets. Finally the outcomes of privatization have to be assessed differently for privatized firms which were already in the 'competitive' sector and state monopolies such as public utilities. However artificial this distinction may be, the former were managed no differently from the comparable private companies or banks.

In East-Central Europe, privatization is an essential part of a political process of overthrowing all the legacies of the communist regime. It cannot rely on a stock exchange mechanism, as sophisticated capital markets do not exist at all in the East, and hence has to develop non-conventional methods. Its outcomes have to be assessed in terms not only of ownership changes but also of changes in management.

False similarities of aims?

Political aims are present in Western European practice. The first wave (1986–8) of the French privatization programme occurred in a highly politicized context (perhaps even more than was the case when Prime Minister Margaret Thatcher came to power in Britain in 1979), when a right-wing government was eager quickly to erase what it considered as a disastrous legacy of the (then seemingly short-lived) first Mitterrand governments; the second wave (1993–) was launched by a right-wing government in a stronger political position. However, there is no real similarity between the end of the communist rule in Eastern Europe after over forty years of existence and the change of the government majority in a democratic society. In France, the 1986 law on privatization had earmarked 65 large state enterprises to be returned to private capital in five years. The programme was interrupted in 1988, due to the return of the left to power after fourteen state companies, employing 333,150 wage-earners, had been privatized. In the wave starting in 1993, the companies earmarked in 1986 and not privatized then are again on the list; nine other companies are included. All belong to the 'competitive' sector (excluding utilities). Most of these French state companies (including state-owned banks) either have shares in foreign public or private companies, or themselves have private minority shareholders.

In France (and for that matter, also in Britain, and, since July 1992, in Italy, where privatization was additionally meant to provide an anti-corruption weapon), the privatization impulse has undoubtedly been political, but however harsh the political struggles between majority and opposition, it could never be likened to the change of regime in the East. The relative speed of privatization has to be evaluated against the rather small size of the privatized sector, whereas in the East the aim is to privatize even more quickly, if possible, a much larger share of the national economy.

Apart from the political aims of reversing the action of the previous government and reducing state control, the economic aims are different. Although in the West the right-wing political rhetoric emphasizes improving the efficiency of the economy through privatization, the main concern of the policy-makers is to decrease public spending and raise revenues. In the East, the proclaimed economic aim of privatization is to create the conditions of a market economy which did not exist and to induce greater efficiency. For political reasons, privatization becomes an aim in itself, which dispenses with the need to assess its economic and financial outcome. The process is generally not considered as a way for the state to increase its revenues, due to the lack of domestic capital. It is seen as a way of reducing subsidies, but in systems in which the most visible part of budget subsidies went to keeping down prices, ending price control is a more radical instrument for cutting subsidies. In addition, the governments have to worry about the restitution of property to former owners or about compensation, a principle which has been recognized in the Central European countries, despite some differences.

Real differences in methods

In any privatizing country one has to find new capital to buy out the former state capital. There are two main sources of capital: foreign and domestic.

Foreign ownership is potentially very appealing. It is, however, politically questionable on the basis of the usual objection to 'selling out' the country. In open market economies, it might seem obvious to let foreign capital in just as the domestic firms are invited to invest abroad. In fact domestic assets are always protected. In France foreigners were allowed to buy up to 20 per cent of the privatized enterprises in the first wave, a limit which could be increased case by case in the second. To prevent foreign capital from buying into these companies later on, and borrowing the mechanism used in Britain, in both programmes the state kept a 'golden share' which allowed it to oppose undesirable foreign participation exceeding 10 per cent of the assets. In Portugal the new privatization programme which was launched in 1991 allowed foreign investors to buy only up to 5 per cent of the shares of the Banco Espirito Santo e Comercial de Lisboa, one of the first large firms to be privatized.

In the countries in transition from communism, the new legislation on foreign investment is increasingly liberal. In the countries of Central Europe, Poland, Hungary and Czechoslovakia (before the latter's split into two countries in 1993, as well as in the Czech Republic thereafter), foreigners can own up to 100 per cent of domestic enterprises. However, licences are usually required for owning more than 50 per cent of the capital. The privatization law in Poland provides that, in the case of state enterprises offered for sale, only 10 per cent of the shares can be bought by foreigners without licence; beyond that, a special permit has to be issued. In Hungary, for the first twenty state enterprises offered for sale in September 1990, non-Hungarian ownership was limited to a proportion of 30 to 50 per cent of the shares as a rule. In Czechoslovakia the sale of some part of state assets was achieved in the framework of 'large-scale privatization', but the 'give-away' scheme of state assets did not include foreigners. The attitudes of the policy-makers are quite ambivalent in this respect. Governments are seeking foreign partners and at the same time expressing anxiety about excessive sell-offs. In fact, the search for foreign capital proved difficult and concern about foreign control was meant mainly to reassure the public as to the value of the domestic assets. Even with proper incentives (tax exemptions, full right of profit repatriation, currency convertibility) foreign capital did not rush to Central Europe once the most attractive deals had been made.

Domestic capital is scarce everywhere, but to different degrees. One usually assumes that a major obstacle to quick privatization in the East is due to the lack of financial market institutions. True, in the West, privatization programmes used a developed network of commercial banks, insurance companies, other institutional investors and full-fledged stock exchanges. But in the countries in transition the main obstacle was the lack of private savings and the poor financial situation of the enterprise sector. Although very dynamic, the emerging financial markets in Central Europe are still very narrow. The Polish Stock Exchange displayed an increase in equity values by 80 per cent in the second half of 1993, but only 22 stocks were traded on this market.[4]

In the Western European market economies, the denationalization realized in the 1980s greatly benefited from the expansion of the financial markets before the 'crash' of October 1987 and from their subsequent recovery. In France, during the first programme, about half of the assets were sold on the Paris Stock Exchange and shareholders had to be rationed as the demand for underpriced shares largely exceeded the supply. Employee participation was limited to 10 per cent of the shares and again demand exceeded supply. One of the major problems encountered in the French case (as well as in the earlier British case and in the later Italian case) was how to prevent, in the conditions of an open, largely deregulated market, an excessive concentration of capital in the hands of a small number of big shareholders, who could easily buy out the shares of thousands of small, not so well-informed new capitalists. This was achieved through the policy of 'hard-core' stable shareholders, which were selected outside the market by a specific procedure conducted through the ministry in charge of the privatizations. Thus it can be said that, in the French case, and more generally in developed market economies undertaking privatization, the problem has not been just *where* to find capital but *what* kind of capital to use. Letting the market do the job can lead to an undesirable concentration of capital. Establishing 'hard-core' shareholders can provoke acrimonious political disputes if it is shown that the government in charge of the privatizations favoured its friends. In France, the 'hard-core' (*noyau dur*) policy in the second programme was based upon a system of intricate cross-shareholdings between industry, banks and insurance companies under the control of the state.

The situation is different in the East. There is simply no available capital, be it from institutional investors collecting private funds or from the business sector. Citizens are more tempted to invest in housing, land or small businesses than in shares in former state enterprises, even when they are employees of the latter. To bypass this obstacle, the countries in transition very early contemplated free or discount distribution of assets to the population. Such transfers of shares to the citizens may involve two main variants: distribution of vouchers, or coupons, to be converted into shares in operating companies; and distribution of shares in investment funds or holding companies that in turn have shares in companies. A combination of both occurs when the citizens are permitted to ask an investment fund to manage their vouchers for them.

Czechoslovakia opted for the first variant as the main method for privatizing large enterprises; the process was launched in the beginning of 1992, involving about 1,500 enterprises. After the partition of the country, while Slovakia postponed launching the second wave, the Czech Republic decided in March 1993 to go ahead for more than 2,000 companies. Poland chose, within its 'Mass Privatization Programme' to experiment with the second method for a significant number of state enterprises (over 400). The programme was announced in June 1991 and prepared during 1992, with great delays due to difficulties in setting up investment funds. The final version of the programme was ultimately approved by the Polish Parliament in April 1993, and endorsed by the government in December 1994. At the same time, in 1993 the Hungarian government seemed to contemplate a shift towards a mass privatization plan, which would, however, include greater involvement of the citizens than in Poland and Czechoslovakia, financed through cheap credit. Due to the approaching general elections, which took place in May 1994, no general scheme was adopted. The project was again revived at the end of 1994.

In any case the voucher plans can provide only a partial solution. Even in the Czech case the state remains the main shareholder in most of the privatized firms. In Poland, the proportion of free 'vouchers' that might be issued to the public has been contemplated as in a range of 10 to 30 per cent of the assets to be privatized in the country. For the enterprises included in the programme, certificates of participation in especially formed investment groups will be distributed to all adult citizens for about one-third of the assets. The investment groups themselves will hold 60 per cent of the assets. More than half of these (i.e., 33 per cent of total assets) will go to 'lead shareholders' so as to provide the 'hard core' in each privatized company. The state itself will retain 30 per cent of the total assets. Thus the plan tries to deal with several constraints at once: the lack of capital (through free distribution of shares, *not* in the companies themselves but in the investment funds), control by the state, and protection against unwanted concentration in domestic or foreign hands. But the ultimate source of finance for the investment funds themselves is still left open and will have to involve foreign assistance. This amounts to acknowledging that, in addition to a large state sector, which is bound to remain, the so-called privatized sector will in fact be controlled by public agencies.

Let us briefly mention the case of employee share ownership, which had been rather widely discussed in the East in association with various schemes of 'market socialism' and is paid a modest tribute in the privatization schemes actually adopted, with no role whatsoever in Czechoslovakia and limited scope in Poland and Hungary. Was it successful in the West? Evidence from Britain in a privatized utility company shows that share ownership has not created better motivation for the workers. In France, shares in the privatized enterprises have been offered to their employees as a form of profit-sharing rather than as a plan for mass capitalism.

To sum up, the most visible difference between the instruments of privatization in the East and in the West is that state assets are disposed of largely by non-capitalist methods in the first case and sold on capital markets in the second. What is the outcome of the process?

Ambiguities in the Outcomes

How can the outcome of privatization be measured? This section will discuss several indicators: the share of the private sector; the gains to the state; the increase in efficiency; the increase of the number of shareholders; the benefits to the public. A non-quantifiable indicator will finally be addressed: does privatization result in a decline of the state?

In the East, victory announcements have been made over the share of private activities (in GDP or employment). By this measure Poland was leading in 1993, with half of its economy already privatized, followed by Hungary and the Czech Republic (between a third and a quarter). These measures are misleading because the calculations do not take into account the share of the state in the privatized companies, or the changes in management and governance. In the West similar assessments are made the other way around, measuring the decrease of the state sector.

A more substantial estimate of the outcome of privatization in the West relates to the financial gains from the process. What was considered in France as a substantial achievement was that privatization brought large revenues into the state budget (in sixteen months, as much as the cumulated deficit of *all* the public sector in 1984 and 1985 – or 40 per cent more than all the subsidies to the industrial state-owned enterprises from 1982 to 1985; see Andreff 1993). Another sign of success was the fact that the stocks of the newly privatized companies were not, on average, more severely affected than financial business generally during the crisis of October 1987, and no massive sale of stocks took place in their case. The three first sales in the second wave also yielded large returns (about thirteen billion dollars). In both Britain and France the issues of shares were heavily oversubscribed, this being due not only to the attractiveness of the companies but also to the fact that the prices were low and the stock exchange bullish. In both countries, privatization was interrupted when the financial markets collapsed in 1987. In 1993 it was crucial for the French government to revive the stock market (by a drop in interest rates) before privatizations would resume.

Thus gains from privatization also mean costs. Such costs are not easily quantifiable. They come under two main headings: the underpricing of the shares in initial public offerings, and the costs of restructuring the public company before privatization. Underpricing is a very widely used practice and is evidenced by the premiums realized in the first day's trading on the stock exchange (Harbury 1989). In the first three cases of privatization in the second French privatization programme, the average premium was 20 per cent. This suggests that the initial price was too low.

The restructuring of the companies, usually with the writing-off of accumulated debts, is a much more costly practice. In order to attract buyers the public company must be in good shape. In the second French programme, the first three companies sold (Banque Nationale de Paris, Rhone-Poulenc, Elf-Aquitaine) were profitable (though Rhone-Poulenc had large debts) but the next companies on the list were less attractive. The European Commission did accept an unprecedented capital injection by France into the computer firm Bull. The debts of the French steel giant Usinor exceeded its assets by 25 per cent at the end of 1992,[5] which implies high restructuring expenditures before privatization. The costs are difficult to estimate because recapitalization is not always done openly and may take oblique forms such as setting up a state-supported company to operate the unprofitable activities of the unit to be privatized. In any case, the more privatization is extended, the less revenue it will yield because the most attractive companies are sold first. The difficulties met in most countries trying to privatize utilities (such as bus or rail transport) evidence the point. The exception is the telecommunications sector, already successfully privatized in Britain in 1983, which is due to be very profitably privatized in most of Western Europe by the end of the century under the pressure of deregulation in the framework of the European Union and of worldwide globalization of the telecommunications market.

Restructuring was also an issue in the East. The very question 'should one restructure first?' is not clear in this case either. Restructuring policies may imply closing firms, or sections of firms judged unprofitable, and laying off workers (Aghion and Blanchard 1993); reorganizing the production process as a whole; recapitalizing the enterprises; and pursuing an anti-monopoly policy and splitting up the enterprises (see Charap and Zemplinerova 1993; Carlin and Mayer 1992; for a clear statement of the issues). The Western advisors and commentators hold divergent opinions. The range of proposals goes from a minimalist approach, advocating the maintenance of the state-owned assets until actual privatization can take place (Aghion 1993) to the 'restructuring first' proposal, on the model of the *Treuhandanstalt* in East Germany (Carlin and Mayer 1992). Roland (1993) has suggested that the best firms should be privatized first, with restructuring following before privatization for the others, on the model of Western privatization. The policy-makers in the East are generally against 'restructuring first', both because of a total aversion to industrial policy reminiscent of planning and because of a lack of resources. A give-away scheme provides an additional argument: as privatization does not procure revenues, it is logical that the state should let the market decide the real value of the enterprise.

If a major aim of privatization is to increase efficiency, is it achieved? The question is premature for the privatization of large firms in the East; it is obviously positive for the small firm privatization (mainly in the service sector). In the West, the answer varies. In the British case performance improved, including that of state monopolies such as British Steel and British Airways, but are the successes to be imputed to privatization or to deregulation and to pre-privatization restructuring, as in the case of British Steel? In the French case, Rhone-Poulenc offers an example of an ambiguous outcome. The company was nationalized in 1982 when making substantial losses and had to be salvaged by the state. Since then it has dramatically recovered, invested heavily abroad and domestically. Just before privatization, it was already only half state-owned, as the French state had sold half of its assets on the stock exchange and to (state) financial institutions. Although in 1992–3 its profits had sharply decreased the company was still faring well, and one may question its privatization for efficiency reasons.

From the political point of view, the number of small shareholders is important as it reflected the move towards mass capitalism. In the West, advertising state company sales emphasized the argument. In Britain the proportion of the adult population owning shares rose from 7 per cent in 1979 to over 20 per cent in 1988 (Harbury 1989), and the number of shareholders reached 13 million in 1991. In France, following the first three sales of the 1993 privatization programme, the number of shareholders reached over five million, i.e., about 12 per cent of the adult population. Such figures are, however, misleading. In Great Britain and France alike, the number of small shareholders dropped after a few weeks. The newly privatized companies in 1993 in France expected the amount of their small shareholders to drop by at least two-thirds in the following months.

In the ex-communist countries in transition, the aim is also to create (in this case, from scratch) a class of capitalists. Give-away schemes automatically ensure such an outcome; in Czechoslovakia, after the first privatization wave, over eight million people could be considered as shareholders. Such a picture is artificial. Most of the new shareholders are ready to sell their shares immediately, especially as the economic situation is bad; they see their assets as an increase in their purchasing power. If trading is not allowed immediately, then they get rid of their shares through black market sales or entrust them to a privatization fund. True 'capitalist' behaviour requires a higher income and a better market environment.

Now we turn to the last question: does privatization really mean state withdrawal? In the West, the state is very active during the process. It controls privatization through *ad hoc* agencies, restructures the companies to be privatized or regulates their markets, and ensures its own continuing presence or influence in the privatized companies through 'golden' shares. It is not the same 'state' as before. When the public sector was expanding under the influence of left-wing governments, the philosophy of the state was dirigiste, emphasizing the public interest, supporting a large involvement of the trade unions in some areas of management (especially in the workplace). The philosophy of a privatizing government is market-friendly, generally anti-unionist (as unions usually try to block privatization and restructuring implies lay-offs) and dedicated to competition as the best way to serve the general interest. However, such a government is also the expression of a party or a coalition of parties, with constituencies to take care of, and is not likely to abandon the political and economic advantages stemming from an involvement in important sectors of the economy. Privatization makes this influence more discreet but not less pervasive.

One should assess in this light the outcome of privatization in Central Europe. The post-communist governments were eager to minimize the involvement of the state, both in the privatization process and in the management of the privatized enterprises, and wanted to get rid of the old state sector as soon as possible. They had, however, to set up state privatization agencies, and, in the case of Hungary, to manage state-owned assets (which meant to acknowledge that the state sector was to remain in some form for a long time). They had, be it unwillingly, to tackle the problem of the bad debts of the enterprises.

They also had to investigate the way the privatized sector was managed. Here one has to distinguish between small assets and large firms. While small-scale privatization most often leads to family businesses, the corporate governance of the privatized large-scale state-owned enterprises is not easy to specify. In all transition countries, the former state-owned enterprises are divided into three groups. First, among the already privatized enterprises, the only identifiable subgroup comprises the companies under foreign control, but these are a minority. The second group is made up of state firms preparing themselves for privatization and submitting projects to that effect. Finally, the third group is residual because there is no clear policy as to what kind of enterprises should remain in the state sector, apart from a few public utilities. Most of the enterprises in this group are, or are being, transformed into companies. All the groups are evolving towards the same kind of corporate governance.

What gradually emerges in the privatized companies is a complex ownership structure involving banks, investment funds, other enterprises, state asset management agencies and local governments, with a network of cross-ownership. The actual managers are the former ones in many cases, owing to the difficulties of finding thousands of able managers willing to do the job (Mihalyi 1992 has an illuminating analysis). There is little the new governments are able to do to control the whole process, apart from rejoicing in witnessing how Western governments confront the same difficulties. But there is an important difference between Eastern and Western conservative governments in this respect. While in both cases the policy-makers claim that they want to divest the state of its involvement and let a competitive market operate freely, they also want to retain political control over the process. In the West the links between big business and the government are close enough to allow for such control. In the East the political decision-makers are deeply distrustful of the managers, whom they suspect of belonging to the old managerial class of the communist *nomenklatura* and of making money on their own account. The 'political-industrial complex', which the French economist Alain Cotta sees as a typical feature of contemporary capitalism (Cotta 1991), has not yet emerged in Eastern Europe.

Conclusion

Is there a European market economy project? A straightforward answer may be found in the Maastricht Treaty signed in 1991, which commits the signatories to the principle of 'an open market economy with free competition' (art. 102B). The project is thus a political commitment to a textbook concept. This concept is, however, constrained by other provisions of the treaty, at least in three ways. To ensure the conditions of competition the market is to be regulated by the states, with supplementary regulation by the European Union on the basis of subsidiarity. The whole bulk of provisions related to the European Monetary Union implies a convergent macro-economic policy. The social provisions based on the concept of 'social cohesion' are a distant echo of the German concept of 'social market economy'. If the EU is to be extended to the whole European area, including Central and Eastern European countries that have signed Association ('Europe') Agreements with the EC in 1991 and 1993, then these principles and constraints are to apply to them as well.

In a broader framework, the market economy 'project' is consistent with the intellectual foundations of the adjustment programmes monitored all over the world by the International Monetary Fund and the Organization for Economic Cooperation and Development. These programmes are based on macro-economic policies aiming at stabilization using monetary instruments and budgetary restraint, and assuming that there will be a proper market response if the state is no longer interfering with price or wage fixing and if it divests itself of its enterprises.

This ideal market economy project is a triple abstraction. It abstracts itself from the state, supposed to be a kind of residual authority external to it. It abstracts itself from finance, as it implicitly belongs to the 'real' world of micro-economics. Finally, though it is defined as an 'open' market, the implicit concept of openness relates to standard international trade theory rather than to international globalization.

As opposed to this project, what we witness is a 'triumphant' capitalism adverse to the state, but making use of the state when the interests of business are at stake. A second feature of this new capitalism is that global industry is interwoven with global finance: the competitive power of firms cannot be measured in terms of management or productive skills but is increasingly dependent on their ability to use the stock markets. Thirdly, as the dark side of the free competition ideal, corruption and economic crime have become a permanent feature of capitalism. In the ex-communist countries in transition the most successful market is the black market. In the sophisticated Western market economies the opportunities offered by insider trading have given a new dimension to individual and organized economic crime. Finally, this new capitalism offers exceptional opportunities of enrichment to a few people while providing less protection to the poor, with chronic unemployment becoming the main source of poverty. Here, too, the countries in transition exemplify the exaggerated image of this division.

These realities do not constitute a stimulating project. In the past, for about a century, socialism offered an alternative to capitalism, even when 'real socialism' tainted the image. Following the collapse of communism, that is no longer an alternative. We have still to define a positive and workable project of a market economy. A mixed economy cannot be a project, even if it is possible to prove that 'market socialism' is theoretically feasible, or that state-owned firms do not necessarily perform worse than private firms, or even if in reality Western and Eastern European economies are mixed economies where the state is involved in the market in various ways. A mixed economy is no longer a credible concept.

Notes

1   'Eastern Europe' is taken here as the set of countries, now in transition to democracy and to the market, which belonged to the Council for Mutual Economic Assistance: Poland, Hungary, the Czech Republic, Slovakia, Romania, Bulgaria. The former GDR is a special case, as explained in the third section. The former USSR is not considered as a part of 'Europe'. In any case, its economy is liberalizing and privatizing so slowly that it would not offer conclusive examples for the matters discussed here. Most of the examples are taken from the first three countries mentioned, where the transition started earlier and proceeds more quickly.
2   Although Fourastié referred to the years 1946–75, the Western European period of stable and high (5 per cent on average) growth lasted from 1951 to 1973; from 1945–6 to 1950 Western Europe only caught up with the war losses. Fourastié's phrase originates from the *Trois Glorieuses*, the three days (July 27–9) of the French Revolution of 1830 which ended the Restoration period and marked the beginning of *bourgeois* capitalism.
3   'Selling the state'. *The Economist*, 21 August 1993.
4   *PlanEcon Report*, vol. 9, nos 46–8, 14 January 1994, p. 44.
5   Jean-Pierre de La Rocque, 'Privatisations: tous partants', *Enjeux-Les Echos*, June 1993.

Bibliography

Aghion, P. (1993). 'Economic reform in Eastern Europe: can theory help?' *European Economic Review* 37 (2/3): 525–32.
Aghion, P. and Blanchard, O. J. (1993). *On the Speed of Transition in Central Europe*. London: EBRD, Working Paper no. 6.
Albert, M. (1991). *Capitalism against Capitalism*. London: Whurr.
Andreff, W. (1993). *La Crise des économies socialistes: la rupture d'un système*. Grenoble: Presses Universitaires de Grenoble.

Beveridge, W. H. (1942). *Social Insurance and Allied Services: the Beveridge Report*. London: HMSO.

—— (1944). *Full Employment in a Free Society*. London: Allen & Unwin [2nd edn, 1960].

Bornstein, M. (ed.) (1994). *Comparative Economic Systems: models and cases*, 7th edn. Boston: Irwin.

Boyer, R. (1986). *Théorie de la régulation: une analyse critique*. Paris: La Découverte.

—— (1987). 'Régulation', in J. Eatwell, M. Milgate and P. Newman (eds), *The New Palgrave: a dictionary of economics*. London: Macmillan, vol. 4, pp. 126–8.

Brabant, J. M. van (1993). *Industrial Policy in Eastern Europe: governing the transition*. Dordrecht: Kluwer Academic.

Carlin, W. and Mayer, C. (1992). 'Restructuring enterprises in Central and Eastern Europe'. *Economic Policy* 15: 311–52.

Cazes, B. (1990). 'Indicative planning in France'. *Journal of Comparative Economics* 14 (4); repr. in Bornstein (1994), pp. 160–72.

Charap, J. and Zemplinerova, A. (1993). *Restructuring in the Czech Economy*. London: EBRD, Working Paper no. 2.

Coase, R. (1960). 'The problem of social cost'. *Journal of Law and Economics* 3: 1–44.

Cotta, A. (1991). *Le capitalisme dans tous ses états*. Paris: Fayard.

Delsen, L. and van Veen, T. (1992). 'The Swedish model: relevant for other European countries'. *British Journal of Industrial Relations* 30 (1); repr. in Bornstein (1994), pp. 137–59.

Eichengreen, B. and Uzan, M. (1992). 'The Marshall Plan: economic effects and implications for Eastern Europe and the former USSR'. *Economic Policy* 14 (April): 13–76.

Fath, J. (1992). *Industrial Policies for Countries in Transition?* Vienna: Wiener Institut für Internationale Wirtschaftsvergleiche, *Forschungsberichte*, no. 187, November.

Fourastié, J. (1983). *Les Trente Glorieuses ou la Révolution invisible de 1946 à 1975*. Paris: Pluriel.

Galbraith, J. K. (1967). *The New Industrial State*. Boston: Houghton Mifflin.

Harbury, C. (1989). 'Privatization: British style'. *Journal of Behavioral Economics* 18 (4): 265–88; repr. in Bornstein (1994), pp. 115–36.

Howells, J. and Wood, M. (1993). *The Globalisation of Production and Technology*. London: Belhaven Press.

Hughes, G. and Hare, P. (1992). *Industrial Policy and Restructuring in Eastern Europe*. London: Centre for Economic Policy Research, Discussion Paper 653.

Kornai, J. (1992). *The Socialist System: the political economy of communism*. Princeton: Princeton University Press.

McKinnon, R. I. (1992). 'Spontaneous order on the road back from socialism: an Asian perspective'. *American Economic Review* 82 (2): 31–6.

Mihalyi, P. (1992). 'Property rights and privatization: the three-agent model (a case study of Hungary)'. *Eastern European Economics* 31 (2): 5–64.

Nuti, D. M. and Portes, R. (1993). 'Central Europe: the way forward', in R. Portes (ed.), *Economic Transformation in Central Europe: a progress report*. London: CEPR; Luxembourg: Office for Official Publications of the European Communities, pp. 1–20.

Roland, G. (1993). 'The political economy of restructuring and privatization in Eastern Europe'. *European Economic Review* 37 (2/3): 533–40.

Stigler, G. (1971). 'The theory of economic regulation'. *Bell Journal of Economics* 2 (1): 3–21.

Tinbergen, J. (1961). 'Do communist and free economies show a convergent pattern?'. *Soviet Studies* 12 (4): 333–41.

Part II

The Political System
at Work

5

A Silent Revolution in Europe?

Herbert Kitschelt

In a seminal article, which he followed up with two books, Inglehart (1971; 1977; 1990) argued that Western democracies are experiencing a 'silent revolution' of changing patterns of political orientation. In post-industrial countries the economic interests of class are gradually complemented, if not displaced, by a post-materialist politics concerned with life styles and political participation. This reorientation of preferences can be empirically identified by changes in public opinion as well as by the rise of social movements that make quality of life claims and engage in political practices with an expressive, not just an instrumental, rational-purposive goal in mind.

In addition to assessing some of the research and scholarly debates on the 'silent revolution' that have prompted a flood of publications since the mid-1970s, this chapter attempts to go beyond that debate in at least two respects. First, I shall reconsider the grounds of political interest formation in contemporary advanced democracies, and especially the relationship between materialist economic and non-materialist cultural and political orientations in the mass electorates of European democracies. Second, I shall develop hypotheses about the likely process of political preference formation in the emerging East European democracies. I shall argue that a convergence between Eastern and Western Europe should not be expected in the foreseeable future.

In a nutshell, I shall advance three hypotheses. First, the critical point about preference formation in Western and Eastern Europe is not a disjunction of material and non-material preferences but the parallel and interrelated transformation of preferences in both realms. In Western Europe, both material and non-material interests have changed and entered a new amalgamation when compared with the first post-Second World War decades and the high point of the Keynesian welfare state. In Eastern Europe, the emerging democracies are also characterized by a specific fusion of economic and non-economic preferences which, however, sharply differs from Western patterns. Second, neither in established West European nor in emerging East European democracies does social class figure prominently in the constitution of interests. With a slight bias towards modernization theory, one might say that Western democracies are 'no longer' shaped by class politics, whereas Eastern democracies are 'not yet' structured by it. Third, variations and change in the content of preference formation are also associated with variations in the organizational forms of interest articulation. Actors choose organizational forms of interest mobilization to promote their cause in the most efficient manner against opposing interests not just with rational-purposive ideas in mind; they also choose them as symbolic-expressive devices to cultivate new collective orientations and influence the process of interest formation. The marginalization of class politics in Western Europe and the new expressive modes of interest mobilization have hastened a certain 'disorganization' of political life that involves an erosion of large political parties and economic interest groups (cf. e.g., Offe 1985a; Lash and Urry 1987). In Eastern Europe, the marginalization of class politics has stalled the organization of interest aggregation as well. As the example of social movements shows, however, the disorganization of political life in Eastern Europe has rather different causes, forms and consequences than in Western Europe.

The 'Post-Materialism' Debate: a Reformulation of the 'Silent Revolution'

In order to assess Inglehart's 'silent revolution' hypothesis critically, we have to keep in mind how studies of the problem have measured materialist and post-materialist orientations in Western Europe. The most commonly used survey instrument asks respondents to rank in order four objectives of government action. Those who rank both (1) 'protecting free speech' and (2) 'giving citizens more say in government' first or second are coded as post-materialists; those who favour (3) 'maintaining law and order' and (4) 'fighting rising prices' over the other two options are coded as materialists. Respondents who rank one 'materialist' and one 'non-materialist' policy goal first are coded as individuals with mixed orientations. Inglehart labels advocates of law and order and of low inflation as 'materialists' because they emphasize personal safety and income over goals of community and creative self-development that are furthered by protecting free speech and political participation. Some surveys employ more complex instruments for measuring value orientations, with batteries of eight or twelve policy goals to be ranked in order by respondents, but the basic measuring tool for which long time-series of opinion surveys, at least for the member states of the European Community, are available is the simple four-item index.

The justification for rating goals as 'materialist' or 'post-materialist' was originally derived from Abraham Maslow's psychological theory of a fixed human hierarchy of needs according to which individuals first attribute highest priority to lower order needs for safety and the satisfaction of material desires (hunger, shelter, sex) and move on to higher order aspirations such as belonging to a group and creative self-development once the lower desires have been satisfied. Maslow's psychological theory, however, has remained highly controversial, and Inglehart abandoned this justification for characterizing and explaining political value orientations after the 1970s in favour of a purely sociological theory. In this theory there are essentially four factors that contribute to the strength of post-materialist value orientations.

1 Period effects: In times of good economic performance, signalled by low inflation, high growth, low unemployment, etc., citizens attribute more importance to non-economic and 'post-materialist' objectives of government.
2 Generational effects: Citizens who receive their political socialization in times of economic well-being develop dispositions towards post-materialist values that are maintained even throughout later periods in life when economic performance declines.
3 Life-cycle effects: 'Post-materialist' values are particularly pronounced among young people who do not have the material obligations and worries that come with raising a family or the risks of catastrophic illness later in life.
4 Educational effects: More educated citizens with a greater ability to articulate political goals and a greater sense of personal effectiveness in the political arena put more emphasis on 'post-materialist' goals of participation and self-development.

Inglehart's (1977, 1990) books as well as his numerous other publications seek to prove that post-materialism is not primarily a life-cycle phenomenon but is more powerfully driven by period, generational and educational effects. Period effects have a varying impact on levels of post-materialism. For example, in the 1970s post-materialist orientations declined with increasing economic insecurity (Inglehart 1981). But period effects may be overcompensated by generational replacements and the upgrading of education among younger age cohorts. These effects explain the presence of a long-term secular trend towards post-materialism despite oscillating economic period effects. In the post-Second World War era, each subsequent generation has been raised under conditions of greater affluence and has enjoyed more education. As a consequence, generational cohorts have maintained rising dispositions towards post-materialism, regardless of period and life-cycle effects (Abramson and Inglehart 1992). Post-industrial society thus brings about a general decline of issues of economic (re)distribution on the public political agenda in favour of questions of life style and political participation (Inglehart 1990, ch. 8). These value orientations are also associated with novel dispositions for political action. Post-materialists typically have a higher propensity to participate in social protest movements that are preoccupied with intangible collective goals (feminism, disarmament, ecology) and tend to vote for leftist parties that support such objectives (cf. Inglehart 1979; 1990, chs 9–11).

The post-materialism thesis has been subject to an avalanche of theoretical, methodological and statistical criticisms, among which I will mention only four important issues. The general gist of my argument is that none of these criticisms convincingly destroys a 'hard core' of the post-materialism thesis, once that thesis has been appropriately amended and qualified. Most import-ant, however, is the need for a reinterpretation of the empirical measure and maybe a relabelling of the phenomenon that post-materialism is meant to measure. Based on this modification, we can then explore the extent to which one may identify a 'silent revolution' in Western and Eastern Europe.

The first criticism of the 'silent revolution' hypothesis is that period and life-cycle effects overwhelm secular generational and educational trends, so that there is no clear evidence for a net increase in post-materialism over time and across countries. Instead, the appearance of such trends derives entirely from changes in the inflation rate. In the 1980s inflation declined in all advanced capitalist countries, and, as the salience of inflation relative to other policy goals decreased, more respondents signalled post-materialist preferences. Had Inglehart substituted unemployment for inflation in the index of policy preferences, no trend towards post-materialism would have occurred (Böltken and Jagodzinski 1985; Clarke and Dutt 1991). Inglehart's response, however, shows that longer time-series of post-materialism than those used by his critics do show a trend towards post-materialism and a sustained increase of post-materialism among younger generations, even once economic period effects are taken into account (Inglehart 1985b; Inglehart and Abramson 1992). Moreover, aggregate data show that in most countries rising unemployment is associated with more materialism, not more post-materialism. The only country where in the long run no trend towards post-materialism can be detected, Belgium, is characterized by an extremely high average of over 12 per cent unemployment in the 1981–8 period.

Nevertheless, the debate about period effects shows that one should not overestimate the extent to which post-materialist orientations overwhelm materialism in advanced capitalist countries. Moreover, the debate shows the importance of analysing cross-national differences in value orientations among countries at similar levels of economic well-being, a task that has not been high on Inglehart's research agenda.[1]

A second criticism is that post-materialist values show no individual-level stability. In other words, people's attitudes are highly volatile so that it is very difficult to interpret what post-materialist orientations really measure. Volatility of respondents' orientations further raises the question whether the index really measures deeper values or only short-term policy preferences. Efforts to test the volatility of post-materialism with sophisticated statistical methodology yield rather conflicting results (for: Inglehart 1985a; against: Clarke and Dutt 1991). Even though this debate is inconclusive, we should keep in mind, however, that individual-level arbitrariness in survey responses is an endemic problem of all attitudinal research. Most importantly, post-materialist orientations hardly ever fail to be strong and consistent predictors of political dispositions to act and of voting behaviour. It would therefore be premature to reject the concept as a methodological artefact.

Two other interrelated criticisms grant there is something important in public opinion that is tapped by the concept of post-materialism, but it is not exactly what Inglehart was initially driving at. The first criticism challenges the linkage between what Inglehart measures and non-materialism. Not everyone who expresses non-materialist orientations supports free speech and political participation. There is also a distinctly authoritarian non-materialism that is lost in Inglehart's conceptualization (Flanagan 1982; 1987; Savage 1985). On an analytical level, this argument is sound, but the critics' empirical data also show that the bulk of non-materialists support participatory goals and locate themselves on the left.

The second criticism focuses on the *meaning* of the post-materialism index and argues that Inglehart's measure taps quite different orientations than concern with security, material affluence and economic self-interest, on the one hand, and non-material interests, on the other. The main division between different responses on the four index components has nothing to do with materialism, but with a political division between libertarians and authoritarians, as well as between economic left and right at a subordinate level. Calls for free speech, more citizens' participation and low priority for a strong law-and-order state express a distinctly anti-authoritarian predisposition. Moreover, because many citizens realize that monetary and fiscal austerity policies to fight inflation hurt the less affluent through rising unemployment, at least in the short run,[2] respondents who attribute little priority to fighting inflation display a distinctly leftist, redistributive materialist preference. In contrast, supporters of law and order and inflation abatement who give little weight to free speech and participation express economically rightist and politically more authoritarian views. In this alternative interpretation of Inglehart's index, then, what is labelled post-materialism really measures a politically libertarian *and* economically redistributive leftist commitment, not primarily a lower appreciation of high and rising standards of material affluence. In fact, there is *nothing* in the index that would allow us to infer how much weight respondents give to material well-being compared with other political goals.

This interpretation is consistent with Schumann's (1989) argument that the index of post-materialism measures only attitudes, not deeper value orientations. The underlying value orientation of which the post-materialism index is a derivative concerns the importance individuals attribute to social stability. Those who endorse discipline, rigidity, intolerance and lack of ambiguity favour 'materialist' priorities, while those who accept flexibility, tolerance, individual autonomy and ambiguity support 'post-materialist' priorities.

Reinterpretation of the post-materialism index as a libertarian-authoritarian index is consistent with all the correlates that Inglehart associates with aggregate changes of index values. Higher education promotes a more libertarian, tolerant and participatory political disposition. In a similar vein, the secular opening of democratic politics to participation and debate reinforces such orientations (period effects), as does the upgrading of education for each successive age cohort (generational effects).

If there is a 'silent revolution' in European politics, then, it involves not so much the displacement of concerns with material well-being and economic self-interest as the rising salience of libertarian political orientations. I will argue in the next two sections that the tension between libertarian and authoritarian orientations and between political practices that are related to these dispositions are relevant in both Western and Eastern Europe, but that these divisions assume characteristically different configurations with economic interests in advanced capitalist stable democracies and in post-communist regimes situated at the beginning of a process of democratic consolidation.

Political Preference Formation and Political Action in Western Europe

Let me begin with two negative general contentions that are in the spirit of the 'silent revolution' hypothesis, as amended and modified in the previous section, and ignore cross-national differences of the extent to which they hold up in comparative research. First, in Western Europe, class structure and class interests play less and less important a role in the political self-conception of citizens and in their political behaviour, as indicated by voting and participation in parties, interest groups and social movements. For example, class is no longer a major predictor of voting for social democratic and socialist parties (Franklin et al. 1992). The trend towards non-class voting is visible everywhere, although the level of class voting is still higher in Scandinavia than in other European countries.

Second, in most European countries a pluralization of forms of political mobilization has set in. Enrolment in political parties for the most part has tended to decline (Katz and Mair 1992), interest groups – particularly trade unions – have become more fragmented (cf. Swenson 1989), and social movements with a limited substantive scope and time-span of operation are complementing, though not effectively displacing, parties and interest groups as important modes of political mobilization (cf. Olsen 1983; Kitschelt 1993b). I will now first examine the nature of political orientations that shape preferences and interests in post-industrial capitalist democracies and then briefly discuss the role of social movements in the new political and economic setting.

Political preferences in advanced capitalism

Contrary to the original 'silent revolution' hypothesis, it would be misleading to postulate a shift of preferences from economic to non-economic concerns. More important is the transformation of economic concerns since the first post-Second World War decades and the emergence of new ways in which they are intertwined with non-economic political and cultural orientations. If there is a silent revolution, it consists in the *joint transformation of economic and non-economic political preferences and interests*. Following Lipset and Rokkan (1967), class and urban/rural divisions constituted the primary lines of conflict along which economic interests were defined in industrial capitalism, whereas religion and (to a lesser extent) ethnicity shaped salient non-economic divisions. In practice, in most countries where both economic and non-economic cleavages were present, they were not completely independent from each other. As the experience of Austria, Belgium, Germany, Italy, the Netherlands and Switzerland shows, large religious parties drew more on rural and middle-class voters than on urban working-class electorates who supported socialist parties. Even in nations without significant religious parties, such as Britain, France and the Scandinavian countries, religious voters tended to support the bourgeois parties. In a similar vein, there is also a linkage between economic and non-economic interests in post-industrial capitalist democracies, but neither class nor religion is the defining component of that linkage.

People's experiences in the production sphere not only influence their economic interests but are also related to their non-economic interests concerning the organization of cultural and political life. In the economic dimension, the main political disagreements are located on a continuum that ranges from those who advocate spontaneous market allocation of scarce resources to those who call for centralized redistribution by the state. In the non-economic political and cultural dimension, the main alternatives vary on a spectrum from 'authoritarian' positions that demand top-down binding political decision-making and cultural conformism with prevailing norms to 'libertarian' views that propose participatory political decision-making procedures and the cultural autonomy of individuals and self-organized communities from the regulatory apparatus of the state and the market economy.

Three macro-structural developments in advanced capitalism influence the way in which citizens construct economic, political and cultural preferences and the linkage among them.[3] First, the exposure of an increasing number of industrial and some service sectors to international competition has eroded the support of further redistributive economic policies also among segments of the working class. The process of economic rationalization in factories and offices which has been induced by international competition has created sharp divisions between winners and losers in the workforce that is also reflected by the decline or the fragmentation of trade unions along sectoral and occupational lines.[4] Those who keep their jobs tend to be skilled workers and technicians who know that the survival of their industries depends on continuous modernization. Sustained modernization, in turn, requires a sufficiently high private profit and accumulation rate that constrains redistributive policies. Whereas white- and blue-collar employees in international competitive industries thus tend to oppose further redistributive policies, their colleagues working in sectors protected from international competition are much more willing to call for redistributive policies because their employment prospects are less affected by reduced business profits and higher production costs.

Second, the rise of comprehensive welfare states influences both economic and non-economic orientations. The economic division runs between private-sector employees, particularly in the internationally competitive sectors, and public-sector employees whose relative and absolute number ballooned in the 1970s and 1980s, though at different national growth rates. The former oppose an ever more expensive public sector, the latter defend it. In non-economic terms, many employees, particularly in those segments of the public sector which have grown strongly over the past thirty years – above all education, health care and social services – work in client-interactive jobs. Client-interactive jobs typically involve relations of social reciprocity with clients and professional collegiality among employees. Such job experiences promote orientations sympathetic towards a reciprocal, egalitarian organization of decision-making processes, respect for the autonomy of the individual and tolerance for disagreements. Client-interactive jobs thus attract people who already hold such orientations or reinforce them through on-the-job experi-

ences. In contrast, people whose work involves processing objects or documents have fewer communicative experiences and are more likely to endorse
a hierarchical and conformist structure of human interaction.

Third, the growth of the welfare state is an element of a broader transformation of advanced capitalism into a service economy. Also, outside the
public sector, client-interactive services and occupations that involve the
production of social meaning and symbols (mass media, consulting, advertising) have multiplied. These 'symbol producers', too, have a more libertarian
orientation than employees and professionals processing documents (most
legal, financial or insurance services). Moreover, regardless of whether service-
sector employment is in client-interactive or in document-processing jobs,
service-sector employees on average have a much higher education than
workers in the industrial sector. Higher education endows individuals with the
competence to master complex social situations, to participate in collective
decision-making, and to demand respect as autonomous, rational-deliberative
persons. Educational qualifications thus generate a demand for and an acceptance of the libertarian tenets of individual autonomy and participatory politics.
In addition to client-interactive jobs and higher education, there is a third
characteristic of employees in the service sector that is related to higher
dispositions towards libertarian politics: gender. By way of childhood
socialization and education, women seek out client-interactive occupations. In
particular, younger women with higher education in client-interactive jobs are
likely to express a very intense disposition towards libertarian politics.[5]

The analytical reference point of my reconstruction of political preference
formation in advanced capitalism in the *production sphere* is less informed by
Marx's theory of property classes or Dahrendorf's theory of authority and
hierarchy in work organizations than by Weber's theory of job-related 'market
chances' and Habermas's theory of communicative interaction. Based on this
framework, two predictions can be made about political orientations, dispositions to act and voting preferences in advanced capitalist countries. Economic 'leftism' is related more to public employment and to sectors and job
categories protected from international competitive exposure than to social
class and property relations. Political and cultural libertarianism is related to
higher education, to client-interactive and symbol-producing occupational
task structures, and to gender.

If the attributes of citizens' market and occupational experiences that
influence their political consciousness were randomly distributed, any combination of economic left or right and political libertarian or authoritarian
positions would be equally likely. Empirically, however, we find a clustering
of market and occupational experiences that makes two combinations of
political consciousness more likely than the opposing pair: left-libertarian
more than right-libertarian views and right-authoritarian more than left-

authoritarian orientations. The vast majority of individuals working in jobs that are associated with libertarian dispositions are employed in the public sector or in private-sector jobs protected from international competition that allow them to develop more 'leftist' economic interests. Thus, 'left' and 'libertarian' political experiences are typically associated with each other on one side of the political spectrum, whereas 'right' and 'authoritarian' experiences characterize the other side of the political spectrum. Highly educated public-sector employees in client-interactive jobs (teachers, health-care and social service employees) constitute the 'hard core' of the libertarian left everywhere in Europe. Less educated businessmen and marginal workers with object-producing task structures in internationally competitive industries (agriculture, manufacturing, retailing) provide the hard core of the new authoritarian right. Between these extremes, of course, there are various market and occupational locations that provide intermediate orientations between authoritarian right and libertarian left.

In addition to the formation of consciousness in the economic sphere, experiences in the *reproduction or consumption sphere* of family, home and neighbourhood also influence political orientations and are irreducible to market or occupational influences. Libertarian orientations are particularly strong among younger women who are engaged in a struggle to redefine gender roles in the family and cultural minorities (homosexuals, religious and ethnic minorities) who demand tolerance and respect from the dominant cultural group. Whereas these groups are involved in a 'politics of individual and collective identity', another relevant strand of political consciousness formation is concerned with a 'politics of space' that enhances both libertarian and leftist orientations and is triggered by people's interaction with the physical environment, particularly close to their residences. Where environmental insults (noise, air and water pollution, risks of catastrophic accidents) affect citizens, they may call for a 'libertarian' politics of participation that gives them a chance to make their grievances heard. Demands concerned with ecology and urban planning usually also imply a 'leftist' bent because they call for restrictions on capitalist investment autonomy either directly through state regulation or indirectly through political measures to increase the scarcity and price of pollution licences in the market-place (emission fees, tradeable pollution vouchers, etc.). In some instances, environmentalists may experience strains in their political orientation, when their residential experiences push them towards demands for more citizens' participation and state intervention in the economy, but their occupational experiences pull them towards rightist and/or authoritarian views. This happens, for example, to workers and managers who are affected by the environmental pollution of their own businesses.

I have now sketched a view of the 'silent revolution' in Western Europe that modifies and amends Inglehart's original thesis rather substantially. The silent revolution involves not one but several interconnected changes in citizens' political preference formation and interests. In the economic sphere, the defining element of more pro- or anti-market orientations is no longer class, but employment sector, occupation and gender. Of course, the speed at which class adherence declines as a structuring element of political orientations and voter choices varies across countries (see Franklin et al. 1992), but in general, with the spread of international competition across business sectors and the growth of the welfare state, support of further redistributive economic policies has faded in Western publics. In the political and cultural sphere, what influences people's orientations is not religion, but the correlates of libertarian or authoritarian orientations – education, occupational task structure and gender. Economic, political and cultural orientations are connected with one another to yield a dominant political cleavage dimension ranging from left-libertarian to right-authoritarian views.

My argument should not suggest a static, immovable pattern of preference formation and preference distribution in advanced capitalist democracies but only a set of mechanisms that influence political orientations. For example, were welfare states to weaken and more segments of the service sectors to experience international competition, it is quite possible that leftist political commitments would decline to the extent that the main axis of preference division would run from right-libertarian to right-authoritarian views. Moreover, with a further upgrading of the educational system and a continued restructuring of the economy, the potential for right-authoritarian politics may decline.

My argument about the 'demand side' of political preferences in the population is insufficient to predict the nature of party systems that appear in the political arena. To explain the fortunes of political parties in general and particularly the rise or demise of new left-libertarian and right-authoritarian parties, we would have to develop a theory of the 'supply side' of political parties and party strategy that goes beyond the scope of this chapter.[6] In a similar vein, the fortunes of interest groups such as trade unions cannot be read directly from changing patterns of political preference formation among mass publics, but must be accounted for in terms of a theory of union organization and bargaining under different institutional constraints. Because parties and interest groups are discussed in other chapters, I will here dwell only on the implications of political preference formation for social movements in advanced capitalist democracies.

Social movements as mode of political action

In comparison with parties and interest groups, social movements involve relatively loosely coupled organizations with ill-defined membership roles and a following that tends to engage in direct political protest action outside the institutionalized channels of interest intermediation to change some undesirable state of affairs.[7] In contrast to parties and interest groups, social movements have a superior capacity to mobilize supporters whenever the grievances they articulate are temporally discontinuous and substantively discrete. Where a grievance is likely to persist over an extended period of time, movement entrepreneurs face an incentive to invest in interest organization and to abandon the pure politics of protest. Where a grievance is tied into a whole host of other policy questions of how to fashion a better social order, movement entrepreneurs are inclined to develop generalized ideologies and to compete as parties in the electoral arena. Conversely, party and interest group elites tend to stay away from 'single issue' divisions because they tend to disorganize their vehicles of interest articulation. Thus, movements occur by default because discrete and discontinuous policy problems are difficult to handle for parties and pressure groups. In other instances, where grievances are temporally continuous and/or substantively generalizable, social movements are only the first step on the path towards a more lasting organization of interests around formal associations and parties.[8]

In advanced capitalist democracies with comprehensive welfare states, traditional issues of economic distribution have been institutionalized through parties and interest groups. The greatest potential of movement mobilization exists at the opposite poles of the new main axis of preference distribution, the left-libertarian and the right-authoritarian pole. Left-libertarian movements revolve around the politics of space and the politics of social identity. In contrast to movements concerned with class and income distribution that focus on the acquisition of tangible individual rights and benefits for underprivileged constituencies, left-libertarian movements demand pure intangible collective goods whose benefits cannot be parcelled out to individuals but generally affect the quality of life in a community. In the politics of space, such collective goods are the protection from pollution and technological hazards. In the politics of social identity, such goods are the respect of cultural or gender difference, personal autonomy and the capacity for collective self-organization without interference by public authorities.

The grievances that left-libertarian movements articulate have one of two sources. They may be based on new deprivations that result from the intervention of business or state regulation into hitherto autonomous spheres of social reproduction. This is most typically the case in movements concerned with the politics of space. Alternatively, they may derive from increasing resources and opportunities aggrieved groups are able to seize in order to fight against existing deprivations. This applies most commonly to movements concerned with the politics of social identity, such as feminist, gay/lesbian and cultural minority movements.[9]

Almost all available empirical studies show that participants in movements concerned with the politics of space or social identity typically experience the market and occupational positions that predispose them towards left-libertarian attitudes. Survey respondents who indicate they might join ecology and disarmament movements in Western Europe, for example, tend to support libertarian (post-materialist) and leftist political positions and have higher education (Inglehart 1990, 390). In occupational terms, social movement supporters come from what sometimes has been misleadingly called the 'new class' of 'symbol producers' (Kirkpatrick 1976), professionals in social and cultural service jobs (see Kriesi 1987 and 1989).

The extent of mobilization in left-libertarian social movements depends on at least four determinants which, taken together, account for the great cross-national and inter-temporal variance in the mobilization of such movements.[10] First, such movements are more likely to appear in the economically most advanced countries with comprehensive welfare states. Where, for example, comprehensive welfare states are absent, as in the United States, social movements will be more concerned with individually appropriable rights and economic rewards (cf. Kitschelt 1985; Plotke 1990). In the same vein, in less advanced industrial economies, such as Greece, Portugal and to a certain extent Spain, social conflicts tend to revolve more around class and economic distribution. Second, where Catholicism continues to be a major cultural force, it constrains the rise of an alternative libertarian versus authoritarian definition of political and cultural stakes. This, for example, has been the case in Belgium or Ireland, where social movements such as feminism have gained strength only recently. Most conducive to the rise of left-libertarian movements are denominationally mixed, Protestant and secular cultural settings that offer little resistance to a redefinition of political and cultural stakes around the authoritarianism-libertarianism axis.

Third, the extent of movement mobilization is greatly influenced by political opportunity structures and institutions.[11] Social movement mobilization will be weak if the elites either coopt movement demands or repress them; mobilization will be high at an intermediate level of repression and facilitation (Eisinger 1973; Kitschelt 1986). This intermediate level of repression typically prevails when the competition among established political parties is very close, so that at least one party may have an incentive to appeal to left-libertarian demands in order to win elections, but at the same time is held back from fully pursuing this strategy by other constituencies (cf. Piven and Cloward 1977; Kitschelt 1994, ch. 4). In a temporal perspective, movements are more likely to grow when they become part of a rising tidal wave of social protest that provides examples on which to model effective protest strategies (Tarrow 1989b).

Fourth, in some countries parties may frame movement issues such as to highlight libertarian versus authoritarian conflicts, or they may attempt to incorporate and to diffuse the new issues within traditional economic left–right divisions concerned with distributive politics. The Netherlands provide an example where leaders of conventional parties early on accepted the new quality of left-libertarian movements and thus indirectly stimulated these movements through a polarized competition between parties supporting and attacking such movements. In Britain or France, in contrast, in the 1970s and the 1980s the parties of the left insisted on the definition of the main political division as a class and distributive cleavage and for a long time succeeded in subordinating left-libertarian concerns to that interpretation of political conflicts.

Regardless of the variable strength of left-libertarian social movements over time and across places, for several reasons they are unlikely to be fully absorbed by existing parties and interest groups. Such movements often articulate discrete and discontinuous policy issues that are difficult to digest for parties and interest groups that organize around permanent and interdependent interests. Even in the case of green or left-socialist parties that have been most eager to embrace left-libertarian issue positions, party politicians are cautious to keep their distance from individual ecological or feminist movement organizations in order to avoid becoming identified with a particularistic pressure group. Conversely, left-libertarian movements themselves usually shun close links even with ideologically friendly parties because they wish to keep their autonomy and do not want to be tied down by the generalized ideological concerns of political parties.[12] The participatory, libertarian message of the movements affects their decentralized, discontinuous form of organization, which is also reflected in the absence of close linkages to political parties.[13] There is no question that political opportunities affect the choice of organizational structure in left-libertarian movements. Nevertheless, the organizational form and mode of interaction among members and sympathizers also have a symbolic meaning that pulls them towards decentralized, horizontally interconnected, loosely coupled networks rather than hierarchical integrated and centrally controlled formal organizations.

As a mirror-image of left-libertarian politics, movements and parties of the authoritarian right have appeared in a number of West European democracies in the 1980s and early 1990s. In ideological terms, they represent a backlash against the libertarian left. They counter feminism, particularly the demand for women's control over their capacity for reproduction, with a new paternalism and opposition to women's choice over abortion. They march against environmental protection under the banner of full employment and 'open roads' without speed limits for car drivers. Most importantly, they reject cultural diversity and tolerance for different life styles in favour of a racist and authoritarian message directed against ethnic minorities and homosexuals. Supporters of right-authoritarian politics tend to be recruited from the ranks of the least educated strata of society, particularly young blue-collar workers, but also farmers and small business people. In all European countries, students, the professions and white-collar employees are under-represented within the extreme new right.[14]

The new authoritarian right differs from the Fascist and national socialist right of the interwar period in a number of respects. In contrast to the interwar right, the contemporary right does not call for a corporatist economy but endorses market liberalism. Whereas the interwar right was particularly strong in those countries where influential components of the business, professional, bureaucratic and military elites in unconsolidated democracies supported it, the new extreme right can count on very little support among the political and economic elites of advanced capitalist democracies.

The extent of right-authoritarian mobilization in skinhead groups, quasi-militarist sects and internally hierarchical rightist parties does not directly depend so much on the strength of left-libertarian movements as on the socio-economic pressures exerted by unemployment, particularly of working class youths and immigration. Furthermore, the mobilization of the extreme right is mediated by the response of the established political elites to racism and authoritarianism. Where a strategic convergence of moderately leftist and rightist conventional parties towards the median voter takes place, the chances for rightist mobilization are good. They are further enhanced if bourgeois parties and governments are divided on how to counter the challenge of rightist-authoritarian movements and parties. In contrast, where conservative politicians incorporate elements of a racist and nationalist message and where left parties remain sharply defined in terms of socialism and economic redistribution, rightist movements and parties have little chance to attract a broad following. This configuration of forces occurred in Thatcher's Britain and Reagan's America in the 1980s.[15]

In my discussion of the 'silent revolution' of left-libertarian and right-authoritarian politics in Western Europe, I have entirely avoided the common terminology of 'new social movements'. The adjective new says nothing about the quality of social movements but only the timing of protest (Melucci 1988, 335–6). Yet not all contemporary social movements are new in a qualitative sense. What is new in contemporary social movement sectors is the prevalence of movements whose stakes can be characterized by left-libertarian or right-authoritarian objectives. Movements with left-libertarian stakes of course also appeared as minor currents in the social movement sectors of previous time periods, for example at the fringe of the women's rights movement in the pre-First World War era in groups that called for the sexual liberation and autonomy of women. But as a mass phenomenon, left-libertarian social movements and their organizational practice of temporary, cyclical, decentralized and horizontally linked communication networks have been confined to advanced capitalist democracies.[16] The same applies to the specific thrust and social following of the authoritarian right that cannot be equated with Fascist and national socialist movements of the interwar period.

Precisely because of the decentralized and intermittent nature of left-libertarian movements, it is often not easy to determine whether they are now or will remain an important element of political interest intermediation in advanced capitalist democracies. Such movements often enter phases of dormancy and latency. What survive, however, are urban networks of shops, cafes, educational projects and new media which cultivate the ideas and dispositions that inspire left-libertarian movements (Melucci 1988). As long as such infrastructures of communication persist, it is easy for renewed left-libertarian movements to move beyond the state of latent presence and organize protests whenever new grievances crystallize calls for politicization.

Returning to the three hypotheses stated at the outset, Western European societies exhibit a distinctive reorganization of political preferences which undermines traditional class and religious cleavages. Economic left–right views are now based more on the individuals' sectoral market position and particular resource endowments than social class. Cultural libertarian–authoritarian orientations are related to occupational task structures and personal competencies. Both types of preferences are also linked to personal experiences in the sphere of reproduction, especially that of primary group relations and residential patterns. Economic and non-economic preferences over politics are related to each other, yielding a left-libertarian versus right-authoritarian main axis of preference distribution in the mass publics of advanced capitalist democracies. Advocates of the ideological extremes are generally most prone to participate in contemporary social movements. Such movements develop different modes of organization depending on whether they are closer to left-libertarian or to right-authoritarian objectives.

Eastern Europe and the 'Silent Revolution'

Does Eastern Europe also provide evidence of a 'silent revolution' after the 'velvet revolutions' pushed communist regimes aside? How do citizens conceive their material interests in the realm of the new competitive democracies? How are such interests related to non-materialist orientations over religion, ethnicity, libertarianism/authoritarianism or post-materialism? Are the same dimensions of political preferences that shape Western European publics also relevant for Eastern Europe? And what kinds of political practices in parties, interest groups and social movements are associated with the prevailing political dispositions?

At the present time, it is difficult to answer these questions because Eastern European political systems are still in a state of flux and have not yet consolidated around institutions of interest aggregation, decision-making and policy implementation. Although many surveys have been conducted, owing to the short history of post-communist democracies social scientists have had little time to analyse patterns and trends in such data that would enlighten us about early tendencies in the development of the new democracies. For this reason, all hypotheses I will advance about the process of preference formation and political practice of social movements in post-communist societies in Eastern Europe are highly tentative. One should always keep in mind the null-hypothesis that political preferences in post-communist societies may not be structured by lasting socio-economic and political experiences at all. Instead, the collapse of communism may have created a political vacuum that is filled by charismatic leaders who craft tenuous and temporary linkages to electoral groups or who appeal to the memory of historical political forces and divisions in the interwar period before the advent of communism. According to this null-hypothesis, stable patterns of preference formation and lines of political cleavage will emerge only once a new distribution of economic resources and new rules of political decision-making have been firmly instituted.

Indeed, many observers of East European politics believe that the exceptional fluidity of socio-economic market and occupational positions renders it impossible at this time to link political preferences to anything other than personal charismatic leadership or traditional national political symbols (cf. Mangott 1992, 106). Whereas in capitalist society the stratification of life chances around relations of property and organizational control clearly structures the aspirations and demands of different groups, characterized by specific market chances, for acquiring scarce resources through political means, post-communist societies create too much uncertainty about the potential economic payoffs of citizens' present jobs and personal marketable resource endowments to lead to any kind of lasting collective political interest formation. Citizens simply don't know whether they will be winners or losers of the economic transformation as individuals with particular resources or as members of a group in the same market position. As a consequence, people have not yet discovered what their preferences are, and even if they believe they know their preferences and interests they still are trying to learn how to pursue them intelligently through the political process. In this situation, free-floating ideas that happen to be seized upon by influential personalities may shape the political arena. This is nicely captured by the title of a recent

German political science paper on reforms in Russia: 'Ideas govern, as long as interests slumber' (Paul 1992).

The formation of preferences and the pursuit of interests may be further hampered by the exceptionally constrained economic options faced by the new democracies. After planned economy and proletarian dictatorship have been discredited, everyone embraces liberal democracy and the virtues of the free market. The liberal-capitalist appeal is not so much a matter of deliberate choice on the part of citizens or politicians, but is enforced by the actual international circumstances in which post-communist societies find themselves. Stripped of the mutual economic integration and support networks within East European socialist economies and exposed to the rough winds of world market competition, these countries see their economies go into free fall and their policies becoming dependent on the guidelines of the World Bank and International Monetary Fund, which support aid in exchange for compliance with economic austerity programmes. The inability to shape one's future may have contributed to the exceptional political apathy and distance between citizens and decision-making elites which many observers of Eastern Europe have detected through survey research (cf. Mangott 1992, 110–12; Plasser and Ulram 1992, 18–20).[17]

In spite of these good reasons to question the usefulness of premature hypotheses about political preference formation in Eastern Europe, I will nevertheless argue that there are emerging patterns of political division in post-communist mass publics. The process of transformation does not proceed in a societal vacuum, but builds on existing economic and political institutions that shape citizens' interpretations of feasible alternatives. The status quo thus provides clues about how citizens interpret their preferences and pursue their interests.

Political preferences in post-communist societies

In advanced capitalism, property classes are now a much less important structuring principle of economic interests than thirty or forty years ago. In Eastern Europe, in contrast, they are not yet a critical divider because a capitalist class in the full sense of the word and a private-sector working class do not yet exist. In the complex and fluid institutional systems of post-communist economies with state companies, syndicalist manager- and worker-governed firms, subsidized private but non-competitive enterprises, and a fledgling private competitive sector, it is *individual assets* which people may hope to convert from providing access to scarce goods in a socialist economy to success in a capitalist market economy that affect their preferences *vis-à-vis* economic reform. Two types of assets are particularly important influences on people's expectations of future gain from a capitalist transformation of the economy: personal cognitive resources and energies, on the one hand, and political and managerial skills that derive from experience in socialist enterprises and the knowledge of social networks and channels of communication in the existing socialist economy, on the other.

Educational qualifications in socialist law, accounting or economics do not help professionals to master business strategies in the emerging capitalist economies, but they produce a cognitive competence in methods of analysis, problem-solving and collective decision-making that are useful and relevant even in a capitalist economy. As a consequence, the more professional educational resources an individual controls and the more recent the vintage of their educational certificates, the more they will be inclined to support economic reform and a market capitalism because their cognitive competence is a scarce and sought-after resource.

Among cognitive resources that may dispose actors towards capitalism, two at first sight ascriptive ones are relevant as well: age and residence. Young people have more energies and time to absorb new information and to adjust to a new economic system. They will therefore be more open to drastic reform. In a similar vein, urban dwellers are exposed to more networks of communication and may therefore be more willing to endorse innovation. Cognitive capabilities and resources in a broad sense, not just educational qualifications, impinge upon political orientations.

Political and managerial skills that were learnt in complex organizational networks are important qualifications not only for planned socialist economies but also for capitalism, where a significant share of transactions is not organized via market exchange but through hierarchical organizations and long-term contracts in horizontal networks of firms (cf. Williamson 1985). As a consequence, individuals with managerial and political competence in creating and working though social networks reckon that their skills are convertible into advantages in a capitalist market economy and will therefore be inclined to endorse economic transformation. Moreover, network membership provides information about the process of economic reform and privatization that may enable well-placed individuals to acquire assets at very advantageous conditions. Obviously those who exercised the greatest managerial authority in the socialist state are too heavily implicated in the responsibility for the communist dictatorship to become players in the post-socialist economy. At the top level, older and high profile apparatchiks are likely to take a dim view of their prospects in capitalism and hence may be more inclined to cling to the status quo. As a consequence, whereas the relationship between endorsement of capitalism and professional-educational skills is linear, it is curvilinear in the case of political-managerial organizational skills.

What combination of professional-educational and political-managerial resources individuals hold, of course, varies across occupational groups. Some groups have neither economic nor political resources (pensioners, lower-level members of the security apparatus and party bureaucracy, farm workers, industrial workers in obsolete enterprises, etc.). Others have primarily professional resources (accountants, lawyers, scientists, etc.), while some have primarily political resources (middle- and higher-level apparatchiks). Many of the younger members of the industrial technocracy in socialist countries, however, combine professional and political resources that promise convertibility in capitalist market arenas. The emergence of the last technocratic elite in communist societies in the 1970s and 1980s thus did not given rise to a 'new class' which some expected to cement the status quo of incrementally modernized socialist societies (Konrad and Szelényi 1979), but a social group was promoted that became the catalyst for dismantling communist regimes, because members of this group could expect to survive the transition from socialism to capitalism without harm to their material or even political life chances.

Moving from the micro-level of individual skills and political orientations to the macro-level of the distribution of pro- and anti-market forces in post-communist countries, the industrially most developed socialist countries with the smallest agrarian sectors are likely to exhibit the greatest proportion of citizens whose educational and managerial resources predispose them to supporting capitalist market economies. The nature of economic development in communist countries, however, is embedded in a whole range of other historical legacies and institutional attributes that can be simplified by constructing three basic types of communist regimes (see table 5.1).[18] The first type, rational-bureaucratic communist regimes with large industrial sectors, includes countries such as the Czech Republic and the former GDR, with a relatively early industrialization in the nineteenth century, an advanced secularization and/or a considerable influence of Protestantism in its religious culture, and longer episodes of competitive democracy before the Second World War in which major communist working-class movements were present. After the Second World War these countries established rational-formal communist bureaucracies with comparatively less corruption and patronage and relied only marginally on nationalism as a mode of regime legitimation. Rational-bureaucratic communism repressed opposition forces quite firmly, but then imploded when faced with a large opposition movement in late 1989.

The second type, national communist regimes, such as Hungary and Poland, are characterized by larger agricultural sectors. Before the Second World War they had only begun to industrialize, had experienced a strong political influence from the Catholic Church, and had established semi-authoritarian regimes in the 1920s that never saw more than weak and isolated communist working-class movements. Under communism, these regimes de-

Table 5.1 *Types of communist regimes*

	Pre-1945 attributes (economy, polity and culture)	Socialist state organization	Level of economic development	Role of national-ism in regime legitimation	Strategy towards dissent/mode of transition	Examples
Rational-bureaucratic communist regimes	* extensive industrialization * pre-1945 period of democracy * strong prewar communist movement * strong Protestant or secular culture	* rational-legal bureaucracy * less patronage and corruption	* large sector of manufacturing industries * small agricultural sector	* weak or medium role of nationalism in communist regime legitimation	* systematic repression, but comparatively predictable treatment of opponents * transition by implosion of the communist elites	Czech Republic German Democratic Republic Slovenia
National communist regimes	* partial industrialization * semi-authoritarian polities * weak communist	* clientelist bureaucracies * more patronage and corruption	* intermediate size industrial and agricul-tural sectors	* strong role of nationalism in communist regime legitimation	* mild repression of opposition in the 1970s and 1980s * transition by	Hungary Poland Slovakia Croatia

Table 5.1   Continued

Pre-1945 attributes (economy, polity and culture)	Socialist state organization	Level of economic development	Role of nationalism in regime legitimation	Strategy towards dissent/mode of transition	Examples
movements * dominance of Catholicism			* exploitation of ethnic divisions	negotiation	[Baltic States]
'Sultanistic' communist regimes * little industrialization pre-1918 * authoritarian despotic regimes * agrarian radicalism instead of working-class movements * Orthodox Christian or Islamic culture	* patrimonial bureaucracy * importance of nepotism in addition to widespread patronage and corruption	* smaller, late developing industries * large agricultural sector	* strong role of nationalism in communist regime legitimation * intense ethno-cultural divisions often promoted by the regime	* intense and arbitrary repression of the opposition * transition by pre-emption through elements of the incumbent elites	Bulgaria Romania Albania most constituents of the former Soviet Union [North Korea]

veloped clientelist bureaucracies with a significant presence of corruption and patronage. Under pressure from nationalist forces in society, they attempted to rely upon national appeals to legitimize the communist regime. Especially after the 1970s, such regimes relied less on repression than on cooptation of dissident forces. This prepared the way to negotiated transitions to democracy in the late 1980s.

The third type are 'sultanistic' or 'despotic' communist regimes,[19] such as Bulgaria and Romania. They were agrarian societies with authoritarian political regimes before 1945. In religious terms, Orthodox Christianity or Islam prevailed, which share in common a monolithic view of religious, political and economic power, whereas Catholicism and even more so Protestantism accept the differentiation of economic, political and religious spheres. In the interwar period radical challenges to the status quo emerged from agrarian rather than from communist working-class movements. After the Second World War the newly installed communist regimes organized patrimonial bureaucracies with a strong reliance on corruption, patronage and nepotism. Following Stalin's death these regimes began to resort to nationalist appeals for legitimation, a strategy that heightened regional, ethnic and even tribal tensions where minorities were present. Democratic opposition forces were more firmly repressed than anywhere else in Eastern Europe and parts of the incumbent communist elites organized the transition to post-communist regimes as pre-emptive strikes to salvage the existing power structure.

Overall, pro-capitalist orientations are most prominent in former rational-bureaucratic communist regimes, where professional skills are most widespread and where a relatively depoliticized technocratic economic elite was most well developed and ready to defect from the existing social order. Interestingly, whereas many professionals in Western Europe, particularly those in the public client-interactive social services, express a more anti-capitalist orientation because they are economically relatively 'saturated' in a public or domestic economic sector protected from international competition, East European professionals are likely to be the most pro-capitalist group in their societies because they have the most to gain from the introduction of new economic institutions.

It is sometimes argued that East European politics will be solely concerned with distributive questions of building market capitalism. At the same time, however, the East European transformation is not confined to a rebuilding of the economic system but also involves momentous changes in the political constitutions and even in the articulation of cultural collective identities that were repressed under the old regimes. In other words, the East European revolution raises questions of political process and of citizenship. It is therefore worth exploring what factors may influence the process of non-economic political preference formation and its relationship to economic interests. Is there a 'silent revolution' in Eastern Europe as well?

To begin with Inglehart's measure of post-materialism, most East European surveys have found a relatively high level of post-materialism, although it remains behind that of most West European countries (Inglehart and Siemienska 1990). According to the 1990 World Values Survey, 4 per cent of Hungarians, but 9.2 per cent of Bulgarians, 10.5 per cent of Czechoslovaks, 10.9 per cent of Poles and 13 per cent of Moscow residents endorsed post-materialist policy priorities on the four-item post-materialism scale. The corresponding proportions within Western Europe ranged from 11 to almost 30 per cent.[20] For the most part, Inglehart and his associates have not attempted to explain cross-national differences in levels of post-materialism among countries with similar levels of affluence and economic systems. Hungarians, for example, might come out as least predisposed towards post-materialism because they have suffered under high inflation longer than the citizens of other East European countries. At the individual level, as Dutch and Taylor (1993, 769–70) have shown, East European support for post-materialism has nothing to do with economic growth at the time of the respondents' maturation to adulthood or with their present material affluence, but primarily with age and education. As in the West European countries, this finding again suggests that what the 'post-materialism' index really measures is a libertarian orientation towards democratic participation and civil liberties. In the words of Dutch and Taylor, 'the items tap certain fundamental democratic values – liberty and rights consciousness, for example – and the better educated simply have had more of an opportunity to learn to appreciate such principles' (1993, 773).

In addition to education, for historical reasons youth should predispose East European respondents towards libertarianism in post-communist societies. Young people have not been indoctrinated into the communist ways for a long time and are therefore more open to participatory, non-hierarchical modes of decision-making and to tolerance for political and cultural diversity. Among older people, the lack of familiarity with democracy and the socialization into communist systems have fostered a 'civilizational incompetence' that makes it hard to accept a civic culture of competition, tolerance for disagreement and political participation (Sztompka 1993). For that reason, Sztompka (pp. 92–3) sees the greatest chance for the development of libertarian and cosmopolitan attitudes among the young and educated. As we have argued above, such individuals also provide the strongest constituencies that support a profound economic transformation towards market capitalism. Hence, whereas in advanced capitalist societies libertarian views go with a moderate left anti-capitalist economic reformism, in post-communist countries libertarians are the most ardent supporters of a rightist, pro-capitalist change of the economy.

The divide over libertarian and authoritarian values is also related to a presently important and historically unique controversy in post-communist societies: how harshly should former communists be treated by the new democratic rulers? Should they be tried for violations of civil rights, the misappropriation of funds, and other crimes committed by those who held high office in communist dictatorships? The founding elections of post-communist regimes were clearly governed by a division between supporters and opponents of communism and constituted plebiscites on the old regimes. Hence, the most pro-capitalist and libertarian voters supported the most anti-communist parties. As time evolved, however, anti-communist 'lustration' laws and other legal instruments to punish former communists have given the communism/anti-communism conflict a new popular interpretation. Now the most libertarian, pro-capitalist forces hesitate to support further anti-communist legislation because of the belief that it is inappropriate under the rule of law to legislate retroactively to punish communist crimes. Moreover, these libertarians advocate that all citizens should start on an equal footing in the new democracy and former communists should not be treated as second-class citizens. To build a functioning democracy in which institutional rules are respected by all citizens, the new democratic rulers should not govern against their own principles to punish former communists. In contrast, authoritarian and nationalist forces with a penchant for a closed national and state regulated redistributive economy often have the greatest inclination to encourage further anti-communist legislation because they are less inhibited by respect for the rule of law and democratic equality of all citizens.

Not only citizens' political rights and the mode of political decision-making, but also the very foundations of citizenship are controversial in many post-communist societies in which competing ethnic and cultural groups have begun to mobilize after communist constraints on channelling cultural identities were removed. Insistence on ethnic particularism and parochialism or on cosmopolitan tolerance is closely related to the economic left–right divide. To a large extent, ethnic and national parochialism can be understood as a defensive reaction against the uncertainties of market competition (cf. Offe 1992b). Because global markets threaten ethnic collectivities (Schöpflin 1991, 53), nationalists and ethnic particularists oppose capitalist economic institutions. By defining the allocation of scarce resources in terms of cultural collectivities, ethnic status becomes a signpost and a bargaining ploy to prevent resource allocation through competitive markets becoming more flexible and individualized. The current mobilization of ethnic differences in the former Eastern bloc is consistent with ethnic competition theory according to which ethnic groups mobilize in periods of rapid change in the relative economic payoffs of competing ethnic groups (Ragin 1987, 135–6). In Eastern Europe, the likely losers of market reforms have the greatest propensity to engage in ethnic or nationalist mobilization: cultural collectivities in more agrarian settings with few viable industrial assets and a weak profile of educational skills convertible into capitalist market advantages. At the individual level, older agricultural and blue-collar workers, the lower salariat, the military and pensioners should be most inclined to support nationalist and ethnic parochialism.

The division between cultural cosmopolitanism and parochialism is related not only to political preferences over market capitalism or statist economics, but also to the alternatives between libertarian and authoritarian views of collective decision-making. Because liberal democracy does not provide an institutional answer to the organization of collective ethnic identities, but instead individualizes the rights to citizenship, national and ethnic particularists tend to oppose democratic competition (Schöpflin 1991, 55). Thus, there is a tendency in post-communist society that citizens who reject free capitalist markets also reject liberal-democratic institutions and endorse national and ethnic parochialism.

The main axis of political division in Eastern Europe thus tends to run from right-libertarian and cosmopolitan supporters of free markets, civil rights and democratic participation to left-authoritarian and parochial proponents of regulated economies, limited individualized civil rights and authoritarian collective decision-making (Kitschelt 1992). In this sense, post-communist societies witness the emergence of a confrontation between democrats and nationalists (Goldfarb 1990, 550). Political tendencies located outside the main axis from right-libertarianism to left-authoritarianism remain weak. For example, economically leftist and libertarian political stirrings, such as in ecology parties or even social democracy (cf. Lindstrom 1991), remain without a broad following, as long as the present structural and institutional makeup of post-communist societies continues to exist. Conversely, the new West European radical right, which combines free market liberalism with political authoritarianism and racism, has no counterpart in Eastern Europe, as long as authoritarian-parochial dispositions are here wedded to socialist economic predilections.

Overall, the potential for a vigorous libertarian, pro-market push in East European mass publics is greatest in the former rational-bureaucratic communist regimes, whereas it is more subdued in the previous national communist countries. By far the lowest potential for libertarian-capitalist politics, however, can be found in former patrimonial and sultanistic communist societies, where few citizens have the skills, the resources and the confidence to adapt to an international market economy and to open democratic competition with uncertainty over winners and losers. Former patrimonial socialism is thus most likely to exhibit a backlash in which economic reforms bog down or are even reversed and statist and semi-authoritarian regimes will seize power. Such propensities have already surfaced in a number of the successor states of the former Soviet Union and also in Romania.

Social movements in post-communist countries

Given the different dynamics of preference formation and articulation in Eastern and Western Europe, social movements in the two regions are also likely to differ in quantitative and qualitative terms. Most importantly, we do not expect to find Eastern equivalents to Western left-libertarian and right-authoritarian movements. Moreover, whatever movements occur, they will find it difficult to articulate their demands and mobilize mass support. In fact, with the exception of brief episodes of mass protest, the East European anti-communist transformation is characterized by an *absence of popular mobilization*. It was instigated by the exhaustion of the incumbent elites and the actions of counter-elites that were sporadically supported by a few mass demonstrations at critical historical junctures. In none of the East European countries were social movements critical in bringing about the destruction of the communist regimes or playing an important role in the building of new post-communist polities and economies thereafter. This assessment even includes Poland, where the Solidarity union certainly constituted a powerful movement in the early 1980s but much less so in the late 1980s (cf. Touraine et al. 1982; Ost 1990).

In most countries, the workers' movements were controlled by the communist apparatus until the very end and since that time have been unable to regain the initiative. Poland's independent Solidarity union was ill-prepared to engineer a transformation of socialist economies to capitalism, a process that entails high unemployment, the emergence of gross inequalities and severe economic hardship for most workers. The fragmentation and loss of power of the various Solidarity unions in Poland is rooted in the inability of workers' movements to develop an alternative future for post-communist political-economic regimes.

In most post-communist countries, the successor organizations to the old communist union apparatus still have the largest enrolment of workers and try to maintain their loyalty by populist anti-market appeals. The spectrum of new unions originating in oppositional elites remains weak and fragmented. In Hungary, for example, the fragmented labour movement has been coopted into quasi-corporatist representative boards with participation of state and business representatives, but the unions are ineffective in defending their members' standard of living and the institutions of social partnership have little power to affect wages, work conditions or job security (cf. Kurtán 1993). In a similar vein, in Poland Solidarity unions have protested against the government's austerity policy but have been defeated. In the 1989 Polish parliament, the legislators elected on the Solidarity ticket supported radical liberal market reform and thus were further removed from the average political opinions of the population, which, like their communist colleagues, preferred economic security and only marginal reforms (cf. Bialecki and Mach 1992, 173–7). In all post-communist countries, working-class movements are ill-designed to take on the tasks of the post-communist transformation and therefore have been unable to stage successful campaigns in defence of their interests.

Women's movements also face great obstacles to mobilization in the post-communist era. They are tainted, if not discredited, by the official communist women's organizations of the past. As a consequence, women in most post-communist countries have been unable to prevent the rapid erosion of their economic and political status and have been forced to shoulder more burdens of the societal transformation than men. Where the Catholic Church has launched a frontal assault on women's control of their reproductive capacities, as in Poland, women's groups have formed late and have been unable to protect their rights, although opinion polls show that the vast majority of women oppose the moral doctrines of Catholicism.

Ecological movements began to thrive in many East European countries in the mid-1980s as an ideologically innocent, pragmatic single-issue protest that confounded the communist elites because the new stirrings of protest could not easily be pressed into the accustomed Cold War left–right stereotypes and branded as counter-revolutionary. For this reason, many regime opponents sought refuge under the shelter of ecology movements as a comparatively harmless but safer way to articulate opposition to the decaying communist regimes. As soon as other avenues of protest against communist rule opened up, however, ecology movements lost their salience. After the revolutions, with the exception of some highly visible protests around particular environmental grievances, ecology movements have further declined and now consist primarily of a hard core of professionals and researchers. In an era when momentous institutional changes in the economy and the polity are on the daily political agenda, ecology is certainly not an issue that can generate mass mobilization.

What is left for social movements if working-class mobilization and 'new' social movements following the West European model of ecology and feminism are bound to stay weak? Two types of movements might gain a mass following. The first type are ethnic and national movements with an intolerant, authoritarian appeal combined with anti-liberal market rhetoric. The reasons why such movements become attractive have already been discussed. The second type are 'poor people's movements' that may mobilize Eastern Europeans in similar ways to American movements of poor workers and inner-city minority communities analysed by Piven and Cloward (1977). They engage in sporadic, disruptive protests against intensely felt deprivations that are meant to force the elites to respond to their needs. At the same time, they have no capacity to build sustained movement organizations that could escalate the scale of political struggles beyond localized acts of resistance. Whatever organizations poor people's movements build will be easily coopted into the existing local power structures and cut off from their moorings in society.

An example of a 'poor people's protest' is the taxi cab strike against petrol price increases in Budapest in October 1990. The strike forced the government to make concessions because poor people rallied to the cab drivers at the critical inner-city traffic jams and immobilized urban life (cf. Szabo 1992, 358). But after this partial success, the protesters dispersed as quickly as they had come together. With its sporadic and anti-institutional character, the cab drivers' strike highlights the populist potential of East European poor people's movements. They are born out of disappointment with the political-economic transformation. Their target of attack is not just the material conditions of life but also the new elite-dominated intermediary institutions of democratic representation, parties and parliament. This thrust of poor people's movements is highlighted by the plebiscitarian drive of the Hungarian 'Movement of People Living under the Threshold of Poverty' in early 1993 to dissolve the Hungarian parliament and schedule new elections immediately.[21] The anti-institutional bias of disruptive protest movements has led especially libertarian parties to abandon protest politics in order to teach citizens to abide by the rules of representative democracy. To make democracy work, libertarian politicians argue that a popular consciousness must be created, so that institutions and rules matter in an order protecting civil liberties and democratic participation, not just interests and passions.[22]

Thus, in addition to the content, the form of social movements in Eastern Europe also differs from practices in the Western advanced capitalist region of the continent. In the West, the institutionalized organizations of economic producer groups, as well as the more fluid left-libertarian movements that build on an infrastructure of well-established social communication networks, are the pillars of societal interest articulation. Even left-libertarian movements advocate modes of direct democratic participation only as a supplement, not as a replacement of representative democracy. In Eastern Europe, in contrast, poor people's protest can resort neither to institutionalized organizations of economic interest groups nor to loosely knit infrastructures of communication that feed into social movements. Because such movements have few resources to stage protests effectively, their supporters are more likely to be alienated from the emerging liberal democracies and to push for an all-out challenge to the rules of representative democracy. The contrast between Eastern and Western patterns of interest mobilization, of course, is a matter of degree. The East European countries whose present democracies were preceded by rational–bureaucratic communist regimes are probably more likely to develop an organized sector of interest representation than countries with a patrimonial 'sultanistic' past.

Patterns of Post-Materialism in Capitalism and Post-Communism: Empirical Illustrations

In 1990, a World Values Survey was conducted in fifty countries, including most of Western and Eastern Europe. Respondents were asked to reveal their materialism or post-materialism index, as introduced by Inglehart, and to indicate their stance on a host of other issues concerning the economic, political, and cultural constitution of society. I will now selectively present some results of this survey for a number of the most important East-Central and West European countries.[23] The lead question is always: how *different* are the attitudes of materialists on each issue from that of post-materialists within each country? Next, I will explore whether the opinion difference between materialists and post-materialists is the *same* in advanced capitalist and post-communist countries, or whether the relationship between material- ists and post-materialists is *different* across the two systems. I have argued that post-materialists will be much more favourably oriented towards a capitalist economic organization in post-communist than in advanced capitalist countries. When it comes to issues related to the libertarian or authoritarian organization of social relations and the state, the difference should be much less pronounced. With respect to the choice between more economic afflu- ence or non-monetary quality of life, it is likely that it is only in Western societies that post-materialists tend to stand out with more non-economic preferences.

Before I interpret the findings, let me indicate what I do not wish to explain in this section. First of all, I shall not explain many of the cross- national differences within the broad groups of capitalist and post-communist countries. Second, I shall ignore the overall levels of support for particular propositions in each country and just examine the relationship between the position of post-materialists and materialists. For that reason, I shall present the respondents' issue positions in each country in tables 5.2A and 5.2B as difference values between materialists' and post-materialists' views on a range of statements. Consider the entry for Austria in row 4 of table 5.2A (−17.5). It subtracts the percentage of materialists who indicate that they have quite a lot or a great deal of confidence in the police from that of post-materialists who express the same view. In this instance, 17.5 per cent *more* of materialists have confidence in the police than of post-materialists, hence a negative difference value (the actual absolute values for each group are 75.1 per cent for materialists, 57.6 per cent for post-materialists). In other words, numbers with a positive sign in tables 5.2A and 5.2B indicate that post-materialists are more likely to endorse a statement, negative numbers that materialists are more likely to approve that statement.

Before we get to the issue items, row 1 in both tables provides the ratio of post-materialists to materialists, revealing that in the capitalist countries (table 5.2A) post-materialists tend to be much more numerous than in post-communist countries (table 5.2B). In both regions, however, there is a tendency that higher education and non-manual white-collar and professional occupations are over-represented among post-materialists (rows 2 and 3). This tendency is very strong in capitalist countries but also moderately so in post-communist countries. Column 7 in table 5.2B provides the difference in the average over- or under-representation of post-materialists for each given statement, as reported in column 7 of table 5.2A for capitalist countries and column 6 of table 5.2B for post-communist countries.

The next block of issues (rows 4 to 8) tests whether Inglehart's measure of post-materialism is associated with libertarian positions on a variety of issues concerning the state and personal conduct. Libertarians emphasize individual autonomy and participatory politics. As a consequence, they tend to have less confidence in the police, less respect for authority, and less pride in one's nation if nationalism is employed as a measure to shore up collective compliance with social norms. Moreover, in private life, they are less insistent on marital fidelity and have more sympathy with women's emancipation. Table 5.2A shows that these relations are borne out without fail in all six capitalist democracies for which I present data. In Eastern Europe, column 6 in table 5.2B reveals a similar tendency for post-materialists to be more libertarian than materialists, but there are some outliers that can be explained by the historical circumstances of the transition. In countries where the transition to democracy began early and could build on opposition movements – Hungary, Poland and to some extent also the Czech Republic – even post-materialists began to have a longing for more authority in 1990, whereas in Bulgaria and the German Democratic Republic, countries with strong communist authority lasting to the bitter end, post-materialists strictly rejected authority and materialists endorsed it. In post-communist countries, post-materialists are also often as proud or more proud than materialists of their nation (row 6). After all, national identity was an important fountain of resistance to Soviet hegemony. In a similar vein, Catholicism as an anti-communist cultural inspiration boosts the approval of marital fidelity among post-materialists in Poland and Hungary to the same level as that of materialists. Finally, approval of the women's movement (row 8) does not exhibit a clearcut association with post-materialism in post-communist societies, because these movements were too often identified with the communist state.

Table 5.2A   Correlates of post-materialism: advanced capitalist democracies

	1 Austria	2 Denmark	3 France	4 Germany	5 Italy	6 Norway	7 Average value
1 Ratio of post-materialists to materialists (% sample)	25:14	15:15	24:20	19:13	24:23	10:28	21.2:18.8
I Socio-economic background							
2 Completed education at age 20 or older (V356 = 9 + 10)	+15.9	+38.7	+40.6	+29.0	+8.3	+37.3	+28.3
3 Non-manual employment or professional (V359 = 3–5)	+33.5	+28.6	+24.9	+24.8	+16.6	+27.5	+26.0
II Libertarian versus authoritarian							
4 Quite a lot or a great deal of confidence in the police (V278 = 1 + 2)	−17.5	−16.7	−13.8	−23.8	−17.3	−8.0	−16.2
5 Greater respect for authority would be good (V268 = 1)	−33.6	−34.2	−40.5	−41.9	−29.3	−28.9	−34.7
6 Very proud to belong to one's own nation (V322 = 1)	−22.7	−28.2	−26.5	−22.1	−15.0	−25.2	−23.3
7 Unacceptable for married men/women to have an affair (V304 = 1–3)	−16.2	−36.2	−25.4	−25.1	−25.2	−17.9	−24.3
8 Approve somewhat or strongly of the women's movement (V294 = 1 + 2)	+9.5	+22.2	+4.7	+29.3	+14.5	+18.4	+16.4

III *Material or non-material quality of life*

9 Willing to pay more taxes for environmental protection (V13 = 1 + 2)	+22.2	+16.6	+21.5	+22.3	+8.1	+17.6	+18.1
10 Disagree that environmental protection is less important than often stated (V17 = 3 + 4)	+18.7	+17.9	+12.9	+19.8	+7.9	+10.6	+14.6
11 Approve somewhat or strongly of the anti-nuclear movement (V291 = 1 + 2)	+0.7	+21.1	+5.1	+28.0	+0.5	+10.9	+12.7
12 Less emphasis on money and material possessions would be a good thing (V264 = 1)	+8.9	+9.2	+9.8	+15.0	+9.4	+19.4	+12.1

IV *Property relations and distribution*

13 Owners should run the business or appoint managers (V126 = 1)	−17.9	−25.0	+1.3	−22.6	−23.1	−19.3	−17.8
14 Private ownership of business should be increased (V251 = 1–3)	+18.9	−11.3	+4.0	−4.4	−10.6	−12.1	−2.6
15 There should be greater incentives for individual effort (V250 = 8–10)	+3.5	−22.1	+4.3	−3.4	+8.0	−7.8	−2.9
16 Competition is good: it makes people work hard and develop new ideas (V254 = 1–3)	+8.2	−14.6	+3.1	−2.0	−9.9	−5.7	−3.5

Note: Entries in rows 2 to 16 are the difference between the percentage of post-materialists and the materialists agreeing with a statement. In brackets: variable numbers and values from the World Values Survey 1990.

Table 5.2B   *Correlates of post-materialism: post-communist democracies*

	1 Bulgaria	2 Czecho-slovakia	3 GDR	4 Hungary	5 Poland	6 Average values	7 Difference between capitalism and post-socialism
1 Ratio of post-materialists to materialists (% sample)	9:27	10:26	23:11	4:45	10:30	11.2:23.2	10.0/4.4
I Socio-economic background							
2 Completed education at age 20 or older (V356 = 9 + 10)	+33.7	+9.3	+20.0	+2.4	+16.3	+16.3	12.0
3 Non-manual employment or professional (V359 = 3–5)	+15.8	+6.0	+22.1	−6.2	+1.5	+7.8	18.2
II Libertarian versus authoritarian							
4 Quite a lot or a great deal of confidence in the police (V278 = 1 + 2)	−33.2	−5.1	−16.1	−7.4	−10.1	−14.4	1.7
5 Greater respect for authority would be good (V268 = 1)	−24.1	+6.3	−32.8	+4.7	+5.4	−8.1	26.6
6 Very proud to belong to one's own nation (V322 = 1)	−40.6	−4.3	−11.3	+12.6	−0.4	−8.8	14.5
7 Unacceptable for married men/women to have an affair (V304 = 1–3)	−35.7	−14.8	−16.4	−0.3	+1.1	−13.2	11.1

8 Approve somewhat or strongly of the women's movement (V294 = 1 + 2)	−12.5	−1.2	+6.4	−8.8	+6.7	−1.9	18.3

III Material or non-material quality of life

9 Willing to pay more taxes for environmental protection (V13 = 1 + 2)	+5.9	+20.8	+23.7	−1.3	no data	+12.3	5.8
10 Disagree that environmental protection is less important than often stated (V17 = 3 + 4)	+13.8	+11.8	+10.5	−5.3	+0.4	+6.2	8.4
11 Approve somewhat or strongly of the anti-nuclear movement (V291 = 1 + 2)	+0.7	−3.3	+1.3	−18.5	−3.6	−4.5	17.2
12 Less emphasis on money and material possessions would be a good thing (V264 = 1)	−4.9	−1.6	+9.6	−10.0	+7.2	+0.1	12.0

IV Property relations and distribution

13 Owners should run the business or appoint managers (V126 = 1)	+26.2	+8.7	−9.7	+8.4	+0.7	+6.9	24.7
14 Private ownership of business should be increased (V251 = 1–3)	+27.4	+26.9	+7.9	+10.2	+21.2	+18.7	21.3
15 There should be greater incentives for individual effort (V250 = 8–10)	+30.3	+8.7	+15.3	+20.3	+5.8	+16.1	19.0
16 Competition is good: it makes people work hard and develop new ideas (V254 = 1–3)	+20.1	+19.2	+7.1	−1.6	+12.1	+11.4	14.9

Note: Entries in rows 2 to 16 are the difference between the percentage of post-materialists and the materialists agreeing with a statement. In brackets: variable numbers and values from the World Values Survey 1990.

The next set of questions concerns the choice between material and non-material goods (rows 9 to 12). Without any inconsistency, in advanced capitalist democracies post-materialists are more willing to pay taxes to fight pollution, to believe in the importance of environmental issues, to support the anti-nuclear power movement and to put less emphasis on money in their lives. Interestingly, the relationship between Inglehart's measure of 'post-materialism' and the only actual statement that operationalizes an orientation beyond material goods, putting less emphasis on money, is *weaker* than the relationship between the formal measure of 'post-materialism' and the various libertarian-authoritarian statements in table 5.2A. This lends some credibility to my contention that Inglehart's post-materialism has less to do with orientations towards material affluence than with a participatory and libertarian political and cultural organization of society.[24]

In post-communist societies, approval for 'intangible' collective goods over tangible material goods is much less clearcut among post-materialists than in capitalism. The different social conditions prevailing in the two systems make themselves felt. While East European post-materialists also have a tendency to be more willing to pay taxes for environmental clean-ups and to emphasize ecology than materialists (rows 9 and 10 in table 5.2B), they are certainly no more anti-nuclear than materialists and also do not believe that less emphasis on money is a good thing (rows 11 and 12 in table 5.2B). The contrast between Western capitalism and East-Central European post-communism shows that, whereas libertarianism is at the core of Inglehart's measure of post-materialism, regardless of the systemic context, the orientation towards money and collective goods is contingent upon specific historical circumstances. Actual non-materialism is not a logical but an empirical and contingent correlate of the measure of 'post-materialism'.

The final block of questions concerns the evaluation of property rights regimes and economic distribution. I have hypothesized that, in advanced capitalist democracies, post-materialist libertarians are more anti-capitalist than materialist authoritarians, whereas in post-communism the reverse is true. Checking first column 7 in table 5.2B, the overall proposition is borne out: The difference in the average evaluation of statements by materialists and post-materialists between the capitalist and the post-communist countries is nowhere greater than in the assessment of economic property rights questions. In post-communist societies, there is a consistent tendency on all four items that post-materialists are much more in favour than materialists of businessmen governing their firms, privatization of the economy, achievement criteria in financial remuneration and competition (column 6, table 5.2B).

In capitalist countries, there is a tendency for post-materialists to be less enthusiastic than materialists about private enterprise, individual income incentives and competition. With regard to three of the four indicators, however, the overall aggregate under-representation of post-materialists in the endorsement of capitalism (row 7, table 5.2A) is not very strong because Austria and France are outliers where post-materialists are actually supporting more pro-capitalist positions. Not by chance, however, Austria and France happen to have a history of state intervention in the economy. Being against statist economics and for private enterprise implies for post-materialists in Austria and France a libertarian protest against what amounted to the most centralist if not 'socialist' policies of economic planning that could be found in European capitalism in the post-Second World War era. In France this is symbolized by the realization of its large nuclear power programme (Kitschelt 1986), in Austria by a large public manufacturing sector and associated strong unions that also pressed for nuclear power. In the other four countries, where capitalist markets had a freer rein and where nuclear power enjoyed more hesitant state support, post-materialism is rather strongly associated with more anti-capitalist positions.

The data I have presented show only where scientific analysis of similar and contrasting patterns of issue positions between capitalism and post-communism should begin, not where it should conclude. The tables pose as many questions as they answer. Nevertheless, they provide some plausibility for the hypothesis that post-materialists, as measured by Inglehart's index, are consistently culturally and politically libertarian, but may support starkly different positions on economics depending on the systemic context. As democracies and capitalism consolidate in post-communist societies, we might expect that the configurations revealed in 1990 will change. In Eastern Europe, post-materialist libertarians will become more decidedly anti-authoritarian, anti-national and pro-feminist, a process that is already in full swing in countries such as Hungary and Poland. For some time to come, they will remain more pro-capitalist than materialists. Eventually, that may also change with economic growth and the transformation of the economy. This process may induce the educated white-collar intelligentsia of Eastern Europe to join its West European counterpart in becoming more sceptical about the blessings of unrestrained capitalism.

Conclusion

If Inglehart's interpretation of the 'silent revolution' in political preference formation implies a dramatic shift from material economic to non-material political and cultural preferences in mass publics, it is likely that neither Eastern Europe nor Western Europe have experienced this revolution. Both regions, however, have undergone silent revolutions, if we interpret Inglehart's research programme more broadly as a study of persistence and change in both economic and non-economic political preferences. In both regions economic interests are now based on market and occupational experiences that have little to do with social classes and ownership in the means of production, whereas class cleavages were more important in past decades, whether based on a spontaneous self-organization of economic groups in Western democracies or a top-down state-corporatist organization in Eastern communist regimes. In both regions we also encounter a new alignment of non-economic political and cultural preferences that is associated with economic concerns in distinctive ways. Even if such 'silent revolutions' have appeared on the whole European continent, they are not the same in East and West. Advanced capitalist social order gives rise to different patterns of political interest formation than a post-communist society. In each region libertarian and authoritarian preferences over collective decision-making practices and cosmopolitan and parochial views of citizenship are associated with different visions of appropriate institutions in the realm of allocating scarce economic resources. If post-communist societies create capitalist classes and market regimes that resemble those of Western Europe, such contrasts are likely to disappear some time in the future. Whether such a convergence will take place, however, is uncertain, given the very different starting-points of capitalist and democratic institutional development in East and West.

Notes

1 Of course, Inglehart in numerous studies has analysed value change in a developmentalist perspective. See Inglehart 1990, ch. 1.

2 Keynesians and monetarists, of course, disagree on whether inflation increases or depresses unemployment in the long run.

3 For a more detailed theoretical elaboration and empirical analysis of the patterns of preference formation discussed on the following pages and their implications for political life, see Kitschelt (1993a), (1994) and (1995).

4 The best study of this process is probably Swenson (1989). Other studies that have analysed the reorganization of the workforce at the shop-floor level include Kern and Schumann (1984) and Piore and Sabel (1984).

5 European and American population surveys usually find that women under 35 form the most leftist and libertarian electorate.

6 For this problem, see Kitschelt (1994, ch. 4) and Kitschelt (1995, ch. 1).

7 For definitions of the concept of social movement, compare Tarrow (1989a, 17–22).

8 I have developed this argument about the choice of modes of interest representation in Kitschelt (1993b, 23–8).

9 Theorists of left-libertarian political movements emphasize new grievances or new capacities for resistance, or both, as triggers of protest mobilization. See Melucci

(1981; 1985) and Offe (1985b).

10 The wide variety of left-libertarian social movement mobilization can be gauged from the country reports in Brand (1985) and Rucht (1991).

11 For a critical discussion of all relevant propositions about the impact of political opportunity structure, see Tarrow 1989a, 32–6.

12 For an analysis of the interaction between left-libertarian movements and sympathetic political parties, see Kitschelt (1989, ch. 9) and Kitschelt (1990).

13 Nevertheless, the movements' organizational form is influenced by opportunity structures. There is no question that left-libertarian social movements that are offered material benefits or rights to participation in institutionalized policy processes are more likely and willing to adopt formal organization than movements not faced with such options.

14 For empirical evidence, at least as far as the supporters of extreme rightist parties are concerned, see Kitschelt (1995, ch. 2). A similar finding about occupational patterns of authoritarian orientations in the United States was reported by Brint (1984). For a general discussion of right-wing backlash movements, see Lo (1982, esp. 113–15).

15 The logic of extreme rightist mobilization in interaction with the strategic choices of conservative party elites is further elaborated in Kitschelt (1995, ch. 1).

16 It is thus insufficient to point at a few isolated movements in some Western countries over the past 150 years which incorporated stakes and practices of contemporary left-libertarian social movements to claim that there is nothing unique about contemporary movement sectors, as is suggested by D'Anieri et al. (1990).

17 On some measures, however, levels of political apathy are no higher in Eastern Europe than they are in established Western democracies. Cf. Mason (1992, table 9a).

18 For a related effort to categorize post-communist regimes, see Offe (1992a).

19 I am employing here Max Weber's terminology for unrestrained authoritarian and personalistic rule, as it was reintroduced by Juan Linz into the contemporary analysis of political regime types. See, e.g., Linz and Stepan (1990).

20 For a similar pattern of responses, see also the Spring 1991 International Social Justice Project (Mason 1992, table 10).

21 The Hungarian Constitutional Court, however, ruled that the dissolution of parliament is not an issue that can be decided by referendum under the terms of the constitution and declared the recall campaign null and void.

22 My rendering of the libertarian position is based on a series of interviews with politicians in Bulgaria, the Czech Republic and Hungary which I conducted in the first six months of 1993.

23 For Western Europe, inclusion of other countries would have revealed the same pattern. In fact, I have included Austria and France because their post-materialists are outliers compared with the economic evaluations of capitalism that characterize post-materialists in other countries. For Eastern Europe, only the five countries shown have decent data sets.

24 Of course, multi-variate analysis would have to probe into this contention.

Bibliography

Abramson, P. R. and Inglehart, R. (1992). 'Generational replacement and value change in eight West European societies'. *British Journal of Political Science* 22: 183–228.

Bialecki, I. and Mach, B. W. (1992). 'The social and economic orientations of Polish legislators against a background of the views of Polish society'. *Polish Sociological Bulletin* 2: 167–86.

Böltken, F. and Jagodzinski, W. (1985). 'In an environment of insecurity: postmaterialism in the European Community, 1970–1980'. *Comparative Political Studies* 17: 453–84.

Brand, K.-W. (ed.) (1985). *Neue soziale Bewegungen in Westeuropa und den USA: ein internationaler Vergleich*. Frankfurt am Main: Campus.

Brint, S. (1984). '"New class" and cumulative trend explanations of the liberal political attitudes of professionals'. *American Sociological Review* 90: 30–71.

Clarke, H. D. and Dutt, N. (1991). 'Measuring value change in Western industrialized society: the impact of unemployment'. *American Political Science Review* 85 (3): 905–20.

D'Anieri, P. et al. (1990). 'New social movements in historical perspective'. *Comparative Politics* 22: 445–58.

Dutch, R. M. and Taylor, M. A. (1993). 'Postmaterialism and the economic condition'. *American Journal of Political Science* 37: 747–79.

Eisinger, P. K. (1973). 'The conditions of protest behavior in American cities'. *American Political Science Review* 67: 11–28.

Flanagan, S. C. (1982). 'Measuring value change in advanced industrial societies: a rejoinder to Inglehart'. *Comparative Political Studies* 15: 99–128.

—— (1987). 'Value change in industrial society'. *American Political Science Review* 81 (4): 1303–19.

Franklin, M. et al. (1992). *Electoral Change: responses to evolving social and attitudinal structures in Western countries*. Cambridge: Cambridge University Press.

Goldfarb, J. C. (1990). 'Post-totalitarian politics: ideology ends again'. *Social Research* 57: 533–56.

Inglehart, R. (1971). 'The silent revolution in Europe: intergenerational change in post-industrial societies'. *American Political Science Review* 65: 991–1017.

—— (1977). *The Silent Revolution: changing values and political styles among Western publics*. Princeton, NJ: Princeton University Press.

—— (1979). 'Political action: the impact of values, cognitive level, and social background', in S. J. Barnes and M. Kaase (eds), *Political Action*. Beverly Hills: Sage, pp. 343–80.

—— (1981). 'Post-materialism in an environment of insecurity'. *American Political Science Review* 75: 880–900.

—— (1985a). 'Aggregate stability and individual level flux in mass belief systems: the level of analysis paradox'. *American Political Science Review* 79: 97–116.

—— (1985b). 'New perspectives on value change: response to Lafferty and Knutsen, Savage, and Böltken and Jagodzinski'. *Comparative Political Studies* 17: 485–532.

—— (1990). *Culture Shift*. Princeton, NJ: Princeton University Press.

Inglehart, R. and Abramson, P. R. (1992). 'Value change in advanced industrial society: problems in conceptualization and measurement'. Prepared for delivery at the 1992 Annual Meeting of the Western Political Science Association, San Francisco.

Inglehart, R. and Siemienska, R. (1990). 'A long-term trend toward democratization? Global and East European perspectives'. Presented at the Annual Meeting of the American Political Science Association, San Francisco.

Katz, R. S. and Mair, P. (1992). *Party Organizations: a data handbook*. London and Beverly Hills, CA: Sage.

Kern, H. and Schumann, M. (1984). *Das Ende der Arbeitsteilung?* Munich: Beck.

Kirkpatrick, J. (1976). *The New Presidential Elite*. New York: Russell Sage.

Kitschelt, H. (1985). 'New social movements in West Germany and the United States', in M. Zeitlin (ed.), *Political Power and Social Theory*, Vol. 5. Greenwich, CT: Jai Press, pp. 273–324.

—— (1986). 'Political opportunity structures and political protest: anti-nuclear movements in four countries'. *British Journal of Political Science* 16 (1): 57–85.

—— (1989). *The Logics of Party Formation*. Ithaca, NY: Cornell University Press.

—— (1990). 'New social movements and the decline of party organization', in R. J. Dalton and M. Kuechler (eds), *Challenging the Political Order: new social and political movements in Western democracies*. New York: Oxford University Press, pp. 179–208.

—— (1992). 'The formation of party systems in East Central Europe'. *Politics and Society* 20: 7–50.

—— (1993a). 'Class structure and social democratic party strategy'. *British Journal of Political Science* 23: 299–337.

—— (1993b). 'Social movements, political parties, and democratic theory'. *Annals of the American Academy of Political and Social Science* 528: 13–29.

—— (1994). *The Transformation of European Social Democracy*. New York: Cambridge University Press.

—— (1995). *The Radical Right in Western Europe: a comparative analysis*. Ann Arbor: University of Michigan Press.

Konrad, G. and Szelényi, I. (1979). *The Intellectuals on the Road to Class Power*. New York: Knopf.

Kriesi, H. (1987). 'Neue soziale Bewegungen: auf der Suche nach ihrem gemeinsamen Nenner'. *Politische Vierteljahresschriften* 28: 315–34.

—— (1989). 'New social movements and the new class in the Netherlands'. *American Journal of Sociology* 94: 1078–116.

Kurtán, S. (1993). 'Sozialpartnerschaft in Ungarn?' in E. Tálos (ed.), *Sozialpartnerschaft: Kontinuität und Wandel eines Modells*. Vienna: Verlag für Gesellschaftskritik, pp. 267–84.

Lash, S. and Urry, J. (1987). *The End of Organized Capitalism*. Cambridge: Polity Press.

Lindstrom, U. (1991). 'East European social democracy: reborn to be rejected', in L. Karvanen and J. Sundberg (eds), *Social Democracy in Transition: Northern, Southern and Eastern Europe*. Aldershot: Dartmouth, pp. 269–301.

Linz, J. J. and Stepan, A. (1990). 'Democratic transitions and consolidation in Southern Europe'. Paper delivered at the Conference on Democratic Consolidation: Spain and the New Southern Europe. Madrid.

Lipset, S. M. and Rokkan, S. (1967). 'Cleavage structures, party systems, and voter alignments: an introduction', in Lipset and Rokkan (eds), *Party Systems and Voter Alignments: cross-national perspectives*. New York: Free Press, pp. 1–64.

Lo, C. Y. H. (1982). 'Countermovements and conservative movements in the contemporary United States'. *Annual Review of Sociology* 8: 107–34.

Mangott, G. (1992). 'Parteienbildung und Parteiensysteme in Ost-Mitteleuropa im Vergleich', in F. Gerlich, F. Plasser and P. A. Ulram (eds), *Regimewechsel: Demokratisierung und politische Kultur in Ost-Mitteleuropa*. Vienna: Böhlau, pp. 99–127.

Mason, D. S. (1992). 'Attitudes towards the market and the state in post-communist Europe'. Paper delivered at the Annual Meeting of the American Political Science Association, Chicago.

Melucci, A. (1981). 'Ten hypotheses for the analysis of new movements', in D. Pinto (ed.), *Contemporary Italian Sociology*. Cambridge: Cambridge University Press, pp. 173–94.

—— (1985). 'The symbolic challenge of contemporary movements'. *Social Research* 52: 789–816.

—— (1988). 'Getting involved: identity and mobilization in social movements', in B. Klandermans, H. Kriesi and S. Tarrow (eds), *From Structure to Action: comparing social movement research across cultures*. Greenwich, CT: Jai Press, pp. 329–48.

Offe, C. (1985a). *Disorganized Capitalism*. Cambridge, MA: MIT Press.

—— (1985b). 'New social movements: challenging the boundaries of institutional politics'. *Social Research* 52: 817–68.

—— (1992a). 'Die Integration nachkommunistischer Gesellschaften: die ehemalige DDR im Vergleich zu ihren osteuropäischen Nachbarn'. Paper delivered at the 26th Conference of the German Sociological Association, Düsseldorf.

—— (1992b). 'Ethnic politics in East European transitions'. MS, Wissenschaftskolleg, Berlin.

Olsen, J. P. (1983). *Organized Democracy: political institutions in a welfare state: the case of Norway*. Bergen: Universitetsforlaget.

Ost, D. (1990). *Solidarity and the Politics of Anti-Politics: opposition and reform in Poland since 1968*. Philadelphia: Temple University Press.

Paul, G. (1992). 'Reformen in Russland: Ideen regieren, solange die Interessen schlummern'. Paper delivered to the Meeting of the East European Section of the German Society for Political Science, 24 April 1992, Berlin.

Piore, M. J. and Sabel, C. F. (1984). *The Second International Divide*. New York: Basic Books.

Piven, F. F. and Cloward, R. (1977). *Poor People's Movements*. New York: Random House.

Plasser, F. and Ulram, P. A. (1992). 'Zwischen Desillusionierung und Konsolidierung: Demokratie- und Politikverständnis in Ungarn, der Tschechoslovakei und Polen', in F. Gerlich, F. Plasser and P. A. Ulram (eds), *Regimewechsel: Demokratisierung und politische Kultur in Ost-Mitteleuropa*. Vienna: Böhlau, pp. 9–78.

Plotke, D. (1990). 'What's so new about new social movements?' *Socialist Review* 20: 81–102.

Ragin, C. (1987). *The Comparative Method*. Berkeley: University of California Press.

Rucht, D. (ed.) (1991). *Research on Social Movements: the state of the art*. Boulder, CO: Westview Press.

Savage, J. (1985). 'Postmaterialism of the left and right: political conflict in postindustrial society'. *Comparative Political Studies* 17 (4): 431–51.

Schöpflin, G. (1991). 'Nationalism and national minorities'. *Journal of International Affairs* 45: 51–65.

Schumann, S. (1989). 'Postmaterialismus: ein entbehrlicher Ansatz?' in J. W. Falter, H. Rattinger and K. G. Troitzsch (eds), *Wahlen und politische Einstellungen in der Bundesrepublik Deutschland*. Frankfurt am Main: Lang, pp. 58–121.

Swenson, P. (1989). *Fair Shares: unions, politics, and pay in Sweden and West Germany*. Ithaca, NY: Cornell University Press.

Szabo, M. (1992). 'The taxi driver demonstration in Hungary: social protest and policy change', in G. Szoboszlai (ed.), *Flying Blind: emerging democracies in East Central Europe*. Budapest: Yearbook of the Hungarian Political Science Association, pp. 357–81.

Sztompka, P. (1993). 'Civilizational incompetence: the trap of post-communist societies'. *Zeitschrift für Soziologie* 22: 85–95.

Tarrow, S. (1989a). *Struggle, Politics, and Reform*. Ithaca, NY: Cornell University Press.

—— (1989b). *Democracy and Disorder: protest and politics in Italy, 1965–1975*. Oxford: Oxford University Press.

Touraine, A. et al. (1982). *Solidarité*. Paris: Fayard.

Williamson, O. E. (1985). *The Economic Institutions of Capitalism: firms, markets, relational contracting*. New York: Free Press.

6

Parties and Elections

Tom Mackie

This chapter investigates the relationship between political parties and civil society in both the well-established democracies of Western Europe and the newly emerging democracies of East-Central Europe. Political parties in the West have gone through distinctive phases of development during the last 150 years. In the contemporary period the distance between political parties and the electorate appears to be increasing, although in some countries this trend is more marked than in others. At the same time an increasingly symbiotic relationship between political parties and the state is emerging. In East-Central Europe too there is evidence of a gap between political parties and the electorate, although the reasons for this distance are very different.

In the second part of the chapter I examine the electoral track records of different kinds of parties in both parts of the continent. In particular I assess the potential and performance of new parties as challengers to established parties in Western Europe and the performance of both the former ruling communist parties and the new political parties in East-Central Europe since 1989. Finally I discuss some of the normative implications of the changes I have described.

The Development of Political Parties in Western Europe

The development of political parties in the heartland of Western Europe shares common characteristics both with respect to the political cleavages which have divided these societies and the organizational forms adopted by political parties. The patterns we find in Southern Europe – Greece, Spain and Portugal and southern Italy – have been rather different in one or both of these respects. They will be discussed later in this section.

The major cleavages which have divided Western European societies during the last century have been social class, religion, centre–periphery and urban–rural (Lipset and Rokkan 1967). All Western European societies have been marked by more or less significant class divisions. In some countries (Ireland would be the extreme case) the class cleavage has been much less significant than in others. In other countries it has been much stronger, with a dominant left party in some (the Norwegian Labour Party, for instance) and much stronger competition within the left in others (Weimar Germany or post-1945 Italy, for instance). In continental Europe a religious cleavage pitting anti-clericals against supporters of the Catholic Church has been very important. Linguistic divisions have impacted upon only a small number of countries, most importantly Belgium, Spain and Switzerland. Urban–rural differences have rarely developed into a strong cleavage in most Western European countries, principally because the Catholic Church has bridged divisions between city and countryside. Only in Protestant Scandinavia and Switzerland has an urban–rural divide spawned well-established agrarian parties.

Although at the level of the voter the linkage between individual social structural characteristics and party choice has weakened in recent decades (Franklin et al. 1991), Western European systems remained relatively stable at least until the 1970s (Bartolini and Mair, 1990). Arguably a post-materialism articulated through new green and left libertarian movements and parties has appeared (Kitschelt 1988). The electoral performance and prospects of these parties will be discussed below.

The organizational development of Western European parties has been conceptualized in terms of a three-stage model of development (Duverger 1954; Kirchheimer 1966; Panebianco 1988). More recently Katz and Mair (1992) have argued that we may be seeing the beginnings of a further stage with the emergence of what they call 'cartel' parties.

In the first stage, in the late nineteenth and early twentieth centuries, the politically relevant sections of civil society and the state were in an almost symbiotic relationship. Parties were typically cadre parties of wealthy notables, relying upon their individual resources to fight election campaigns. Typically cadre parties were dominated by their parliamentary members.

In the second stage, with the expansion of the electorate, came the development of mass parties which sought control of the state as the agents of the working class or sometimes other social groups, especially churches or small farmers. Unlike the cadre parties they relied upon their own mass membership or that of associated organizations such as trade unions, religious organizations or farmers' cooperatives to provide financial backing and organizational help at election time. Collective resources countered the individual resources of the notables of the cadre parties. In principle, parliamentarians were delegates of a section of civil society rather than trustees for the whole of a more limited part of civil society, as were the parliamentarians of the cadre parties. Mass parties performed an important function in integrating sections of civil society into the polity. Even when they were excluded from political office at national level, they were often in government at the local level. In response to this development, the old cadre parties often sought to deepen their links with the broader civil society. But the motives for this adjustment were largely electoral and these parties tended to remain dominated by their parliamentary elite. The political consequences of the increasing electoral successes of the mass parties and of broader changes in civil society created conditions which impacted upon the relations between parties and civil society.

From the 1930s onwards the mass parties increasingly became governing parties. During the generation of rapid economic growth and social change which characterized post-1945 Western Europe their originally rather homogeneous social bases became more and more heterogeneous, as higher incomes and greater social and geographical mobility became the norm. These developments and the expansion of the welfare state eroded to some extent the solidarity of the support bases for working-class mass parties, while secularization and the flight from the land eroded the organizational bases of religious and agrarian parties.

As a result of these economic and political changes, many mass parties began to develop 'catch-all' characteristics (Kirchheimer 1966).[1] In this third stage parties became brokers between civil society and the state rather than agents of parts of civil society. Parties became essentially teams of leaders who have ditched much of their ideological baggage and sought electoral support from a much wider constituency. Catch-all parties are essentially electoral rather than membership parties. Party activists may still be employed in election campaigns, but direct communication between the party and the electorate, especially by the electronic media, becomes central. Increasingly parties are funded not by their individual members and allied organizations but by a much broader range of interest groups and by the state.

Katz and Mair (1992) argue that catch-all parties are progressively becoming cartel parties. Cartel parties can be differentiated from catch-all parties in three respects. Firstly, they are becoming more reliant upon the state for financial support. Not surprisingly such support favours the traditional parties of government. Secondly, as governing parties they regulate the electronic media – the most influential communications link between parties and the citizenry. Finally, almost all the larger parties in Western Europe are now governing parties.[2] To summarize, political parties increasingly use the resources, financial and regulatory, of the state to protect their own interests as organizations, thus even further removing them from the influence of the wider civil society. The characterization of such parties as 'cartel parties' nicely makes the analogy with oligopoly in the economic market. Parties, Katz and Mair argue, are becoming agents of the state. In a sense, then, the wheel has turned full circle, with a symbiotic relationship between the parties and the state becoming more and more similar to that in the nineteenth century. The essential difference, of course, is that, unlike cadre parties, cartel parties do not encompass civil society, but are detached from, even above it.

It is important to emphasize that what we are describing is an ideal-typical model of political party development. Parties only more or less share the characteristics of ideal-typical, cadre, mass, catch-all or cartel parties. In the real world parties of an earlier era persist into later ones. for instance, cadre parties remained the typical form of the centre-right in France until the birth of the Fifth Republic in 1958. The transformation of mass parties into catch-all parties may depend upon factors such as the degree of institutionalization before the process begins. Strongly institutionalized parties, such as the French or Portuguese Communist parties, will be slower to change than weakly institutionalized ones, such as the French or Italian Socialists. Less fragmented party systems dominated by a few large parties may change more quickly (Panebianco 1988, 265).

Table 6.1 delineates the principal characteristics of parties in each of the four stages. It also identifies some parties and time periods typical of each stage. The expansion of the electorate is the necessary but not the sufficient condition for the development of mass parties, which typically develop as agents of part of a broader civil society and seek to wrest control of government form traditional elites. These parties' roles as delegates in parliament was combined, not always easily, with attempts to create a counter-culture within 'their' sector of civil society. Mainstream European social democrat parties and their communist opponents comprise most of the clear cases of mass parties.

The role of such parties and their relationship to the state and civil society are quite different from those of parties in an earlier period. The emergence of such parties necessarily changes the character of cadre parties in some respects. In a wider civil society and facing competition from mass parties, their symbiotic relationship with civil society is ended and identification with the state threatened. Organizationally they may attempt to reform by building their own mass associations, although these will be vehicles to mobilize votes on behalf of traditional elites rather than bottom-up organizations like the newer mass parties. The British Conservatives' Primrose League or the German Conservatives' Agrarian League would be examples of this kind of adaptation. In more traditional societies cadre parties typically depended on

Table 6.1   *The development of party types in Western Europe*

	Electorate	Party role	Relationship to Civil society	State	Party goals
Cadre party	Restricted	Trustee	Symbiotic	Symbiotic	Patronage
Examples:	German Conservatives, Wilhelmine Empire				
	Italian Liberals, nineteenth and early twentieth century				
Mass Party	Broad Loyal voters	Delegate	Agent of part of society	Seeks control	Comprehensive social reform
Examples:	Italian Socialist Party until the 1960s				
	German Social Democrats until the 1960s				
	French Communist Party in the 1990s				
Catch-all party	Broad Floating	Entrepreneur	Broker	Seeks control	Social amelioration
Examples:	German Social Democrats after the 1959 Bad Godesberg Congress				
	British Conservative Party after 1945				
Cartel party	Broad Floating	Agent of the state	Detached	Symbiotic	Patronage
Examples:	Italian Socialist Party in the 1980s				
	Spanish Socialist Party in the 1980s				

clientelistic relationships with local notables or on electoral manipulation by government officials. The Italian Liberals before the First World War characterize such parties.

Both mass and modified cadre parties began to develop catch-all tendencies. On the left the forerunner in this process was the German Social Democratic Party, whose new programme agreed at the party's Bad Godesberg Congress in 1959 was the most explicit negation of the concept of a party committed to comprehensive social reform to one committed only to piecemeal change. Kirchheimer's description of this transformation as the 'vanishing opposition' (Kirchheimer 1966) nicely picks up the characteristics of catch-all parties and their era.

Cartel parties are likely to develop in polities where state support for parties and opportunities for patronage are strongest. Katz and Mair (1992, 22) suggest that Norway, Sweden, Austria and Italy would fit this mould very well. More generally, all the Southern European countries, with their strong traditions of party patronage politics, as well as some of the most advanced welfare societies, may belong in the same camp. The mix of social amelioration and patronage as party goals will clearly be very different in these two groups of countries, but the increasing autonomy of their parties from civil society is a characteristic they share.

Party Development in Southern Europe

In Southern Europe party development was rather different. In the case of Spain and Portugal the lengthy period of dictatorship, forty years in the case of the former and fifty in the latter, was clearly an important factor, distinguishing these countries from the rest of Western Europe. In Greece, on the other hand, democracy was interrupted only rather briefly from 1967 to 1974 by the military dictatorship.

In Portugal, political parties had only barely begun to develop beyond the cadre form before the 1926 coup ended parliamentary rule. Mass parties had developed a vigorous life in Second Republic Spain, but were vigorously repressed during the Franco dictatorship. In both countries only the communist parties, well organized and with strong roots in sections of the working class, survived underground during the dictatorships. The new parties which emerged were very much top-down groups of politicians. On the right they tended to have links with the reform elements of the previous regime. On the left they were parties of lawyers and intellectuals rather than workers. Organizationally these new parties were initially rather weak, though during the founding period of the new regimes they benefited from the financial and technical assistance of friendly parties abroad, and as governing parties they soon benefited from extensive state support. Moreover, in civil societies, in which economic interest meso-organizations were also very poorly coordinated and financed, and where the Church had largely taken itself out of partisan politics, political parties were at a considerable organizational advantage (Gillespie 1990, 235).

The new governing parties soon began to exercise an extensive patronage of the civil service, the state-owned media and to some extent other groups. In other words, although in form and rhetoric the new Iberian parties look very like mass political parties, they seem in practice to behave very much like cartel parties. Their rather weak ties with social groups at the electoral level reinforce this picture (Lancaster 1991, 332).

In some respects the pattern in Greece is different. As in Iberia, there is in Greece a well organized communist party with strong links to sections of the traditional working class but a minority position in electoral politics. The two major parties, Pasok and New Democracy, which have alternated in office since 1974, have links with the parties which existed before 1967, and there are very clear ideological differences between them which centre on whether

Greece should be closely tied to Western Europe (Dimitras 1991, 213–15). In this respect, then, Greece is different, but as in Iberia the governing parties function in a rather undeveloped civil society with weak meso-organizations and have developed into patronage parties.

In all three 'new democracies' of Southern Europe, then, the political parties, with the important exception of the communist parties, have skipped the mass party politics stage. Parties, in their relationships both with the electorate and with civil society, are catch-all parties which are increasingly developing characteristics of the cartel party. These differences must be evaluated in the context of societies in which the structures of civil society were much less well developed than in Western Europe and in which the role of the state in the economy and long experience of authoritarian rule suggest some similarities with Central rather than Western Europe. In many respects southern Italy shares these societal and political characteristics, so it is not surprising that the parties in this region, too, are basically patronage parties.

Electoral Change in Western Europe

One of the best documented changes in Western Europe over the last twenty years has been in individual-level voting behaviour. There are several aspects to this. One is declining attachment to political parties. For the countries of the European Union several scholars (Mair 1984; Schmitt 1989) have documented this change, as have Lane et al. (1993) for the four Scandinavian countries and Plasser et al. (1992) for Austria. A second and related change is a decline in the linkage between parties and social groups. One study of electoral support for left-wing parties in sixteen Western countries from the 1960s through the 1980s shows how dramatic this change has been. In the 1960s social structural variables explained 35 per cent of the variance between voters supporting parties of the left and those supporting other parties. By the end of the 1980s the average percentage of variance explained had dropped to only 13 per cent (Franklin et al. 1991, 384–90). Party politics in Western Europe increasingly lack a social base, as electors become essentially free floating. 'The particularization of voting choice' (van der Eijk et al. 1991, 411) captures the implications of this phenomenon, but in using this phrase these changes should not be exaggerated. Class and religious differences still differentiate the electorates of West European parties.[3]

Elections in the 1980s, therefore, were opportunities both for existing parties to retain support and for new parties to gain votes. This potential for electoral volatility is clearly important, but it would be a mistake to interpret it necessarily as a challenge to existing political parties as a whole, let alone to the existing political order. Indeed, it could be welcomed as a 'political emancipation of individual citizens who can now choose rather than being predestined by social position' (van der Eijk and Niemoller 1985, 367).

What, then, are the implications of these changes in the character of political parties and of individual voting behaviour? Two major scenarios can be put forward. Firstly, existing and increasingly catch-all parties may prove flexible in terms of addressing new issues and incorporating groups in civil society. In other words, their progression towards the cartel-party type will be arrested. Alternatively, parties may become or may already be becoming increasingly distant from civil society. What options are available for an increasingly independent electorate in either of these scenarios? In our benign scenario, the electors may vote against the governing parties, but will probably support another established party instead. In our pessimistic scenario, electors have more options. If the rascals they wish to throw out are all the normal parties of government, those who by definition are the only ones who may or have already become 'cartel' parties, they may declare against them either by not voting at all, or by voting for a party which is opposed to the existing political order. In the next section I examine the electoral record in Western Europe since 1980 to discover which of these scenarios carries most conviction.

The Electoral Performance of Governing Parties since 1980

In this section I look at the electoral performance of governing parties since 1980 in comparison with the period from 1948 to 1979. Previous research covering a rather wider range of countries (Rose and Mackie 1983) has shown that incumbency in government is (very modestly) a net electoral liability. Two-thirds of governments in Western countries in elections from 1948 to 1979 lost votes, though their mean penalty was only 1 per cent. From 1980 the electorate's sanctions have become more severe. Eighty per cent of incumbent parties have lost votes during the latter period, and their mean penalty has increased to 4 per cent, as table 6.2 shows. These figures need to be interpreted with some care. It would not be unreasonable to expect that governments presiding over economies whose performance has been as poor as Western Europe's in the last decade should themselves suffer from poor electoral performance. But it is worth noting that governments were not so sanctioned during the economically challenged 1970s, when support barely declined more than during the economically successful 1950s and 1960s (Rose and Mackie 1983, 31).

So far we have assumed that the only option facing the electorate is voting 'agin the government'. Another option of course is not to vote at all. If parties

Table 6.2   *Gains and losses of governing parties in Western Europe, 1948–93*

	Gain votes		Lose votes		Average change
	N	%	N	%	
1948–79	93	36	166	64	−1.0
1980–93	12	19	53	81	−4.1

Sources: Rose and Mackie (1983, 137); Mackie and Rose (1991); Mackie (1991); Mackie (1992); Koole and Mair (1992); Koole and Mair (1993); Woldendorp et al. (1993); and figures provided by national election agencies.

are becoming increasingly remote from civil society, then citizens may choose one version of a 'plague on all your houses' and simply stay at home. Historically, rates of turnout have varied considerably *between* countries.[4] So it is important to look at *intra-country* trends in the first instance rather than comparing countries. Table 6.3 shows the average percentage of the valid vote cast for each of the last three decades and for the most recent national election. Valid votes rather than turnout are chosen to help to iron out the differences between countries with compulsory voting and the rest. In countries where voting is not obligatory invalid votes tend to be very low. When electors are obliged to go to the polls, as in Belgium, Italy and Luxembourg and until 1971 the Netherlands, they are much higher. Writing in 1984, Peter Mair was able to argue convincingly that from 1950 onwards there had been virtually no change in electoral participation (Mair 1984, 175). But this is no longer the case. During the 1980s participation declined by nearly 3 per cent. Moreover, at the most recent general election, participation dropped on average by a further 2 per cent compared with polls earlier in this period. Some of these decreases are quite large. Participation in France in 1993, for instance, was only 66 per cent, a uniquely low figure for a parliamentary election that did not follow a presidential contest.

Voting for 'Challenger' Parties

Those citizens who do not stay at home may either vote for governing parties, as they are increasingly disinclined to do, vote for other parties who may reasonably be expected on past performance to participate in government, or

Table 6.3   *Turnout in national elections in Western Europe since the 1960s*[1]

	1960s	*1970s*	*1980s*	*Most recent election*
Austria	92.7	91.4	87.9	83.7
Belgium[2]	85.4	85.7	86.9	86.2
Denmark	87.1	87.0	84.8	82.2
Finland	84.7	80.8	76.1	71.4
France	74.8	80.6	68.9	65.6
Germany	84.7	90.2	84.1	76.9
Greece	81.7	79.4	81.5	81.5
Iceland	89.6	88.8	87.7	87.6
Ireland	73.5	75.7	71.5	67.5
Italy[2]	89.7	89.2	83.8	82.7
Luxembourg[2]	84.2	84.0	85.0	82.5
Netherlands[3]	92.5	83.0	83.2	80.0
Norway	82.5	81.5	83.0	76.4
Portugal	–	83.4	72.1	67.4
Spain	–	71.3	72.7	76.3
Sweden	85.9	90.8	87.5	85.3
Switzerland	63.0	51.9	46.5	45.3
United Kingdom	76.5	74.9	75.2	77.7
Average	83.1	81.6	78.8	76.4

Notes: [1] Valid votes as a percentage of the electorate
    [2] Compulsory voting
    [3] Compulsory voting in the 1960s

Sources: Mackie and Rose (1991); Mackie (1991); Mackie (1992); Koole and Mair (1992); Koole and Mair (1993); and figures provided by national election agencies.

vote for parties who are not serious contenders for government office, either because they are explicitly anti-system or because they are not regarded as suitable partners by existing government parties. Anti-system here should be generously defined so as to include not only anti-constitutional parties, but also parties who are overt challengers to the status quo in terms of major policy issues or the nature of political activity. This category is *not* coterminous with new parties, in the sense of parties established in the 1980s or in the latter half of the 1970s, such as the green parties. It will not include new parties which break away from governing parties on the basis of personality or single policy issues. These parties usually remain a part of normal politics and may well expect to become governing parties themselves in due course. Parties such as the Progressive Democrats in Ireland and the Centre Democrats in Denmark have already followed such a course. Conversely, it *may* include existing parties, sometimes even ones which have served in government in the past, providing that they are 'challengers' in the sense indicated above. A clear case in point would be the Austrian Freedom Party, briefly in government in the early 1980s, but under the leadership of Kurt Heidar since 1986 clearly a 'challenger' party. (For a complete listing of these 'challenger' parties, see Appendix 6A.)

The overwhelming majority of these challenger parties belong to two, at first inspection very different, categories: parties of the libertarian left and parties of the far right. The left-libertarian category encompasses most, but not all, green parties; they are the electoral party vehicles of the new social movements which mushroomed in the late 1960s and early 1970s. They advocate environmentalism, feminism, the rights of ethnic and sexual minorities, opposition to nuclear energy, etc. When these movements began to develop it was widely believed that they would seriously weaken the roles of political parties as linkages with civil society (Berger 1973). This was both because they had introduced new issues onto the political agenda which could not easily be accommodated by the traditional parties and because their emphasis on participatory politics was so much at odds with the increasingly top-down leaderships of those parties. Inglehart's argument that post-materialist values were becoming more prevalent in Western societies and that the division between materialism and post-materialism was becoming a new political cleavage (Inglehart 1990) has obvious resonance in this context. In fact left-libertarian political action soon came to include conventional electoral politics, and activists and ordinary voters with post-materialist values began to develop strong affinities with these parties (Reiter 1993), especially where existing parties proved particularly inflexible in adjusting to this new issue agenda. During the 1980s these parties became established features of the electoral landscape. But their electoral success varied greatly across the continent. (See Appendix 6B for a record of their electoral performance since 1980.)

The parties of the libertarian left were the children of the late 1960s and early 1970s. By the late 1980s the electoral successes of what were rather loosely termed far right or neo-Fascist parties began to attract attention (Cheles et al. 1991; Ford 1992; Hainsworth 1992). (See Appendix 6C for the electoral track record of these parties.)

As with left-libertarian and green parties, two major questions arise: does it make sense to treat these parties as a single category, and how can the very varying levels of support for such parties by explained? One approach which seeks to address both these questions argues that a distinction needs to be made between two groups, the avowedly neo-Fascist parties of tradition or nostalgia whose electoral support has been and remains rather modest, and 'new right wing parties' (Ignazi 1992) or the new populism (Taggart 1993; see also Betz 1993). Like the traditional neo-Fascist parties, the new populists clearly lie on the right of the political spectrum. But unlike historic Fascists they support new right free market economics rather than corporatist autarky, and while they may argue for constitutional reform (for instance, the French National Front calls for a fully presidential regime and the Italian National Alliance for a popularly elected president), they are not avowedly anti-democratic. Neo-Fascist parties have tended to be single-issue anti-immigrant parties, while the new populists have picked up nation-specific issues as well. The Progress parties in Denmark and Norway and New Democracy in Sweden have attacked high taxation and the welfare state. The Northern League in Italy has opposed subsidies to the south and called for the transformation of the country into a federation. The Motorists' Party in Switzerland has opposed environmental regulation.

To some extent the new populist parties are the mirror-image of the parties of the libertarian left. They too inveigh against the democratic leviathan which excludes the people from political life. Their programmes are very different, as are their organizations; the left is participatory, the new populist parties are typically one-man bands, the party of a Le Pen, a Bossi or a Haidar. However, they share common enemies, including each other.

The electoral base of new populist parties is obviously distinct from that of the supporters of the libertarian left, but it is far from the unemployed, under-educated lumpen proletariat characteristic of support for neo-Fascist parties (Falter and Schumann 1988). New populist voters tend to be young males drawn from right across the socio-economic spectrum and employed pre-dominantly in the private sector (Taggart 1993, 8). Their geographical base of support includes some of the most prosperous countries and regions in Europe: Scandinavia, Flanders in Belgium rather than Wallonia, the north and especially Lombardy rather than the Mezzogiorno in Italy. Of course all these parties appeal to and obtain support from less well-educated blue-collar workers, who are unemployed or threatened with unemployment and who fear job competition from immigrant workers. But it would be incorrect, if tempting, to classify these parties' voters or the parties themselves as *Poujadist* defendants of sections of society threatened by economic change – the 1980s equivalents of the small shopkeepers and artisans of the 1950s. At the indi-vidual level, as well as in terms of region and nationality, they represent the successful rather than the marginal and the threatened.

Apart from the 'challenger' parties, a few parties have made some impact since 1980. Only eight of them have won 5 per cent of the vote in national elections and half of them have been short-lived. Six were breakaways from established major parties: the Irish Progressive Democrats (ex Fianna Fail), the Social Democratic Federation and Citizens' parties (splinters from two major centre-right Icelandic parties), Political Spring (a splinter from the Greek New Democracy), and Italy's Rifondazione Comunista and Finland's Democratic Alternative, both fundamentalist Marxist-Leninist breakaways from their country's reform communist parties. The first four cases all involved personality as well as policy differences. Both the Icelandic parties have now disappeared. The remaining two parties were election vehicles for former Portuguese President Antonio Eanes and former Spanish Prime Minister Adolfo Suarez. Although both were extremely popular public figures and their parties enjoyed some initial successes, winning 19 and 9 per cent of the vote respectively at their first appearance at the polls, they were unable to sustain momentum, their vote declined and they eventually disappeared.

If, then, we wish to establish how far 'challenger' parties have made an electoral impact in Western Europe we need only to track the record of both left-libertarian and rightist parties. And if, as we suggested earlier, their enemy is the same, we might expect libertarian and new populist parties to do well and to fare badly in the same countries. Tables 6.4 and 6.5 show that this is indeed the case. In nine of our eighteen countries, *both* left and right perform well. In five countries, Greece, Ireland, Portugal, Spain and the United Kingdom, *both* left and right fare badly. In four countries the left is strong but the right is weak. In one of these countries, Germany, the right has done very well in *Land* and local elections. In other words, only three of our eighteen countries, Iceland, Luxembourg and the Netherlands, do not fit the mould, in all cases because of the absence or extreme weakness of either traditional neo-Fascism or the new populism.

How can this pattern and the exceptions be explained? Nearly thirty years ago a perspicacious scholar predicted new forms of opposition to what he called a 'new democratic leviathan' characterized as 'welfare-oriented, central-ised, bureaucratic, tamed and controlled by competition amongst highly or-ganised elites, and, in the perspectives of the ordinary citizen, somewhat remote' (Dahl 1966, 399). Dahl went on to argue that in Western Europe this opposition was likely to come from the youthful, well-educated left – a premonition of the post-materialism of the coming decade. Kitschelt's argu-ment about the conditions for left-libertarian party success since the early 1980s (Kitschelt 1988 and 1990) echoes the same theme. Left-libertarian parties were found to fare well in countries with comprehensive welfare states, corporatist bargaining between government, labour and capital, and long-standing participation by socialists in government. Taggart (1993) argues that a well-developed welfare state, an advanced post-industrial economy and a cartelized (in Katz and Mair's sense) party system are conducive to the

Table 6.4   *Best electoral performance of green/left-libertarian and neo-Fascist/new populist parties in Western Europe, since 1980 (% of seats)*

Country	Green/ left-libertarian	Neo-Fascist/ new populist	Both
Austria	6.8 (1990)	16.6 (1990)	23.4 (1990)
Belgium	10.2 (1991)	10.8 (1991)	21.0 (1991)
Denmark	15.9 (1987)	10.4 (1988)	20.4 (1988)
Finland	6.8 (1991)	9.7 (1983)	11.6 (1991)
France	10.9 (1993)	12.8 (1993)	23.7 (1993)
Germany	8.3 (1987)	2.6 (1990)	8.9 (1987)
Greece	1.1 (1990)	0.6 (1985)	1.2 (1990)
Iceland	10.2 (1987)	–	10.2 (1987)
Ireland	1.5 (1989)	–	1.5 (1989)
Italy[1]	5.1 (1994)	42.9 (1994)	48.0 (1994)
Luxembourg	8.5 (1989)	2.3 (1989)	10.8 (1989)
Netherlands	4.5 (1989)	0.9 (1989)	7.4 (1982)
Norway	10.1 (1989)	13.1 (1989)	23.2 (1989)
Portugal[2]	less than 1	0.7 (1985)	0.7+ (1985)
Spain	1.6 (1989)	1.1 (1989)	2.7 (1989)
Sweden	11.3 (1988)	6.7 (1991)	14.6 (1991)
Switzerland	8.2 (1991)	9.8 (1991)	18.0 (1991)
United Kingdom	0.5 (1992)	0.6 (1974)	0.6 (1979)

Notes: [1]In 1992 left-libertarian parties won 5.1 per cent and neo-Fascist/new populist parties won 14.5 per cent.
[2]The greens have always run on Communist Party lists. They have won one seat in a 250-seat legislature at every election since 1983.

mobilization of new populist parties. The limited success of parties of both types in five of our countries fits in well with both these arguments, as they are laggards in economic development, corporatism and the welfare state. Although the United Kingdom is considerably richer than the other countries, it is also poorer than the rest of Western Europe. The political differences between these five and the overwhelming majority of other European countries is also worth pointing out. All are countries with a basically bipolar party system in which alternation in government between single parties has been the norm (or, in the case of Ireland, competition between Fianna Fail on the one hand and Fine Gael plus assorted allies on the other). These countries are, in this respect at least, those with the least cartel-like parties in Europe.

Table 6.5　*Strong and weak green/left-libertarian and neo-Fascist/new populist parties*[1]

| | | Green/left-libertarian | |
		Strong	Weak
Neo-Fascist/ new populist	Strong	Austria Belgium Denmark Finland France Italy Norway Sweden Switzerland	
	Weak	Germany Iceland Luxembourg Netherlands	Greece Ireland Portugal Spain UK

Note: [1] Strong parties (or groups of parties) are those winning an average of at least 5 per cent of the vote over the last two elections.

At the other extreme from our five countries lies Italy. The political crisis beginning in 1992 led to a massive haemorrhage of support for the mainstream governing parties. In national elections in 1992 and local elections in the following year this benefited both new populism, represented by the Northern League, and the forces of left-libertarianism in junior partnership with the Democratic Left – the former Communist Party. In March 1994 the traditional governing parties, which had won 53 per cent of the vote only two years previously, were reduced to a mere 16 per cent. The parties of the left were able to improve modestly on their 1992 performance, increasing their share of the vote from 27 to 32 per cent. But the real victors were on the right. The neo-Fascist National Alliance (significantly styling itself a post-Fascist rather than a neo-Fascist party) more than doubled its vote to 14 per cent. The Northern League maintained its share at 8 per cent, but the major surprise was the performance of Forza Italia, founded only three months before the election by the business and media tycoon Silvio Berlusconi, which won a fifth of the vote. The three allied parties of the right, all mouthing a neo-populist rhetoric, thus won 43 per cent of the vote, compared with 14 per cent in 1992 and only 6 per cent in 1988.

The significance of the Italian example for the argument being put forward here is that it is the extreme case of a country governed by cartel parties. Italian governing parties have long ceased to be in any sense agents of a broader civil society. Rather, they were mechanisms for the colonization of as large a part of that society as possible by those parties' servants. The consequential corruption and involvement with criminality such as the Mafia was probably on a much more massive scale than anywhere else in Western Europe (Allum 1993; Cazzola 1988; Harris 1994). But Italy is an extreme case rather than an isolated example.

A case which at first sight looks deviant in fact provides further support for this argument. In March 1993 the ruling Socialist Party in France was toppled from office by an alliance of the neo-Gaullist Rally for the Republic (RPR) and the conservative Union for French Democracy (UDF). The conservative parties won 485 out of 577 seats in parliament. At first sight this looks like the conventional workings of a bipolar party system. Despite the election's outcome this was not the case, except at the level of parliamentary seats. Like the governing parties in Italy, the French Socialists suffered an electoral haemorrhage. The vote for the parties supporting President Mitterrand fell from 38 per cent to 19 per cent. However, the vote for the traditional opposition parties, the RPR and the UDF, rose by only 2 per cent. Instead voters either abstained or turned to the National Front and various green parties, whose combined share of the vote increased from 10 to 24 per cent. The number of persons who did not register to vote also increased. French voters repudiated an administration marred by numerous cases of high-level political corruption and distant from even those sections of civil society on which, rhetorically, it rested (Hyest 1993, 10).

Because of the focus of the new populist/neo-Fascist parties on immigration control, it is tempting to argue that the relative importance of this issue in national politics is another variable which should be discussed. However, recent surveys across the European Union (Eurobarometer 1993, A51–A55) suggest relatively little variance across these twelve countries. Just over half of all respondents felt that there were too many non-union immigrants in their country. Only Ireland (where emigration is seen as a major problem), Spain, Portugal and Luxembourg differ dramatically from the European norm. None of these countries have successful new populist parties. But neither does the United Kingdom or the Netherlands, where 50 and 47 per cent of respondents think their country has too many immigrants. The relationship between perceptions of the number of immigrants, the salience of the issue to ordinary citizens, and their perception of their government's handling of the issue are obviously germane to its importance in explaining support for the new populist/neo-Fascist parties. It cannot be understood simply in terms of varying proportions of citizens identifying immigration as a problem.

To summarize, during the period since 1980 and more especially in the early 1990s, there has been growing evidence that political parties in Western Europe are becoming increasingly removed from the electorate. Turnout at general elections has begun to decline, as has voting for the normal parties of government, and support for challenger parties has increased. In some countries this trend is more pronounced than in others. In the poorer European countries and in those countries where the traditional parties have developed fewer of the characteristics of a cartel party, change is much less evident.

Political Parties in East-Central Europe

Elections and political movements were central mechanisms in the collapse of communist power in East-Central Europe in 1989 and 1990. The first free or founding election (Korosenyi 1991) was typically a referendum on communist party rule. These elections produced four different types of outcome. First, in most cases, broad national anti-Soviet and anti-communist liberation movements won. This was the case in 1989 in Poland with Solidarity and in the following year in the three Baltic republics of Latvia, Lithuania and Estonia, in Czechoslovakia, and in Slovenia and Croatia within Yugoslavia. A second route was followed in four countries where the ruling communist parties initially remained in office. In Albania and Bulgaria the communist parties were ousted in the next elections, held in 1991, but in the rump of Yugoslavia (the republics of Serbia and Montenegro) and in Romania former communists remained in power after later elections – though in both cases without winning a majority of votes. A third route was taken in Hungary and the German Democratic Republic (DDR), where a competitive multi-party system characterized the first free elections. In the case of Hungary this reflected the much more open political life of the last years of the communist regime. Opponents of the regime were not obliged to operate as a single movement because it was clear, well before the founding election, that free political competition would be allowed. In the DDR the popular anti-regime movements, associated largely with the Lutheran Church and left-libertarian opposition to the regime, were overwhelmed by the impact of Western German parties and the central issue of reunification. In East Germany German unity was the local version of national liberation from Soviet rule. Finally, in the two remaining Yugoslav republics events took a rather different course. In Bosnia-Herzegovina ethnic parties dominated the first free elections, presaging the civil war and external intervention following that republic's declaration of independence. In Macedonia both Macedonian and Albanian nationalist parties and the former communist party supported independence.

If the core issue in 1989–90 was whether the communist parties' monopoly of political power should continue, what political issues and cleavages are likely to develop in East-Central Europe following the collapse of communist rule? The starting-point will clearly be different from that in the Western part of the continent in the nineteenth century. Contemporary Eastern European societies are much more industrialized and their populations much better educated. The virtues of universal suffrage and parliamentary government are not in general in contention, if only because the need to secure financial support from Western European countries will pressurize Eastern European regimes to, at the very least, parrot these virtues.

One major source of political cleavage will certainly be the social differentiation consequent upon the attempt, whether successful or not, to transform socialist into market economies (Kitschelt 1992; Evans and Whitefield 1993). Kitschelt argues that the linkage between the electorate and the parties in the period of transition will be based upon the way individuals perceive their interests in a post-socialist society. Those with convertible skills, such as higher education or skills learnt in the second economy, who believe that they will benefit from economic transformation, will support pro-market parties. Those with non-transferable or no skills, for instance unskilled heavy industrial and farm workers and pensioners, who expect to lose out, will favour parties that protect them from market forces. In other words, as in Western Europe, a left–right division based on socio-economic cleavages will appear.

While not disagreeing with the thrust of Kitschelt's argument, Evans and Whitefield point to the central importance of ethnic differences and argue that the relative success or failure of the attempt to transform the economy must also be taken into account. In ethnically homogeneous countries, where the chances of successful economic transformation are high, left–right competition based upon socio-economic cleavages will prevail. They suggest that the Czech Republic, Hungary, Lithuania and Poland most clearly belong in this category. To this list one could plausibly add Slovenia (former Yugoslavia is omitted from their discussion). Estonia and Latvia are also regarded as candidates for successful market transformation, but the presence of very large ethnic minorities belonging to the former ruling power will, Evans and Whitefield argue, ensure ethnic cleavage a central place in those countries' politics. Finally, in ethnically heterogeneous countries, where economic transformation proves much more difficult (the remaining states of the former Soviet Union, Slovakia, the Balkan republics – and arguably the remaining states of the former Yugoslavia as well), stable left-right cleavages will not establish themselves and populist politics often based upon scapegoating of national minorities or chauvinism will appear. In summary, both relatively conventional left–right politics and nationalist/ethnic cleavages in different combinations will be the popular bases for party competition in the future.

Neither of these arguments, building upon a rational choice approach (Kitschelt 1992, 42) or upon a more social-structural approach (Evans and Whitefield), leave much room for the impact of parties themselves in setting agendas. The electoral arena opened up in 1989–90 was not an empty one. In all countries the former ruling communist parties and in many countries the new national liberation movements clearly had the potential to establish themselves as major catch-all political parties. Other parties also had some electoral potential. Everywhere traditional parties which predated the communist era sought to re-establish themselves. In three countries, Bulgaria, Czechoslovakia and Poland, some of these parties had maintained some organizational continuity during the communist era as satellite parties. As the communist regimes began to fall apart, these satellite parties sought genuine independence. The former satellite parties could, like their former communist masters, rely upon already existing organizational resources. Other traditional parties, often styled 'parties of nostalgia', could often rely upon support from emigré sources, and, indeed, ex-emigrés and even politicians who had been active in the pre-communist period were candidates for these parties in national elections.

In all countries the former communist parties remained significant electoral forces. The communist parties sought to present themselves as reformist parties which had sloughed off Marxism-Leninism and embraced both pluralist democracy and the mixed economy.[5] In doing so they changed their names. The title Socialist Party, adopted in Albania, Bulgaria, Hungary and rump Yugoslavia, was the most popular choice. In three countries, Hungary, Estonia and Latvia, the reform communists were opposed by traditionalist parties which continued to espouse Marxism-Leninism. In Lithuania the post-independence government banned the pro-Moscow communist party, which had won 13 per cent of the vote in 1990. Although the electoral performance of the communist parties varied considerably between countries, they in all cases maintained a considerable organizational capacity and were therefore an obvious potential base for a broad catch-all party in the future.

The wide-ranging anti-regime movements which had taken power in seven countries were another potential base for establishing political parties. They had demonstrated formidable abilities to mobilize anti-regime feeling. For instance, in Poland in 1989, Solidarity won 72 per cent of the vote (Pelczynski and Kowalski 1990, 350). The Czech Civic Forum and its Slovak counterpart Public Against Violence won the support of half the electorate the following year. But having achieved their initial aim of regime change, the question of whether these single-issue movements could maintain their unity was inevitably raised.

What has been the track record of different kinds of parties in the early free elections and what does this tell us about likely future developments? Predicting even short-term trends on the basis of what are thus far merely snap-shots based upon the experience of perhaps one or two elections is obviously very hazardous. However, some general observations are worth making. Firstly, the national liberation movements have signally failed to hold together once their initial objective had been achieved. Secondly, reform communist parties have maintained a substantial presence, although their vote has varied considerably across the region. Thirdly, former satellite parties and parties of nostalgia have made little impact. Fourthly, parties which are largely vehicles for individual politicians have been much in evidence. Finally, nationalist/ethnic parties and nationalist/ethnic issues have appeared in amost every country.

One common characteristic in all countries has been the failure of the national liberation movements to institutionalize themselves once they had achieved their initial objectives. Indeed, some of them were already beginning to fray at the edges before the founding election. For instance, in Czechoslovakia Christian Democrat, Green and Social Democrat parties all broke away from the Civic Forum/Public Against Violence to compete independently. In Poland Solidarity was unable to agree on a single candidate for the 1990 presidential election, and at least thirteen post-Solidarity groups contested the parliamentary elections the following year. A similar picture can be seen in the Baltic States. Latvia's Way, which won two-thirds of the seats in parliament in 1990, gained only 3 per cent of the vote in the next elections three years later. Only in Bulgaria has the United Democratic Front managed largely to maintain its coherence, perhaps because a relatively unreconstructed communist party remains a serious electoral competitor and therefore the securing of a non-communist regime is still uncertain.

A much stronger element of continuity has been provided by the former communist parties. Elections in 1992 and 1993 brought these parties back into office in Lithuania and Poland respectively (in the latter case in alliance with a former satellite farmers' party). In Hungary the Socialist Party won 32 per cent of the vote in the May 1994 elections compared with 9 per cent four years previously. None of these parties claim to be nostalgic for the previous regime. Both the Hungarian and Lithuanian parties have had to compete with traditional Marxist-Leninist parties, and they have beaten them soundly. Although parties openly supporting the political practices of the former regimes have made no impact, calls for greater protection for groups suffering from the transition costs of marketization have met with a warmer reception from the electorate.

In general the parties of nostalgia have not fared well. In Romania the Liberal and National Peasant parties, which dominated prewar politics, won only 11 per cent of the vote in 1990. In Hungary these parties did better. The Smallholders, Social Democrat and Christian Democrat parties together won about a fifth of the vote in the same year. In particular the revived social democratic parties fared very poorly, despite their importance in several pre-communist regimes, especially in the Czech Republic and Hungary. Presumably they suffered from association with the communist regime, as these parties had been forcibly merged with the communists in the late 1940s.

What has filled the gap left by the decay of the national liberation movements? In the Baltic Republics and in the Czech Republic, centre-right pro-market parties have become the main competitors to the former communists. A somewhat similar picture has emerged in Slovenia and Poland. Arguably the dominance of the Hungarian Democratic Forum on the Hungarian right ensured a similar dimension of political competition in that country as well. The pro-market right rarely consists of a single party, but a left–right dimension clearly exists at party level in these countries. Moreover, in all these countries the former communist parties compete primarily in terms of economic and social policy. This is much less the case in the more economically backward and more ethnically heterogeneous countries, where the former communists have stressed calls for national unity and attacked ethnic minorities.

Ethnic minority parties have reappeared in virtually all the countries of East-Central Europe. In the more homogeneous countries these represent relatively small groups whose demands can be acceded to at relatively little cost. Elsewhere, ethnic divisions form a major political cleavage. One important exception is the gypsy community, which may number as many as three million people. This community, unlike other ethnic minorities, has been unable to mobilize itself politically, even though it is commonly a target of social and political abuse. It is an object rather than a participant in national politics.

Right-wing populist parties have made an impact in a number of countries, even in ethnically relatively homogeneous ones. In the Czech Republic the Republican Party won nearly 7 per cent of the vote in the 1992 elections on a law-and-order and anti-German platform. A number of extreme nationalist parties took about the same share of the vote in Poland in 1993 (Vinton 1994), and in Slovenia the National Party gained one-tenth of the vote in the previous year, largely on an anti-refugee/foreign worker platform.

Presidential elections provided a particular opportunity for right-wing anti-party politicians to make an impact. The 18 per cent of the vote won by Wladislaw Tyminski in the 1990 Polish elections and the 17 per cent won by Georgi Ganchev in the Bulgarian elections were not translated into success in parliamentary elections, but the support given to two politicians with no real platform beyond the expertise resulting from their presumed successes as businessmen in the West pointed to the weak anchoring of parties in the electorate. In parliamentary elections Tyminski and Ganchev's followers made much less impact, but a very similar figure, Jur Toomepuu, a United States Army veteran, won nearly 7 per cent of the vote in the 1992 parliamentary elections in Estonia. The names of their parties, respectively Party 'X', the Bulgarian Business Block and Estonian Citizens, reflect the nebulous programmes they espoused.

Are we then seeing the 'Europeanization' of East-Central Europe, as von Beyme (1992) has argued? Certainly Western Europe, and specifically the European Union, has been at least rhetorically a reference point for most East European political parties. Future membership of the Union has been espoused not only by conservative parties but also by many of the ex-communist parties. As part of this quest, East European parties have been eager to seek legitimacy (and hopefully as a result financial and organizational support) from Western European parties by soliciting membership of Conservative, Christian Democrat, Green, Liberal and Socialist internationals. For instance, the Hungarian Socialist Party has been accepted as an observer by the Socialist International. But too much should not be made of these links as indicators of a party's ideological position, and 'mistakes' have sometimes been made. For example, the Hungarian Independent Smallholders' Party's membership of both the European Democratic Union and the European Christian Democratic Union has been suspended (Agh 1993).

The installation of the formal procedures of parliamentary democracy in East-Central Europe has been a success. Free elections have been held, and only in Romania and the rump of Yugoslavia have international observers seriously questioned the probity of the polls. Even in these countries the governing parties face serious electoral competition. In several countries governments have lost elections and freely transferred office to their opponents.

The role of the parties in the broader democratization of these societies is rather more problematic, however. Most of them are very much top-down parties 'in search of cleavage', in Charles Taylor's evocative phrase (Taylor 1992). With the exception of the former communists, most are really caucus parties of small, basically parliamentary elites. In consequence party systems are very fragmented. For instance, 29 parties won seats in the 1991 election in Poland. Moreover, the membership of these elite groupings is itself very unstable. Six parties gained seats in the 1990 elections in Hungary, but by the end of 1993 there were sixteen party groups in parliament. Superficially only three parties won seats in the 1991 elections in Bulgaria, but these three parties are actually alliances of 28 different groups (Szajkowski 1992b, 28–9).

Conclusion

What are the longer-term prospects for political parties in both parts of the continent? We have argued that in many Western European countries the traditional parties are becoming increasingly removed from the electorate. Voters have responded either by deserting electoral politics or by voting for new parties of the libertarian left or the new populist right. East-Central Europe mirrors this picture. Parties there are also to some extent removed from the electorate on account of their unformed character and very weak links with the developing institutions of civil society. And the governing parties face challenges from more or less anti-system parties, usually of the political right. More generally throughout the continent, the normative implications of these developments threaten to be malign. The traditional and central role of political parties as a means of holding government accountable to citizens is compromised. This creates conditions which may lead to the gradual alienation of the citizenry from the regime and offers an opportunity for anti-system parties and movements. In East-Central Europe these dangers are stronger because parties are so weakly institutionalized and because the simultaneous tasks of economic reform and building democratic institutions are so very difficult. In Western countries, political parties and especially working-class parties played a key role in the democratization process (Rueschmeyer et al. 1992). But these were fundamentally bottom-up parties acting as agents of working people. If the success of democratization in East-Central Europe also depends upon the creation of parties of this kind, then the top-down governing parties currently in place may not be equal to the task.

Appendix 6A   *Green/left-libertarian and neo-Fascist/new populist parties contesting Western European elections since 1980*

Austria	Freedom Party (FPO); Greens
Belgium	Democratic Union for the Respect of Labour (UDRT); Flemish Greens (Agalev); Flemish Block (VL BLOK); Francophone Greens (ECOLO); Radical Reformers Fighting For an Upright Society (ROSSEM-ROSSUM); National Front (FNB); Rainbow (Regenboog)
Denmark	Progress Party; Greens; Common Course
Finland	Greens
Germany	Greens; National Democratic Party; Republicans; Ecological Democratic Party
France	Greens; National Front
Greece	Greens; National Political Union/National Party (EPEN)
Ireland	Greens
Italy	Greens; Italian Social Movement/National Alliance; The Network; Radical Party; Northern League
Luxembourg	Greens; Luxembourg for the Luxembourgers; Why Not?
Netherlands	Centre Party; Centre Democrats; Green Left (and previously independent parties which united to found Green Left in 1990, namely the Communist Party, the Radical Party, the Pacifist Socialist Party and the Evangelical People's Party)
Norway	Progress Party; Greens; Socialist People's Party/Socialist Left
Portugal	Greens; Christian Democratic Party
Spain	Greens; New Force; National Alliance; Ruiz Mateos List
Sweden	Greens; New Democracy; Left Party-Communists
Switzerland	Greens; Motorists' Party; Swiss Democrats (formerly National Action); Ticino League; Progressive Organizations of Switzerland; United Socialist Party
United Kingdom	Greens

Appendix 6B   Percentage support for green/left-libertarian parties in Western Europe, 1981–93

Country	1981	1982	1983	1984	1985	1986	1987	1988	1989	1990	1991	1992	1993
Austria	4.8		3.3			4.8			6.8				
Belgium	11.3			11.5			7.1				10.0		
Denmark							15.9	14.4		9.2			
Finland			1.4				4.0				6.8		
France	1.1					1.2		0.4					10.9
Germany			5.6				8.3			5.0			
Greece	0.0				0.0				0.9	1.1			0.8
Iceland			5.5				10.2				8.3		
Ireland	0.0	0.0					0.4		1.5			1.4	
Italy			2.2				5.1					5.9	
Luxembourg				4.2					8.5				
Netherlands	5.8	6.2				3.6			4.1				
Norway	4.9				5.5				10.1				7.9
Portugal		1.0	1.0		1.0			1.0	1.6		1.0		
Spain		0.0				0.4							
Sweden		7.3			6.9			11.3			7.9		
Switzerland			4.4				6.8				7.4		
UK			0.2				0.3					0.5	

Appendix 6C   *Percentage support for neo-Fascist and new populist parties in Western Europe, 1981–93*

Country	1981	1982	1983	1984	1985	1986	1987	1988	1989	1990	1991	1992	1993
Austria			5.0				9.7			16.6			
Belgium	4.8				2.5		2.0				7.6		
Denmark	8.9			3.6			4.8	9.0		6.4			
Finland			9.7				6.3				4.8		
France	0.2					9.8		9.8					12.8
Germany			0.2		0.2		0.6			2.8			
Greece									0.0	0.1			0.1
Iceland			0.0				0.0		0.0				
Ireland		0.0					0.0		0.0		0.0	0.0	
Italy			7.1				7.6		2.3			14.5	
Luxembourg			0.0										
Netherlands	0.5	0.7			3.7	0.2				0.9			
Norway	4.5				0.6		0.6		13.0		0.0		6.3
Portugal		0.2											
Spain		0.5			0.0			0.0	1.0				1.0
Sweden		0.0						5.8			6.7		
Switzerland			3.4								8.4		
UK		0.1					0.0				0.0		

Notes

1   Panebianco (1988, 311) calls these parties 'professional-electoral' rather than 'catch-all' to emphasize the central importance of organizational change in distinguishing these parties from mass parties – which he calls 'mass bureaucratic' parties. Terminologically this makes sense, but Kirchheimer's classification will be used here on grounds of familiarity.

2   Katz and Mair can find only two large parties which have been permanently excluded from government since 1945: the British Liberal Democrats and Italy's Democratic Left (formerly the Communist Party). To this modest list one should add the Spanish Popular Party.

3   For a sceptical analysis of this account, see Heath et al. (1985) and Reiter (1989).

4   For a discussion of the possible explanations for these differences, see the debate in Powell (1986) and Jackman (1987).

5   In Romania the Communist Party was formally banned, after the overthrow of President Ceauçescu in December 1989, but the dominance of former communists in the so-called National Salvation Front was so clear that its claim to be a non-party national movement was clearly fraudulent.

Bibliography

Agh, A. (1992). 'The Europeanization of the Hungarian Polity'. *Budapest Papers on Democratic Transition* No. 72.

—— (1993). 'The "comparative revolution" and the transition in Southern and Eastern Europe'. *Journal of Theoretical Politics* 5: 231–52.

—— (1994). 'The Hungarian party system and party theory in the transition in Central Europe', *Journal of Theoretical Politics* 6: 217–38.

Allum, P. (1993). 'Chronicle of a death foretold: the First Italian Republic'. *Reading Papers in Politics* No. 12.

Bartolini, S. and Mair, P. (1990). *Identity, Competition and Electoral Availability: the stabilisation of European electorates, 1885–1985.* Cambridge: Cambridge University Press.

Berger, S. (1973). 'Politics and anti-politics in Western Europe in the seventies'. *Daedalus* 108: 27–50.

Betz, H.-G. (1993). 'The new politics of resentment: radical right wing populist parties in Western Europe'. *Comparative Politics* 25: 413–27.

von Beyme, K. (1992). 'L'europeizzazione dell'Europa occidentale', in M. Calise (ed.), *Come cambiano i partiti.* Bologna: Il Mulino.

Cazzola, F. (1988). *Dalla corruzione: fisiologia e patologia di una sistema politico.* Bologna: Il Mulino.

Cheles, L. et al. (eds) (1991). *Neo-Fascism in Europe.* London: Longman.

Daalder, H. (1992). 'A crisis of party?' *Scandinavian Political Studies* 15: 269–88.

Dahl, R. (ed.) (1966). *Political Oppositions in Western Democracies.* New Haven, CT: Yale University Press.

Dalton, R. and Kuechler, M. (eds) (1990). *Challenging the Political Order: new social and political movements in Western democracies*. Cambridge: Polity Press.

Dimitras, P. (1991). 'Greece', in M. Franklin et al. (eds), *Electoral Change*. Cambridge: Cambridge University Press, 205–18.

Doukas, G. (1993). 'Party elites and democratisation in Greece'. *Parliamentary Affairs* 46: 506–16.

Duverger, M. (1954). *Political Parties: their organisation and activity in the modern state*. London: Methuen.

van der Eijk, C. and Niemoller, K. (1985). 'The Netherlands', in I. Crewe and D. Denver (eds), *Electoral Change in Western Democracies*. London: Croom Helm.

van der Eijk, C. et al. (1991). 'Cleavages, conflict resolution and democracy', in M. Franklin et al. (eds), *Electoral Change*. Cambridge: Cambridge University Press, 406–31.

Eurobarometer: Public Opinion in the European Community No. 39, June 1993: *Trends, 1974–1992*. Brussels: Directorate General for Information, Communications and Culture.

Evans, G. and Whitefield, S. (1993). 'Identifying the bases of party competition in Eastern Europe'. *British Journal of Political Science* 23: 521–48.

Falter, J. and Schumann, S. (1988). 'Affinity towards right-wing extremism in Western Europe'. *West European Politics* 11: 96–110.

Ford, G. (1992). *Fascist Europe: the rise of racism and xenophobia*. London: Pluto Press.

Franklin, M. et al. (1991). *Electoral Change: responses to evolving social and attitudinal structures in Western Countries*. Cambridge: Cambridge University Press.

Gillespie, R. (1990). 'The consolidation of new democracies', in D. Urwin and W. Paterson (eds), *Politics in Western Europe since 1980: perspectives, policies and problems*. Harlow: Longman.

—— (1993). 'The continuing debate on democratisation in Spain'. *Parliamentary Affairs* 46: 534–48.

Hainsworth, P. (ed.) (1992). *The Extreme Right in Europe and the USA*. London: Pinter.

Harris, W. (1994). 'Italy: purgatorio'. *New York Review of Books* 3 March: 38–41.

Heath, A. et al. (1985). *How Britain Votes*. Oxford: Pergamon.

Hockenos, P. (1993). *Free to Hate: the rise of the right in post-communist Eastern Europe*. London: Macmillan.

Hyest, J. J. (1993). 'L'argent obsédant', in A. Chausseborg and T. Ferenczi (eds), *Les élections législatives de mars 1993*. Paris: Le Monde: 12–14.

Ignazi, P. (1989). *Il Polo Escluso: profilo del movimento sociale Italiano*. Bologna: Il Mulino.

—— (1992). 'The silent counter-revolution: hypotheses on the emergence of extreme right wing parties in Europe'. *European Journal of Political Research* 22: 3–34.

Iliescu, D. (1992). 'Another front for Romanian salvation'. *RFE/RL Research Report* 1 (21 August): 16–23.

Inglehart, R. (1990). *Culture Shift in Advanced Industrial Societies*. Princeton, NJ: Princeton University Press.

Jackman, R. (1987). 'Political institutions and voter turnout in industrial democracies'. *American Political Science Review* 81: 405–23.

Katz, R. and Mair, P. (1992). 'Changing models of party organization: the emergence of the cartel party'. Paper presented at the European Consortium for Political

Research, Joint Sessions, Limerick, Ireland.

Katz, R. et al. (1992). 'The membership of political parties in European democracies'. *European Journal of Political Research* 22: 329–45.

Kirchheimer, O. (1966). 'The transformation of West European party systems', in J. LaPalombara and M. Weiner (eds), *Political Parties and Political Development*. Princeton, NJ: Princeton University Press, 177–200.

Kitschelt, H. (1988). 'Left-libertarian parties: explaining innovation in competitive party systems'. *World Politics* 40: 194–234.

—— (1990). 'New social movements and the decline of party organization', in R. Dalton and M. Kuechler (eds), *Challenging the Political Order: new social and political movements in Western democracies*. Cambridge: Polity Press.

—— (1992). 'The formation of party systems in East Central Europe'. *Politics and Society* 20: 7–50.

Koole, R. and Mair, P. (eds) (1992). European Political Data Yearbook 1992. *European Journal of Political Research* 22.

—— (1993). European Political Data Yearbook 1993. *European Journal of Political Research* 23.

Korosenyi, A. (1991). 'Revival of the past or new beginning? The nature of post communist politics'. *Political Quarterly* 62: 52–74.

Lancaster, T. (1991). 'Spain', in M. Franklin et al. (eds), *Electoral Change*. Cambridge: Cambridge University Press, 327–38.

Lane, J.-E. et al. (1993). 'Scandinavian exceptionalism reconsidered'. *Journal of Theoretical Politics* 5: 195–230.

Lawson, K. and Merkl, P. (eds) (1988). *When Parties Fail: emerging alternative organizations*. Princeton, NJ: Princeton University Press.

Lipset, S. M. and Rokkan, S. (eds) (1967). *Party Systems and Voter Alignments: cross-national perspectives*. New York: Free Press.

Mackie, T. (1991). 'General elections in Western nations during 1989'. *European Journal of Political Research* 19: 157–62.

—— (1992). 'General elections in Western nations during 1990'. *European Journal of Political Research* 21: 317–22.

Mackie, T. and Rose, R. (1991). *The International Almanac of Electoral History*. London: Macmillan; Washington, DC: Congressional Quarterly Press.

Mair, P. (1984). 'Party politics in contemporary Europe: a challenge to party?' *West European Politics* 7: 170–84.

—— (1993). 'Myths of electoral change and the survival of traditional parties'. *European Journal of Political Research*.

McGregor, J. (1993). 'How electoral laws shape Eastern European Parliaments'. *RFE/RL Research Reports* 2 (22 January): 11–18.

Mouzelis, N. (1986). *Politics in the Semi-Periphery: early parliamentarism and late industrialisation in the Balkans and Latin America*. London: Macmillan.

Panebianco, A. (1988). *Political Parties: organization and power*. Cambridge: Cambridge University Press.

Pelczynski, Z. and Kowalski, S. (1990). 'Poland'. *Electoral Studies* 9: 346–54.

Plasser, F. et al. (1992). 'The decline of "lager mentality" and the new model of electoral competition in Austria'. *West European Politics* 15: 16–44.

Powell, B. (1986). 'American voter turnout in comparative perspective'. *American Political Science Review* 80: 17–44.

Reiter, H. (1989). 'Party decline in the West: a skeptic's view'. *Journal of Theoretical Politics* 1: 325–48.

—— (1993). 'The rise of the "new agenda" and the decline of partisanship'. *West European Politics* 16: 89–104.

Rose, R. and Mackie, T. (1983). 'Incumbency in government: asset or liability?' in H. Daalder and P. Mair (eds), *Western European Party Systems: continuity and change*. Beverly Hills: Sage.

Rueschmeyer, D. et al. (1992). *Capitalist Development and Democracy*. Cambridge: Polity Press.

Schmitt, H. (1989). 'On party attachment in Western Europe and the utility of the Eurobarometer data'. *West European Politics* 12: 122–39.

Szajkowski, B. (ed.) (1991). *New Political Parties of Eastern Europe and the Soviet Union*. Harlow: Longman.

—— (1992a). 'The 1992 Albanian elections'. *Journal of Communist Studies* 8: 129–35.

—— (1992b). *Coping with Communist Legacy: the complexity of the emerging party system in Bulgaria and Romania*. Paper presented at the European Consortium for Political Research joint sessions, Limerick, Ireland.

Taggart, P. (1993). 'Muted radicals: the emerging "new populism" in West European party systems'. Paper delivered at the 1993 Meeting of the American Political Science Association, Washington, DC.

Taylor, C. (1992). 'Parties in search of cleavage: elite mass linkage in Hungary'. *Budapest Papers on Democratic Transition* No. 16.

Urwin, D. (1980). *From Ploughshare to Ballot Box: the politics of agrarian defence in Europe*. Oslo: Universitetsforlaget.

Vinton, L. (1994). ' "Outsider" parties and the political process in Poland'. *RFE/RL Research Report* 3 (21 January): 13–22.

Waters, S. (1994). ' "Tangentopoli" and the emergence of a new political order in Italy'. *West European Politics* 17: 169–80.

Woldendorp, J. et al. (1993). 'Political data 1945–1990: party government in 20 democracies'. Special Issue of *European Journal of Political Research* 24: 1–120.

Woods, D. (1992). 'The rise of regional leagues in Italian politics'. *West European Politics* 15: 56–76.

7

Parliament in the New Europe

Michael L. Mezey

In the period following the Second World War the description usually applied to parliaments, especially those in Europe, was 'in decline'. Legislatures were said to have lost their prominence and influence to some combination of dominant political parties, popularly elected, often charismatic presidents, policy experts resident in the bureaucracy and military leaders (see Wheare 1963; Bracher 1968). Although the theme of legislative decline was seldom supported by empirical data and seemed to be based on the largely unsubstantiated premise that at some time in the past a golden age of parliaments existed, the idea of decline nonetheless persisted as part of the conventional wisdom in the area of legislative studies (see Loewenberg 1971, 15).

For Americans studying European legislatures, the theme of historical decline was joined with the assumption of political marginality. Implicitly setting European legislatures against the model of the United States Congress, these institutions typically were dismissed as peripheral to national policy-making processes. It was not until the comparative study of legislative institutions moved forward during the mid- and late 1970s that a more sophisticated and nuanced understanding of the power and functions of all of the world's legislatures, including European parliaments, began to emerge (Loewenberg and Patterson 1979; Mezey 1979).

If the decline and marginality themes were problematic at an earlier time, they have been largely vitiated by current events. Today, throughout Europe, indeed throughout the world, one sees an enhanced role for parliaments.

- In 1974 Greece ended a seven-year period of rule by military junta and returned to parliamentary government. Shortly thereafter, Portugal and Spain emerged from long years of right-wing dictatorship with parliamentary bodies at the centre of their new democratic societies. Today, in all three of these nations, parliamentary democracy appears to rest on quite stable foundations (see Alivizatos 1990; Giol et al. 1990; Da Cruz and Antunes 1990).

- In 1988 the Soviet Empire began to break up. With these events new parliaments with new powers replaced minimal legislatures with little if any policy-making power in most Central and Eastern European nations as well as in several of the newly independent nations of the former Soviet Union. Many of these legislatures became the primary arenas for democratic institution building and for the deliberation of policies designed to shift these nations to market economies.

- In Denmark, Sweden and Norway, majority party coalitions that had dominated the parliaments of these countries for most of the postwar period fell apart and minority governments became more common. With this change came more active, more powerful parliaments, less subordinate to the government of the day (Strom 1990; Damgaard 1992; Rommetvedt 1992; Sannerstedt and Sjolin 1992).

- In Britain, the textbook Westminster system of strong party government and a parliament subject to executive domination has changed. Towards the end of the 1970s party discipline diminished somewhat, especially among a newly professionalized class of MPs. Members began to solicit a 'personal vote' from their constituents, the select committee system was strengthened, and more members came to expect that they would exercise a significant policy-making role (Cain et al. 1987; Norton and Wood 1993; Jogerst 1993; Searing 1994).

- Outside of Europe, several Latin American and East Asian nations underwent transitions from authoritarian political systems characterized by weak parliaments and strong presidents backed by military strength to more democratic societies with more active legislatures. Examples of the recent converts are Brazil, Chile and South Korea (see Held 1993; Pereira 1993).

- In Japan, the ruling Liberal Democratic Party that had dominated both the Diet and the Cabinet from the end of the Second World War collapsed in 1992 under the accumulated weight of scandal and corruption. Replacing it in power was a weak coalition government and a suddenly more powerful legislature capable of exerting significant pressure on the government.

- In the United States, the theme of the late 1960s and early 1970s was an 'imperial presidency' and a subordinated Congress. By the end of the 1970s terms such as a 'no-win' presidency, a 'resurgent' Congress and legislative-executive 'stalemate' began to dominate discussions of national political institutions (Light 1982; Sundquist 1981; Mezey 1989).

What is going on here and what does it imply for the role of parliaments both in the New Europe and the world at large? By the New Europe, I mean a Europe transformed by at least two phenomena. The first is the movement towards the economic and political integration of Western Europe and the second the economic and political revolutions that are going forward in the nations of Central and Eastern Europe as a result of the collapse of the Soviet Union.

Parliament and the State

Legislatures affect and are affected by the state and the political system in which they exist. Put in more formal terms, the legislature can be viewed as both an independent and a dependent variable.

Parliament as an independent variable

Functionalism provides the terminology most frequently employed by political scientists in discussions of the legislature as an independent variable. Such analyses begin by asking what functions the legislature performs for the larger political system in which it operates. The answers to such enquiries have been grouped into three broad categories: policy-making, representation and legitimization (see Mezey 1979). In regard to representation and legitimization, the evidence is that legislatures wherever they are found tend to be quite similar; the greatest variation in legislative activity occurs along the policy-making dimension, with the powerless minimal legislatures associated with one-party states or dictatorships at one end of the continuum, the uniquely activist United States Congress at the other, and the rest of the world's legislatures, including most of those in Europe, lying somewhere in between.

Changes in the status of a legislature typically involve movement along this policy-making continuum. Just as the 'decline of the legislature' theme implied a movement towards a more peripheral policy-making role for legislatures, the current state of the legislature in many nations suggests movement towards a more central policy-making role. In some nations this change is dramatic, as was the case for the minimal legislatures of the Iberian Peninsula in the mid-1970s and those of Central and Eastern Europe after 1990. In other instances the changes are more incremental, as was the increased frequency of intra-party dissent among British MPs during the 1970s, or the enhanced policy-making influence of Scandinavian parliaments during the 1980s.

Parliament as a dependent variable

These changes in the policy-making prominence of the legislature have not been self-induced. These legislatures did not create a more active policy-making role for themselves. As one seeks explanations for why the role of these legislatures has changed, the focus of enquiry shifts to parliament as a dependent variable. The legislature is nested in a set of political institutions, which in turn is nested in a larger socio-economic-political context. Although what the legislature does or fails to do affects this larger environment, changes in the latter can also alter the role and status of the legislature. This perspective shifts our attention towards changes in the nature of executive power, such as occurred with the deaths of Franco in Spain and Salazar in Portugal, or the massive political upheavals caused by the fall of communism in Eastern and Central Europe, or the decline in class consciousness that seems to characterize post-industrial Western Europe.

In the context of the New Europe, one sees changes of extraordinary breadth that affect the nature of all political institutions, including the parliament. In Western Europe, the movement towards economic and quasi-political unity has created a set of transnational institutions that have subsumed some of the prerogatives of national institutions while at the same time creating new issues for national legislatures to deal with. Simultaneously, economic insecurity has become more pronounced among important sectors and the traditional class distinctions upon which many party organizations have rested have been undermined.

These changes in the West, important as they are, pale in comparison with the collapse of the Marxist systems of Central and Eastern Europe. This change literally redefined the idea of Europe; one now can speak seriously of pan-Europeanism, exemplified by the desire of the Central European nations to join the EU and NATO and the prospect of democratic institutions from London to Moscow and from Riga to Athens. For the political parties of Western Europe, the demise of the Soviet Union and the Warsaw Pact removed an important external reference point for inter-party conflict. Parties of the left could no longer be accused of being agents of Moscow and parties of the centre and right could no longer contest elections simply on the grounds that they alone stood as the bulwark against Marxism.

For the countries of Central and Eastern Europe, the challenge of change is enormous. Simply put, these countries face the task of moving simultaneously towards a more democratic political system and a more open, market-oriented economy. They do so in an environment of economic crisis, major social and cultural changes, extraordinarily high public expectations and few political leaders with much experience of either democratic or capitalist forms.

All of this puts great pressures upon political institutions in general and legislative institutions in particular. In the West, the economic sea change provoked by a united Europe has created domestic pressures on representative institutions to protect established national traditions and interests. For the parliaments of Central and Eastern Europe, much more is expected of them than they appear institutionally capable of delivering. Typically, these legislatures have multiple parties and fragile governing coalitions which significantly reduce their capacity to act. Naturally, they have a membership with little if any parliamentary experience, and if they have staff support, they too are inexperienced. Nonetheless, these legislatures have been charged with guiding economic and political change of a virtually unprecedented character while at the same time transforming themselves from peripheral to central decision-making arenas. It has proved difficult enough for established parliaments to design public policies that incorporate important economic changes; the difficulty is increased exponentially for new legislatures that are also engaged in designing electoral laws, parliamentary procedures and constitutional provisions that define their own status and prerogatives.

Constitutional Forms

The challenges facing the nations of Central and Eastern Europe have provoked renewed interest in constitutional forms. Those charged with designing new constitutions for these countries seek among other things to create legislatures with enough power to influence policy and to check the excesses of the government while at the same time retaining enough power in the hands of the executive so that the business of the nation can be conducted.

Parliamentary versus presidential forms

Many students of comparative politics have supported parliamentary rather than presidential systems of government for these states. From their point of view, a presidential system characterized by a legislature and an executive structurally independent of each other is a guarantee of policy-making inefficiency and, ultimately, political instability. Juan Linz (1994, 6ff) argues that presidential systems lead to such results for two reasons. First, because both the president and the legislature are elected by the people, both enjoy 'democratic legitimacy', and so it is not possible to resolve disputes between the two institutions by appeals to democratic criteria. Second, because the terms of both the legislature and the president are fixed and independent of each other, presidential systems are 'rigid'. If the political lines shift or new challenges confront the system, it is not possible to adjust the personnel of government until the next scheduled election.

Other scholars have pointed out that the capacity of the government to act may have more to do with the relative strength of parties in the parliament, and specifically with the presence of a majority party, than with the existence of a parliamentary form. In parliaments with no majority party and a fragile governing coalition, policy-making may be as slow and as inefficient as in a presidential system. In such systems, the introduction of a mixed premier-presidential system – or semi-presidential government, to use Duverger's (1980) term – following the model of the Fifth French Republic, may enhance policy-making efficiency. In a deeply divided nation, an elected presidency, the argument goes, may actually enhance stability, especially if the presidential election system is designed to encourage the election of a centrist (Shugart and Carey 1992; Horowitz 1990).

Semi-presidential government

Whether or not the Fifth French Republic is truly a mixed form lying midway between presidentialism and parliamentarianism, as suggested by Shugart and Carey, is open to debate. Lijphart (1994, 94–5) argues that there are no actual examples of intermediate systems between parliamentarianism and presidentialism. In the case of France, he says that the two forms have alternated, with the typical system of presidentialism occasionally interrupted by parliamentarianism. Exactly which it has been depends upon whether or not the president's party enjoys a majority in the parliament. As long as the president had such a majority, the system operated presidentially. But during periods of co-habitation between a president of one party and a premier of another, as occurred between 1986 and 1988 and reappeared with the election results of March 1993, the role of the president is limited. Then what appears to be semi-presidential government in fact operates along parliamentary lines.

Furthermore, there is some question as to whether semi-presidential systems are actually associated with greater levels of stability. Linz (1994, 48) reminds us that the Weimar Republic was a semi-presidential system in which the president could dissolve the Reichstag. Although the consent of the chancellor was required for such a step, this was not a problem because the president appointed the chancellor. It was exactly this sequence of events that led to the end of the Republic, with the election of a Nazi majority in March 1933. And those who point to the stability of the Fifth French Republic over its predecessors as testimony to the stabilizing influence of mixed systems sometimes slight the importance of the consolidation of the party system that resulted from the abandonment of the proportional representation system of parliamentary elections in favour of the single member system (Linz 1994, 51; but see also Suleiman 1994).

The West: the parliamentary model persists

In Europe, this debate over appropriate constitutional forms and particularly the efficacy of the French model is most relevant for the new democracies of

Central and Eastern Europe. In Western Europe, constitutional changes with a significant effect on the relative balance of power between the legislature and the executive have been restricted in recent years to Portugal and Spain. The modal constitutional form has been the parliamentary system, with Belgium, Denmark, Germany, Greece, Ireland, Italy, Luxembourg, the Netherlands, Norway, Spain, Sweden and the United Kingdom clearly falling into this category, and Austria, Finland and Portugal operating largely in that manner despite constitutions that appear to be semi-presidential (see Duverger 1980). Switzerland remains a special case, with an executive selected, but not removable, by its parliament (see Shugart and Carey 1992, 41).

The only Western European nations that have undergone significant constitutional renovation have been Spain and Portugal. In Spain, the presence of the monarchy ensured the creation of a conventional parliamentary system, with most powers vested in the legislature. However, the position of that government was strengthened by the inclusion of the constructive vote of no confidence, a device borrowed from the German Constitution which requires that the new prime minister to be is named in the text of the no-confidence vote (Giol et al. 1990, 124). The Portuguese system originally resembled the French, with a popularly elected president sharing power with a prime minister responsible to a parliamentary majority. However, this proved to be an interim situation designed primarily to reassure the military leadership during the period of democratic transition. Constitutional changes adopted in 1982 reduced the president's powers, and restricted his right to dissolve the Assembly, to dismiss the prime minister and to veto legislation. Also, the military's Council of the Revolution, which had exercised a strong influence over the president, was abolished and replaced by a strictly consultative Council of State with no direct military membership (Gladdish 1990a, 107; Da Cruz and Antunes 1990, 159–60).

The gross similarity in parliamentary forms throughout most of Western Europe should not be mistaken for a similarity in the status of parliament. That there is a gap between what is written on constitutional paper and what happens in practice is an old lesson of comparative politics. Obviously, there is great variation among these systems in regard to the role that their legislatures play, a variation having mostly to do, as we shall see, with the nature of the party system.

The East and semi-presidentialism

As the nations of Eastern Europe moved towards more democratic forms, the legislature was usually at the centre of the process. This was because the written constitutions of the old regime endowed these legislatures with a great deal of formal power. Informally, of course, these legislatures were dominated by the single party. As the power of the party began to erode, the legislature took a leading role in the transition to democracy, but within its midst were office-holders from the past, often including many members of the communist party. Thus, these parliaments quite paradoxically were at the centre of change yet, in the view of many, inhibitors of change.

This led to a rewriting of constitutions to shift more power to the hands of executive leaders and away from the legislature. Typically, mixed systems that seemed to follow the model of the Fifth Republic were created, with independently elected presidents exercising their own prerogatives in tandem with a prime minister and cabinet responsible to the parliament. Thus, in October 1992, the Polish Parliament ratified the so-called Small Constitution. It gave the president rather than the parliament the power to appoint the prime minister and cabinet, maintained the power of the president to dissolve parliament, and enhanced the formal powers of the government as compared to the parliament (Rapaczynski 1993; Holc 1993). In Russia, a new constitution approved by referendum in December 1993 also shifted significant powers to the president and away from the parliament. Similar premier-presidential models have been adopted in most of the other Central European nations. However, the balance of power between the premier and the elected president is subject to great variation, with countries such as Slovenia, Estonia and Bulgaria having strong parliamentary features (see Stepan and Skach 1994, 124).

Along with the newly created Czech Republic and Slovakia, Hungary is among the few nations that has not turned to an independently elected president. Although the president is appointed by the parliament, he is somewhat more than a figurehead. Real power, however, lies with the prime minister and his cabinet, and, in the time since the shift to a democratic system, further steps were taken to strengthen the power of the government of the day. Under constitutional changes approved in 1990 the president is elected by the parliament; he in turn nominates a prime minister who must have the support of a majority of the parliament. The prime minister then appoints a cabinet the members of which need not be confirmed by a parliamentary vote. As in Germany and Spain, the government can be voted out only through a constructive vote of no-confidence (Paczolay 1993, 36ff).

Political Parties

Although the status of the legislatures of Portugal and Spain and, more recently, the countries of Eastern and Central Europe has been subject to significant constitutional changes, the role of these parliaments as well as those throughout Europe has also been affected by changes in political party systems.

These, in turn, have triggered changes in the pattern of legislative–executive relations.

Parties and legislative strength

The strength of a nation's political party system is the key variable explaining the prominence of its legislature. Party system strength is measured by a number of variables, including the complexity of party organization, the connection between citizens and their parties, the control of the electoral process by political party organizations, the dominance of government decisions by party leaders and the number of political parties.

At one end of the continuum of party system strength are single-party systems of the sort found until recently in Eastern and Central Europe. Here the power of the party was firmly institutionalized, its connections with the public were strong although not always amicable, and the party's control of the electoral process and political decision-making was unquestioned. In nations such as these, a minimal legislature with virtually no autonomy existed. All decisions were made by the governing party; its members in the legislature, who were usually the *only* members of the legislature, might under certain circumstances affect the shape of public policy at the margins (see Mezey 1979, ch. 7), but in general, and certainly on major matters, they were obliged to follow the party line.

Next in party system strength are dominant two-party systems in which one party commands a reliable and disciplined legislative majority. Although the party in power might alternate from election to election, the governing party always has a majority and its legislative members can usually be counted on to support party positions. This has been the case for much of the postwar period in the United Kingdom and in Scandinavia. These legislatures are certainly more autonomous than minimal legislatures; their members are able to exercise real influence on government policy and they are always the site for unfettered criticism of the government by opposition members. Nonetheless, on major issues the legislature is largely subordinate to a government party that can be depended upon to muster its majority and get its way. Rank and file legislators are usually asked to react to and approve government proposals rather than initiate policies of their own.

When two-party systems yield to multi-party systems with no party holding a majority in the legislature, parliamentary prominence inevitably increases. In postwar Italy, for example, no single party has ever held a majority in the parliament. Thus, even though the political parties are firmly institutionalized in Italian society and their parliamentary wings are internally disciplined, party leaders have regularly steered their members into and out of government coalitions, the legislature has been the scene of regular no-confidence votes in the government, and therefore the legislature has been a force to which the government has always had to attend. The result has been a parliament that, although frequently immobilized by party factionalism, nonetheless holds more power than the usually short-lived Italian governments (see Cotta 1990).

No matter how many parties are functioning, when party discipline decreases, the power of the legislature increases. The dependence of legislators on their party leaders has two sources. Members may remain loyal to their party because of a strong commitment to a discernible party ideology. Also, when members depend for their re-election on the continued good will of their party leaders, they themselves are very likely to be loyal partisans. But to the extent that members' election and re-election turns on their own efforts and their own connections with their constituencies, their loyalty to the party will be at risk. Weak or vague ideologies among partisans put loyalty at further risk. The independence of members of the United States Congress from their party leaders, although frequently exaggerated, has always been premised on both the non-ideological nature of American political parties and their electoral dependence on their own political entrepreneurship.

Finally, there are nations in which political parties lack internal cohesion and have very little in the way of governmental or extra-governmental organization, where parties form and re-form from day to day, and where candidates regularly shift from one group to another while others stand outside the party system, running as independents. In such countries, legislatures may exercise considerable power in the short run, but often will be at risk from non-democratic elements, especially the military. A disintegrated party system suggests that representative democracy itself is weak, and the legislature in such a context becomes vulnerable to extra-legal attacks on its prerogatives and even its existence. This is exactly the situation in most of the nations of Eastern and Central Europe; the end of the single-party state left an atomized party system in its wake.

The East: the collapse of party system strength

Although there are exceptions, what we see throughout much of Europe, from East to West, is the weakening and, in some cases, the destruction of the party systems that have dominated these nations during the postwar period. In the case of the hegemonic one-party states of Eastern and Central Europe, the single communist party has been replaced by a chaotic multi-party system that sometimes appears to be more like a no-party system. After years of nearly totalitarian domination by a single party, citizens of these nations have little experience with alternative political movements or ideologies. In countries such as Poland and Russia, parties seem to come and go almost daily. Some organizations are simply personal vehicles of popular politicians. Others hark back to old pre-communist ideologies and alliances and still others represent groups that had been united against the old order but now have disintegrated into warring factions. Some parties have the makings of complex political organizations and are at work building strong popular bases, but many are what have been called 'couch' parties; that is, all of the party members – usually political activists – could sit comfortably on one couch.

These nations have tenuously strong parliaments – parliaments that can exercise significant authority as long as they are permitted to do so. The problem is that, although they may be strong, they may be incapable of acting because of multiple, weak and feuding party groupings. This puts them at risk to populist and ultimately authoritarian leaders who promise simple and quick solutions to intricate problems. As the leaders of the Russian Parliament discovered in October 1993, a reluctance to bend to the will of a president who has the support of the armed forces can end rather unpleasantly. And the alternative to Yeltsin, it seems, may not be a more powerful parliament, but an even more authoritarian presidency in the hands of someone like Zhirinovsky.

Even in those former Marxist systems where the armed forces are not particularly strong, the parliament may still be quite vulnerable. Janine Holc (1994) describes the manner in which the powers of the Polish Sejm were undermined by President Walesa, who succeeded in associating the Sejm with anarchy and substituting a stronger presidential and plebiscitary approach to governance. In 1993 Walesa dissolved the parliament, branding the institution as debased, corrupt and a threat to democracy itself. He, in contrast, described himself as above special interests and, most importantly, above political parties. Walesa's characterization of an anarchic parliamentary situation was given credence by the presence as a result of the 1991 elections of eighteen political parties with at least two Sejm members, eleven seats in the hands of independents, and no party with more than 13.5 per cent of the seats (Bielasiak 1994, 243).

Even if such parliaments are not threatened by strong executives and/or military force, their capacity to act in a decisive manner will be quite problematic. Without the ability to muster reliable majorities, such parliaments are unable to come to decisions and are usually at odds with the presidents and technocrats with whom they share power. In the case of Poland, there were extraordinary difficulties forming a government, let alone acting on policy issues (Bielasiak 1994). In Hungary, it was just this fear of immobilism which moved the parliament to approve constitutional provisions that strengthened the hand of the prime minister and the cabinet (Ilonszki 1994).

The West: the erosion of party strength

In Western Europe, a somewhat more complex situation obtains. In most nations the partisan players have remained largely the same, but the nature of inter-party politics has changed. One of the more enduring discriminators among European political parties during the twentieth century was their position on the relationship between the state and the economy, with parties of the left supporting welfare state policies against the more capitalist and business oriented attitudes of the centre and the right. Party allegiances built on the appropriate class lines remained relatively stable.

In the post-industrial, Maastricht era of the New Europe, these class-based party alliances have become somewhat anachronistic, and such distinctions have begun to erode. For the right, the fall of communism in Eastern Europe and the elimination of a military threat from the Warsaw Pact deprived the non-socialist elements of a major unifying theme. With the left in disarray because of a decline in class consciousness and the right in disarray because of the absence of a common enemy, party alliances began to shift. In some countries new parties such as the greens have emerged, with new issues that crosscut the old class divisions. The powerful and emotional issue of immigration has brought other new alliances into being, with working-class whites finding common cause with neo-Fascist movements. The economic uncertainty that permeates all post-industrial systems has loosened party allegiances and created a pool of voters ripe for seemingly anyone who promises to deliver economic security to an increasingly insecure populace.

In postwar Italy, the parliament has been consistently strong because no party has ever had a majority of the seats, the number of parties participating in governing coalitions has been high, and the leading party in the governing coalition, the Christian Democratic Party, has always been factionalized (Cotta 1990, 78). In the 1980s the percentage of seats held by the Christian Democrats dropped from the low 40 per cent range to the mid-30 per cent range, and more recently the party has virtually collapsed in the face of a seemingly endless series of scandals. The Communist Party has moved towards the centre, positioning itself and its allies in the Democratic Party of the Left as one alternative to the Christian Democrats. However, the other alternative, a loose coalition of right-wing and neo-Fascist groups, emerged victorious in the March 1994 elections, suggesting that a resurgence of authoritarianism as a reaction to conditions of parliamentary immobilism and corruption is a threat that is not restricted to the newer, more fragile democracies of Eastern and Central Europe.

The erosion of its class base is not the only cause of the weakening of the West European party systems. As is the case throughout the world, the rise of the mass electronic media has dealt a serious blow to party strength. At one time, strong party systems were the major institution that linked citizens to the state. They recruited candidates, organized their campaigns, turned out the vote and, after the elections, organized the government and the opposition. For most voters, most of what they knew about candidates, their politics and government came from political parties.

The world of television has changed all of this. Candidates now have direct access to the voters and have less need for an organized political party. In some cases this has led to the rapid rise of new leaders who stand outside the party system. Although this phenomenon has been most apparent in presidential politics – the Perot movement in the United States, Le Pen in France, Zhirinovsky in Russia – it also appeared in the 1994 Italian parliamentary elections. Silvio Berlusconi, a wealthy businessman with no previous political experience but with a huge media empire and a compelling media presence, led his new party, Forza Italia, to victory.

In other nations, the electronic media has reduced the electoral control of the party and thus enhanced the electoral independence of the legislator or the legislative candidate. A candidate with access to the media need not rely as heavily on the party organization for election and therefore may not rely as heavily on party directives once in office.

Legislative–Executive Relations

Throughout Europe, in sum, an increasingly contentious and heterogeneous society has eroded old party lines. These factors manifest themselves in parliaments increasingly fractionalized among more parties, and in some instances by a decline in internal discipline within these parties. All of this, in turn, has produced governments with less dependable parliamentary majorities and therefore governments less able to act on the problems that their nations confront. In this sense, strengthened parliaments may be associated with weak governments which in turn may be an indicator of a weakened state.

As the capacity of the government to control the legislature erodes, parliamentary influence on executive activity will increase, or, put differently, the independence of members of parliament from the executive will increase. Such influence can be apparent in a number of ways – the frequency with which government proposals are challenged in debates, the frequency with which such challenges lead to the amendment or rejection of such proposals, the frequency with which private members' bills succeed, and the frequency of questions or interpellations of the government. Less visible, but possibly even more important, would be evidence that the government is taking seriously the opinions of members of the legislature as it shapes its policy proposals. If this is the case, what appears to be government success in having its proposals pass the legislature in virtually unamended form may in fact be the result of accommodations privately made with legislators prior to the submission of proposals.

The connection between changes in the party system and the enhanced prominence of parliament is evident in Denmark, Norway and Sweden. As these nations moved from majority to minority governments, they experienced increases in virtually every indicator of legislative activity: in Denmark, in bills and resolutions considered and adopted, interpellations, questions to ministers and hours in session (Damgaard 1992, 42–3); in Norway, in the number of questions asked and the frequency of dissenting remarks in committee recommendations (Rommetvedt 1992, 86); and in Sweden, in committee dissents, member motions and questions asked (Sannerstedt and Sjolin 1992).

In Great Britain, parliamentary activity has also increased. Comparing the late 1980s with the late 1970s, Philip Norton notes that MP to Minister communications have risen by 50 per cent, the number of questions by 25 per cent and early day motions fourfold (Norton 1990, 19–20). From the 1970s, MPs began to cast votes against their party leadership with some degree of regularity. In the 1974–9 parliament, 44 per cent of the Labour MPs voted against their party leadership ten or more times. Even in the more cohesive Conservative Party, nearly all members voted against the party leadership at least twice, with the median number of dissenting votes at six (Rose 1986, 24–5). Although government defeats in parliament were more common in the 1970s than in the 1980s, Norton (1990) argues that this is because government majorities have been somewhat larger in recent years and also because governments have become more deferential to their members, seeking to avoid defeat by early consultation and even by the withdrawal of bills that might provoke members to desert the party.

There have also been significant changes in Dutch politics from the early 1970s. In the previous two decades the Netherlands had been characterized by a broad consensus across the major party groupings. But this consensus dissolved with a decline in support for the traditional parties, the emergence of new parties, and the movement of elements within the traditional parties towards a more polarized politics. All of this was accompanied by what Gladdish terms a 'startling rise' in parliamentary amendments, in parliamentary policy initiatives, in motions and in questions to ministers. Questions rose from 689 in 1971–2 to 1,481 in 1981–2; motions from 196 in 1973–4 to 1,214 in 1983–4; and budgetary amendments from 41 in 1974 to 115 in 1984 (Gladdish 1990b, 112–14). Whether or not this increase in activity means an increase in the power and influence of the Dutch Parliament is open to question; one view is that activity has increased but that the parliament continues to have no real influence (Andeweg and Irwin 1993, 150–1).

A recent review of the role of the Spanish Parliament after the end of the Franco period traces a direct relationship between changes in party power and changes in the status of the Cortes. Between 1977 and 1982, according to Alda and Nieto (1994, 181), a situation of minority centrist governments 'resulted in Parliament taking a leadership role'. However, between 1982 and 1988, the Socialist Party won two outright electoral victories and parliament declined in the face of a 'partisan *rodillo*, or steamroller'. In the earlier period, 16 per cent of the bills passed by parliament originated there; in the latter period, the figure was 6 per cent. In the earlier period, 72 per cent of the government's proposals passed; in the latter, the figure was 91 per cent (Giol et al. 1990, 111). With the weakening of the socialist majority after 1988, parliamentary power once again increased, although not to the pre-1982 levels.

In Austria, Wolfgang Muller (1993) reports that the parliamentary groups have become less disciplined and that the parliament itself has achieved greater importance in the policy-making process; it now possesses considerable leeway in a substantial proportion of decisions.

But the deterioration of party power and the consequent enhancement of legislative power has not been uniform across Europe. In the united Germany and France, for example, party discipline remains strong, and by all accounts the legislatures of these countries remain relatively docile. In the case of the united German Bundestag, there has been no increase in non-governmental legislative initiatives or any decline in party loyalty. However, Thomas Saalfeld (1990, 78–86) indicates that extensive consultation and bargaining between the parliamentary party and the government is now the norm. He also notes that the 1983–7 Bundestag was the occasion for a marked increase in the number of interpellations, the number of oral questions and the number of requests for short debates.

In France, the situation is not as clear. Howard Machin (1993, 136) detects a greater willingness upon the part of the government to accommodate parliamentary amendments; in 1989, of 5,181 amendments tabled, 2,285 were adopted, with only 18 per cent of the adopted amendments offered by the government. He also reports a greater willingness upon the part of the government to consider opposition amendments and a rise in the use of parliamentary questions. John Frears (1990, 50) comes to a somewhat different conclusion, arguing that the 'greatest weakness' of parliament is as a watchdog. He concludes that the procedures for controlling executive power, for scrutinizing or debating or questioning executive acts, are completely inadequate.

Professionalism

As the legislature becomes a more active policy-making institution, it is more likely to attract professional politicians to its membership – people who view government service in vocational rather than avocational terms. Such members are more likely to be policy activists, and parliamentary service will become a full-time rather than a part-time occupation. Professionalization can be traced to several factors. First, politicians are attracted to offices where they can exercise influence. As the influence of the legislature increases, the office of legislator becomes more attractive to the more politically ambitious. Second, as legislatures become more prominent they become more active, and service in an active legislature is likely to be a full-time occupation.

Of course, the causal arrow can also run in the other direction. In Great Britain, for example, the shift from part-time to full-time MPs seems to have begun before the strengthening of the select committee system (see Rose 1986). As these more professional members came to constitute a larger percentage of the membership of the House of Commons they sought a greater policy-making role, which in turn led to the ultimately successful demand for the strengthening of the select committee system (see Jogerst 1993).

Evidence from several European legislatures suggests that more professionalized legislators have begun to emerge, especially in those parliaments that have increased their policy-making influence. An increase in full-time legislators who bridle at the passive backbench role and seek opportunities to influence public policy has been observed in the United Kingdom (see Jogerst 1993; Norton and Wood 1993; Searing 1994), Denmark (Damgaard 1992) and Spain (Giol et al. 1990).

In the case of the legislatures of Eastern Europe and the former Soviet Union, one sees an odd mixture of parliamentarians. Some are relics from the old regime, people who had made political careers within the party, state or local bureaucracies. Some of these members of the *nomenklatura* moved from bureaucratic to electoral politics as the centre of political gravity in these states shifted from the executive to the legislature. Others are political amateurs, drawn from universities, the arts and the nascent business class. Few, however, among either the *nomenklatura* or the amateurs had served in legislative bodies before. In Poland, the elections of June 1989 produced 422 Sejm members (92 per cent of the total) who were serving in the legislature for the first time (Lewis 1993, 304). In Hungary, 96 per cent of those elected in the April 1990 elections had had no previous parliamentary experience (Ilonszki 1994, 264), and of those elected to the Russian Congress of People's Deputies in May

1990, 94 per cent had never been deputies before (Remington et al. 1994, 290).

Constituency Service

Although the evidence is that all legislators, no matter what their nation, devote some of their time to serving the particularized needs of their constituents, there is a theoretical reason to suggest that, as the strength of political parties begins to erode, even greater emphasis is placed on such representational activities. That is, if parties are less able to control or guarantee the re-election of their members, then members who wish to be re-elected may well feel the need to protect their careers by strengthening their relationships with their constituents.

At this point there is more evidence supporting the universality of service activities than the electoral impact of such activities. In terms of their frequency, there is reason to believe that such activities are more prevalent in single-member district systems than in multi-member proportional representation systems. This is because the former creates a more direct bond between the individual legislator and the constituency than the latter. In Britain, for example, the constituency service activities of MPs have long been documented (Dowse 1972; Barker and Rush 1970) and recent evidence suggests that they are increasing (Norton and Wood 1993). One new study concludes that today 'nearly all MPs, including those in the highest ministerial offices, do at least some constituency service' (Searing 1994, 371). Similarly, in France, one analysis of the role of the deputies concludes that they are dominated by local preoccupations, with members averaging approximately thirty letters a day, most asking for some sort of service (Frears, 1985, 109–11).

In countries with proportional representation, the service link between legislators and their constituents seems weaker. This is especially so when local constituencies either do not exist or are very large. Thus, in the Netherlands, a proportional representation country where there are no local constituencies and all candidates run on nationwide lists, voters say that they are unlikely to go to MPs with their problems; for their part, MPs, in describing their roles, place little emphasis on dealing with voters' problems (Gladdish 1991, 100–2). In Germany, service activities are more likely among that portion of the Bundestag members elected from single-member constituencies than from those deputies elected from party lists (Lancaster and Patterson 1990). In Belgium, however, service activities by legislators seem to be high despite a proportional system, perhaps because members act at the behest of their party leaders, who use such activities to shore up the party's level of public support (MacMullen 1985).

Some versions of proportional representation can encourage service activities. In Ireland, the single transferable vote system allows voters to indicate their preferences among candidates, and in one study a plurality of voters indicated that constituency service was their most important criterion in making such preference decisions (Farrell 1985).

What is not clear is the electoral impact of these activities. Although it is now an article of faith among American political scientists that constituency service activities provide an important explanation for the re-election success of incumbent members of the United States Congress, there is little research and therefore little evidence of such an impact in other nations.

One exception is Great Britain. Using public opinion data, Cain et al. (1987) documented an increase in constituency service activities from the mid-1960s to the late 1970s, an increase in constituency awareness of these activities, and an apparent increase in the frequency with which evaluations of service formed the basis for constituent evaluation of MP job performance. MPs who engaged in constituency service were better known and more favourably evaluated than those who did less, and some evidence was found of an electoral advantage for the former group. A more recent analysis, working with voting returns and interviews with MPs, finds 'strong, if not conclusive, evidence' that incumbents do gain a personal vote through their efforts on behalf of constituents, and that first termers in particular make an effort to impress local leaders with their diligent approach to constituency affairs (Norton and Wood 1993, 141). Both of these studies attempt to link the increase in constituency service activities and the emergence of a personal vote to the weakening of British parties.

The local activities of parliamentarians are not always a guarantee of their electoral independence from their parties or of a personal vote. In France, for example, nearly three-quarters of the deputies in the National Assembly hold local offices and many define their roles as representing the needs of their constituencies to the central government. On the other hand, discipline within the French parties continues to be strong despite this degree of legislative parochialism (Frears 1985).

In the case of the new legislatures of Central and Eastern Europe, the evidence in regard to constituency service is slim and ambiguous. Under the old regime, members were expected to serve as a link between their constituents and the leadership at the centre. Under the new regime, these activities, at least for the time being, seem to be somewhat less in evidence. Werner Patzelt (1994) finds that linkage and other constituency oriented roles are less likely to be articulated by East German than West German legislators. He suggests that this may be because the former have been preoccupied with state and institution-building activities, an explanation that may apply to other nations undergoing democratic transitions.

Structure

As legislatures become more active, and as they attract more members who wish to be actively involved in the policy-making process, they become more structurally complex. Usually, this is reflected in a strengthened committee system and enhanced resources for staff and other support services. Such structural features were unnecessary if parliament's primary responsibility was to endorse the policy proposals of the government of the day. But as legislatures become more autonomous their workload increases, as does their need for additional resources to do their jobs effectively.

A recent study by Michael Jogerst (1993) of changes in the select committee system of the British House of Commons demonstrates this process. As parliament attracted a more professionalized class of legislators who began to seek arenas in which they could assume a more active policy-making role, the long-standing opposition of party leaders to a strengthened committee system began to weaken. As a result, in recent years the number of members wishing to serve on these committees has exceeded the number of places available. Where at one time backbenchers involved in committee work might reduce their chances of promotion to their party's frontbench, Jogerst finds no evidence of this now.

In several other European countries, the committee system is either well established or has been strengthened. In Spain, committees now have their own permanent staff members (Liebert 1990, 257). In Germany, committees have long been central arenas for parliamentary decision-making despite the presence of disciplined political parties (see Loewenberg 1967, 334ff; Saalfeld 1990, 81). In postwar Italy, committees have possessed the unique power of enacting legislation on their own. Committee activity has expanded steadily since 1971; now there is more emphasis on the preliminary scrutiny of proposed legislation and on oversight activities, and somewhat less emphasis on bill enactment (Di Palma 1977, 194ff; Della Salla 1993).

Public Support

In terms of public support for the legislatures of Europe, these may be the best of times and the worst of times. Certainly, the increasing prominence of the legislature across the continent is beyond dispute. Yet the effects of greater legislative activity on the public stature of the legislature is uncertain. If, as is the case in Central Europe and the countries of the former Soviet Union, legislative power rises in the context of a movement towards democratization, a movement to which the legislature is a central component, then in the short term the reputation and prestige of the legislature might well be enhanced. When the first post-communist institutions were installed in Poland, all of them, including the legislature, enjoyed very high levels of public confidence (Przeworski 1993, 170). Mishler and Rose (1994, 12) found in their analysis of 1991 survey data gathered in Bulgaria, Czechoslovakia, Hungary, Poland, Romania and Slovenia that 77 per cent of their respondents said that they would oppose a suspension of the parliament, and nearly three-quarters of these respondents were confident that their parliaments would not be suspended.

However, if economic conditions deteriorate following the establishment of democratic institutions and the legislature is unable to respond, or if the legislature and the executive are in constant conflict over what is to be done, the public prestige of all institutions, including the legislature, can be expected to suffer. Hibbing and Patterson (1994, 95) analysed survey data gathered between 1990 and 1991 in nine nations in Eastern and Central Europe. They found that trust in parliament was directly connected with the level of citizen satisfaction with their economic circumstances and was highly correlated with a more general sense of trust in government and trust in the leading government party.

Keith Crawford's (1994, 257) discussion of the parliament of Czechoslovakia indicates that parliamentary immobilism after January 1991 coincided with a steady decline in public confidence in the Federal Assembly. In Poland, net confidence (the difference between the percentage of those supportive and the percentage of those non-supportive) in the Polish Sejm dropped from a high of 84 in November 1989 to 21 in November 1990, and to −33 by July 1991. This plunge in support coincided with a period of deepening economic problems, particularly mounting unemployment. According to Przeworski (1993, 172–4), unemployment figures alone explain 82 per cent of the variance in confidence in the Sejm.

When conditions deteriorate, the legislature is more likely than the executive to lose public support, especially in presidential systems. Presidents typically have easier access to the mass media than the parliament and can more effectively bring their case to the public. They can project an image of action and decisiveness, and they can label the legislators as argumentative, dilatory and perhaps corrupt. And, to the extent that presidents can project themselves as representatives of the national interest rather than of the more parochial concerns that find expression in the legislature, they can marshal public support behind them in their disputes with a recalcitrant parliament. Thus, during the 1989–91 period when confidence in the Polish Sejm was falling, confidence in the executive also fell, but to a lesser extent. In part this was due to the continuing message from Walesa that the problem with Poland was the Sejm (Przeworski 1993, 176–7), a theme that he continued in later months, and one which Yeltsin also used in his confrontation with the Russian Parliament in October 1993.

Ironically, legislatures that are subordinate to a dominant executive or political party may well have higher levels of public support than a more active legislature, because it is difficult to blame the former for public policy failures. A more prominent legislature is the object of higher public expectations, which may well be disappointed in the face of very difficult problems. Such disappointed expectations can lead to lower levels of public support. Low levels of support are not necessarily fatal to a legislature; the United States Congress itself is notorious for the low esteem in which the public holds it. But such low levels of support may be more dangerous for a new institution struggling to establish itself than for a well-entrenched legislature.

Legislatures and Change

The policy-making power of legislative institutions and the degree to which they are supported by mass publics is subject to change. These changes most often can be traced to changes in the larger context within which the legislature operates. For example, Norton and Wood (1993) argue that economic tensions in Great Britain provoked by the problems of post-industrialism and de-industrialism eroded the class base of British parties. This in turn made the electoral situation of MPs a good deal more uncertain and provided an incentive for them to devote even more of their energies to constituency work as a way of generating a personal vote. Economic uncertainty among the public created strong demands that MPs work to protect local constituency interests. And, as MPs became more active in this respect, the assumption that this was indeed their responsibility became more widespread (Searing 1994, 383). In Scandinavia, according to Damgaard and his colleagues, the shift to minority governments was the product of a growing heterogeneity and an increased level of conflict in these societies. The consensus that had created majority governments in the past was shaken, minority governments became typical and thus the legislature rose in prominence.

The clearest examples of the impact of contextual change on legislative institutions are from Central and Eastern Europe. The current salience of these parliaments is directly connected to the withdrawal of Soviet power, and in Russia itself economic collapse was the largest factor provoking these political changes. Disastrous policies had left the party and the bureaucracy discredited and so the legislature in some sense was the last institution left standing. It alone was capable of changing its membership through elections and thereby establishing its legitimacy in the new order.

What the future holds for the 'old' legislatures of Western Europe and the new legislatures of the East is open to question. In the West, if strengthened legislatures are a sign of weak or minority governments, the capacity of the state to act will be reduced. Damgaard (1992, 48–9) concludes that, in the case of the Danish Parliament, its enhanced status has been accompanied by a reduced governmental capacity to manage serious economic problems, a disposition towards short-term thinking and temporary solutions and unclear lines of responsibility.

Although it is unlikely to happen in Denmark, such situations can invite challenges to the legislature from its traditional enemy, the authoritarian right. If economic problems mount, if popular disaffection with government increases, and if governmental immobilism becomes more apparent, citizens will continue to be vulnerable to the siren call of the outsider who blames everything on the corrupt parliamentary politicians, who offers quick and simple solutions to complex problems, and who promises to restore lost national pride. In its most dangerous form, such demands are joined with xenophobia and racism. The victory of the right in the 1994 Italian elections, the increasing frequency of neo-Fascist violence in Germany, and the persistent strength of the extreme right in France are reminders that it can indeed happen again in Western Europe.

In Central and Eastern Europe, the future of legislatures is even more uncertain. These are societies undergoing the broadest transformations, economically, socially, politically, and, in some cases, in terms of geography and national identity. Many of these nations have instituted popularly elected presidents and they have done so for a number of good reasons. In some instances, the likelihood of a factionalized parliament created the need for a person who in certain circumstances could act without parliamentary consent. In some instances the presidency was a symbol for the nation, an affirmation of its new sense of nationhood. This was particularly so in Poland and Czechoslovakia, where national heros of the resistance to Soviet domination were installed in the presidency. Finally, in some cases, a presidency was necessary to reassure the military, an institution congenitally distrustful of legislative institutions. In Russia, it was not surprising that the military cast its lot with President Yeltsin in his 1993 confrontation with the parliament.

Despite the utility of an elective president in these states, it is also important to note the potential dangers that this can create for parliamentary institutions. Alfred Stepan and Cindy Skach (1994) discuss Guillermo O'Donnell's concept of 'delegative democracy', a term he used to describe Latin American presidential systems and which is to be taken as the opposite of representative democracy. Delegative democracy is characterized by presidents who present themselves as above parties, who view legislative institutions as nuisances to which they should not be required to account, and who concentrate power in their own offices, sharing decision-making only with their closest advisors.

Delegative democracy is ultimately destabilizing and a threat to parliamentary autonomy. However, it is not clear if the experience of Latin America with presidentialism, and models such as O'Donnell's developed in that context, are applicable to Eastern Europe (see Whitehead 1993, 324–5; Przeworski 1991; Lewis 1993). On the one hand, President Walesa's verbal degradation of the Polish Sejm, President Yeltsin's military attack on the Russian Parliament, the tenuous relationship of both men with political parties and a tendency in both cases towards power gravitating to the president and his advisors fit O'Donnell's model of delegative democracy. However, the military is a key element in Latin American systems, and outside the former Soviet Union the military is not much of a factor in Central and Eastern Europe. If the parliament should fall in Hungary, in the Czech Republic or in Slovakia, for example, it is unlikely to fall to a military coup, as is the typical fate of parliaments in Latin America.

The most interesting comparison between Latin America and Central and Eastern Europe turns on the manner in which political institutions manage economic change. In Latin America, delegative democracy has been justified by the need for strong government action to deal with severe economic crises. Although exact comparisons are difficult, the economic crises confronting the new governments of Europe are in many respects more profound than those confronting Latin America. Worse yet, severe economic privations and radical changes in the distribution of wealth are very recent phenomena in these countries, and have the potential to create strong public discontent with democratic institutions – as can be seen from the Polish confidence data cited earlier. In such an environment, people may turn away from representative institutions and towards strong, executive-based leaders, as they have in several Latin American nations. On the other hand, the experience of Spain and Portugal, in which democratization and economic development went forward successfully, suggests another alternative (Maravall 1993).

No matter whether Latin America or Southern Europe ultimately proves to be the model for Eastern Europe, the fact is that the nations in the latter group face the necessity of profound economic reform. Such initiatives may be helped or hindered by democratic institutions. From one perspective, parliaments can build support for such initiatives by providing an arena for broad consultation, consensus building and legitimacy. From another perspective, such a process may open reform initiatives to political pressures that can ultimately weaken them and render them ineffectual. Przeworski (1991, 180–7) hypothesizes that this will lead to a certain oscillation between executive dominance and executive solicitation of parliamentary support, and therefore towards a 'stop–go' approach to economic reform. He argues that such an approach eventually undermines respect for representative institutions and in the end may harm the process of economic change.

To the extent that the consolidation of democratic institutions in Central and Eastern Europe ultimately depends upon economic reform, very powerful parliaments may not be helpful, at least in the short term. If such a legislature is simply an indicator of fragmented power that makes legislative majorities difficult to come by, it may signal a deterioration in the capacity of the government to govern. Put simply, there are circumstances in which a strengthened legislature may denote a weakened and deeply divided state with a decreased capacity to act on crucial problems. If that is the case, strong parliaments may undermine their own prospects for long-term success. On the other hand, by ceding the control of economic reform to popularly elected presidents, parliaments may undermine their own legitimacy and pave the way for more long-term control by the executive, to the ultimate detriment of representative institutions.

Bibliography

Alda, M. and Nieto, L. L. (1994). 'Parliament in the transition and in the consolidation process: the case of Spain', in L. D. Longley (ed.), *Working Papers on Comparative Legislative Studies*. Appleton, WI: International Political Science Association Research Committee of Legislative Specialists.

Alivizatos, N. (1990). 'The difficulties of "rationalization" in a polarized political system: the Greek Chamber of Deputies', in U. Liebert and M. Cotta (eds), *Parliament and Democratic Consolidation in Southern Europe*. London: Pinter.

Andeweg, R. B. and Irwin, G. A. (1993). *Dutch Government and Politics*. New York: St Martin's Press.

Barker, A. and Rush, M. (1970). *The Member of Parliament and his Information*. London: Allen & Unwin.

Bielasiak, J. (1994). 'Institution building in a transformative system: party fragmentation in Poland's parliament', in L. D. Longley (ed.), *Working Papers on Comparative Legislative Studies*. Appleton, WI: International Political Science Association Research Committee of Legislative Specialists.

Bracher, K. D. (1968). 'The crisis of modern parliaments', in R. C. Macridis and B. E. Brown (eds), *Comparative Politics: notes and readings*, 3rd edn. Homewood, IL: Dorsey Press.

Cain, B. et al. (1987). *The Personal Vote: constituency service and electoral independence*. Cambridge, MA: Harvard University Press.

Cotta, M. (1990). 'The centrality of parliament in a protracted democratic consolidation: the Italian case', in U. Liebert and M. Cotta (eds), *Parliament and Democratic Consolidation in Southern Europe*. London: Pinter.

Crawford, K. (1994). 'Problems of institutionalization of parliamentary democracy: the federal assembly of the Czech and Slovak Federative Republic, 1990–1993', in L. D. Longley (ed.), *Working Papers on Comparative Legislative Studies*. Appleton, WI: International Political Science Association Research Committee of Legislative Specialists.

Da Cruz, M. B. and Antunes, M. L. (1990). 'Revolutionary transition and problems of parliamentary institutionalization: the case of the Portuguese national assembly', in U. Liebert and M. Cotta (eds), *Parliament and Democratic Consolidation in Southern Europe*. London: Pinter.

Damgaard, E. (1992). 'Denmark: experiments in parliamentary government', in E. Damgaard (ed.), *Parliamentary Change in the Nordic Countries*. Oslo: Scandinavian University Press.

Della Salla, V. (1993). 'The permanent committees of the Italian chamber of deputies: parliament at work?' *Legislative Studies Quarterly* 18 (May): 157–84.

Di Palma, G. (1977). *Surviving Without Governing: the Italian parties in parliament*. Berkeley: University of California Press.

Dowse, R. E. (1972). 'The MP and his surgery', in D. Leonard and V. Herman (eds), *The Backbencher and Parliament*. London: St Martin's Press.

Duverger, M. (1980). 'A new political system model: semi-presidential government'. *European Journal of Political Research* 8 (June): 165–87.

Farrell, B. (1985). 'Ireland: from friends and neighbours to clients and partisans: some dimensions of parliamentary representation under PR-STV', in V. Bogdanor (ed.), *Representatives of the People: parliamentarians and constituents in Western democracies*. Brookfield, VT: Gower.

Frears, J. (1985). 'The role of the député in France', in V. Bogdanor (ed.), *Representatives of the People: parliamentarians and constituents in Western democracies*. Brookfield, VT: Gower.

—— (1990). 'The French parliament: loyal workhorse, poor watchdog', in P. Norton (ed.), *Parliaments in Western Europe*. London: Frank Cass.

Giol, J. C. et al. (1990). 'By consociationalism to a majoritarian parliamentary system: the rise and decline of the Spanish Cortes', in U. Liebert and M. Cotta (eds), *Parliament and Democratic Consolidation in Southern Europe*. London: Pinter.

Gladdish, K. (1990a). 'Portugal: an open verdict', in G. Pridham (ed.), *Securing Democracy: political parties and democratic consolidation in Southern Europe*. London: Routledge.

—— (1990b). 'Parliamentary activity and legitimacy in the Netherlands', in P. Norton (ed.), *Parliaments in Western Europe*. London: Frank Cass.

—— (1991). *Governing from the Center: politics and policy-making in the Netherlands*. DeKalb: Northern Illinois University Press.

Held, D. (ed.) (1993). *Prospects for Democracy: North, South, East, West*. Cambridge: Polity Press; Stanford: Stanford University Press.

Hibbing, J. R. and Patterson, S. C. (1994). 'Public trust in the new parliaments of Central and Eastern Europe', in L. D. Longley (ed.), *Working Papers on Comparative Legislative Studies*. Appleton, WI: International Political Science Association Research Committee of Legislative Specialists.

Holc, J. P. (1993). 'Representations of parliament in Polish political discourse, 1990–1993'. Prepared for presentation at the Annual Meeting of the American Political

Science Association, Washington, DC, September.

—— (1994). 'Institution in post-communist polities: executive – legislative relations in Poland, 1990–1993', in L. D. Longley (ed.), *Working Papers on Comparative Legislative Studies*. Appleton, WI: International Political Science Association Research Committee of Legislative Specialists.

Horowitz, D. L. (1990). 'Comparing democratic systems'. *Journal of Democracy* 1 (fall): 73–9.

Ilonszki, G. (1994). 'From systemic change to consolidation: the Hungarian legislature – an institution in search of roles', in L. D. Longley (ed.), *Working Papers on Comparative Legislative Studies*. Appleton, WI: International Political Science Association Research Committee of Legislative Specialists.

Jogerst, M. (1993). *Reform in the House of Commons: the select committee system*. Lexington: University Press of Kentucky.

Lancaster, T. D. and Patterson, W. D. (1990). 'Comparative pork barrel politics: perceptions from the West German Bundestag'. *Comparative Political Studies* 22: 458–77.

Lewis, P. G. (1993). 'Democracy and its future in Eastern Europe', in D. Held (ed.), *Prospects for Democracy: North, South, East, West*. Cambridge: Polity Press; Stanford: Stanford University Press.

Liebert, U. (1990). 'Parliament in the consolidation of democracy: a comparative assessment of Southern European experiences', in U. Liebert and M. Cotta (eds), *Parliament and Democratic Consolidation in Southern Europe*. London: Pinter.

Light, P. (1982). *The President's Agenda: domestic policy choice from Kennedy to Carter*. Baltimore: Johns Hopkins University Press.

Lijphart, A. (1994). 'Presidentialism and majoritarian democracy: theoretical observations', in J. J. Linz and A. Valenzuela (eds), *The Failure of Presidential Democracy*. Baltimore: Johns Hopkins University Press.

Linz, J. J. (1994). 'Presidential or parliamentary democracy: does it make a difference', in J. J. Linz and A. Valenzuela (eds), *The Failure of Presidential Democracy*. Baltimore: Johns Hopkins University Press.

Loewenberg, G. (1967). *Parliament in the German Political System*. Ithaca, NY: Cornell University Press.

—— (1971). 'The role of parliament in modern political systems', in G. Loewenberg (ed.), *Modern Parliaments: change or decline*. Chicago: Aldine-Atherton.

Loewenberg, G. and Patterson, S. (1979). *Comparing Legislatures*. Boston: Little, Brown.

Machin, H. (1993). 'The president, the parties, and parliament', in J. Hayward (ed.), *De Gaulle to Mitterrand: presidential power in France*. New York: New York University Press.

MacMullen, A. (1985). 'Citizens and national parliamentarians in Belgium: sectional representation in a multi-party system', in V. Bogdanor (ed.), *Representatives of the People: parliamentarians and constituents in Western democracies*. Brookfield, VT: Gower.

Maravall, J. M. (1993). 'Politics and policy: economic reforms in Southern Europe', in L. C. B. Pereira, J. M. Maravall and A. Przeworski, *Economic Reforms in New Democracies: a social democratic approach*. Cambridge: Cambridge University Press.

Mezey, M. L. (1979). *Comparative Legislatures*. Durham, NC: Duke University Press.

—— (1989). *Congress, the President, and Public Policy*. Boulder, CO: Westview Press.

Mishler, W. and Rose, R. (1994). 'Support for parliaments and regimes in the transition to democracy in Eastern Europe'. *Legislative Studies Quarterly* 19 (February): 5–32.

Muller, W. (1993). 'Executive – legislative relations in Austria, 1945–1992'. *Legislative Studies Quarterly* 18 (November): 467–94.

Norton, P. (1990). 'Parliament in the United Kingdom: balancing effectiveness and consent?' in P. Norton (ed.), *Parliaments in Western Europe*. London: Frank Cass.

Norton, P. and Wood, D. M. (1993). *Back From Westminster: constituency service by British members of parliament*. Lexington: University Press of Kentucky.

Paczolay, P. (1993). 'The new Hungarian constitutional state: challenges and perspectives', in A. E. D. Howard (ed.), *Constitution Making in Eastern Europe*. Washington, DC: Woodrow Wilson Center Press.

Patzelt, W. J. (1994). 'Legislators of new parliaments: the case of East Germany', in L. D. Longley (ed.), *Working Papers on Comparative Legislative Studies*. Appleton, WI: International Political Science Association Research Committee of Legislative Specialists.

Pereira, L. C. B. (1993). 'Economic reforms and economic growth: efficiency and politics in Latin America', in L. C. B. Pereira et al., *Economic Reforms in New Democracies: a social democratic approach*. Cambridge: Cambridge University Press.

Przeworski, A. (1991). *Democracy and the Market: political and economic reforms in Eastern Europe and Latin America*. Cambridge: Cambridge University Press.

—— (1993). 'Economic reforms, public opinion, and political institutions in the Eastern European perspective', in L. C. B. Pereira et al., *Economic Reforms in New Democracies: a social democratic approach*. Cambridge: Cambridge University Press.

Rapaczynski, A. (1993). 'Constitutional politics in Poland: a report on the constitutional committee of the Polish parliament', in A. E. D. Howard (ed.), *Constitution Making in Eastern Europe*. Washington, DC: Woodrow Wilson Center Press.

Remington, T. F. et al. (1994). 'Voting alignments in the Russian Congress of People's Deputies', in L. D. Longley (ed.), *Working Papers on Comparative Legislative Studies*. Appleton, WI: International Political Science Association Research Committee of Legislative Specialists.

Rommetvedt, H. (1992). 'Norway: from consensus majority parliamentarism to dissensual minority parliamentarism', in E. Damgaard (ed.), *Parliamentary Change in the Nordic Countries*. Oslo: Scandinavian University Press.

Rose, R. (1986). 'British MPs: more bark than bite?' in E. Suleiman (ed.), *Parliament and Parliamentarians in Democratic Politics*. New York: Holmes & Meier.

Saalfeld, T. (1990). 'The West German Bundestag after forty years: the role of parliament in a "party democracy" ', in P. Norton (ed.), *Parliaments in Western Europe*. London: Frank Cass.

Sannerstedt, A. and Sjolin, M. (1992). 'Sweden: changing party relations in a more active parliament', in Erik Damgaard (ed.), *Parliamentary Change in the Nordic Countries*. Oslo: Scandinavian University Press.

Searing, D. D. (1994). *Westminster's World: understanding political roles*. Cambridge, MA: Harvard University Press.

Shugart, M. S. and Carey, J. M. (1992). *Presidents and Assemblies: constitutional design and electoral dynamics*. Cambridge: Cambridge University Press.

Stepan, A. and Skach, C. (1994). 'Presidentialism and parliamentarism in comparative perspective', in J. J. Linz and A. Valenzuela (eds), *The Failure of Presidential Democracy*. Baltimore: Johns Hopkins University Press.

Strom, K. (1990). *Minority Government and Majority Rule*. Cambridge: Cambridge University Press.

Suleiman, E. N. (1994). 'Presidentialism and political stability in France', in J. J. Linz and A. Valenzuela (eds), *The Failure of Presidential Democracy*. Baltimore: Johns Hopkins University Press.

Sundquist, J. L. (1981). *The Decline and Resurgence of Congress*. Washington, DC: Brookings Institution.

Wheare, K. C. (1963). *Legislatures*. London: Oxford University Press.

Whitehead, L. (1993). 'The alternative to "liberal democracy": a Latin American perspective', in D. Held (ed.), *Prospects for Democracy: North, South, East, West*. Cambridge: Polity Press; Stanford: Stanford University Press.

8

Organized Interests and Public Policies

Jack Hayward

In their diversity, European states seem to be located between a Western pole represented by the USA as the model 'society-led state' and the former Soviet Union as embodying the typical 'state-led society'. The latter has withered away, not through the attainment of communism but its decomposition. It rejected the Anglo-American view that legitimate state authority derived from society, because it was deemed to be made up of selfish, sectional interests collectively damned as capitalist in inspiration and motivation. Despite its claim to have given power to the proletariat, the subordination of all the manifestations of the wishes of working people to the will of the leaders of the Communist Party and their bureaucratic minions in the state apparatus – collectively known as the *nomenklatura* – meant that an immense effort was made to deprive the individual, group and community components of society of all autonomy. This totalitarian urge failed in practice to achieve its ambition, but it paralysed the pluralist forces that had provided both the impetus and the countervailing constraints in the liberal democratic market societies.

For their part, the 'society-led states' were not able to confine governmental activities to a minimally instrumental and persistently suspect subordinate role. With a range of variation that reflects the oversimplifying nature of the state – society distinction, continental Western European polities sometimes accorded a priority to the state–when conjoined with the nation – as an all-embracing community comparable to the Eastern European polities when the state and working class were conflated. Even in those polities which sought hardest to limit government intervention, the demands made politically effective by democracy compelled increased social and economic public provision, leading to spectacular increases in the number of state employees and public expenditure. The initiation, elaboration and implementation of a proliferation of public policies provide the focus for the encounter between organized interests and the other actors in the intricate process which constitutes the political system at work.

As society became increasingly diversified, between the mass of individuals and families on the one hand and government on the other, there emerged intermediate bodies that organized the plurality of people's interests as they related to their collective political, social and economic activities. While they might be primarily for the purpose of regulating wealth creation or social protection, like the medieval guilds, such bodies would have dealings with governmental authorities, if only in relation to taxation to pay for the public services that were confined largely to the military sphere. However, particularly with the industrialization of the market economy and urbanization, the process of diversification became such that the belief that an undifferentiated public interest could subsume all sectional interests increasingly lost its credibility. In any case, both state and society shed their relatively monolithic character.

Pluralism became, by the late nineteenth century, not merely a plausible way of conceptualizing the advanced industrial societies of Western and to a lesser extent Central Europe; it was on the whole empirically accurate, albeit struggling for expression within the straitjacket of state legalism. Despite attempts to curb their activities or even to deny them legal recognition, trade unions were established to defend the interests of industrial workers. Business organizations – chambers of commerce and trade associations – were also created, though in their case official encouragement rather than repression reflected a bias in the enforcement of the traditional view that there were no legitimate interests other than the public interest in matters of collective concern or of individuals in matters of private concern.

As political activity was not merely a matter of defending or promoting material interests, some people were recruited to organizations promoting a cause, such as the abolition of the slave trade and then of slavery or the prevention of cruelty to children or animals. These bodies were regarded as pressure groups because they represented members of society seeking to influence the exercise of power by state authorities to coerce, regulate or subsidize, without themselves taking over governmental functions. As such, the institutional separation between society and state appeared to be preserved, but, because the same name was used to describe both groups that were continuously and mainly or only intermittently and secondarily concerned with influencing government, the term 'pressure group' was a source of confusion.

Furthermore, in stressing the unilateral pressure of societal groups on the state and its agencies, the early Anglo-American studies of organized interests unconsciously expressed their liberal bias about the priority and legitimacy of groups over governments. They neglected the bilateral nature of group–government relationships, as a consequence of which groups could be pressured as well as exert pressure. Just as the market economy was supposed to work harmoniously through the automatically self-regulating mechanisms of supply and demand, so the plurality of interest organizations were assumed to interact in ways that would ensure that all needs were articulated prior to being satisfied.

However, the public interest could not be expected to emerge from the interaction of private interests. In authoritarian political systems, even – perhaps especially – those where democracy had replaced autocracy, once the official bodies deemed to express the one and indivisible public interest had taken a decision, they were entitled to bend all and sundry to their will. Any opposition was by definition illegitimate, betraying its nature as a partial or even sinister interest. While such a repressive attitude was far from unknown in Western Europe, being a legacy of absolute monarchy via the Jacobin First French Republic to its successors and emulators, it had its fullest expression in the communist regimes of East-Central Europe modelled on the USSR. However, a form of pluralism took its revenge within such systems, through the fragmentation of their bureaucratic apparatus, with the paradoxical result that their comprehensive effort to coerce into conformity was partially frustrated and distorted by the very instrument dedicated to its enforcement.

Parts of the would-be monolithic public authority also entered into collusive relationships with selected outside interests, particularly those that were regarded as cooperative or could provide information or support that was necessary to effective public action. These were accorded 'insider' status. Where the intimacy of such ties between public and private bodies reached the point of virtual symbiosis, it has been customary to describe them as neo-corporatist. As we shall see, this is only one of several types of relationship, ranging from voluntary association to compulsory association, that can exist when one leaves the polarized world of a separated state and society to explore the space in between them. We shall consider the many forms that their confrontation, consultation, concertation and cooptation take as they collaborate in loose issue networks, tighter patron–client networks or closed policy communities across the spectrum of European states.

Group–Government Relations

The great diversity that we encounter in group–government interaction suggests the need for simplicity's sake to distinguish the main forms it takes. These can be envisaged as varying between forms of association that are completely voluntary to those that are entirely compulsory, as they are formed in state-led societies or society-led states. Four predominant types can be derived form the distinctions made, and they are set out in figure 8.1.

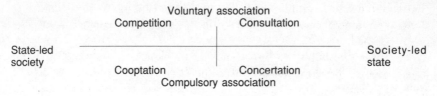

Figure 8.1   *Four stereotypes of group–government relations*

1   Voluntary association in society-led states readily lends itself to a plural-ist analysis. This liberal approach treats the relations between organized 'private' interests and government as similar to market interaction between organizations. In its extreme version, the self-effacing government divests itself of as many of its functions as possible to society and market. It has become the new prescriptive model for parts of East-Central Europe by extension from its Anglo-American progenitors. The competitive nature of the interaction be-tween groups and with government, while it may take the form of mutual tolerance, can easily degenerate into adversarial confrontation, which is the form in which it poses a political problem as group pressure by 'outsiders' on those who take official decisions.

2   Voluntary association in state-led societies corresponds to a semi-struc-tured pluralism in which public action cannot simply be confined to policing and creating suitable conditions in which voluntary organization can freely operate. Between the preferences of organized private interests and the government decisions taken in the name of the public interest, some accom-modation is necessary. This mutual accommodation will characteristically take the form of a loose policy network between 'private' and 'public' actors but may acquire the more permanent and closely integrated form of a policy community. Those organizations judged by governments to be representative and 'responsible' will be accorded non-commital consultative status. What these interests lose in relative autonomy may be compensated by the influence that they hope to exercise over public decisions. The danger is that they may be confined to inducing their interest group members to act in conformity with government preferences in return for modest concessions and 'insider' status.

3   Compulsory association in society-led states assumes that people are clustered in vertically segmented subsystems in which neither organized groups nor governments are able to exert unilateral control over the agenda,

groups nor governments are able to exert unilateral control over the agenda, timing, scope and content of the decisions concerning their interaction. Interdependence between the private interests and the public administration has reached the point that some type of joint control becomes desirable or even indispensable. Concertation becomes the continuous practice and in some cases may go as far as acquiring the cartellized characteristic associated with neo-corporatism. However, just as consultation can verge on concertation – leading to a blurring of the boundaries between types 2 and 3 – so concertation can, when fully developed, become difficult to distinguish from weak forms of cooptation.

4   Compulsory association in state-led societies in its extreme form corresponds to the virtually total subordination of organized interests to the all-absorbing state apparatus in the Fascist and Nazi regimes of the 1920s to the 1940s and the communist regimes imposed upon East-Central Europe on the model of the Soviet Union. Groups lose all 'privacy' and become incorporated by the government as agents of the state. Although it seems as far removed as possible from voluntary association in the society-led category, we shall see in the case of Poland in the late 1970s how this totalitarian type can lead to confrontation, as the repressed organizations of civil society seek to assert themselves, before the comprehensive collapse of this system a decade later throughout East-Central Europe as well as the USSR.

These four stereotypes have the merit of focusing attention on some salient features of group–government relations, but they are static in character. To impart a more dynamic way of looking at the interaction of organized interest and the public authorities, it is necessary first to consider the contrasting contexts in which they operate and then to describe the main stages of the policy agenda setting and implementing process. This will allow us to link our typology to a comparison of the ways in which organized interests have acted in actual European states and in attempting to resolve specific policy problems.

Policy Contexts

The contextual dimensions with which organized interests are confronted in deciding how to defend or promote their policy objectives are, first, whether they are concerned with everyday, humdrum, routine situations or with exceptional, heroic crisis situations. Second, is the political system in which they are operating one in which it is customary to reach decisions by imposition or by consensus? In combination, these two criteria may help us to distinguish the four ways (figure 8.2) in which group–government relations vary both cross-nationally and between policy sectors, as well as over time.

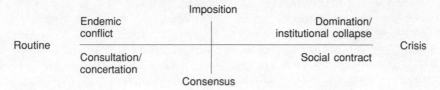

Figure 8.2   *Four contexts of group—government relations*

The first situation, endemic conflict, corresponds to that of 'outsider' interests in permanent conflict with government. This situation was character- istic of communist East-Central Europe whenever organized interests tried to achieve an autonomous existence. It began to break down in the 1980s as governments, notably in Poland and Hungary, found that routine imposition was proving doubly ineffective. It was neither yielding the results desired by government nor was it being successful in imposing the government's will. This was especially true of the relations between the Roman Catholic Church and the KOR trade union with the Polish Government. The party-state was manifestly losing its grip. However, in France and Italy, where communists controlled the major trade unions, the relations of the latter with governments and other organized interests were also characterized by endemic conflict. Even in Britain, where the major trade unions adopted an extra-legal, 'outlaw' attitude towards governments – especially but not exclusively Conservative governments – strikes were the normal, routine way of resolving conflict. In the 1980s, however, British trade unions were increasingly subjected to legal regulation, as the Conservative Government curbed their capacity to paralyse the industrial or transport system.

The second situation, that of consultation or concertation, could be re- garded as the harmonious, routine way of resolving policy problems between organized interests and government. The less committed, arms-length version is that of consultation, government bodies listening to the views of various concerned interests. The latter may present their proposals or reactions separ- ately or in joint meetings but, while they are listened to, they are unlikely to get their way except from time to time and in part. Consultation is the antechamber to the closer, sustained collaboration of concertation, corre- sponding to a shift from involvement in a policy network to a more selective, intimate policy community, where a greater measure of consensus can be expected and is generally and regularly achieved. Thus, whereas in the 1950s and 1960s, when French national planning was a relatively effective part of economic policy-making, the process of committee concertation between senior civil servants, businessmen and trade unionists had an effect both on government decisions and on the behaviour of those participating in the meetings, this subsequently ceased to be true. The Soviet-style planning prevalent in East-Central Europe was conducted without the need to persuade autonomous organized interests to cooperate, so that it corresponded to the bureaucratic pluralism of intra-administrative bargaining and clientelism.

Going even further than concertation, where the links between organized interests and government do not deprive either side of their autonomy, neo-corporatism – which we shall discuss later – draws upon an older tradition of Social Catholicism that had strong roots in Austria, Italy and Spain, where it took the Fascist form of corporatism. However, there it was imposed rather than negotiated between state and society, and was an attempt to replace territorial, democratic party representation by functional, anti-democratic interest representation. In the diluted form of neo-corporatism, characteristic of postwar Austria and to a more limited extent Germany, Sweden and Switzerland, it sought to counteract the tendency of a pluralist and interest group system to generate conflicts, substituting state control for market competititon. Interdependence was considered to require a loss of autonomy in the service of maximizing consensus. However, it presupposed so large a loss of independence and so much organizational discipline that it proved impractical in most policy areas in countries like Britain, France and Italy, while communist state corporatism was a thinly disguised form of party-state control. Whereas consultation leaves ideological divisions intact and concertation may blunt them, corporatist practices require a commitment to a social Catholic, social democratic or communist ideological orthodoxy in terms of which freedom of action can be foregone.

The shift from the routine side of figure 8.2 to the crisis side requires clarification of the term 'crisis'. It may not be a short-term convulsion but a protracted period of breakdown in the 'normal' policy-making process, such as many East-Central European countries are currently experiencing. During a crisis it is tempting to believe that it will be possible to get over the transitional difficulties, but in East-Central Europe the difficulty in setting up effective organizations of the major interests ensures that the temporary will endure indefinitely. The legacy of 'You pretend to pay us, we pretend to work' is a perverse version of the 'social contract' that it is hard to shake off. Western-style 'social contracts' between interests and governments – to restrain inflation by a summit agreement on prices and incomes – have proved ephemeral but worked for a while in Britain and Germany in the latter half of the 1960s. They broke down because they imposed too great a strain upon the natural inclinations of firms to raise prices and trade unions to increase wages for consensus to hold. The temptation to infringe even 'solemn and binding' agreements meant that such contracts could not be more than temporary expedients. This was the case even when the British or Polish trade unions backed the policies of governments to which they had given life, once they took the form of restraining or reducing the living standards of their members. This points up the difficulties of political parties that seek to aggregate the interests of organizations belonging to the same 'movement' – like the Labour Party and trade unions in Britain – because their priorities and purposes are not necessarily convergent.

Finally, the fourth context – imposition of crisis solutions to policy problems – is characteristic of East-Central Europe and the successor states of the former Soviet Union, especially in conditions of institutional collapse. However, the authoritarian style of decision-making appears appropriate, even in the liberal democracies of Western Europe, at times of crisis. Thus, in 1958, faced by the imminent institutional collapse of the Fourth Republic, de Gaulle imposed not merely new institutions but a whole series of policies that had hitherto been victims of an immobilism in which organized interests were able to paralyse weak and ephemeral governments. In Italy, the corrupt clientelist system collapsed during the 1993 avalanche of politico-economic scandals, rendering it possible to undertake reforms of the policy-making process, as well as restructuring policy networks that had seemed impregnably entrenched.

In the case of the post-communist regimes, the reaction against a style of decision-making characterized by party-state domination has led to what may be a more or less prolonged period of institutional collapse and semi-paralysis of the policy process. Various scenarios can be envisaged in this situation, ranging from the most reassuring – movement in the next five years to a consultation/concertation normality – via pathological versions of the social contract and endemic conflict, to a new form of domination. What is clear is that the massive shift from public to private ownership has changed the post-communist context of interest group–government relations even more dramatically than have the privatization programmes of Britain in the 1980s and France and Italy in the 1990s. At the same time, the increase of unemployment across Europe has so weakened the position of the trade unions, both in the labour market and within the political process, that the balance of power among organized interests and between them and governments has been drastically modified.

Policy Process

To see how organized interests intervene in the policy process in dynamic rather than static terms, we need to consider them in a more elaborate version of the policy agenda setting and implementing process. We shall distinguish pre-policy, policy-making proper and post-policy-making stages. Somewhat government nor organized interests have become aware of the existence of a problem requiring their attention. Before we can move to identification of a policy issue, something must occur or someone must act to engender the political birth of a problem. While the communist regimes of Eastern Europe were in control, their party/governments sought to ensure a monopoly over this potentially threatening source of innovation. Where they could not control the external agencies through which problems were placed on the agenda, such as the media, these 'closed societies' sought to eliminate them altogether by jamming foreign broadcasts. The result was that these would-be revolutionary regimes became relatively immune to change until the eruption of movements such as Solidarity in Poland or the Chernobyl nuclear disaster in the Ukraine meant that it was no longer possible to confine policy-making to officially approved channels. Overindulgence in inertia eventually precipitated institutional collapse. By contrast, the 'open societies' of liberal democratic Western Europe are much more exposed to the innovative pressures of policy problems, whose existence they are compelled to acknowledge. While they might be reluctant to act at all, governments will usually endeavour to muddle along. By a combination of *ad hoc* incrementalism and crisis management, environmental or industrial policies, for example, can be avoided until specific problems assume proportions that prevent attempts to sidestep the need to formulate a new policy.

In moving to the *policy-making process* proper, we need to separate the three phases concerned with the 'insiders' and excluding the 'outsiders' from the three phases concerned with making and legitimating the policy choices. Once an issue has been thrust onto the policy agenda the decision-making structures allocate it to an existing subsystem or create a new one. This sectorization of policies raises difficulties because many problems overlap a number of sectors. Can the electro-nuclear energy sector be separated from the environmental or military-industrial sectors, for example? Nevertheless, if only for reasons of orderly bureaucratic organization, a subsystem with the main responsibility must be selected and this will have important implications for the way the policy problem is subsequently handled. In particular, it will influence the constitution of the personal and organizational networks of actors accepted as partners in the consultation or concertation processes to deal with the problem. Where those concerned share sufficient common policies and purposes – a characteristic particularly of producer and professional interests – they are more inclined to engage in continuous collaboration within a 'closed' sectoral policy community. This nucleus of policy 'insiders' may achieve sufficient stability to reintroduce some of the predictability and continuity that was disturbed by the initial disruption of policy inertia.

The policy issue having been identified and allocated to a set of public and

The policy issue having been identified and allocated to a set of public and private policy actors, we move to the process of fitting the solutions that are worked out in these arenas into the wider normative, institutional and legitimizing processes. The micro-political or macro-political norms at the local and sectoral levels have to be reconciled with the macro-political norms that prevail more generally. Thus in Eastern Europe, the meso-political shift from nationalization to privatization of industry has to be related to micro-political adjustments at the level of the firm and macro-political changes substituting market competitiveness for state control. Similar changes – of a less cataclysmic nature – occurred in Western Europe, although the timing, extent and manner of the policy upheaval was different in individual countries and sectors. The switch from the macro-economic norm of full employment to reducing inflation occurred more gradually and surreptitiously in the late 1960s and early 1970s in Western Europe (although delayed in Sweden until the end of the 1980s), whereas in Eastern Europe full employment ceased to be a public policy priority very quickly and sweepingly after the demise of their communist regimes. However, they have frequently suffered from extreme versions of stagflation: massive unemployment and inflation.

The task of working out a detailed, practicable solution to the policy problem passes from the covert discussions between organized interests and bureaucrats to the overt, partisan political process. Parties, outsider groups and public opinion may want to have their say if the issue is not simply a routine matter; the more controversial the issue, the more adversarial the discussion may become, with the possibility of the solution more or less laboriously negotiated being significantly modified. Until the late 1980s this was seldom likely in the former communist states, hence the traumatic effect upon their party/government leaders when opposition, in the form of incipient parties and interest organizations, emerged from illegality. The adjustment to a process that has taken centuries in Western Europe – tolerating opposition as non-subversive and then welcoming it as a constructive contribution to the policy process – is still painfully in its experimental stage in Central Europe, most advanced in the Czech Republic and Hungary, with Eastern Europe further behind.

The process of policy legitimization by parliament and the courts is again one where until recently the two halves of Europe were sharply contrasted, although the capacity of these institutions to change policy proposals worked out earlier should not be exaggerated. Nevertheless, between the rubber-stamping parliaments of Eastern Europe, which met for a handful of days each year to transact their literally formal business, and those of Western Europe, we have all the difference between political systems where intermediation and representation have been reduced to a caricature and those where they can still legitimate because they are more than a formality. As far as the courts are concerned, organized interests such as trade unions have had a curious experience with them. Declared illegal for restraining trade in labour during the era of laissez-faire in Britain and France, they were first tolerated and then legalized only to be subjected in Britain in the 1980s to a legislative onslaught because they had become powerful enough to defy or even unseat governments, as occurred after the coal miners' strike in Britain in 1973–4. In the 1980s, the shipyard workers at Gdansk in Poland spearheaded the creation of Solidarity, first repressed and then triumphant, only to split once it had helped overthrow the communist regime and was faced with the task of governing. Having been much more than a trade union it has found it difficult to revert to a more modest role.

The *post-policy-making stages* are the least spectacular but in many ways the most significant from the standpoint of the consumers of public policy as well as the organized producer and professional interests. The agreed policy must be implemented and it is only then that it begins to make a real impact. It is often adapted at this stage in ways that were not intended to meet the unanticipated difficulties encountered or to placate interests that were frustrated at earlier stages in the policy process. 'Dynamic conservatism' comes into play to ensure that the changes made are those necessary to keep things as they are. This leads naturally into the phase of routine administration, in which the problems that initiated the process we have been tracing have found their resolution. This would be the end of the story if routine placidity was not disturbed by the emergence of new problems or the evaluation of existing policies exposing unresolved old problems. Faced with either or both of these predicaments, there will be a need to return to the second stage of the policy cycle owing to the rebirth of a problem to be resolved.

Networks and Communities: the Neo-Pluralist Public Policy Process

In East-Central Europe, much of what follows cannot apply in a generally meaningful way because, although the party-state monopoly of power had begun to decompose even before the collapse of the communist regimes, they have so far seldom been capable of creating effective organizations of interest intermediation. Although Hankiss detected the emergence in Hungary of a 'second society' in the years 1965 to 1985, in which the slow re-emergence of the social networks destroyed in the immediate postwar period allowed some 'informal interest mediation' through 'behind-the-scenes interest group politics', this was of a very limited character (Hankiss 1990, 83). '. . . It was characterized by client–patron relationships, oligarchic and nepotistic mechanisms, corruption, informal bargaining between state agencies and dependent economic and social actors' (Hankiss 1990, 107; cf. 105–10). Although these are features which are far from unfamiliar elsewhere in Europe and are especially well documented in Italy, it led to a dysfunctional policy stalemate because it was subsidiary to a statist and monopolistic first society that prevented the emergence of a competitive market economy. Instead, it 'produced vicious hybrids, low-efficiency mixes' (Hankiss 1990, 109), owing to the incompatibility of this unofficial proto-pluralism with the official centralized, hierarchical structures. So, although the 'second economy' was tolerated, attempts to build networks of interest intermediation were successfully obstructed by the party-state elites. Hankiss concluded that, 'when the second economy had already been completely atomized, politically neutralized, and colonized by the ruling elite, then it could be legalized' (Hankiss 1990, 120). If Hungary has not yet extricated itself from the subsequent attempt to dismantle and reconstruct this counter-productive system, how much more is this true of the other post-communist polities.

We have seen earlier that, between an explanation based exclusively on market interaction and one based wholly on intra-state interaction, there are several neo-pluralist types of inter-organizational explanation of the agencies of interest intermediation. Without going into the confusions over nomenclature used by different exponents of the policy networks–community approach, let us briefly consider its salient features. It has been motivated by a wish to 'go beyond the ever more elaborately qualified versions of pluralism and corporatism to capture more directly the central features of policy making' and does so from a 'broadly pluralistic perspective' aimed at reconciling competition between interest organizations with 'the stable and sectorised patterns of policy-making uncovered in case studies' (Jordan and Schubert 1992, 8–9; see also Marsh and Rhodes 1992, 181–205, and Rhodes 1990, 293–317). The generic term 'network' relativizes the unilateral dichotomies between statism and pluralism, between statist and societal corporatism and so forth. We need a sufficiently elastic concept to embrace a multitude of diverse and shifting policy situations which can be distinguished into segmented subtypes. Networks are characteristic of a policy environment that contains a plurality of reciprocally recognized, informally interacting, public and private sectorized organizations. They may be more or less open and enduring. Although most of the findings on policy networks have been of a sectoral kind, they can be transectoral and can become global in their scope if only because the interdependent nature of policies makes it difficult to avoid relating sectoral activities to a more comprehensive setting.

A policy network is an identifiable group of interacting bureaucrats, interest group representatives and (to a lesser extent) politicians whose purposes are sufficiently interdependent to seek to cooperate in achieving them. It is intermediate between the individualist world of the market and the formal organization of government. Only when it acquires the cohesive form of a structured pluralism will a network become a more stable policy community of 'insiders', who are prepared to subordinate their disagreements about objectives to their wish to preserve the solidarity of the community. The reasons why such relationships develop can be simply stated, bearing in mind the stages of the policy process described earlier.

> Administrators need political support, legitimacy, information, coalition partners in their competition with other sections of the bureaucracy, and assistance in the implementation. Interest groups on the other hand desire access to public policy formation and implementation, and concessions in their interests or those of their constituents. These different needs motivate and produce exchanges and transactions. When repeated often these exchanges may become institutionalised in network structures [which] constrain the successive options open to the actors . . . (Van Waarden 1992a, 31)

Van Waarden has distinguished between types of policy network according to seven major dimensions. First, there is the number of network *actors*, their interests and conception of their role, their degree of professionalization and whether they have a representational monopoly. Second, the network *functions* range between lobbying and concertation. They include channelling access to decision-makers, consultation, negotiation, coordination, cooperation in policy formation and implementation, going as far under corporatism as the delegation to the selected interest group of public authority. Third, the network *structures* vary in whether they are open or closed, whether membership is voluntary or compulsory, the frequency and duration of member interaction, the multiplicity of links, whether the relations are hierarchical or based upon bargaining, cooperative or conflictual, centralized or decentralized. Fourth, is the network highly *institutionalized* and stable? Fifth, are the *behavioural relations* of an adversarial, or consensual kind, explicitly aimed at serving the public rather than private interests, formal or informal, secretive or open, politicized or depoliticized, ideological or pragmatic? Sixth, the *power* of the government relative to the organized interests – state autonomy, state capture or symbiosis – needs to be ascertained, Seventh, what are the strategies of government and groups in seeking or rejecting official recognition, providing/ receiving support, changing bureaucratic or group structures? (Van Waarden 1992a, 33–41).

Despite being concerned mainly with non-controversial decisions which belong in the routine-consensus stereotype of group–government relations (see figure 8.2 above), we are clearly faced with a highly complex and unpredictable kind of decision-making. Fortunately, 'public policy is largely the aggregation of minor matters of little interest to those not immediately affected' (Jordan 1992, 11). When we move from the world of low politics to controversial high politics, the policy issues usually have to be reduced to what is manageable within the confines of a particular policy community. Uncertainty is a great source of anxiety to those involved in policy-making. Policy networks and policy communities help to reduce political uncertainty by giving advance warning of problems and providing serviceable structures and procedures for dealing with them. Although they generally have a bias towards the status quo or to incremental change, their prime function is to keep state and society in step.

A Diversity of Group–Government Relations

In applying these ways of conceptualizing the role of organized interests, some of the contrasts between different countries, notably between Western and Eastern Europe, have begun to emerge. For example, it is clear that the growth of state intervention in markets, even in countries such as Britain where the policy commitment to free trade can be regarded as an early manifestation of the effectiveness of group pressure, was a major impetus to the development of organized interests. Otherwise, the state would lose touch with society except in its coercive capacity. However, in post-communist Eastern Europe, it required the retreat of state intervention to allow enough free space for autonomous organized interests to emerge or re-emerge and mediate between enfeebled governments and the nascent markets and civil society.

This is an oversimplified dichotomy because in many Western European countries, such as Germany and France but not Britain and the Netherlands, the normative priority of state over society placed organized interests in a position of dubious legitimacy. While this usually took a statist form, it could also assume a societal disguise in the unattractive shape of Fascist corporatism in Italy and Spain with the aim of denying market capitalism, group pluralism and liberal democracy, whereas the totalitarian conception of communist systems in East-Central Europe exaggerated the extent to which a non-autonomous society could be comprehensively subordinated to the party-state. Especially in former Yugoslavia but also in Central European Czechoslavakia, East Germany, Hungary and Poland, stern repression should not be equated with successful suppression.

Although references to the existence of partial and limited forms of socialist pluralism – intended to correct the rival totalitarian exaggeration – lend themselves to ambiguous and misleading interpretations (Brown 1974, ch. 3; Skilling 1966 and 1983; Brunner and Kaschkat 1979; and Holmes, 1986), they help us avoid the assumption that post-communist countries had no dissentient and dissident group basis from which to construct or reconstruct a fully fledged pluralist economy, society and polity. However, it was because of official denial of their right to autonomous organization that interests which resisted party-state domination were driven into either the twilight *samizdat* existence of endemic confrontation with the political authorities or open political revolt against them.

Confrontation between organized interests and government

This can take a statist and a pluralist form of an extreme kind. In the first case, governments seek to dominate the organized interests; in the second case, the interests try to 'capture' the government body or bodies concerned. They are both attempts at 'winner takes all'. State domination may be justified as the only legitimate authority because it represents the national interest as against sectional interests or because it represents the dictatorship of 'the proletariat' over 'the bourgoisie'. Interest group capture – which is seldom achieved except at the sectoral level, unless one is going to treat the military or the bureaucracy as an interest group – may take the form of Church or business domination of public policy, although even in these instances it is generally only partial, like farm organizations dominating the policies pursued by the Ministry of Agriculture. However, in the case of the Polish Solidarity movement, we have an example of what purported to be a trade union, supported by the Catholic Church and a section of the intelligentsia, initially making piecemeal demands upon the communist party-state but in the ensuing confrontation becoming engaged in a life and death struggle. While the Communist Party gained the upper hand thanks to a military coup in December 1981, Solidarity had the last laugh at the end of the decade. Its triumph was due to international events beyond the control of either adversary but proved short-lived because of the problems of becoming a party in power. Let us consider the contrasting Soviet and Polish cases of pseudo-pluralism in turn.

Before the collapse of the communist regimes at the end of the 1980s, Archie Brown exposed the pseudo-pluralist interpretation of Soviet politics to searching criticism. Not merely was pluralism in the Western sense anathema to the communists; they denied even relative autonomy from state-party control to interest organizations. Acknowledging that institutional rivalries existed between different branches of the state and public sector apparatus – bureaucratic, managerial and territorial – just as these existed in liberal democratic political systems, he argued that interest group pluralism is stretched so far that 'it plays down differences that are substantially more important than the similarities between the Soviet system and certain Western systems . . . and less important distinctions between different Communist systems at different times' (Brown 1984, 61; cf. 58–64). Thus Czechoslovakia before, during and after the Prague Spring of 1968 or Poland before, during and after the toleration of Solidarity in 1980–1 did not involve differences of pluralist degree but a difference in kind of political regime.

In the Soviet Union, it was only after the Gorbachev *glasnost* destabilization of 'the structure of simulated assent' in the late 1980s that dissident intellectuals, youth or environmentalists created autonomous organizations. However, unlike the nationalist movements notably in the Baltic states and Armenia, the Russians were not able to develop effective 'popular fronts' of intellectuals and workers because the intellectual dissidents of the 'shadow culture' based on shared values rather than shared interests were unable to create a mass based alliance (Hosking 1992, 2–23, 31–4, 54; Rigby 1992, 312–16). Hopes that the miners' strikes of 1989 and 1991 would lay the foundations of a Solidarity-style Russia-wide trade union movement proved illusory. The mass of Russian workers 'rarely wavered in their hostility to the old régime and in their support for market reform but the organisational cohesion that was required for this to develop into a powerful movement continuously eluded them' (Aves 1992, 139; cf. 153). Not only did regional and local differences prevent the emergence of a national solidarity such as that achieved in Poland; conflicts of interest between profitable and unprofitable mines and factories were exposed by the tentative introduction of market methods. Potentially more effective are 'organisations for people leasing enterprises from the state, new independent entrepreneurs, cooperative members, managers of state enterprises, and chairmen and directors of state farms', but 'as yet the employers have not developed clear local or industry-based organisational structures, and there is no regular or established framework for negotiation with government or organised labour' (Cox 1993, 80–1).

The failure of Gorbachev's 'belief that interest groups could be co-opted into a grand pro-perestroika alliance under the leadership of a reformed Communist Party', based on the assumption that 'there was a basic harmony of interests underlying the Soviet system' (Cox 1993, 84), might have been inferred from the Polish experience, despite the striking differences of the two political contexts. The so-called Polish United Workers Party in power had tried to achieve a compromise with the embodiment of the survival of national culture after centuries of foreign occupation and dismemberment: the Roman Catholic Church. It did so by conceding a substantial measure of religious and some cultural and socio-economic autonomy, in particular to private farmers. However, in the 1970s the strong 'kinship' link between the Church and important bodies of Catholic intellectuals and workers led to the development of a network through which popular discontent with declining living standards and lack of freedom could take an organized form, assisted by the election of a Polish Pope in John Paul II in 1978. While the failure of the post-1968 Czech attempt to achieve a reform communism led to a fight for human rights in the Charter 77 non-mass movement, in Poland the intellectual dissidents were able to win mass support from both the Church and the industrial working classes. It was the KOR Workers Defence Committee, set up in 1976 to support the workers tried for anti-price rise strikes, followed by the Gdansk Shipyard Free Trade Union in 1978, that created the 'nationwide opposition network' that rallied to the 1980 Gdansk shipyard strike and made Solidarity possible (Garton Ash 1991a, 27; cf. 20–33, 83 and 1991b).

That Solidarity was to be much more than a trade union was symbolized by the fact that its progenitors in KOR had by 1977 widened the name of their organization from *Workers* Defence to *Social* Self-Defence. The lack of both an autonomous civil and political society meant that, if the Polish people were to acquire the capacity to assert their interests against party-state domination, they would have to acquire independent trade unions that were more than defensive of their sectional interests. Whereas in Hungary it was possible to follow a strategy of 'getting around the system rather than confronting it, of finding loopholes and niches rather than making demands of the state' (Garton Ash 1991b, 133; see also Pelczynski 1988, 368–75 and Pravda 1983, 248–57), in Poland Solidarity became the organization focusing society-wide demands for self-government that forced it into self-restrained confrontation with the communist party-state. Whereas both sides talked of the need for 'partnership', suggesting a 'social contract' approach to group–government relations, in fact the party-state authorities meant no more than 'consultative authoritarianism' with the major interest groups, which would carry responsibilities without power to bargain or negotiate, leading to concertation and compromise. For its part, Solidarity was tempted by the anarcho-syndicalist vision of workers by-passing an oppressive state and controlling their own enterprises within a 'self-governing republic' and mixed economy. Compelled in practice, in 1980–1, to yield repeatedly to pressure backed by threats of a general strike from Solidarity, which could boast some 9.5 million members out of about 12.5 million employees, the humiliated Polish party-state retrieved its dominant position by the military coup of December 1981 (Garton Ash 1991a, 115, 121, 163, 196–202, 209–10, 232–4). Although it looked as though pressure for change from below had failed as disastrously as change from above was to fail in the Soviet Union, Solidarity's defeat was a signal that, although an apparently toothless totalitarian could still bite in 1981, it would lose this capacity by the end of the decade.

It may seem a far cry from the imposition of martial law to the deliberately confrontationist destabilization tactics pursued by the Thatcher Government in Britain towards the major organized interests, the trade unions in particular. Nevertheless, they both represented a deliberate attempt to shift group–government relations from a conciliatory desire to achieve consensus to domination through conflict. Whereas in Poland, virtually no interest apart from the Church had been allowed to organize freely, in Britain the opposite was true. Most groups were treated as legitimate and representative of their interests even when they did not fully merit the honour. Committed to consensus, senior civil servants often went beyond seeking advice through consultation with select groups into a policy community relationship that had become institutionalized. This applied to a whole range of public services, notably the doctors' and teachers' organizations in health and education, as well as with the Trade Union Congress, the Confederation of British Industry and the National Farmers' Union at the peak association level and thousands of more specialized organizations. The consensus style worked best in the aftermath of the Second World War and during the years of economic expansion, but the harsher post-1973 climate led to confrontations. These occurred first between the coal miners and the Conservative Government in 1973–4, leading to Prime Minister Heath's electoral defeat and, after the breakdown of the mid-1970s 'Social Contract', between the trade unions and the Labour Government in 1978–9, contributing to Prime Minister Callaghan's electoral defeat. Learning the lessons of the 1970s, Mrs Thatcher led a confrontationist counter-attack, mobilizing all the partisan resources that British adversary politics gave the government.

Instead of accepting the consensus politics that had prevailed with the major interest organizations under both Conservative and Labour governments, Mrs Thatcher adopted the position of an anti-establishment outsider, committed to a radical reversal of past relationships. Her successive governments from 1979–90 were not merely aimed at destroying the veto power of the overmighty trade union movement but sought to redistribute power between government and interests. By 'setting one member of the old policy community against another . . . this destabilization of policy communities – evident in such diverse areas as health, education, law reform and the structure of the legal profession, and water policy' (Richardson 1993, 96–7; see also Marsh and Rhodes 1992) – was extended to relations with the civil service, business and local government. As the public sector was privatized, hand-picked business friends displaced the CBI as the government's policy partners, and local government was deprived of both resources and functions. A country that had prided itself on its pluralism and self-government experienced a decade in which the mania to shake up every institution in sight witnessed a massive centralization of power in the name of freeing market forces from interest-group-induced inertia at the risk of engineering institutional collapse. It makes an ironic contrast with the Polish attempt to use worker power to destroy party-state-perpetuated inertia in the name of a self-governing plurality of autonomous organizations. In retrospect, despite the Thatcherite urge to curb producers and professional organizations, it has been the survival of their policy networks and communities that has sheltered the partially deindustrialized British economy and dismantled welfare state from some of the worst excesses of the marketing and centralizing whirlwind.

While Thatcherite Britain was unusual in rounding on the insider groups with which governments had been accustomed to discuss public policy, there are still numerous 'outsider' groups that are denied access, much less bargaining and negotiating status. Anti-nuclear and animal rights groups have remained in this excluded position, while others – feminist and environmentalist groups – have had a measure of success in coming in from the cold. In some countries, such as France and Italy, the major trade unions have been in this situation, being controlled by communist leaders who are opposed to the capitalist market system. A majority of those workers who joined a trade union at all gave their loyalty to organizations that challenged the legitimacy of the economic system and did not merely demand a greater share of the wealth they produced. A former French right-wing minister admitted: 'There is hardly a single achievement of the workers – wages, paid holidays, social security, length of workweek and tempo of workrate – that has not been torn from their private or state employers at the end of a serious crisis. How could workers not be tempted to join trade unions committed to confrontation rather than concertation?' (Peyrefitte 1976, 376; see Cox and Hayward 1983, 229–37). However, this was behaviour characteristic of weakness. In those European countries where trade unions have not been divided, underfinanced and usually without friends in government, abrasive rhetoric and intransigent confrontation tactics can be replaced with bland conformism and collusive concertation.

Between cooptation and consultation: concerting interest–government activities

Although it is generally agreed, even by those who were its greatest protagonists in what they retrospectively recognize as the 'heyday of corporatism in the 1970s', that corporatism has largely ceased to be an accurate way of conceiving interest intermediation in the 1990s (Streeck and Schmitter 1992, 143; cf. 144), it is still useful to consider why it was a popular way of characterizing many of the smaller European democracies. Katzenstein regarded democratic corporatism as a feature of small states in world markets particularly exposed to foreign trade competition. He distinguished between the 'depoliticized, private and decentralized liberal corporatism' of Belgium, the Netherlands and Switzerland on the one hand, and the 'politicized, public and centralized social corporatism' of Austria, Norway and Denmark on the other, with Sweden combining features of both variants (Katzenstein 1984, 244–5; cf. Katzenstein 1985, 24, 81–2, and Van den Bulck 1992, 35–55). While they all shared a commitment to achieving stable policy consensus through the practice of elite social partnership within a mixed economy framework, Austria and the Scandinavian countries were more social demo-cratic, giving greater weight to the trade unions, while in the Low Countries and Switzerland the predominance of bankers and industrialists imparted a more firmly capitalist emphasis.

While we shall draw our examples from social corporatism, the Dutch combination of a historically strong civil society controlled by a decentralized mercantile oligarchy, with a weak form of centralized, French-style bureauc-racy, accustomed to cooperating with self-regulating business interests, is worthy of note. Government regulation accorded interest organizations an important role not merely in policy advisory committees; 'many implemen-tation tasks were delegated to private associations or intermediary semi-state agencies which so characterise Dutch corporate policy networks' (Van Waarden 1992b, 157; cf. 147–54; see also Andeweg and Irwin 1993, 164–75). Such highly institutionalized representation of all interests at all stages of the policy process has been counteracted by a strong commitment to liberal economic and political practices, which curbed the neo-corporatist developments that were such a feature of the Scandinavian and especially the Austrian postwar political systems. It is the self-same commitment to liberal democracy that has prevented the functionally representative chambers like the Dutch and French Economic and Social Councils from achieving more than consultative status, and the same is true of the EC Economic and Social Committee.

Austria has been the most widely acknowledged model of neo-corporatist stable social partnership – two-thirds of the population regarding this partner-ship as of more importance than parliament. The willingness to conclude comprehensive contractual agreements, based on mutual trust between the major organized interests, is founded on deep-rooted agrarian and pre-indus-trial values, reinforced during the Fascist 1930s (Gerlich et al. 1988, 215). Authoritarian corporatism promoted the Chambers of Business, Labour and Agriculture as statutory centralized and compulsory interest organizations with taxing powers. Such chambers exist in most countries, but there is a great difference between the voluntary associations such as exist in Britain, the statutory but consultative chambers in France and the Austrian chambers which exercise functions on behalf of the state. The three Austrian chambers, together with the Austrian Trade Union Federation, have since 1957 formed part of the Joint Commission chaired by the Federal Chancellor, which has been described as 'a kind of second cabinet' (Gerlich 1992, 135; see also Marin 1983, 201–16). Through three subcommittees dealing with wages, prices and general economic and social affairs, the major organized interests institutionalized and extended the earlier wage- and price-bargaining practices. More generally, the interest organizations used to be closely involved from the preparatory to the implementation stages of draft Bills and their comments were usually incorporated into legislation. Interest organization leaders have been accustomed to rely upon a disciplined response from their members. 'For example, Austrian workers will ask themselves much more often than their colleagues in other countries whether they are actually *allowed* to go on strike – and they are likely to answer this question in the negative' (Gerlich et al. 1988, 217).

Whereas gentlemen's agreements, notably between the presidents of the Chamber of Business and the Austrian Trade Union Federation – both of whom held office continuously throughout the 1970s and 1980s – personified social partnership in its intimacy and informality, by the 1990s this type of policy compromise had ceased to operate effectively owing to a number of converging causes. The liberalizing impact of competition – both nationally between political parties and internationally, with Austria's desire to join the EC – substituted an open for a closed type of politics, in which autonomy and rivalry rather than consensus and coordination were given pride of place. The declining popularity of established interests – reflected in the falling turnout in chamber elections – delegitimized the interest groups. They are less consulted and their policy advice is more frequently disregarded. Reflecting this change of status, 'the Constitutional Court has discontinued its long-term practice of more or less accepting even questionable legislation as constitutional, as long as the social partners had agreed' on its desirability (Gerlich 1992, 140; cf. 138–44). Preparing to become part of a Common EC Market, the neo-corporatist practices that had served it well are no longer appropriate. Regulating prices ceases to be possible, so such activities of the Joint Commission will disappear. Like existing EC countries, Austria will have to learn to be less 'exceptional' and has begun to do so by anticipation (Gerlich 1992, 144–5).

The Scandinavian countries never fitted the neo-corporatist model as readily as Austria. Characterized by the decisive policy influence exercised by highly organized interests through concertation with the public authorities, these practices are rooted in the early twentieth century wartime experience of Denmark and Norway, which were expanded with increased state economic intervention and the development of the welfare state there, as well as in Sweden and Finland. In the latter countries, interest group participation in commissions of enquiry play a crucial part in the preparation of legislation, whereas in 'Denmark and Norway concertation in the formulation of legislative projects takes place more in departmental advisory committees . . .' (Elder et al. 1982, 182; cf. Ruin 1982, 153–7).

Scandinavian societies are among the most highly organized in the world, reflected in the high membership and organizational unity of their interest groups. As with Austria, the most important organizations are those representing employers, workers and farmers, though in Scandinavia these are not official Chambers but voluntary organizations. They have worked closely with the social democratic parties that were in power for long periods – in the case of Denmark almost without interruption from 1924 to 1982. Whereas this suited the trade unions admirably, the employers had to concentrate on other points of access, not simply treat them as supplementary to privileged political contacts. 'They based their strategy for political influence on professional contact and expertise in relation to civil servants and through the widespread network of public committees and commissions' (Buksti 1993, 105; on Norway, see Kvavik 1974 and Olsen 1983, chs 5–6). Such activity is less visible to the media but no less effective for that.

As in the case of Austria, there has been a liberalization of the role of organized interests, notably during more than a decade of liberal-conservative government in Denmark from 1982 to 1993, which deliberately reversed the previous integration of interest groups in the process of policy-making. While unable to go as far as Mrs Thatcher in destabilizing the policy communities, they have been weakened by comparison with the years of social democratic consensus building. Similar changes can be identified in Norway and Sweden, confirming that such national neo-corporatism as existed has been in general retreat and there is no likelihood that it will be revived.

In Germany, the role of organized interests is subject to greater legal regulation than in other European countries. As in Austria, there are chambers to which farmers, businessmen, lawyers and doctors are required to belong, although they are less centralized and influential at the federal level. Such functional representation is more active at the *Länder* level, where they sometimes enjoy more than consultative status. For example, 'spokesmen for all the major interest groups sit on the supervisory boards of the states' radio and television networks along with representatives of the principal political parties' (Edinger 1993, 178). At the federal level, draft legislation is submitted to peak interest organizations as a matter of routine administrative procedure, and this facilitates the subsequent concertation with them in decision-making and implementation. Furthermore, *pantouflage* between interest organizations and sponsor ministries makes public policy particularly responsive to private interests. 'Key officials in federal ministries have frequently been recruited from corresponding interest groups and sometimes returned to them after leaving office. For instance, the heads and leading members of the Ministry of Labour usually come from the trade unions and those of the Ministry of Agriculture from the farmers' organisations' (Edinger 1993, 182).

Although the interest organizations concentrate their activities on the bureaucracy, they do not neglect parliamentary committees and party study groups. Nevertheless, even the business, trade union and farmers' organizations have been less effective in the political arena because they exert less and restrictions on electoral expenditure following financial scandals that discredited the practice of depending upon the support of outside interests. The CDU/CSU personnel and programme still reflect business and farmers' interests, while the SPD has symmetrically close links with the DGB trade union movement. However, just as the close links between the Swedish trade union movement and the Social Democratic Party failed to implement the radical and imaginative Meidner Plan to shift ownership and control over industry from the employers to the unions through wage-earner funds, so the more modest codetermination plans of the DGB were blocked in Germany, notably by the SPD's coalition partners, the FDP (Markovits 1984, 95–8, 162–4; Martin 1984, 272–5, 283; Sabel 1981, 212–23). Since the 1980s, a challenge to the established interests–government agencies nexus from more unconventional manifestations of German civil society – through 'citizen initiatives' – has shifted the emphasis somewhat from insiders to outsiders within looser policy issue networks. The Green Party and the environmentalist movement may not have had an influence comparable with that of the establishment organizations but they have forced issues onto the policy agenda that had been excluded by agreement between insider interests and government officials (Edinger 1993, 188–90). However, marginal impact from outsiders is a far cry from the threat drastically to change the balance of power among insiders which the German and Swedish trade unions had sought and failed to achieve.

Between fragmentation and collapse: the pathology of interest–government relations

Whereas in the pluralist conception of politics the activities of interest organizations are regarded as not merely normal but indispensable to the harmonious relations between state and society, they may not work as intended. We have already seen that the relationship may become so close that they can no longer play the countervailing role of separated powers that in liberal doctrine is intended to ensure no single actor is strong enough to dominate the others. However, when their activities are dysfunctional to the working of democratic politics, 'interest group activity is not studied and described, it is *denounced* as if it were intrinsically dangerous for democracy' (Lanzalaco 1993, 117; see also Lapalombara 1964, 6). Italian experience suggests that the danger is real.

As early as 1964, Lapalombara's seminal study *Interest Groups in Italian Politics* contrasted the 'physiological' situation of a strong government capable of withstanding pressures from external interests with the 'pathological' situation of a feeble government facing more powerful organized interests. 'Where, as in Italy, political power is weak or in a state of coll-

'Where, as in Italy, political power is weak or in a state of collapse . . . attempts to regulate or to limit the activities of interest groups fail and
"the most immoral and corrupt methods come to prevail". When this occurs,
the state disintegrates, branches of government begin to operate as interest
groups', leading to 'one of the worst kinds of feudalism that can corrupt and
mortify a society' (Lapalombara 1964, 6–7; see also Lapalombara, 1987). As if
this were not a sufficiently prophetic description of what was revealed in the
scandals that surfaced in 1992–3, Lapalombara paraphrased into the functionalist language of political science a response to a 1960 survey on Italian
pressure groups. It argued that, 'whereas political parties should serve to filter
and aggregate the demands on the political system, they function instead as
instruments of the groups, transmitting to government structures demands that
are selfish and that do not in any way represent a willingness to compromise'
(Lapalombara 1964, 8).

Summing up the findings of the 1960 survey, Lapalombara reported that
'the most pernicious influence on Italian politics is exercised by organised
business and organised religion' (Lapalombara 1964, 8). So, it is not surprising
that he devoted his study to the clientelist relationship between *Confindustria*
– the General Confederation of Italian Industry – and the Ministry of Industry
and Commerce and to the kinship relationship between the Christian Democratic Party and various branches of Catholic Action. Subsequent experience
and revelations have shown that, while it is neither *Confindustria* nor Catholic
Action as such that have been responsible for the generalized corruption of
Italian politics, this is because fragmentation has prevented these peak organizations from aggregating the interests they have tried to represent. 'Kinship'
and 'clientelism' have disintegrated into piecemeal links between factions of
catch-all political parties and specific firms or localities, dismembering public
interest concerns for the satisfaction of private business or partisan interests. In
such a context, it is seldom clear whether specific interests are colonizing parts
of government or vice versa.

With such interest organization and governmental fragmentation and their
associated *ad hoc* deals, it is not surprising that attempts at centralized bargaining or concertation, such as were tried in the early 1960s essay at national
economic planning, were doomed to failure. This has been compensated
partially through the development of cohesive political communities at the
local or regional level among interest organizations and public authorities
united by political 'kinship', which take over the tasks that the inability to
achieve concerted action at the centre have left unattended.

The policy networks and communities that are present in territorial subcultures,
and the clientelistic relationship between local interest groups and national
politicians have an important role not only in explaining what happens at the

sub-national level but at the *national* level as well. The local and regional levels of governance provide interest groups, at least in Italy, with an alternative channel of access to policy-making and implementation that strengthens their position vis à vis the national organs. (Lanzalaco 1993, 127; cf. 123–9)

However, the linkage between centre and periphery has meant that the nexus between party and business corruption prevents national policies being developed that can deal with public interest matters such as rapid rates of inflation and growth of the public debt. It required the major political crisis of 1993 to put Italy's government-party-interest system into the melting pot.

The failure to achieve a clear distinction between organized interests and political parties has also been a salient feature of the post-communist systems of East-Central Europe, experiencing institutional collapse of a different kind from Italy but with instructive analogies. They have arrived at fragmentation from an attempt at filling the abyss between the party-state and society through the creation of rigidly monolithic mass organizations that

> tried to reach down into the depths of society and control even its micro-mechanisms . . . The inefficiency of these institutions led to the development of various informal networks of power and influence. It led to the generation of oligarchic, client-patron, and nepotistic networks, which were able to penetrate, and to build themselves into, the very tissues of society . . . They became the channels of crypto-politiking, latent interest-mongering, corruption, implementation or mis-implementation of central decisions, etc. They soon became as much a barrier as a link between the party-state and society. (Hankiss 1990, 164–5)

More formal attempts at legitimizing interest organizations in Hungary, with the 1967–8 launch of the 'New Economic Mechanism', notably the Labour Code liberalization of trade union law and the Agricultural Cooperatives Law providing for prior negotiation and consultation with the National Council of Agricultural Cooperatives, failed because they were incapable of creating autonomous markets and interest groups. All the attemps to simulate the operation of a market achieved was to encourage managers and workers to compete for 'preferential treatments, bonuses, subventions, exemptions, and the favours of the bureaucracy' and the Communist Party (Hankiss 1990, 202; cf. 59–60, 158, 201, and Toma and Volgyes 1977, 62–3, 68–70). In Italy the government was too weak and ill-organized, and in Hungary the groups were too weak and ill-organized. Both reached in the early 1990s a pathological situation in which the ruling elites are desperately trying to create a viable system of interest intermediation between a reformed or resurrected liberal democratic political system and an economy purged of its degeneration into segmented, politically administered markets that have yet to be firmly established.

National Policy Styles, Sectorization and Organized Interests

In making transnational comparisons of the way in which public policy relates to the system of interest organizations, we quickly face the problem of which of two contrasting starting-points we should adopt. Should we commence with a comparison of national cultural policy inputs or specific policy sector outputs? Traditionally, the macro-political approach through distinctive national policy styles carried with it a number of consequences that derive from an assumption that 'politics determines policy'. There is a 'where there's a will there's a way' presumption that the actors in the policy process can shape the context within which they interact. They are not simply at the mercy of external constraints but can exercise some discretionary control with a real if circumscribed margin of choice (Freeman 1985, 469). This has led to a discussion of whether, if such state autonomy existed, it could be said to vary as between 'strong' and 'weak' states (Atkinson and Coleman 1989; Suleiman 1987, 302–3). While this may be in part a function of size – the smaller states being less able to act autonomously – those countries that still like to think of themselves as capable of independent action like Britain and France have in recent years had to accept that they are decreasingly able to do so in practice. Although national policy style reflects the normative framework of prescriptive values that set the standard by which the conduct of both government agencies and organized interests is judged, this should not be confused with their actual achievements. This leads us to a further consequence of the 'politics determines policy' presumption.

National policy as a consequence of national politics assumes that the elite intentions, preferences and practices of those making policy will determine outcomes. Especially legalistic in Germany and Italy, they are more techno-bureaucratic in France, more politicized and adversarial in Britain, more corporatist in Austria and more professional in Sweden. However, outcomes seldom work out in practice as intended, because policy-makers can seldom impose as they choose. Even in the case of traditionally authoritarian France, which has a conspicuously assertive and activist elite style of decision-making, it has proved difficult to perpetuate its ambitious attempt to direct rather than respond to wants. So although it has a relatively great '*capacity* for policy initiative, a *potential* for far-sighted planning and a *propensity* to impose its will when this is necessary to attain public objectives', it has usually adopted a 'reactive, short-term and piecemeal approach to problem-solving' (Hayward 1982, 116). Political leaders in France become prisoners of the need to adopt a heroic style of leadership, so that Prime Minister Balladur in presenting his government's programme on taking office in 1993 felt the need to describe it as setting a 'new French example' even when compelled to improvise and adapt to domestic and foreign constraints.

In Germany, the reaction against Nazi dictatorship led to the adoption of a predominantly reactive policy style, based on interdependent power sharing with 'insider' organized interests by governments that acknowledged them as legitimate partners (Dyson 1982, 18–19). Where the autonomy of public authorities is given special protection, as in the case of the Central Bank and the judiciary, this is to prevent interference by political parties rather than by organized interests. Concertation and negotiation between interests and government has been the norm, with important variations between policy sectors. Thus, as in France, there was an exclusive, closed policy community dealing with nuclear energy policy, but whereas in France this survived both the onslaught of the anti-nuclear movement and the arrival of the left in power in the 1980s, in Germany there was a breakdown in the 'insider' nuclear policy community under the impact of 'outsider' citizen action groups. Unwillingness of government to impose policy led to an effective blocking of the building of nuclear power stations, whereas in France the 1970s drive to expand nuclear electricity went on virtually unabated (Dyson 1982, 26–30, and Lucas 1979).

Adopting instead a sectoral policy subsystems, meso-political approach, which assumes that 'policy determines politics' and focuses on outcomes rather than inputs, we have to face the increasing prevalence of the phenomenon of sectorization which has been identified in many European political systems (Richardson 1982, 45, 82–4, 152–3, 178–82). This has led to a diversity of policy styles within nations which, in conjunction with the need to involve more groups in the policy process, threatens the national government as a policy-making centre with disintegration. Before assessing how far this approach weakens the plausibility of an analysis based on a national styles starting-point, let us try to clarify the meaning of sectorization to see whether it is not itself open to serious objections as a way of understanding interest organization–government interaction.

Sectorization has three main features. First, it assumes that policy-making has been impenetrably compartmentalized into discrete areas which are the preserve of specific policy networks or communities. Second, within each sector, a specific policy issue or set of issues attracts the attention of governmental actors and organized interests who bargain over the way in which the issue(s) should be handled. The interests are involved because governments need to avoid controversy, secure compliance or seek information, and the need for the latter and the capacity of interest organizations to manage controversy/compliance varies substantially. Third, as it is the functional necessities of particular policy problems that decide policy outputs, one should start with the policy and work backwards to the actors clustered in specific 'self-contained policymaking systems' (Freeman 1985, 483; cf. 482; see also Richardson and Jordan 1979, and Page 1986). Taken together, these three features suggest that one can identify relatively autonomous policy sectors in which particular actors pursuing joint programmes to deal with problems in an issue area are capable of achieving a durable consensus.

The national policy styles approach implies that the government–interest organizations relationships will have a predominant form in each country, cutting across all policy sectors and surviving major crises or even changes of regime: from Fourth to Fifth Republic in France, pre- and post-Franco Spain, perhaps even pre- and post-communism in Central Europe. By contrast, the sectoral policy subsystems approach suggests that there will be cross-national convergence in specific policies and divergence across policy sectors in the same country. Thus, the oil shock of 1973 should have led to strong similarities in national energy policies. In fact, France – thanks to the leadership of the public electricity corporation EDF, supported by the nuclear energy policy community and with the enthusiastic approval of the President of the Republic – went for an all-out electro-nuclear investment programme, which no other European country matched. This suggests that national style did have a major impact, although the French oil national champion ELF did work with the international oil policy community (Hayward 1986, 35–8). So, within the energy policy sector, we have divergent evidence within a single country.

A factor making for partial cross-national convergence both in macro- and meso-political policy is the phenomenon of fashion which prompts imitation. So, in matters of macro-economic policy, the late 1940s and 1950s witnessed the differential triumph of Keynesianism as offering the solution to the interwar problem of mass unemployment reconciling the interests of labour and capital within a market economy (Hall 1989). In the 1960s, planning, not Soviet-style but French-style, was all the rage, as offering the efficient secret of sustained and rapid economic growth in concert with the organized interests (Shonfield 1965, 122–3 and pt 2; Hayward and Narkiewicz 1979). In the 1970s national neo-corporatism – of both Austrian and Swedish varieties – seemed to offer the way of achieving stable economic prosperity, while in the 1980s Thatcherite marketizing, monetarist and privatization policies permitted transnational businesses to call the tune to which many felt compelled to dance. In fact, the results of such attempts at transferring national policies between nations underline how difficult such exercises are. The venture by the Conservative British Chancellor of the Exchequer, who sought to imitate

French national economic planning in 1961, has been compared to Christopher Columbus's celebrated voyage of discovery. When he set out, he did not know where he was going; when he got there he did not know that he had arrived; when he returned (dismissed from office in 1962) he did not know where he had been (Hayward 1975, 287). Such are the perils of ignoring the persistence of national policy styles inhibiting institutional transfers.

Similar lessons could serve as salutary warnings to the post-communist attempts to import wholesale from 'the West' both this or that version of interest intermediation between market economy and liberal democratic institutions in a desperate attempt to repair past damage and prepare for possible membership of the European Community. This is complicated by the fact that the EC represents an especially pluralistic framework for the activities of organized interests. The dispersal of power among a multiplicity of national and multi-national policy actors compounds the unpredictability arising from competition between firms, government departments, regions and sectional interests to gain control over the EC agenda. The relative absence of policy communities, with the notable exceptions of COPA in agriculture and EUROFER in steel, has meant that 'it is virtually impossible for any single interest or national association to secure exclusive access to the relevant officials', so that loose issue networks predominate (Mazey and Richardson 1993, 209; cf. 194, 206–12). Although some 525 organized interests make representations at the EC level – business interests being much more effective than trade unions, still less consumer or environmental groups – they are still much more inclined to use national channels of access. 'Paradoxically, the growing importance of EC legislation has in many cases reinforced the dependency which exists at the national level between groups and "their" ministries, since the latter are effectively *intermediaries* between groups and the EC in the final stages of Community decision-making' (Mazey and Richardson 1993, 211; cf. 193–9). However, because of the importance of the European market to American and Japanese firms, they are present in Brussels individually and through bodies such as the American Chamber of Commerce, as well as through the employment of professional lobbyists and law firms, whose services are increasingly used by many interest organizations from inside and outside the EC.

The pluralistic and competitive character of the EC has been marked by 'growing interdependence between national economies due to progressing market integration without proportionate growth of regulatory institutions' (Streeck and Schmitter 1992, 142; cf. 149, 159, and Sandholtz and Zysman 1989, 116–17). A major consequence has been that big business has benefited from the deregulation filling the gap left by the reduction in national regulation, notably in the sphere of social regulation of working conditions and protection of the workplace rights of the employed. We have known for a long time that some organized interests are much more influential than others, so we should not be surprised that what is true at the national level should be at least as true within the EC.

As power shifts from the national to the supra-national level in Europe and the organized interests adapt accordingly, the EC has assumed the shape of a *community of networks* in which national styles and sectoral subsystems contend yet cohere under the pressure of external forces and events. Not only a common market, nor yet a state, 'The EC can best be viewed as a set of complex overlapping networks, in which a supranational style of decision-making, characterised by compromise upgrading common interests, can under favourable conditions lead to the pooling of sovereignty' (Keohane and Hoffmann 1990, 277; cf. 282). This flexible way of deciding policy issues makes it easier to contemplate enlarging the community and its networks to new members in Northern and Central Europe because past experience suggests that such enlargement will encourage the impetus towards integration to counteract the consequent increased heterogenity.

Having considered the 'question of whether the sovereignty lost by individual states can be focused at all – or whether Europe will become simply a network without a decisive or accountable centre of authority', Keohane and Hoffmann concluded in 1990 that it was more likely that the 'ties of European networks will deepen as habits of pooling sovereignty develop' (Keohane and Hoffmann 1990, 293, 296). The organized interests, through their role in transnational sectoral networks, will assist in the neo-pluralistic process of elite power sharing within a community that has filled some of the political space between retreating national authorities and an as yet non-existent supranational authority. That it continues to do so by fits and starts does not mean that the many-sided impulses towards integration have spent their force, although the EC has given signs of reverting from a community to a common market, less cooperative and more competitive. In the multitude of committees into which so much EC decision-making has diffused, interest organization interaction with intergovernmental processes will both extend and complicate their task in shaping public policies to conform with their objectives. Without necessarily bringing about policy paralysis, a propensity to pluralistic stagnation may slow down political impetus.

Bibliography

Andeweg, R. and Irwin, G. (1993). *Dutch Government and Politics*. London: Macmillan.

Atkinson, M. and Coleman, W. (1989). 'Strong states and weak states: sectoral policy networks in advanced capitalist economies'. *British Journal of Political Science*

14 (1): 46–67.

Aves, J. (1992). 'The Russian labour movement', in G. Hosking et al., *The Road to Post-Communism*. London: Pinter.

Brown, A. H. (1974). *Soviet Politics and Political Science*. London: Macmillan.

—— (1984). 'Political power and the Soviet state: Western and Soviet perspectives', in N. Harding (ed.), *The State in Socialist Society*. London: Macmillan.

Brunner, G. and Kaschkat, H. (1979). 'Party, state and groups in Eastern Europe', in J. Hayward and R. N. Berki (eds), *State and Society in Contemporary Europe*. Oxford: Martin Robertson.

Buksti, J. (1993). 'Interest groups in Denmark', in J. Richardson (ed.), *Pressure Groups*. Oxford: Oxford University Press.

Cox, A. and Hayward, J. (1983). 'The inapplicability of the corporatist model in Britain and France: the case of labour'. *International Political Science Review* 4 (2): 217–40.

Cox, T. (1993). 'Democratisation and the growth of pressure groups in Soviet and post-Soviet politics', in J. Richardson (ed.), *Pressure Groups*. Oxford: Oxford University Press.

Dyson, K. (1982). 'West Germany: the search for a rationalist consensus', in J. Richardson (ed.), *Policy Styles in Western Europe*. London: Allen & Unwin.

Edinger, L. (1993). 'Pressure group politics in West Germany', in J. Richardson (ed.), *Pressure Groups*. Oxford: Oxford University Press.

Elder, N. et al. (1982). *The Consensual Democracies: the government and politics of the Scandinavian states*. Oxford: Martin Robertson.

Freeman, G. (1985). 'National styles and policy sectors: explaining structural variation'. *Journal of Public Policy* 5 (4): 467–96.

Garton Ash, T. (1991a). *The Polish Revolution: Solidarity*. London: Granta Books.

—— (1991b). *The Uses of Adversity: essays on the fate of Central Europe*. Cambridge: Granta Books.

Gerlich, P. (1992). 'A farewell to corporatism'. *West European Politics* 15 (1): 132–46.

Gerlich, P. et al. (1988). 'Corporatism in crisis: stability and change in social partnership in Austria'. *Political Studies* 26 (2): 209–23.

Hall, P. (1989). *The Political Power of Economic Ideas: Keynesianism across nations*. Princeton: Princeton University Press.

Hankiss, E. (1990). *East European Alternatives*. Oxford: Clarendon Press.

Hayward, J. (1975). 'The politics of planning in France and Britain'. *Comparative Politics* 7 (2).

—— (1982). 'Mobilising private interests in the service of public ambitions: the salient element in the dual French policy style', in J. Richardson (ed.), *Policy Styles in Western Europe*. London: Allen & Unwin.

—— (1986). *The State and the Market Economy*. Brighton: Wheatsheaf.

Hayward, J. and Narkiewicz, O. (eds) (1979). *Planning in Europe*. London: Croom Helm.

Holmes, L. (1986). *Politics in the Communist World*. Oxford: Clarendon Press.

Hosking, G. (1992). 'The beginnings of independent political activity', in Hosking et al., *The Road to Post-Communism: independent political movements in the Soviet Union, 1985–91*. London: Pinter.

Jordan, G. (1992). 'Assumptions about the role of groups in the policy process: the British Policy Community Approach'. University of Aberdeen Working Paper No. 4.

Jordan, G. and Schubert, K. (1992). 'A preliminary ordering of policy network labels'. *European Journal of Political Research* 21 (1–2): 7–27.

Katzenstein, P. (1984). *Corporatism and Change: Austria, Switzerland and the politics of Industry.* Ithaca: Cornell University Press.

—— (1985). *Small States in World Markets.* Ithaca: Cornell University Press.

Keohane, R. and Hoffmann, S. (1990). 'Community politics and institutional change', in W. Wallace (ed.), *The Dynamics of European Integration,* London: Pinter.

Kvavik, R. (1974). 'Interest groups in a "cooptive" political system', in M. Heisler (ed.), *Politics in Europe.* New York: David McKay.

Lanzalaco, L. (1993). 'Interest groups in Italy: from pressure activity to policy networks', in J. Richardson (ed.), *Pressure Groups.* Oxford: Oxford University Press.

Lapalombara, J. (1964). *Interest Groups in Italian Politics.* Princeton: Princeton University Press.

—— (1987). *Democracy Italian Style.* New Haven: Yale University Press.

Lucas, N. J. D. (1979). *Energy in France: planning, politics and policy.* London: Europa.

Marin, B. (1983). 'Organising interests by interest organisations: associational prerequisites of cooperation in Austria'. *International Political Science Review* 4 (2): 197–216.

Markovits, A. (1984). 'Trade unions and the economic crisis: the West German case', in P. Gourevitch et al. *Unions and Economic Crisis: Britain, West Germany and Sweden.* London: Allen & Unwin.

Marsh, D. and Rhodes, R. A. W. (eds) (1992). *Implementing Thatcherite Policies: audit of an era.* Buckingham: Open University Press.

Martin, A. (1984). 'Trade unions in Sweden: strategic response to change and crisis', in P. Gourevitch et al. *Unions and Economic Crisis: Britain, West Germany and Sweden.* London: Allen & Unwin.

Mazey, S. and Richardson, J. (1993). 'Interest groups in the European Community', in J. Richardson (ed.), *Pressure Groups.* Oxford: Oxford University Press.

Olsen, J. (1983). *Organized Democracy: political institutions in a welfare state – the case of Norway.* Oslo: Universitets Forlaget.

Page, E. (1986). 'Sectorisation and uniformity in the government of Western nations'. American Political Science Association, mimeo.

Pelczynski, L. A. (1988). 'Solidarity and "The Rebirth of Civil Society" in Poland, 1976–81', in J. Keane (ed.), *Civil Society and the State: new European perspectives.* London: Verso.

Peyrefitte, A. (1976). *Le mal français.* Paris: Plon.

Pravda, A. (1983). 'Trade unions in East European communist systems: towards corporatism?'. *International Political Science Review* 4 (2): 241–60.

Rhodes, R. (1990). 'Policy networks: a British perspective'. *Journal of Theoretical Politics* 2/3: 293–317.

Richardson, J. (ed.) (1982). *Policy Styles in Western Europe.* London: Allen & Unwin.

—— (ed.) (1993). *Pressure Groups.* Oxford: Oxford University Press.

Richardson, J. and Jordan, G. (1979). *Governing Under Pressure.* Oxford: Martin Robertson.

Rigby, T. H. (1992). 'Reconceptualising the Soviet System', in S. White et al., *Developments in Soviet and Post-Soviet Politics*, 2nd edn. London: Macmillan.

Ruin, O. (1982). 'Sweden in the 1970s', in J. Richardson (ed.), *Policy Styles in Western Europe*. London: Allen & Unwin.

Sabel, C. (1981). 'The internal politics of trade unions' in S. Berger (ed.), *Organising Interests in Western Europe*. Cambridge: Cambridge University Press.

Sandholtz, W. and Zysman, J. (1989). '1992: recasting the European bargain'. *World Politics* October: 95–128.

Shonfield, A. (1965). *Modern Capitalism*. Oxford: Oxford University Press.

Skilling, G. (1966). 'Interest groups and communist politics'. *World Politics* 18: 435–51.

—— (1983). 'Interest groups and communist politics revisited'. *World Politics* 36: 1–27.

Streeck, W. and Schmitter, P. (1992). 'From national corporatism to transnational pluralism: organised interests in the single European market'. *Politics and Society* 19 (2).

Suleiman, E. (1987). *Private Power and Centralization in France*. Princeton: Princeton University Press.

Toma, P. and Volgyes, I. (1977). *Politics in Hungary*. San Francisco: Freeman.

Van den Bulck, J. (1992). 'Neo-corporatism and policy networks in Belgium'. *West European Politics* 15 (2): 35–55.

Van Waarden, F. (1992a). 'Dimensions and types of policy networks'. *European Journal of Political Research* 21 (1–2): 29–52.

—— (1992b). 'The historical institutionalisation of typical national patterns in policy networks between state and industry: a comparison of the USA and the Netherlands'. *European Journal of Political Research* 21 (1–2): 131–62.

9

Administering Europe

Edward C. Page

The Problem of Bureaucratic Character

Bureaucrats are expected to obey orders. A traditional model, of the sort found in the work of the political sociologist Max Weber, views an administrative organization very much as an army; as a continuous set of superior–subordinate relationships with the chief at the top indirectly guiding the actions of all subordinates. This armed forces simile is understandable since military necessity has for centuries constituted one of the most potent of stimuli towards bureaucratization in Europe, and pioneers of bureaucratic organization, such as Charlemagne, Cromwell, Napoleon or Scharnhorst, were above all concerned with the organization of the military. In this sense a modern state bureaucracy might be comfortingly seen as a vast army with elected politicians as its generals. However, we know that bureaucrats do not *only* obey orders. They participate in decision-making. Their experience and technical skills are likely to make their advice carry a lot of weight in the policy-making process. An unimaginative or reticent official in a senior position would, in most cases, be useless. At first glance, the fact that unelected officials have an important role to play in shaping public policy appears to run counter to the conception of a liberal democracy based on political power concentrated in the hands of elected politicians, yet to argue that bureaucrats have power one does not have to believe that they should have none. Such a view of bureaucratic power as illegitimate would be mistaken since advice is central to the role of a top bureaucrat within a democracy. Failing to advise a politician of the known or likely consequences of an action could also be reckless as well as illegitimate.

What sort of power do bureaucrats have in modern European states? It is impossible to give a direct answer to this question not only because we have no common denominator for measuring power, but also because even within the same country the role of civil servant is likely to vary according to the time, the place, the issue and the individuals involved. For example, as Catherine Grémion (1979) has shown in France and Robert Putnam (1973) in Germany, it is possible to identify different types of civil servants who seek to take more or less active roles in the process of policy-making. Moreover, the influence of officials is likely to depend upon the nature of the issue. Policy issues which are 'politically sensitive' – a term that itself defies any constant definition – are less likely to be left to the routines of civil service interactions with pressure groups than the sort of routine legislation referred to by Richard Rose as the product of an 'ongoing Whitehall process' (Mackie and Hogwood 1985).

Certainly the influence of senior officials is highly variable. Yet it is difficult to miss the point that administrative systems have distinctive national characteristics. Thus many studies give an overall impression of the way in which civil services affect policy-making in any one polity by emphasizing one distinctive aspect and basing much of their description on that. Hugh Heclo (1977) emphasizes the fact that top civil servants and political appointees in the United States do not know one another and cannot be said to be part of a united governing elite. With Aaron Wildavsky, Heclo (1981) argues almost the opposite in the case of Britain, where the higher levels of the civil service are characterized as a 'village community' in which top officials not only know each other but have developed a distinctive set of norms and *mores*. Anton (1980) emphasizes the 'consensual' style of Swedish policy-making, Eldersveld, Kooiman and van der Tak (1981) the importance of 'consociationalism' in the Dutch bureaucratic elite, and studies of the French civil service, most notably the works of Suleiman (1975) and Thoenig (1973), show the importance of techno-bureaucratic training and the career patterns related to it as a major key to understanding the relationship between civil service and politics.

The problem with discussions of national characteristics of a civil service, along with related terms such as 'style' and 'culture', is that they are often indeterminate and impressionistic. Kjellberg described the concept of 'policy style' as used by Jordan and Richardson as simply 'armchair generalizations', with little by way of benchmarks against which to measure or otherwise assess the dimensions which go to make up 'style' (Kjellberg 1984). A similar argument could be levelled against the notion of 'weak states' and 'strong states' (or 'stateless' or 'state' traditions of government); there appear to be no criteria according to which a nation can be allocated as being in one or the other category (see, for example, Suleiman 1987). The concept of style essentially involves a circular argument; policy is habitually or preferably made in the following way because that is the way policy is made. It has a useful function of conveying a flavour or atmosphere of the way things are done, yet it cannot identify the causes of such habitual behaviour or factors which are likely to change it or its consequences.

If such national characterizations are possible, the number of factors involved mean any analysis would become exceptionally unwieldy, with a relatively large number of variables involving relatively few cases. It is, however, possible to point to five major factors that are repeatedly found in the literature on national civil services which differentiate European administrative systems from one another. These factors, the pervasiveness of national bureaucracies, their cohesion, the nature of political control, their permeability as well as their caste-like character, can be found in existing national studies of bureaucracies, as will be set out in the following discussion. Moreover, in discussions of national bureaucracies, the impact of such variables can be assessed in a comparative context. This allows us to draw up a typology of bureaucratic systems and say something about their general properties.

Components of Bureaucratic Character

Pervasiveness

The pervasiveness of national administration refers to the range of competences which come under its direct influence. In some countries the power of national civil servants is limited by the power of the executive of national or federal government itself. In such systems one can expect the role of the national bureaucracy to be far more pervasive than in systems where the extent of national administration is smaller. Thus in France national administrators have for a long time been involved in local decision-making: the studies of the mayors and notables by Crozier and his colleagues show that, while French local politicians are not as dominated by national government as the formal legal conceptions of tutelage suggest, they also show national administrators were routinely involved in making the most parochial of decisions (see Crozier 1970; Grémion 1976).

There is quite clearly a difference between those countries in which local government is a major provider of services and those countries where local government's role is far more limited. Figure 9.1 shows graphically that there is a marked contrast between countries such as Greece, Portugal, Belgium, France and even Italy on the one hand, and the Nordic countries along with the federal systems of Germany, Switzerland and Austria on the other. Localities in the Netherlands, the United Kingdom and Poland tend to be responsible for a larger portion of public spending than those in Southern European countries.

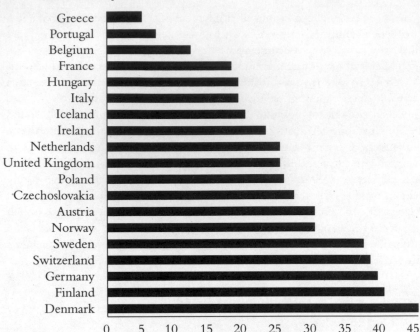

Figure 9.1   *Percentage of total government spending channelled through state and local government, 1990*

Source: IMF, *International Monetary Fund Government Finance Statistics 1992*. Washington, DC: IMF.

The degree of influence of the national executive over state and local government is not simply a matter of the functions which state and local government carry out. Differences in the nature of the regime of control of national over regional and local government also affect the ability of national administrators to shape subnational decisions. For example, although France may have decentralized in the 1980s, we know that even the reformed prefectoral system offers a routine involvement of superior authorities in the daily affairs of a French *commune* that go beyond the formal powers of the prefect (see Page 1991). However, such direct intervention is not necessarily guaranteed by the existence of a prefect-type figure which has been an almost universal feature of subnational government throughout Europe – and indeed remains so. The prefect or the prefectoral figure was not a creation of a Napoleonic system of government but became a standard feature of public administration in the seventeenth and eighteenth centuries. The Scandinavians have their governors, as do the Belgians, Greeks and French. Only Britain is unusual in this respect, as the medieval equivalent of the prefect, the justice of the peace, became increasingly a figure of local self-government rather than the king's agent.

There are three broad types of system of control of central over local government. Moreover, these coincide largely with the degree of functional allocation so that we may use them to describe three types of administrative system from the point of view of the extent of national bureaucratic influence. First, there are federal systems – Germany, Belgium, Austria and Switzerland – where the power of the federal bureaucracy is highly limited. As a legal concept, federalism means that states or provinces have a constitutional right to protection from the encroachment of a central government. This federal model would also best describe the administration of the European Union (EU), since the authority of EU institutions, although extensive and still growing, is defined through international treaties. Second, there are unitary systems with administrative control of local government. A unitary system is one where there is no constitutional limitation on the power of the national government. In principle it can reorganize, reform or even abolish local government. Of course there are political limitations to the form of change that national governments may impose on local government but no formal legal restrictions. Where local government is continually supervised by an active national administrative structure, such as through prefects or regional courts of accounts, then we may term the form of supervision administrative. Such administrative forms of supervision are found in France, Luxembourg, Italy, Spain, Portugal and Greece. Certainly the powers of central state officials have changed in some of these countries, most notably in France, where the prefects briefly changed their names to Commissioners of the Republic in the 1980s to indicate a changing role.

Hungary comes closer to the statutory model, as does Ireland. Hungarian commissioners have limited rights: they can 'note' that a law has been violated, but if the local authority takes no action, then the commissioner can only take the council to court (Szábo 1993, 96). In Ireland top officials, above all the powerful city or county managers, are selected by the Local Appointments Commission, although this was introduced less as a means of exerting central control and more as a means of combating patronage in local public services (Tannam 1993, 277–8).

Cohesion

Perhaps the most common aspect of bureaucracies to feature in single country studies is the *cohesion* of the senior levels of the administration. The cohesion of the 'village community' of Heclo and Wildavsky's (1981) study of Britain contrasts with the isolated 'issue networks' Heclo (1977) identifies in the United States as well as with the *Ressortpartikularismus* of the German civil service discussed by Mayntz and Scharpf (1975), according to which individual ministries, or even parts of individual ministries, see themselves as distinct and in competition with other ministries or parts of ministries. In the United States the Senior Executive Service was launched in the late 1970s in part in order to combat this fragmentation at the higher levels of the civil service (see Perry and Miller 1991). Moreover, the nature of potential divisions is also important here since the traditional departmental loyalties which serve even in Britain to counteract the cohesion in the higher levels of the senior civil service are cross-cut by the *corps* pattern of recruitment and career development in France, which can both create cross-ministerial cohesion and interministerial division.

Cohesion among top civil servants is commonly claimed to have two main effects upon the policy process. First, it is generally argued to strengthen the role of the civil service in decision-making. An internally divided body does not have the status or power of one that speaks as if with a single voice. Moreover, where there are close links between officials from different ministries, interdepartmental negotiations can be conducted predominantly by bureaucrats. Hence in France the forces of cohesion in the French civil service, the *Grands Corps*, are one of the mainstays of civil service power. As Suleiman (1978, 276) concludes, 'The entire elite-forming process – from initial recruitment to the mutual aid and support that members of the elite learn to give one another throughout their careers – creates a self-conscious, self-confident elite, unhampered by self-doubt', and this is mirrored by acceptance of the status and power of the civil service among politicians and citizens alike. It is a common perception among critics of the British civil service that civil servants can arrange deals behind the backs of ministers, in gentlemen's clubs if not in the corridors of Whitehall (this was satirized in Lynn and Jay 1981). One can find some evidence of this in Heclo and Wildavsky's (1981, 139) study of the budgetary process, where 'the minister who is not only unaggressive but also dull will be kept out of sight as much as possible. His officials will go to great lengths to settle matters with their Treasury counterparts; they will seek to make a deal, make an arrangement, accept losses they would rather not take – anything but let their feeble lamb go up to the slaughter.'

Second, cohesion imparts a set of interests: since an elite is a distinctive group, it may have distinctive group interests. This observation is the basis of the whole 'bureaucratic politics' thesis which suggests that support for policy positions is influenced by institutional affiliation, or rather where you stand depends on where you sit (see Allison 1971). There is plenty of evidence to demonstrate that different ministries or agencies within government develop distinctive ideologies, and it is a commonplace observation that civil servants in finance ministries seek to restrain spending while those in, say, social welfare service ministries seek to increase it (Wynia 1974). Occasionally, group identity and interests can extend beyond departments. Again, the French bureaucracy and the material interests of members of the *Grands Corps* in the fate of their particular *corps* may shape attitudes to substantive policy proposals. For example, Thoenig (1973) argues that for decades the building of motorways in France was successfully opposed by the *Ponts et Chaussées* because of the feared consequences for its power base within the *départements*. Or the identity and thus interests can be service-wide, attempts to shape the system of recruitment to the higher civil service provoking a common response. It was a service-wide group interest which, according to Kellner and Crowther Hunt, led the civil service to oppose and ultimately 'defeat' many of the reform proposals set out in the 1969 Fulton Committee report (Kellner and Crowther-Hunt 1980).

In the Commission of the European Union there is substantial mobility between Directorates General among senior officials. The extent to which this creates a cohesive civil service identity is, however, open to some doubt. While there is certainly a dominant perception of belonging to a European administrative elite among officials (Shore and Black 1992), access to the more senior positions is somewhat restricted by the practice of 'parachuting' in candidates from outside the EU service or the rapid promotion of those with good political contacts within it (see below). Parachutists are more mobile within the EU than those who reach senior positions after years of service in the Commission. Consequently, Rotacher and Colling (1987, 25) conclude that 'able and dynamic junior and middle level European officials . . . increasingly may see themselves deprived of joining the European meritocracy through truly European service.'

In fact, cohesion is greatest within the British, Irish and French civil service. In most other European states, it is more conventional to pursue a senior career in a department or agency than in the civil service. In comparison with Italy and Germany, 'the much higher level of interministerial mobility in Britain . . . marks an important idiosyncrasy of British administrative career patterns' (Aberbach et al. 1981, 70–1). Daalder (1989, 8) writes of the Netherlands that 'there is *no* real central recruitment of civil servants. These is *hardly* anything like conscious career planning within let alone between departments. There is *no* rotation of posts: such movement as there is between departments is a matter of individual motivation rather than of conscious government policies. In short there is *no* national civil service.' While Daalder contrasts Dutch with British and French practice, such features are widespread in continental Europe. In France, although the focus for cohesion is the *corps*, career patterns can also erode *corps* loyalty: the principle of *détachement* gives officials pursuing a senior career path the opportunity of working in organizations outside the traditional areas colonized by the *corps*, in another ministry, in a public agency or in a semi-public industry. Grémion (1979) argues that this is creating a new breed of civil servant whose open-mindedness and extended range of contacts mark them off from those who retain a narrow concern with the *corps* and its interests. In Ireland, reforms introduced in 1984 sought to secure greater mobility in the civil service, and this has had some success, especially at the very top, since around 40 per cent of appointees come from other ministries (see O'Nuallain 1990, 455).

Institutionalized political control

A third component of the character of the bureaucracy is the form of *institutionalized political control* found within it. Political control can be institutionalized in three main ways, although they are not mutually exclusive. First, it can be institutionalized by making top officials the appointees of politicians. These can be selected on the basis of their sympathies towards the ideology and policies of the ruling parties. One such form of politicization is found in countries such as France and Germany, where the 'commanding heights' of a ministry are subject to party political appointment. Below this relatively thin layer the bulk of civil service positions, even senior ones, are subject to rules of appointment and promotion established and run by civil servants themselves. Thus the *politische Beamte* of Germany, referring to the top posts of *Staatssekretär* and *Ministerialdirektor*, are subject to political appointment, and in France new ministers can seek to change their *directeurs d'administration*. Overall, the use of the power to appoint officials in France and Germany is exercised relatively sparingly. Moreover, the choice of top ministerial appointees is effectively limited to senior civil servants who have sufficient experience to be eligible for such posts.

In the Commission of the European Union the appointment of officials from outside the EU civil service, or the unusually rapid promotion of serving officials, is associated with the principle that the very top posts, from A1 (Director General) to A3 (Director), should be roughly proportionate to the size of member states. This is euphemistically called the principle of 'geographical balance'. It effectively means that appointments to these senior positions involve not only Commissioners but also the Permanent Representations of the member states as well as the Council of Ministers. Although the explicit use of nationality as a criterion for any appointment is illegal, it is widely practised and tolerated by member states if not the career Commission officials, who might justifiably believe that the top levels of the EU civil service were closed to them. Often, officials are 'parachuted' into top positions from national civil services or, somewhat less frequently, senior executive positions within the private or public sector. Alternatively, rapid promotion within the service may follow service within the *cabinets* or advisory bodies of the Commissioners. The members of these *cabinets* generally, but not invariably, share the same nationality as the Commissioner they advise.

More extensive forms of politicization, going beyond the top levels of government, are found where membership of the correct party is a precondition for promotion to civil service posts, with in some cases different ministries requiring different party membership. Where 'party book administration' is extensive throughout the whole national bureaucracy, and not just at its most senior levels (as in Germany and to a lesser extent France), one might expect it to have the effect of reducing the political status of civil servants. The proposition that political affiliation rather than competence or even seniority is a crucial qualification for career advancement undermines the claim of civil servants to a distinctive expertise and professionalism. One would not expect this to be the case where only the most senior positions are subject to 'party book administration', since seniority and professional competence are likely to have been important in advancing the careers of officials to the point where they are eligible for top jobs. Given that party membership rather than personal loyalty is the major criterion for promotion, the control offered politicians by this form of linkage between politics and administration must remain questionable. This view is reinforced by the practice in Austria and Belgium of officials frequently holding simultaneous membership of several parties.

In Belgium there is extensive politicization of the higher levels of the civil service, the top level (Level I) containing around 10,000 employees subject to party nomination, albeit under the proviso that they are eligible (i.e., qualified and have experience within the service). In practice this often means people from the second rank within a ministry being promoted to top positions. In Austria it is extensive. The 'imperial halves', according to which the ÖVP and the SPÖ coalition divided ministries into Catholic and socialist spheres of influence up until 1970, declined in the socialist years between 1970 and 1986 but re-emerged after the coming to power in 1987 of the new Catholic-socialist grand coalition (Neisser 1991, 147). It is impossible to have a career within the higher civil service without at least being nominally a member of a political organization affiliated to a political party; clever and ambitious bureaucrats will hold two party cards (Neisser 1982, 241). In Italy the hegemony of the Christian Democrats until 1994 makes it difficult to evaluate the extent of political appointments. Moreover, promotion is supposed to conform to abstract merit principles. Although evidence is hard to come by, patronage is generally agreed to be extensive in the Italian civil service. In addition, the traditional dominance of party appointments to para-state agencies was formally extended to ministries in 1972 with a decree allowing political appointments to 'general leadership' posts (Berti 1981, 143).

The former communist countries are exceptionally difficult to classify here, since the system of *nomenklatura* (according to which high or even middle-ranking official positions were for Communist Party nominees and almost always went to party members) as well as the absence of free elections meant that a bureaucratic career was a political career and vice versa. How the Czech and Slovak Republics, Poland and Hungary will develop is difficult to determine. In former Czechoslovakia, a 'screening law' envisaged banning all officials identified as sympathizers with the communist regime until 1996 (Pomohac 1993, 63). The changeover from communism in Poland brought about extensive turnover of personnel as those associated with the former regime resigned or were dismissed (Taras 1993). Since then there has been widespread instability within the bureaucracy, and it is difficult to see whether the networks of clientelism that characterized Poland under the communist regime will develop within the parties to produce a form of politicization close to that of Southern European nations (Tarkowski 1981). In Hungary the turnover in administrative staff after the collapse of communism appears to have been far less extensive (Horvath 1992). Moreover, separation of political from administrative functions at the very top of the Hungarian ministerial civil service suggests the development of a 'commanding heights' approach to politicization (Szábo 1993, 99), although the tradition of the interwar years where different ministries and even different local government authorities belonged to different parties and factions bears similarities with subsequent Austrian practice (Janos 1982, 294–5). East-Central European bureaucracies have a variety of diverse historical experiences of distinctive bureaucratic cultures and it is hard to see whether any or none of these is likely to re-emerge (for a discussion of diverse administrative traditions in East-Central Europe, see Seton-Watson 1962, 146–50); the future development of these systems is difficult to predict from the vantage point of the mid-1990s. Politicization is an inevitable part of the transition from communism, yet it is limited by the availability of qualified and experienced officials, just as was the transition to communism after the Second World War. At present in East-Central Europe, 'many ministries exist with a gulf of distrust between top level political appointees and the permanent staff' (Curry 1993, 453). Whether this will persist once the generation of ex-communist appointees has been replaced or moved on, and what forms of politicization will emerge, remain open questions.

A second approach to political control of the bureaucracy can be found in the *norm of neutrality*. Through insisting on the neutrality of the civil service, the bureaucracy can be relied upon, in the words of Max Weber (1972, 128), to 'carry on working normally for the regime that comes to power after a violent revolution, for the enemy government of occupation just as it did for the legitimate governments they replace.' A prime example here is Britain, where even those who point to the 'politicization' of the civil service under the Conservatives since 1979, with ministers (and above all Mrs Thatcher) suspected of influencing civil service careers because of party political preferences, can identify only one or two cases, and even these are open to serious question (Page 1992, 39–40). Similarly, in many of the Scandinavian countries, party political appointments are relatively rare. Olsen (1983, 128–9) argues that, although party political and interest group affiliations in Norway are more likely among civil servants than the mass public and although 'there is a tendency to take political affiliations into account when choosing between several well qualified candidates', the merit principle dominates. Even during the lengthy period in office of the Labour Party, there were fewer Labour Party members in the higher civil service than one would expect on the basis of its proportionate strength in the nation as a whole. The 'recruitment process takes place within a framework of strong norms based on the merit principle, as traditionally defined by the ministries themselves, and disallowing political promotions and intervention by special interests.' Anton (1980, 34) argues similarly for Sweden, which represents a 'guild' model of the civil service, since 'entry is rigidly controlled, leadership is derived from within the system and outside penetration is minimized.' In Denmark a similar pattern obtains. Alone among the Scandinavian countries, Finland has developed since the 1960s an extensive party politicization, although it is of dubious legality. Available posts are divided up between the ruling parties (Modeen 1980, 42).

The norm of neutrality can, curiously, coexist with extensive patronage throughout the political and administrative system. In the Netherlands, despite the importance of the principle of proportionality in the old consociational system that preserved social and political stability, posts within the higher levels of the national civil service appeared to be relatively immune to political appointments; there are no formal procedures for political appointments, and 'for all its . . . potential for political spoils, in practice the Dutch administration cannot be said to be highly politicised' (Daalder 1989, 8). Given the degree of patronage in public sector jobs generally, as well as the tendency for top civil service jobs to be filled by political appointees, albeit from within the service, it is also somewhat surprising that a similar neutralization of the top levels of the civil service is characteristic of both the image and self-image of civil servants in Italy (see Hine 1993).

A third means of institutionalizing political influence is through some form of administrative body which acts as the eyes, the ears and possibly also the voice of the politician within the bureaucracy. In authoritarian systems this was carried out by an extensive, frequently party-based, administration (although in both the Soviet Union and Nazi Germany the degree to which this meant a takeover of the state by the party can be exaggerated; see Lane and Ross 1994; Caplan 1988). In European democracies such a function has

been exercised to a more limited degree by the *cabinets* of ministers: a group
of advisers appointed by ministers who generally have authority to act in the
minister's name as well as be informed of developments within the ministry.
Such *cabinet* systems are found in Belgium, France, the Netherlands, Italy,
Spain and Portugal, and also in the Commission of the European Union. In
a much weaker form, ministers in many other countries without formal
cabinets, such as Britain, use advisers on an *ad hoc* basis to sustain their influence
within their ministry.

All three forms of institutionalization of political control are used to some
degree in most countries; civil servants, like most professional groups, generally claim some form of ability to serve others irrespective of their political
views. Moreover, the impact of any single institution is not common across all
countries that have adopted it. For example, while the *cabinet* system is central
to the bureaucratization of politics in France, being a stepping stone from an
administrative to a political career, it has no such significance and impact in
Italy.

There are three broad forms of impact produced by different types of
institutionalization of political control. The first can be found in the potential
of such institutionalization in the form of political appointments and *cabinets*
for introducing conflict at the top of the executive organization. It is not
necessarily the case that the top career officials feel in competition with *cabinet*
members or political appointees. Rather, career officials on the one hand and
political appointees and *cabinet* members on the other have different bases of
legitimacy and can have different loyalties and perceptions which may frequently conflict. Heclo's (1977) study makes this point in the context of
presidential appointees and career officials in the United States. In the Commission of the European Union, the Director General may come into conflict
with the *chef de cabinet* of the Commissioner. In France the distinction
between *cabinet* director and permanent *directeur* is a 'particularly acute conflict
at the apex of the French administrative system' (Suleiman 1975, 234). Yet,
for the most part, in France the potential conflict is substantially reduced by
the fact that *cabinet* members are generally senior career civil servants.

A second consequence comes from the degree to which the institutionalization of political control creates opportunities for career officials to participate in overtly party political decisions. Of course all civil servants are
involved to some degree or other in political decision-making, otherwise the
civil service would have relatively little importance for political science. Yet
the form of institutionalization of political control can encourage the development of a distinctive form of bureaucratic politician who, as a political
appointee of one sort or another, can advance his career by playing the
political field. The two clearest examples of these are the French civil servant
politicians who pursue a career within the 'politico-administrative' elite, for

which a period in a ministerial *cabinet* is a major springboard, and the American 'technopols', people who move into and out of the Washington establishment as political appointees and lobbyists (Heclo 1984). There are others: in Sweden the advisory bodies surrounding ministers create a group of bureaucratic politicians known as *politruker*. However, it cannot be assumed that every *cabinet* system creates such a group of bureaucratic politicians. In Italy the *gabinetti* of ministers have failed to do so. The reasons for this are instructive: the Italian ministerial *gabinetti*, composed of a large proportion of Council of State officials, are primarily legalistic bodies, and see their role as principally technical and not as policy-making. Thus only where it has extensive decision-making powers can we expect a *cabinet* body to generate a distinctive form of bureaucratic politician.

A third consequence is in the impact on the *status* of the profession of civil servant. Politicization subordinates a career within the civil service to patronage from politicians. It ceases to be a self-governing profession with its own rules and criteria for advancement and is dependent upon political favour of one form or another. While there is no certainty that a political appointee will do the bidding of a political master, this is not the central point. A bureaucratic career is subordinated to the political in some countries and inhibits the development of a strong professionalized bureaucracy; this is most noticeably the case in Belgium and Italy, where the status of ministerial officials is relatively low.

Caste or category

The higher levels of the bureaucracy are not composed of random selections from the populations of the countries they serve. In Western nations they tend to be male, from professional backgrounds with university degrees – the usual backgrounds for people in high status jobs in elected politics as well as in the private sector. However, beyond this, the higher reaches of many civil services are dominated by people with educational backgrounds that give them the characteristics of a bureaucratic *caste*, sharing a similar culture or even set of values, rather than simply a collection of high status individuals. In some systems, recruitment patterns create such castes. In Germany recruitment to the civil service as a *Beamte* (official) in the top flight *höherer Dienst* (higher civil service) is still predominantly through a *Staatsexamen* (state examination) taken after studying law. Consequently, lawyers tend to dominate still in the higher levels of German administration. In France the *Grandes Écoles* such as the *École Polytechnique* or the *École National d'Administration* are the training ground for senior administrators, and in Britain the universities of Oxford and Cambridge still provide nearly two-thirds of Permanent Secretaries. In other countries, top administrators are a more heterogeneous category; in Sweden the traditional dominance of legal scholars in the higher reaches of administration has to some degree given way to a greater diversity of educational backgrounds.

The nature of the higher levels of the civil service as a caste has two implications for the role of the civil service in the decision-making process. The first is that a caste is more likely to be cohesive, and this in turn may be expected to affect the role of bureaucracy in the political process in the manner already outlined. Second, the nature of the caste is likely to influence the bureaucratic elite's perception of its role in the decision-making process. For example, a training in law on the European continent has conventionally been associated with a role perception of administration as a subordinate and largely separate world to that of politics: the 'traditional' bureaucrat of Putnam's (1973) study of Germany and Italy in the 1960s. This has been associated with the conception of the role of the judge in continental European Roman law, especially in its Germanic version, as a *Paragraphenautomat*, an expert who makes no judgements but merely interprets facts in the light of existing law (Page 1995). In Italy this legal background, combined with the fact that a large proportion of civil servants are from the south, is LaPalombara's main explanation for the fact that civil servants appear to be 'dialectically minded' (LaPalombara 1987, 208–9). A different perception can be found among French civil servants, whose training and career give them a key role in politics:

> The members of the Grands Corps . . . benefit from an aura of elitism and from a reputation for impartiality; they occupy important positions in the administrative, para-administrative and private sectors; they form part of a network within and beyond the administration, which enables them to arbitrate conflicts and coordinate policies – all of which means that they are profoundly involved in the decision making process. (Suleiman 1975, 269)

In Britain the humanistic Oxford-Cambridge training that has been so characteristic of the upper reaches of the bureaucracy since the middle of the nineteenth century is passed on to new recruits, since the 'civil service . . . is very proficient at moulding its bright and its young. They very quickly rub shoulders with the great, the seasoned and the established in the upper ranks and are indulged in the way that dons treat bright, sparky undergraduates who are fun to teach' (Hennessy 1989, 521). Such a training certainly does not emphasize subordination to politicians. One former permanent secretary recalls how a mentor 'showed me how to negotiate, how to draw breath mid-sentence so as to discourage interruption, how to draft, and why the service belongs neither to politicians nor to officials but to the Crown and the nation' (Sir Ian Bancroft quoted in Hennessy 1989, 521).

In much of continental Europe the predominant qualification for senior civil servants is a law degree. Lawyers predominate in the higher reaches of the civil service in Germany, Italy, Spain, Portugal, Austria, Switzerland, Belgium and Luxembourg. Although in the Scandinavian countries this used to be the case, it remains so only in Finland. While a law degree is not, as has been discussed above, a necessary or sufficient qualification for entry into the *Grands Corps*, nevertheless training in the *École National d'Administration* contains substantial emphasis on constitutional law and its application. In Sweden, Denmark and Norway, the traditional reliance upon law graduates has declined steadily in the twentieth century and has been replaced by a variety of qualifications, above all in the social sciences. In the European Union a legal qualification is the most common degree held by top officials – about 40 per cent have law as a first qualification, another 30 per cent hold an economics degree and 16 per cent studied politics (Rotacher and Colling 1987, 15). In the *nomenklatura* systems of East-Central Europe before the collapse of communism, a qualification in law was held by a small proportion of senior appointees. In Hungary, for example, *nomenklatura* elites were predominantly teachers, engineers or technicians; less than 3 per cent were lawyers (Tökés 1991, 278–80).

Permeability

The permeability of civil services refers to the relationship with interest groups, a high level of permeability being found where groups are difficult if not impossible to exclude from the policy-making process. Conversely, where interest groups are relatively easily excluded, the level of permeability is low. Of course the precise influence of interest groups in policy-making will vary over time and over the issue involved. Nevertheless, some generalizations about the accessibility of the bureaucracy to interest groups have been possible. For example, observers have examined cross-national differences under the rubric of 'non-negotiable policy-making', while others have sought to use the distinction between 'strong states' and 'weak states' (see Nettl 1968; Atkinson and Coleman 1989).

The classic case of the 'weak state' or the political system in which the scope for non-negotiable policy-making is very small is the United States. In the 1970s the growth of interest organizations was one of the most profound changes affecting decision-making in Washington; large numbers of new groups, or rather groups new to Washington, transformed the existing structure of close relationships between groups and government, known as 'iron triangles', to create a series of 'issue networks' – fluid and unstable groups consisting of group representatives, congressional committee and executive agency members, personnel and advisers, as well as 'policy watchers' (see

Heclo 1978). This contrasts strongly with France, where the political status of interest groups within the national policy-making networks is much weaker. As Hayward (1986, 50) writes in his discussion of industrial policy-making, the products of the *Grandes Écoles* are 'regarded as entitled to influence public policy decisions because they embody a disinterested and elevated conception of the public interest. When pushed to extremes, this statism can amount to a desire to dominate all private group manifestations of a potentially disorderly society, prone to the seductions of sinister sectional interests.' Consequently, Suleiman's (1975, 327) survey of the French administrative elite finds that even the suggestion that groups influenced decisions was initially considered offensive. Although this does not mean that groups are excluded from the policy process, which groups are included is a matter of discretion for the executive; in Hayward's (1986, 39–55) terms they are 'pressured' groups rather than pressure groups.

The main relevance of this distinction for our purposes is its significance for the role of bureaucrats in policy-making. In a system where the executive dominates and can exclude groups from the policy-making process, or include them on its terms, the role of the civil servant is different from that in a system in which the bureaucrat is one player among many others. In the former, senior officials make decisions or advise those who make decisions; in the latter, they are more cautious participants in a wider game of bureaucratic politics in which outcomes are more likely to be negotiated among governmental and non-governmental actors. Bureaucratic leadership in systems where the scope for non-negotiable policy-making is small is more likely to resemble Kaufman's (1981) description of 'nudging agendas' than making decisions. As Aberbach et al. (1981, 98) put it:

> American bureaucrats are clearly more political in their role focus than their European counterparts ... The fragile and uncertain nature of political authority in America makes for bureaucratic orientations that emphasize the building of political support. ... In this system of fragmented responsibilities each institutional actor [whether politician or bureaucrat] plays a major role and each, to a degree unknown in Europe, has come to speak the other's language.

The fusion between executive and legislative power in Europe means that such an American model of a weak state is less likely to exist. But there are other aspects of political systems which similarly make the executive and thus the bureaucracy particularly vulnerable to group pressures.

The executive may be permeated by group pressures due to the central position that political parties hold in the policy-making process, making them the prime route through which interests can reduce the scope for non-negotiable policy-making. This is especially noticeable in Italy, where the 'party centred dynamic' of policy-making means that the focus of interest activity is with 'the secretaries general of the political parties, . . . the party factions and their leaders, and . . . the local political notables and patrons who constitute the base of the power system' (LaPalombara 1987, 221). In the early years of the Bonn Republic, some interest groups even had power over appointments within the bureaucracy due to their close association with governing parties (Eschenburg 1963). The 'corporatist' patterns of policy-making in the Netherlands before the 1980s, which gave major groups regular access to forums of executive decision-making, were closely related to the 'consociational' model of democracy according to which the different 'pillars' in Dutch society shared political power (Gladdish 1991).

In other countries, the involvement of groups in executive decision-making is not so obviously and directly underpinned by the relationship of groups to governing political parties. In such countries the extensive consultation is generally viewed as an element of 'style' or 'culture'. One of the prime examples of this is the elaborate arrangements for consulting interests that one finds in the 'consensual democracies' of Scandinavia and above all Sweden. 'Style' and 'culture' in this context may serve as a proxy for a pattern of behaviour, the cause of which is inexplicable. In the Swedish case Elder, Thomas and Arter (1982, 159–60) point out that such cultural explanations may have concrete causes, since

> politicians in Scandinavia are [not] somehow differently constituted from politicians anywhere else in the world. As an American historian of Sweden [FR Scott] put it, referring to the confused period of minority government that followed the breakthrough of the parliamentary principle in that country in 1918–21, 'The politics of compromise was forced by the electoral situation not by the fact that the Swedes loved compromise'.

They add that 'concertation' of policy was forced upon political elites not only in Sweden but throughout Scandinavia in the early part of this century, 'because no single party found itself within striking distance of a majority'. Nevertheless, whatever the precise explanation in countries such as Sweden, such consultations have become a significant feature of the policy-making process. This contrasts with Britain and France, where consultation with outside interests, indeed the securing of consensus on policy proposals, might be desirable, yet it is quite possible for the executive to pay little or no attention to these consultations.

Thus we may talk of three forms of permeability; one which is underpinned by strong parties and a relationship between groups and leading parties, such as in Italy and 'corporatist' systems such as those in the Netherlands, Belgium and Austria. The degree to which this pattern persists is uncertain in these countries, since in Italy the party system has all but collapsed and in the others the traditional consociational model no longer applies, at least not to the degree found in the 1960s (see Gladdish 1991, ch. 9; Luther 1992; Van den Bulck 1992) – in which case one might expect the systems in these countries increasingly to resemble one of the other two forms. The second is a system where extensive consultation is an institutionalized if not entrenched feature of policy-making. To some extent we might explain this as a 'style' of policy-making in default of other obvious concrete political imperatives, apart from a historical legacy which can explain why incorporation of groups into the policy-making process has become such an established feature of the political process. Sweden, Norway and Denmark would fall into this category. In Germany, where opposition parties and a wide range of groups are involved in policy formulation, the 'style' is explained at least in part by the necessities of cross-party collaboration fostered by the federal system. A third form of permeability is rather weak. It is found in political systems such as in France and Britain where extensive dialogue is a 'preferred' form of interest consultation, yet there are few general imperatives, either political or cultural, which ensure that key aspects of government policy must remain entirely negotiable.

The Role of the Minister

While so far this chapter has concentrated on the character of the civil service, to some extent the impact of the bureaucracy is a function of the degree to which political leaders are capable of giving direction to it. The military analogy used at the start of this chapter breaks down, since those who give orders are not simply organizational superiors, they also have a separate source of legitimacy and authority: the political authority of public election. Alongside the control that legislatures may exert over the bureaucracy through their capacity to exercise scrutiny of the executive and control of legislation, the concept of political leadership of executive organizations by elected politicians remains a fundamental component of democratic responsiveness in contemporary government. The degree to which this form of leadership can be found in different countries, of course, varies from individual to individual, from case to case. From Headey's (1974) study of British cabinet ministers we know that some ministers tend to take on roles as ambassadors representing the ministry to the outside world, others are executives, concentrating on running the ministry, while still others are actually policy initiators. Yet there are some general features of the political system that limit or strengthen the ability of ministers to exercise leadership within it.

Firstly there is the structure of the executive. The traditional European pattern of executive organization is the ministry, where policy-makers and service providers in specific policy areas are part of the same hierarchical organization. Thus it is common in many European countries for a teacher to be an employee of the Ministry of Education. Not all public services, not even those which are carried out by national government, are executed by ministerial employees – in France those who pay out social security benefits are employees of the *Caisses de Securité Sociale* rather than the ministry, just as hospital workers are mostly employees of local health trusts in Britain. In Sweden the structure of the executive limits the scope for ministerial leadership through the board structure of the executive. Ministries in Sweden generally engage few employees. They have responsibility for policy planning and the issue of guidelines concerning the execution of legislation, yet operational decisions affecting service delivery are the responsibility of the *ambetsverke* (boards) answerable to the ministries yet over which there is no direct administrative control. This principle has formed the basis of Swedish administration since the seventeenth century. In Britain it has developed since the 1988 Next Steps initiative, which similarly sought to confine ministries to a policy-making role, while implementation is a function of the agencies – although it must be acknowledged that policy-making and implementation cannot be separated very easily. In Germany a number of ministerial functions are carried out by *Anstalten des öffentlichen Rechtes* (public law institutes) or similar agencies, most notably the provision of many social security benefits, as well as the delivery of labour market services, which is the responsibility of the *Bundesanstalt für Arbeit*. Systematic information about the relations between the ministry and its agencies is unavailable. For example, we have only limited knowledge of just how independent Swedish agencies or Next Steps agencies are in practice. This means that it is not possible to do more than point to internal organization as a possible limitation to the exercise of ministerial political leadership.

A second factor influencing forms of executive political leadership consists of the skills with which politicians reach ministerial office. Ministers do not have to be elected members of the legislature. In some countries such as France, Norway and the Netherlands there is an incompatibility rule that forces members of the legislature to resign once appointed to ministerial office. In Belgium, Italy, Britain and Ireland, over four-fifths of ministers have been MPs (see table 9.1). In the Netherlands, as well as the Scandinavian countries, with the exception of Denmark, the number of ministers reaching office through parliament is much lower, at between one half and two-thirds. Germany, Austria and Denmark fall in between these two groups.

A third factor is broadly related to this. The importance of career officials is generally believed to derive from their permanence. They have both the technical knowledge and the experience of policy-making that temporary politicians lack. According to Aberbach et al. (1981, 110–11), politicians, and here they base their analysis on MPs rather than ministers in particular, are

Table 9.1   *Characteristics of ministers*

	Single-post ministers (%)	Civil servants (%)	Duration in post (years)	Elected as MPs (%)	Interrupted careers (%)
Austria	83	17	4.9	68	7
Belgium	55	6	2.1	87	32
Denmark	63	15	2.9	79	37
Finland	67	24	1.9	62	41
France	53	35	2.0	69	18
Germany	64	6	3.9	74	11
Ireland	35	4	2.9	96	62
Italy	42	4	1.6	94	44
Netherlands	79	16	3.1	53	14
Norway	75	25	2.9	57	21
Sweden	71	25	3.9	61	21
UK	38	9	2.5	95	26

Source: Blondel and Thiébault (1991)

'informed by a broad-gauged view of society . . . Politicians are generalists motivated by political ideals and broad interests, and the world view of the generalists is usually keyed to simple explanations. Thus personal or social forces rather than technical capacities or complex intertwining forces are seen as the causes of social problems more frequently by politicians than by bureaucrats.' However, if one examines the structure of ministerial careers, there is some difference between individual countries on this, since in some countries there is a greater emphasis upon the specialization in ministerial careers than others. Put simply, Britain, Ireland, Italy and Belgium tend to have ministers who have broader political skills, whereas Finland, Sweden, Norway, Austria and the Netherlands tend to have ministers who specialize to a greater extent. While not all the indicators point in the anticipated direction, if we look at table 9.1 the four countries in this first group tend to have fewer ministers whose career is spent entirely in one ministry (an average of 42.5 per cent) compared with the others (75.2 per cent). Ministers are more likely to have been civil servants in the more specialized group (21.2 per cent) than the other group (5.8 per cent) and specialization is also reflected in the average length of tenure of a ministerial office (3.34 years) in the more specialized countries than the others (2.28 years). Fewer ministers in the specialist group (20.6 per cent) have 'interrupted careers' – that is to say, have returned to ministerial office after having left the cabinet – than in the other (41.1 per cent).

The other countries, Germany, France and Denmark, tend to fall in between these two groups. France is particularly interesting since the most striking feature of ministerial recruitment is the importance of a civil service background for high ministerial office. Dogan's (1979) study shows how 'mandarin ascent', an education and career as a civil servant enhanced by participation in the political process, above all through a *cabinet* position, became one of the prime routes to ministerial office under the Fifth Republic. This is certainly supported by the data in table 9.1. The German position, intermediate between the groups of countries with specialized and less specialized ministers, may reflect the legacy of the early years of the Bonn Republic when relatively more ministers were technical experts.

The significance of this specialist dimension of variation lies in the type of ministers different systems tend to produce. While the distinctive contribution of politicians as ministers to policy-making is the political authority that they represent and the concern with 'broad gauged' issues, in some countries this is less evident than in others, indicating a greater propensity to the bureaucratization of politics in countries such as Sweden, Norway, Austria and the Netherlands above all. France is peculiar in the sense that a bureaucratic career can contribute, paradoxically, to a non-specialized political career, with an elite education generally regarded as an appropriate training for a wide range of jobs, whether in politics, the civil service or even in the public or private sector.

In the European Union there is, of course, no direct counterpart to the minister. As appointees of the member states, the Commissioners are the nearest equivalent. They are similar in many respects. They generally have political experience; 80 per cent of them have been regional, local or national representatives, and many (58 per cent) have held ministerial office. They differ, however, in three key respects. First, while they tend to have experience as elected politicians in their home states, they no longer have the direct political authority that comes from successful active participation in public elections (see Page and Wouters 1994). In fact the oath of office for a Commissioner almost by definition excludes it when it requires that they neither seek nor accept instructions from their home state, thus severing the direct political linkages between their political constituency at home and their duties in Brussels. Second, they do not belong to a collegial body, a Cabinet, which has, through its control of the legislature via the party system, access to legislation. While cabinet ministers of member states have to compete with others for time for their ministry's legislation, Commissioners face the altogether more daunting task of mobilizing sufficient nation-states to back their proposals, and increasingly the European Parliament too. While Commissioners certainly have the skills and the ability to give leadership through bureaucratic entrepreneurship, they lack the direct electoral mandate that enables them to mobilize political authority.

Six National Patterns of Bureaucracy in Europe

On the basis of the five characteristics – pervasiveness, cohesion, politicization, caste and permeability – as well as the nature of ministerial control, each country in Europe is unique. However, it is possible to take things a little further than this and point to some broad similarities between countries across a number of the indicators discussed here. Although such groupings should not be taken too far, they are useful for two main reasons. First, they point out major contours of cross-national similarities and differences, and second, in doing so, they suggest ways in which we may begin to start accounting for these differences.

One pattern of administration–politics interaction is a *Southern European pattern*, characterized by a bureaucracy which has a relatively low status, in part because it is generally politically appointed. In fact, patronage is generally widespread throughout the civil service in such countries. Nevertheless, in this pattern officials still regard themselves as the neutral servants of the state. They perceive their roles in formal legalistic terms as interpreters of the law, and most senior civil servants will be trained lawyers. While the scope for central intervention in the affairs of subnational government is extensive, the legalistic culture of national administration, the lack of cohesion within the national civil service, and the large possibilities for networks of political patronage to bypass formal intergovernmental administrative channels mean that this potential for central control is manifested more in procedures to detect and limit illegal actions by regional and local governments than any active role in shaping their policies. The weakness of the bureaucratic elite as well as its self-image as the representative of a neutral legal order further mean that patterns of interest group–government relations are likely to emphasize routine linkages with political parties rather than with ministries. Such a model is more likely to be approximated in Italy, Spain, Portugal and Greece. Belgium to a certain degree also corresponds to this model, although the federal structure of the country means that it is difficult to talk of an extensive national bureaucracy. Nevertheless, at the level of the central state as well as within the Flemish and Walloon communities, the civil services bear some resemblance to the Southern model.

A second clear pattern is that of the *Scandinavian political systems*, with a professional, largely non-politicized civil service in which the advances made by social and natural scientists have eroded the traditional dominance of lawyers. Here the status of civil servants is high. Their participation in the affairs of local government is far less direct than in the Southern European model, and, apart from the setting of the legal framework through national statutes, takes the form of cooperative planning. The bureaucracy in these countries can scarcely be called a single administrative elite, since careers are pursued within a ministry or agency. Moreover, the routine involvement of major interests in the decision-making process, often through mechanisms which are constructed to maximize the chances of finding consensual policies, means that, although they enjoy a status and power far higher in general than Southern European bureaucratic elites, there is much less scope for sustaining the 'non-negotiable' forms of policy-making characteristic of states such as France and Britain. Included in this category would be Norway, Sweden and Denmark and possibly also Finland, although the degree of politicization of the bureaucracy there makes it very different from the other Scandinavian countries. In the Netherlands where, even at the height of the consociational democracy, a non-politicized senior civil service was maintained, there are some similarities with the Scandinavian group.

A somewhat looser third grouping, incorporating Switzerland, Germany and Austria, might be termed a *Germanic* form of bureaucracy. These are federal systems and thus the role of senior officials is generally less extensive than in unitary states. Civil servants are predominantly lawyers, although it is important to note that the Germanic tradition of Roman law has tended to emphasize the technical and abstract as opposed to the form and style associated with Italian and French traditions (Zweiggert and Kötz 1992). Like civil servants in both the Scandinavian and the Southern European patterns, civil servants in Germanic systems are likely to be parts of a sectorized executive and make their careers within single ministries or *Ressorts*. In Austria and Germany the higher levels of the bureaucracy are politicized, although this does not appear to have had the impact on the status of the bureaucracy found elsewhere. Possibly this is because of the formalism of 'party book administration' (Dyson 1977), according to which membership of a political party is regarded as a normal prerequisite for any high flier. Thus party membership is not associated with rapid promotion for the less well qualified but is a prudent measure for the professionally qualified to ensure that they can rise as high as they deserve. This might possibly also be a consequence of the traditional high status accorded to the bureaucracies of Germany and Austria from the eighteenth century to the Second World War. In these countries, unlike in Southern Europe, the high status of administration makes the bureaucracy an important focus of government–group relations.

The *East European* systems of bureaucracy belong together only because they currently face common problems: creating a new democratic administrative system with limited economic and personnel resources. So far, because democratic institutions are still in their infancy, it is not possible to point to a clear role of the civil service in these countries. Neither has any substantial body of literature on the matter yet been made available outside of East-Central Europe. It is possible that eventually the East European democracies will develop along similar lines in this respect, but since they have different traditions – different indigenous as well as Austrian, Russian and Prussian influences – diversity is just as likely.

The *British and Irish model* is distinctive since it has probably the least politicized senior civil service. It has a high status within the policy-making process and, in its senior ranks, can be seen as a government-wide *service*. The *French model* is also on its own, since its bureaucracy enjoys an enormous social and political prestige that allows it to lay successful claim to a degree of expertise required to run major governmental and non-governmental organizations. While the French administrative system is open to political appointment at the senior levels, its self-perception as standing aloof from the conflicts of party and group politics as the representative of the interests of the state is generally unchallenged by either elite or public opinion. Its status is such that an administrative training and career can be, and often is, an important component of a political career. Nevertheless, the corporative system, not unique in principle to France but unique in the power of *corps* loyalties that it generates, serves to fragment the bureaucratic elite of France significantly.

The European Union has elements from different systems. The French influence is especially noticeable in the form of *cabinet* found in the Commission, where the *chef de cabinet* has important executive powers which are exercised in the name of the Commissioner. Also characteristic of the French system is the fusion between the administrative and political elites, where administrative careers are furthered by service in a *cabinet* which has some similarities with the top A1 and A2 level within the Commission. Service-wide careers at the top level make it resemble the English and Irish model more than those which predominate on the European continent. In terms of the educational qualifications held by top officials, the EU resembles more closely the Scandinavian model, where legal qualifications still dominate at the most senior levels but where social sciences are studied by a large number of top officials. In terms of its pervasiveness, the EU appears to be an emerging federal institution with defined spheres of authority relating to member states and their regions, provinces and localities.

How might one account for the differences in bureaucratic systems? One possibility would be to interpret them as results of 'culture'. In fact this is an especially attractive explanation, since administrative cultures have been the subject of survey analysis by Hofstede, whose resultant cross-national typology of cultures in public and private organizations mirrors very closely the groupings discussed here. Using survey analysis from 39 countries, he derived a typology constructed largely from an 'uncertainty avoidance index', a measure which reflects, among other things, the willingness to tolerate ambiguity, and a 'power distance' index, reflecting among other things the inability of different strata within an organization to communicate with one another. He places European nation-states into an Anglo cluster (Britain, Ireland), a developed Latin cluster (France, Spain, Italy, Belgium), a less developed Latin cluster (Portugal), a Nordic cluster (Norway, Netherlands, Finland, Sweden and Denmark) and a Germanic cluster (Switzerland, Germany and Austria). Greece belongs to a 'near eastern' cluster, related to the developed Latin cluster (Hofstede 1980, 336).

If the cultural explanation is in fact an accurate one, we still have the problem of explaining how these cultures developed. It might be the case that patterns of state formation, such as the experience of feudalism, Roman law or absolutism, had decisive impacts on bureaucratic cultures (Page 1995). However, the explanation is not likely to be a simple one, since the linkage between the bureaucratic groupings discussed here, or even those set out by Hofstede, and geographic variations in patterns of state formation are not obvious. While, for example, France, Spain, Italy and Belgium share a 'cultural' cluster, they have very different patterns of state development (see Chapter 1). Alternatively, far more specific experiences, such as the collapse of the Weimar regime and the Nazi era in Germany, the early years of parliamentary government in Scandinavia or the experience of Napoleonic rule on the European continent, may have a decisive influence on the forms of bureaucratic organization and behaviour found in each country. Certainly it is possible to identify the proximate causes of radical changes in administrative systems in discrete policies or events that seem to have little to do directly with either the tide of history or administrative culture. For example, the move towards a 'new public management' in Britain, with the creation of executive agencies, the introduction of merit pay and more developed use of performance targets, is associated with the ideology of the British Conservative party since the late 1970s.

Probably to a greater extent than in the recent past, the quest for any such explanation of differences will be trying to hit a moving target. Privatization and the attempt to introduce management methods borrowed from the private sector are certainly not unique to Britain. In the expanding European Union, there is the possibility that the changes that EU membership has brought into the national policy-making process in member states, in matters ranging from agriculture and employment to road safety, will eventually have a more profound effect upon the internal structure of national civil services than they have had so far. The forms of administration and political leadership that emerge in East-Central Europe are at present very unclear, if not fluid. There is certainly no evidence of a general movement towards a 'bureaucratization of the world' (Jacoby 1973). If the traditional model of the bureaucracy as an army obeying the orders of its commanders breaks down even further, it will not be because the privates have taken over.

Bibliography

Aberbach, J. T. et al. (1981). *Bureaucrats and Politicians in Western Democracies*. Cambridge, MA: Harvard University Press.

Allison, G. (1971). *Essence of Decision: explaining the Cuban missile crisis*. Boston: Little, Brown.

Anton, T. J. (1980). *Administered Politics: elite political culture in Sweden*. Boston: Nijhoff.

Atkinson, M. M. and Coleman, W. D. (1989). 'Strong states and weak states: sectoral networks in advanced capitalist economies'. *British Journal of Political Science* 19 (1): 47–62.

Berti, G. (1981). 'La politique de choix des fonctionnaires en Italie', in C. Debbasch (ed.), *La fonction publique en Europe*. Paris: CNRS.

Blondel, J. and Thiébault, J.-L. (eds) (1991). *The Profession of Government Minister in Western Europe*. London: Macmillan.

Caplan, J. (1988). *Government without Administration: state and civil society in Weimar and Nazi Germany*. Oxford: Clarendon Press.

Crozier, M. (1970). *La société bloquée*. Paris: Seuil.

Curry, J. L. (1993). 'Pluralism in East Central Europe: not will it last but what is it?' *Communist and Post Communist Studies* 26 (4): 446–61.

Daalder, H. (1989). 'The mould of Dutch politics: themes for comparative inquiry'. *West European Politics* 12 (1): 1–20.

Dogan, M. (1979). 'How to become a minister in France: career pathways 1870– 1978'. *Comparative Politics* 12 (1): 1–26.

Dyson, K. (1977). 'The West German party book administration: an evaluation'. *Public Administration Bulletin* 25: 3–23.

Elder, N. C. M. et al. (1982). *The Consensual Democracies? The government and politics of the Scandinavian states*. Oxford: Martin Robertson.

Eldersveld, S. J. et al. (1981). *Elite Images of Dutch Politics: accommodation and conflict*. Ann Arbor: University of Michigan Press.

Eschenburg, T. (1963). *Herrschaft der Verbände?*, 2nd edn. Stuttgart: Deutsche Verlagsanstalt.

Gladdish, K. (1991). *Governing from the Centre: politics and policy making in the Netherlands*. London: Hurst.

Grémion, C. (1979). *Professions décideurs: pouvoir des hauts fonctionnaires et reforme de l'Etat*. Paris: Gauthier-Villars.

Grémion, P. (1976). *Le pouvoir périphérique: bureaucrates et notables dans le système politique français*. Paris: Seuil.

Hayward, J. E. S. (1986). *The State and the Market Economy: industrial patriotism and economic intervention in France*. Brighton: Wheatsheaf.

Headey, B. (1974). *British Cabinet Ministers*. London: Allen & Unwin.

Heclo, H. (1977). *A Government of Strangers*. Washington, DC: Brookings.

—— (1978). 'Issue networks and the executive establishment', in A. King (ed.), *The New American Political System*. Washington, DC: American Enterprise Institute.

—— (1984). 'In search of a role: America's higher civil service', in E. N. Suleiman (ed.), *Bureaucracy and Policy Making*. New York: Holmes & Meier.

Heclo, H. and Wildavsky, A. (1981). *Private Government of Public Money*, 2nd edn. London: Macmillan.

Hennessy, P. (1989). *Whitehall*. London: Secker & Warburg.

Hine, D. (1993). *Governing Italy: the politics of bargained pluralism*. Oxford: Oxford University Press.

Hofstede, G. (1980). *Culture's Consequences*. London and Beverly Hills, CA: Sage.

Horvath, T. (1992). 'The structure of Hungarian local government past and present', in I. Elander and M. Gustafsson (eds), *The Re-emergence of Local Self-Government in Central Europe: the first experience*. Örebro: University of Örebro Centre for Housing and Urban Research.

Jacoby, H. (1973). *The Bureaucratisation of the World*. Berkeley: University of California Press.

Janos, A. C. (1982). *The Politics of Backwardness in Hungary, 1825–1945*. Princeton, NJ: Princeton University Press.

Kaufman, H. (1981). *The Administrative Behavior of Federal Bureau Chiefs*. Washington, DC: Brookings.

Kellner, P. and Crowther-Hunt, Lord (1980). *The Civil Servants*. London: Futura.

Kjellberg, F. (1984). Review of J. Richardson (ed.), *Policy Styles in Western Europe*. *Journal of Public Policy* 4 (3): 271–73.

Lane, D. E. and Ross, C. (1994). 'The limitations of party control: the government bureaucracy in the USSR'. *Communist and Post-Communist Studies* 27 (1): 19–38.

LaPalombara, J. (1987). *Democracy Italian Style*. New Haven, CT: Yale University Press.

Luther, K. R. (1992). 'Consociationalism, parties and the party system'. *West European Politics* 15 (1): 99–131.

Lynn, J. and Jay, A. (1981). *Yes Minister: the diaries of a cabinet minister by the Rt Hon. James Hacker MP*, Vol. 1. London: British Broadcasting Corporation.

Mackie, T. T. and Hogwood, B. W. (1985). 'The United Kingdom: decision sifting in a secret garden', in T. T. Mackie and B. W. Hogwood (eds), *Unlocking the Cabinet: cabinet structures in comparative perspective*. London and Beverly Hills CA: Sage.

Mayntz, R. and Scharpf, F. W. (1975). *Policy Making in the German Federal Bureaucracy*. Amsterdam: Elsevier.

Modeen, T. (1980). 'La politique de choix des fonctionnaires en Finlande', in C. Debbasch (ed.), *La fonction publique en Europe*. Paris: CNRS.

Neisser, H. (1982). 'Die Rolle der Bürokratie', in Heinz Fischer (ed.), *Das politische System Österreichs*, 3rd edn. Vienna: Europaverlag.

—— (1991). 'Verwaltung', in H. Dachs (ed.), *Handbuch des politischen Systems Österreichs*. Vienna: Manz.

Nettl, J. P. (1968). 'The state as a conceptual variable'. *World Politics* 20: 559–92.

Olsen, J. P. (1983). *Organized Democracy: political institutions in a welfare state – the case of Norway*. Oslo: Universitetsforlaget.

O'Nuallain, C. (1990). 'Irlande: maitrise des coûts, efficacité et politique des cadres'. *Revue française d'administration publique* 55 (July–Sept): 451–60.

Page, E. C. (1991). *Localism and Centralism in Europe: the political and legal bases of local self-government*. Oxford: Oxford University Press.

—— (1992). *Political Authority and Bureaucratic Power: a comparative analysis*, 2nd edn. Brighton: Harvester Wheatsheaf.

—— (1995). 'Bureaucrats and their brothers in law', in B. G. Peters (ed.), *Comparing Public Bureaucracies*. Aldershot: Edward Elgar.

Page, E. C. and Wouters, L. (1994). 'Paying the top people in Europe', in C. C. Hood and B. G. Peters (eds), *The Rewards of High Public Office*. London: Sage.

Perry, J. L. and Miller, T. K. (1991). 'The senior executive service: is it improving managerial performance?' *Public Administration Review* 51 (6): 554–63.

Pomohac, R. (1993). 'Administrative modernization in Czechoslovakia between constitutional and administrative reform', in J. J. Hesse (ed.), *Administrative Transformation in Central and Eastern Europe*. Oxford: Blackwell.

Putnam, R. D. (1973). 'The political status of senior civil servants in Western Europe: a preliminary analysis'. *British Journal of Political Science* 3 (3): 257–90.

Rotacher, A. and Colling, M. (1987). 'The community's top management: a meritocracy in the making'. *Staff Courier* 489.

Seton-Watson, H. (1962). *Eastern Europe between the Wars, 1918–1941*. New York: Harper & Row.

Shore, C. and Black, A. (1992). 'The European communities and the construction of Europe'. *Anthropology Today* 8 (3): 11–12.

Suleiman, E. N. (1975). *Politics, Power and Bureaucracy in France*. Princeton, NJ: Princeton University Press.

—— (1978). *Elites in French Society*. Princeton, NJ: Princeton University Press.

—— (1987). *Private Power and Centralization in France: the notaires and the state*. Princeton, NJ: Princeton University Press.

Szábo, G. (1993). 'Administrative transition in a post-communist society: the case of Hungary', in J. J. Hesse (ed.), *Administrative Transformation in Central and Eastern Europe*. Oxford: Blackwell.

Tannam, E. (1993). 'Influence or power? European regional policy and the Irish administrative system'. *Governance* 6 (2).

Taras, W. (1993). 'Changes in Polish public administration, 1989–1992', in J. J. Hesse (ed.), *Administrative Transformation in Central and Eastern Europe*. Oxford: Blackwell.

Tarkowski, J. (1981). 'Poland: patrons and clients in a planned economy', in S. N. Eisenstadt and R. Lemarchand (eds), *Political Clientelism, Patronage and Development*. London and Beverly Hills CA: Sage.

Thoenig, J.-C. (1973). *L'ère des technocrates*. Paris: Éditions d'Organisation.

Tökés, R. L. (1991). 'Hungary's new political elites: adaptation and change, 1989–1990', in G. Szoboszlai (ed.), *Democracy and Political Transformation: theories and East Central European realities*. Budapest: Hungarian Political Science Association.

Van den Bulck, J. (1992). 'Pillars and politics: neo-corporatism and policy networks in Belgium'. *West European Politics* 15 (2): 35–55.

Weber, M. (1972). *Wirtschaft und Gesellschaft*, 5th edn. Tübingen: Mohr.

Wynia, B. (1974). 'Federal bureaucrats' attitudes towards a democratic ideology'. *Public Administration Review* 34 (2): 156–67.

Zweiggert, K. and Kötz, H. (1992). *Introduction to Comparative Law*, trans. T. Weir, 2nd edn. Oxford: Clarendon Press.

10

Governing with Judges:
the New Constitutionalism

Alec Stone

Parliamentary supremacy, understood by most students of European politics to be a constitutive principle of European politics, has lost its vitality. After a polite, nostalgic nod across the channel to Westminster, we can declare it dead. In contrast to central tenets of the British parliamentary model, contemporary European constitutional theory has it that legislation, in order to be considered legally valid, must conform to the dictates of the constitution *as interpreted by constitutional courts*. In practice, the work of continental governments and parliaments is meaningfully structured by an ever-expanding web of constitutional constraints. Constitutional judges, for their part, routinely intervene in policy-making processes, establishing limits on legislative behaviour, but also drafting the precise terms of legislation. Further, the development of European constitutionalism has not been limited to national political systems, but has instead infected the politics of the European Community. The European Court of Justice, the constitutional court of the EC, has fashioned a kind of supra-national constitution, and this constitution binds – again – governments and the parliaments they control. European politics is today, in part, constitutional politics.

A comprehensive analysis of the political impact of constitutional courts on European politics remains impossible. Until very recently, little social-science, policy-relevant research on European constitutions or courts existed. Comparative political science is now in the process of (re)discovering courts, and especially European constitutional courts (Jackson and Tate 1990; Kommers 1989; Landfried 1989; Shapiro and Stone 1994; Stone 1992a; Volcansek 1992). I seek to build on this new research and to extend it to new cases and concerns. The chapter is divided into three parts. In part 1, I contrast the 'European model' of constitutional review with the 'American model' of judicial review, and then provide a comparative overview of the structure of the French, German, Italian and Spanish constitutional courts. In part 2, I evaluate the impact of these courts on policy-making processes and outcomes. In part 3, I examine the role and impact of the European Court of Justice in the construction of supra-national constitutionalism.

The 'European Model' of Constitutional Review

Constitutional review is the authority of an institution to invalidate laws, administrative decisions and judicial rulings on the grounds that they violate constitutional norms. The consolidation of review in Europe after 1945 has definitively repudiated certain dogmas of continental state theory, the most important of which subjugated constitutional to legislative authority. To cite just three common examples, European constitutions could be revised and even replaced by a simple majority vote of a legislative assembly, could not be protected by the judiciary, and did not contain substantive constraints – such as those contained in bills of rights – binding on law-makers. In nearly all European polities, American-style judicial review – the exercise of consti-tutional review by the judiciary – remains expressly prohibited. Review powers have instead been vested in quasi-judicial organs called constitutional courts. Such courts have been established in Austria (1945), Italy (1948), the Federal Republic of Germany (1949), France (1958), Portugal (1976), Spain (1978), Belgium (1985) and, after 1989, in the post-communist Czech Re-public, Hungary, Poland, Romania, Russia and Slovakia.[1]

The European model versus the American model

Viewed in comparative perspective, European constitutional courts can be said to make up an institutional 'family', to the extent that they share certain attributes distinguishing them from institutions that exercise constitutional review elsewhere. The point is perhaps best made by contrasting the European and American 'models' of review (Favoreu 1990). In American judicial review, 'any judge of any court, in any case, at any time, at the behest of any litigating party, has the power to declare a law unconstitutional' (Shapiro and Stone 1994). Although formulated broadly, the power is in practice conditioned by a number of doctrines designed to distinguish 'the judicial function' – *the settlement of legal disputes* – from 'the political function' – *legislating*. Most important, judicial review powers are said to be exercised only to the extent that they are necessary to settle a concrete 'case or controversy', one brought to trial by real-life litigants, with concrete interests in the outcome of the case. It can then be further said that the power of judicial review is not wished for, in and of itself, but at times *must* be exercised in order to resolve a pending legal conflict. Advisory opinions on constitutionality are necessarily precluded, as a judicial usurpation of the legislative function. American separation of powers notions – which rest on the formal equality of the executive, legislative and judicial branches of government – both enable and restrict the exercise of judicial review.

In contrast, the subordination of the work of the judiciary to that of the legislature is a central principle of continental constitutional law. As in the United States, the function of the European judiciary is to settle legal conflicts according to the law. But continental judges may not invalidate or refuse to apply a statute (legislation) as unconstitutional. From 1780 in Germanic states and from 1790 in France, for example, the prohibition of judicial review was explicitly proclaimed in written constitutions, and penalties were incorporated into the penal codes for any transgression. The paradigmatic statement of this prohibition is the French law of 16 August 1790, which remains in force today and has never been violated: 'Courts cannot interfere with the exercise of legislative powers or suspend the application of the laws'. This constitutional orthodoxy spread across Europe during the nineteenth century. In it, American-style judicial review is not defended in terms of a *separation* of powers, but attacked as establishing a permanent *confusion* of powers, since it enables the judiciary to participate in the political function. American judges are responsible for defending the integrity of a hierarchy of legal norms, the apex of which is the constitution; and, because legislative norms are juridically inferior to constitutional norms, constitutional provisions must prevail in any legal conflict between them and statutory provisions. Continental courts are also charged with defending a normative hierarchy, the apex of which, however, is the statute: legislative norms (as in the United States) trump conflicting, inferior norms (regulations, decrees, local rules). Put simply, European judiciaries have never possessed jurisdiction over the constitution, that is, the constitutional law is detached from the hierarchy of laws which judges are otherwise responsible for applying and defending.

A problem is posed: who will defend the constitutional law, arguably the law most in need of protection, if not the judiciary? The solution to this problem, it turned out, was the invention of the constitutional court. Constitutional courts enable the effective exercise of constitutional review while preserving the traditional separation of powers between the legislative and judicial branches. We can break the European model of constitutional review down into a number of interrelated, constituent components. The first of these is that, within the legal order, constitutional courts enjoy exclusive constitutional jurisdiction. That is, constitutional courts possess a monopoly on the exercise of constitutional review, and other judicial bodies remain formally precluded from engaging in review. Second, the jurisdiction of constitutional courts is formally restricted to settling constitutional disputes.

Unlike the US Supreme Court, constitutional courts do not preside over judicial disputes or litigation, which remains the function of the judiciary. Instead, specifically designated authorities refer constitutional questions to constitutional judges for rulings. Third, constitutional courts are formally detached from the judiciary. They occupy their own 'constitutional' space, a space neither wholly judicial nor political. Fourth, constitutional courts are at times empowered to render advisory opinions as a means of eliminating unconstitutional legislation and practices *before* they can do harm. Thus, in the European model, the judiciary remains bound by the supremacy of statute, while a constitutional court is responsible for preserving the supremacy of the constitution.

The historico–political origins of this institutional innovation are complex and beyond the scope of this chapter (Kommers 1989, chs. 1–3; Stone 1992a, chs. 1, 9), but two points deserve attention. First, contemporary European constitutional courts had important antecedents, to be found in the federal states of Austria, Germany and Switzerland. In these states, constitutional review functioned above all else to preserve the integrity of the distribution of authority between the federation and the federated states. The most important of these institutions was the constitutional court of the Austrian Second Republic (1920–34). The Austrian court was the brainchild of Hans Kelsen, an influential legal theorist who drafted the constitution of 1920, and who wrote a widely translated article elaborating and defending the European model of review (Kelsen 1928). Kelsen understood that politicians would not accept the establishment of judicial review in Europe. Nevertheless, he believed that a constitutional court, if granted carefully prescribed powers, could function to protect the constitution and enhance long-term regime stability. Present-day constitutional courts conform to nearly all of the central dictates of Kelsen's model.

Second, the bitter experience of Fascism before the Second World War and the huge American presence after it conspired to undermine the dogma of legislative supremacy, while placing the question of enforceable constitutional rights at the top of the European agenda. In Germany and Italy, the Americans insisted that new constitutions include a charter of rights, as well as some form of constitutional review to enforce these rights. American-style judicial review was rejected in these states and across Europe for diverse reasons. Most important, political elites remained hostile to sharing policy-making authority with judiciaries. Kelsenian constitutional review was an attractive option because it could easily be attached to the existing architecture of the state. Nevertheless, the Kelsenian model had to be modified in one crucial respect. Kelsen had forcefully argued that, in order to ensure that judicial and legislative functions remained as separate as possible, constitutional courts should be denied jurisdiction over constitutional rights, since rights provisions would inevitably enable or require courts to legislate. If judges were given the power to substitute their opinions about the meaning of rights claims for the opinions of the legislature, a 'government of judges' would develop. Since the Second World War Western Europe has experienced a kind of rights revolution, a hugely important movement to codify human rights at both the national and supra-national levels. The burden of protecting these rights has fallen to modern Kelsenian courts.

The scope of these rights is far more extensive than that of the American Bill of Rights. European charters (in, for example, France, Germany, Italy, Spain and Portugal) include not only the traditional 'liberal' rights and freedoms of speech, assembly, religion, equality before the law and due process. They also enshrine newer, more 'collective' rights, to education, employment, trade union activity, health care, the development of 'person-ality' and leisure. In practice, in any given legislative process, one right may conflict with another. Do the right to life provisions of the German and Spanish constitutions protect foetal life and thus prohibit abortion, or does the right to develop freely one's own personality protect a woman's choice whether or not to become a mother? To what extent can rights to property be set aside to enable workers' rights to participate in managing the workplace, or the government's right to nationalize industry? Constitutional courts are constantly being asked to answer such questions and to balance or harmonize conflicting rights claims. In doing so, as Kelsen predicted, consti-tutional courts legislate.

In summary, the European model of review was widely diffused after 1945 because it permitted the retention of orthodox separation of powers doctrines (the prohibition of *judicial* review) while providing a means of defending constitutional law – which includes constitutional rights – as higher law.

Jurisdiction

Table 10.1 simplifies and summarizes constitutional review mechanisms in four European states: France, Germany, Italy and Spain.[2] There are two main types of review – abstract and concrete. Abstract review processes result in decisions on the constitutionality of legislation that has recently been adopted by parliaments but has either not yet entered into force (France), or whose force has been suspended pending the constitutional court's decision (Germany, Italy, Spain). As the table shows, abstract review is initiated by elected politicians. Executives and legislators (France, Germany, Spain) or federated member-states or regional governments (Germany, Italy, Spain) may, within prescribed time limits, attack legislation as unconstitutional before the constitutional court.[3] The constitutional court is then required to render a decision. Abstract review processes are, in essence, constitutional

Table 10.1 *European constitutional courts and the constitutional review of legislation*

	France (1959)	Germany (1951)	Italy (1948)	Spain (1978)
Constitutional court	Constitutional Council (Council)	Federal Constitutional Court (FCC)	Italian Constitutional Court (ICC)	Spanish Constitutional Tribunal (STC)
Year created/ began operations	1958/9	1949, 1951	1948, 1956	1978, 1981
Abstract review	Yes	Yes	Yes	Yes
Authority to initiate abstract review of legislation	President Pres. Assembly Pres. Senate *Since 1974*: 60 Assembly deputies 60 Senators	Federal government Länder governments 1/3 Bundestag	National government (against regional laws) Regional governments (against national laws)	Prime Minister Pres. of Parliament 50 Deputies 50 Senators Executives of autonomous regions Ombudsman ('Defender of the People')
Laws referred	National legislation	Federal and Länder (federated member state) legislation	National and regional legislation	National and regional legislation
Laws must be referred	Within 15 days following adoption by parliament	Within 30 days following adoption by federal or Länder parliament	Within 30 days following adoption by regional or national government	Within 90 days following adoption by parliament or regional government
Concrete review	No	Yes	Yes	Yes
Authority to initiate concrete review of legislation		Judiciary Individuals (after judicial remedies exhausted)	Judiciary	Judiciary Ombudsman Individuals (after judicial remedies exhausted)

dialogues between elected politicians and constitutional judges in the making of legislation.

Concrete review processes are initiated by the judiciary (Germany, Italy, Spain), by individuals (Germany, Spain) or by an ombudsman (Spain), in the course of, or following, litigation in the courts. The logic of concrete review may seem somewhat convoluted. Recall that the constitution is today considered to be higher law binding upon all public authorities including the judiciary; but also recall that this same judiciary is not allowed to engage in judicial review. In the solution adopted, ordinary judges are authorized to refer constitutional questions – is a given law, legal rule or administrative act constitutional? – to constitutional judges. In general, the judiciary is required to refer such questions to the constitutional court if there is substantial doubt about the constitutionality of a given act or rule being applied, or if the settlement of a case depends on the answer to such questions. The judiciary is then obligated to apply faithfully the constitutional court's decision to the case at hand. Individuals (Germany, Spain) and an ombudsman (Spain) also have the right to refer constitutional questions – what the Germans call a constitutional complaint – directly to constitutional courts, once judicial remedies have been exhausted. In concrete review processes, a constitutional dialogue is established between the judiciary and constitutional courts in the defence of the supremacy of the constitution in the administration of justice.

Composition

Table 10.2 compares rules governing the recruitment of constitutional judges in France, Germany, Italy and Spain. Two appointment procedures exist, nomination and election. Where nomination procedures are used, the appointing authority simply names a judge or a slate of judges; no countervailing confirmation or veto procedures exist. Such is the case in France, where all constitutional judges are named by political authorities, whereas in Germany they are all elected. Italy and Spain have mixed nomination and election systems. Where election systems are used, a qualified majority (a two-thirds or three-fifths vote) within a parliamentary body is necessary for appointment. Because the German, Italian and Spanish polities are multi-party systems, and because no single party has ever possessed such a super-majority on its own, the qualified majority requirement effectively obliges the parties to bargain with each other in order to achieve consensus on a slate of candidates. This bargaining process occurs in intense, behind-closed-doors negotiations. In practice, these negotiations determine which party will fill vacancies on the court, with allocations strictly controlled by the parties with the greatest parliamentary strength.

Table 10.2 European constitutional courts: recruitment and composition

	France (1958)	Germany (1949)	Italy (1948)	Spain (1978)
Number of judges	9	16	15	12
Recruiting authorities	*Named:* President (3) Pres. Assembly (3) Pres. Senate (3)	*Elected:* Bundestag (8) Bundesrat (8) (both by 2/3 majorities)	*Named:* National Govt (5) Judiciary (5) *Elected:* Parliament (5) (by 2/3 majority of joint session of parliament)	*Named:* National Govt (2) Judiciary (2) *Elected:* Congress (4) Senate (4) (by 3/5 majorities)
Length of term	9 years	12 years	9 years	9 years
Age limits	None	40 year minimum 68 year maximum	None	None
Requisite qualifications	None	6/16 must be federal judges; all must be qualified to be judges	All must be judges, lawyers with 20 years in practice, or tenured law professors	May be judges, lawyers, law professors or civil servants with at least 15 years experience and whose 'judicial competence is well known'

Table 10.2 also indicates who may serve as a constitutional judge. All German, Italian and Spanish judges must have had advanced legal training, as well as professional experience in some domain of law. The constitution may also contain precise quotas, guaranteeing a minimal number of professional judges. In Germany the sixteen-member court must always contain at least six federal judges, in Italy representatives of the judiciary control the appointment of five out of fifteen seats, and in Spain they control two out of twelve. In France no legal training is required. Perhaps, in consequence, a majority of the French Council has always been made up of former ministers and parliamentarians, although many of these had studied or practised some law. Several influential law professors and a few judges have served on the French Council but far fewer than in the other countries. In Germany, Italy and Spain, law professors make up the largest group of appointees, followed by judges and lawyers. Only in Italy does the number of politicians appointed approach that of France: of the judges elected by parliament to the end of 1988, fifteen out of twenty had been at one time parliamentarians; but factoring in double careers, the great majority of all appointees have been either law professors (28 out of 64) or judges (26 out of 64).[4]

It is virtually impossible for social scientists to study the impact of composition (or changes in composition) on political (jurisprudential) outcomes as they have studied the American or Canadian supreme courts. In France and Italy, where dissenting opinions are formally prohibited, decisions are always unanimous, presented as if they were the only ones possible. In Germany and Spain dissents are extremely rare, if important, indications of schisms within the court. In all cases internal deliberations are secret. As the rest of this chapter seeks to demonstrate, a social science of the political behaviour of constitutional courts can nevertheless be constructed on the basis of the *impact* of such courts on policy-making processes.

Constitutional Politics

Conceived broadly, constitutional politics are the intimate, highly structured interactions between constitutional courts, legislators and judicial authorities in the making of public policy. The intensity of this interaction has increased over time. In consequence, the influence of constitutional judges over legislative outcomes has widened and deepened. Indeed, it can be argued that within legislative processes constitutional courts function as specialized legislative chambers. In consequence, legislators have come to behave 'judicially'. They deliberate questions of constitutionality and help to construct constitutional law.

Constitutional dialogues: legislating

From a policy-making perspective, one that focuses on the *impact* of constitutional review on legislation, constitutional courts can be said to function as specialized chambers of parliament, specialized because their powers are meaningfully limited to decisions on constitutionality. This function is most visible in abstract review processes. In European parliamentary systems, important legislative bills are drafted by government ministers. The bills are then sent to parliament for amendment and adoption. After adoption, within certain time limits (see table 10.1), any law can be attacked before the constitutional court as unconstitutional. In practice, national legislation is referred to the court by parliamentary oppositions, or – in the case of Germany and Spain – by the subnational wings of national opposition parties in control of state-level or regional governments. (Executives and parliamentary majorities have no incentives to refer their own bills to the court, and thus do not normally make use of review authority.) Every abstract review referral lengthens the policy-making process by adding another stage to it. The court's decision, then, constitutes the final 'reading' of a bill or law.

Concrete review jurisdiction, too, enables constitutional judges to participate in law-making. But unlike abstract review processes, concrete review is costly, time-consuming and virtually always less politically charged. It may often take years if not decades for a given statute to come before the constitutional court, and only subsequent to one or more trials in the ordinary judiciary. By the time the constitutional court renders a decision on a given law, partisan bickering over it (if there ever was any) has usually calmed or even disappeared. The invalidation of legislation pursuant to concrete review, therefore, is generally viewed as more benign, and far less politically provocative, than rulings of unconstitutionality pursuant to referrals by parliamentary minorities.

The impact of constitutional courts on legislative outcomes, complex and multi-dimensional, is both direct – the formal, immediate effect of any particular decision – and indirect – the feedback or pedagogical effects of a given decision (or line of jurisprudence) on ongoing or future legislative processes.

Direct effects

When a constitutional court annuls a legislative provision as unconstitutional, its impact on policy outcomes is direct and negative: the court has exercised its veto authority. Statistical summaries of the activities of constitutional courts provide some indication of the presence and impact of constitutional courts in legislative processes. In France, where abstract review is the only type of review possible, Constitutional Council intervention in the policy-making process can be characterized as systematic. Since 1974, when the right of referral was granted to any sixty members of the National Assembly or the Senate, every annual budget (with only one exception) and the major pieces of legislation adopted since 1981 have been referred to the Council. The number of referrals grew dramatically after 1981, and has since stabilized. In the period 1974–80, the Giscard presidency, 46 laws were referred to the Council, or 6.6 per year; in the period 1981–7, the first Mitterrand presidency, 92 laws were referred, or 13.1 per year. The average number of laws referred has remained above ten per year since 1987. Expressed in different terms, since 1981, about one-third of all legislation adopted[5] has been referred, an extraordinary ratio given the fact that most legislation passed is politically uncontroversial. Referrals have a high success rate: during the period 1974–80, 14 out of 46 (or 30 per cent) of the laws referred were judged to be in whole or in part unconstitutional; in the period 1981–90, 66 out of 123 (or 54 per cent) of all laws referred resulted in censure (statistics in Stone 1994)!

Compared with the French case, the importance of abstract review to German policy-making would, at least at first glance, appear to be far more limited. Up to 1991, the German FCC received 112 referrals, or 2.7 per year. These referrals have led to definitive decisions on 43 laws, 23 (or 53 per cent) of which were declared to be at least partly unconstitutional.[6] These figures underestimate the impact of abstract review in two crucial ways. First, to be discussed below, the very threat of referral – whether or not such referrals are eventually made – can profoundly alter the conduct of German policy-making, and by some indications even more so than in France. Second, the German policy-making process is veto-ridden, while the French process is relatively veto-free. The demands of coalition government (in practice, the Liberal Democrats have effectively reoriented reform-minded governments of both the left and right to the pragmatic centre), cooperative federalism (the necessity of coordinating national and member-state policies) and the existence of a strong second chamber (the *Bundesrat*) possessed of substantial veto authority combine to encourage inter-party compromises and to filter out controversial legislative initiatives. The constitutional court 'is only the third filter of legislative ambition', whereas, in France, 'the Council is the *only* policymaking institution which can impose its will on the government and its majority', accounting for its popularity with the opposition (Stone 1994). While less salient to the day-to-day life of parliamentary policy-making than abstract review, the FCC spent most of its first four decades processing concrete review referrals (nearly 3,000) and constitutional complaints (nearly 85,000). Taking its constitutional review activities as a whole, the FCC (up to 1991) has invalidated some two hundred laws (and another 223 administrative and other legal rules). The court has reviewed 20 per cent of all federal laws adopted and has annulled 4.6 per cent of all federal laws adopted (statistics in Kommers 1994; Landfried 1992; Stone 1994).

In Spain, the instances of abstract review exceed those of concrete review. During its first decade in operation, 1981–90, the STC received 143 abstract review referrals, leading to the review of 101 laws. Of these, 53 were declared in whole or in part unconstitutional, a success rate for petitioners of 52 per cent. Since 1986 the rhythm of such referrals has quickened, surpassing French levels. Of the 143 referrals received during the STC's first decade, 103 (or 72 per cent) were made during the period 1986–90, leading to 63 decisions and 37 rulings of unconstitutionality (70 per cent of all such invalidations). Spanish – like German – abstract review implicates the constitutional court not only in partisan disputes over national legislation but also in the ongoing construction of regionalism. Of the 143 abstract review referrals to the STC, 33 (23 per cent) were made by parliamentary oppositions; 44 (31 per cent) by the national government, usually against legislation passed by the autonomous regions; sixty (42 per cent) by the autonomous regions attacking national legislation; and six (4 per cent) by the ombudsman. During the period 1981–90, the STC also received 83 concrete review referrals – resulting in 32 invalidations of statutes for unconstitutionality – and 1,300 constitutional complaints.[7]

Because Italian parliamentarians do not possess the power of abstract review, the constitutional dialogue between the ICC and elected politicians is, at least formally, indirect. Further, research on the political role and functioning of the ICC have emphasized that Italian constitutional judges have been conscientiously passive in their relations with sitting legislators (Furlong 1988; Volcansek 1994). That said, the court has clearly been more assertive when confronting the work of legislators past and gone, gradually but systematically 'dismantling', for instance, the 'offensive legislation from the fascist regime' (Volcansek 1994). While this essentially defensive posture may have been consciously fashioned by the judges, the court has been able to remain in the shadows by exploiting the delays inherent in concrete review processes. Until recently, the court actively (and successfully) 'encouraged the judiciary to refer the maximum number of constitutional questions' to it (Escarras 1987, 520 – 21), questions it was in fact unable to process efficiently. In the decade 1976– 85, for example, the ICC rendered over 1,200 decisions. But the backlog of cases facing the judges rose, during this same period, from 1,138 to 2,748 (a backlog representing about three years of full time work!). About 85 per cent of these pending cases were concrete review referrals (Escarras 1987, 550).

There are some extremely important indications that the policy-making role of the Italian court is in the process of being transformed into a more present and visible one, in line with that of other constitutional courts. In 1988 the ICC announced that it would process all concrete review referrals within six months, and it has since begun to keep that promise. This change could well have the effect of blurring the distinction between abstract and concrete review processes, since a law may be immediately attacked before a judicial body and then passed on to the constitutional court for what is in effect an immediate ruling. Indeed, for the first time, the ICC has begun to confront legislation adopted by a sitting parliament. In 1990, 60 per cent of all constitutional review cases involved legal texts adopted during the period 1980–90, and over 30 per cent were laws passed in the period 1988–90; of the 65 texts annulled as unconstitutional in 1990, 23 were promulgated in the 1980s and ten in the period 1988–90 (statistics in Di Manno 1992). This development has been the source of hand-wringing among leading professors of constitutional law worried about judges making 'political choices', about the potential for 'the constitutional review process to become a continuation of the politico-party debate' in parliament, and about the ICC coming to resemble the French Constitutional Council – more a 'third chamber' and a 'political counselor' than a 'constitutional judge' (Di Manno 1992, 793–4).

Decisions which invalidate an entire law, or 'total annulments', are rare but potentially explosive. In 1975 the German FCC annulled an attempt on the part of the Social-Liberal (SPD-FDP) coalition to decriminalize abortion, declaring that the foetus possessed constitutional rights, including the 'right to life' mentioned in article 2 of the constitution. An attempt in 1985 to decriminalize abortion in Spain by the Socialist-Workers' government met with a similar fate. Both of these decisions were accompanied by unusually shrill dissenting opinions within the court and are among the most widely cited as evidence of unwarranted judicial activism (Landfried 1992). In France the Constitutional Council annulled the 1982 nationalization law, on the grounds that it did not provide for adequate compensation to shareholders of companies to be nationalized, provoking vague threats by the Socialists to abolish the Council. In these cases and many others, constitutional courts went on to tell legislatures exactly how legislators could correct invalidated legislation to make it constitutional (see below).

The great majority of all invalidations are 'partial annulments'; the constitutional court 'deletes' from the referred law those provisions judged unconstitutional but allows what remains to enter into force. Partial annulments are generally a more flexible means of controlling legislative outcomes than total annulments, since they allow governments and their legislative majorities to claim at least partial absolution. Some partial annulments have nevertheless had spectacular policy effects, obstructing central legislative priorities. In 1984, to take just one example, the French Council thwarted the Socialists' attempt to dismantle Robert Hersant's newspaper empire, of which *Le Figaro* is the flagship daily. The government, anxious to enshrine press 'pluralism' (the right of the public to have access to a range of newspapers expressing a diversity of views) as a constitutional right, and angered by the Hersant group's unrelenting opposition to socialist government, sought to place strict limits on the percentage of the total national market any press group could control (15 per cent). The Council declared that pluralism did have constitutional status but ruled that the new limits could apply only to future situations and not to Hersant's. The result was that Hersant's dominance, which rose to over 30 per cent in 1986 (the highest percentage of the national market then controlled by any press group in any Western country), was frozen into place. Most partial annulments are less dramatic but can, over time, add up to the virtual 'constitutionalization' of rules binding law-makers in any given sector. The best cross-national example of this phenomenon is probably the constitutionalization of penal law, the legal codes specifying crimes and penalties for committing them and the codes governing judicial procedures. Constitutional courts have vetoed hundreds of particular legislative revisions of these codes, while laying down rules for how they must or must not be revised in the future. In consequence, law-makers must now be sure to maintain, and sometimes even extend, standards of due process, non-retroactivity, equality before the law, etc. These standards have been constructed by constitutional judges, from constitutional rights texts, in interaction with legislators.

Constitutional courts have also developed a host of techniques to control the constitutionality of a law without invalidating it. In Germany, for example, the FCC can rule that a law is 'not compatible' with the constitution (as opposed to strictly unconstitutional), a decision that allows the law to remain in force for a specified period of time, pending its revision by the legislature. Such decisions, of which there have been 151 up to 1991, are in essence constitutional commands issued by the FCC to the government and parliament to (re)legislate in a given area. All four constitutional courts also use the technique of attaching 'strict guidelines (or "reserves") of interpretation' to legislation under review. Such guidelines are formal declarations that a law or legislative provision can (and will in the future) be considered constitutional only if it is interpreted as the constitutional court has stipulated. Put differently, the court rules that only one interpretation of a given legislative text saves that text from being declared unconstitutional. Statistics show a rising tide of these declarations. In France, for example, the percentage of decisions containing guidelines has risen from 11 per cent (1959–74), to 14.5 per cent (1974–81), to 19.5 per cent (1981–5); in 1986, a year of ferocious political attacks on the Council by the Chirac Government (right), 56 per cent (nine out of sixteen) of the decisions the Council rendered contained them (Stone 1992a, 135). In Italy the level of decisions containing guidelines was below 15 per cent until the end of the 1980s but since 1990 has risen to 25 per cent. Perhaps revelatory of the ICC's new, more politicized role, more than two-thirds of the decisions rendered by the ICC on legal texts promulgated during the period 1987–90 contained guidelines of interpretation (Di Manno 1992).

As Landfried has noted with respect to the German case, this technique can have the effect of giving constitutional judges 'pre-eminence' over policy outcomes, not by 'invalidating' but 'prescribing' (Landfried 1992, 53). These techniques place legislators, administrators and judges under a kind of constitutional surveillance.

Indirect effects

The authority to veto legislation as unconstitutional is only one dimension – *direct and negative* – of the policy impact of constitutional courts. We must also account for another dimension of this impact, *indirect and creative*. Indirect effects are governmental or parliamentary decisions to draft, amend or abrogate (void) legislation in order to take account of the dictates, real or divined, of constitutional jurisprudence. Put differently, indirect effects constitute the reception or implementation of constitutional jurisprudence by legislators. Such effects, capable of being registered at each stage of the legislative process, are crucial to understanding the pattern of legislative outcomes in a wide range of policy sectors.

The impact of constitutional courts on policy-making processes results from a combination of two main factors. The first of these is the existence of a leading decision (or line of decisions) relevant to the legislation currently being debated in the government or parliament. By 'leading decision' I mean a constitutional ruling that either specifies, for the first time, those rules governing policy-making in a given legislative sector or radically reinterprets existing rules. Nearly all leading decisions are invalidations, precisely because the best moment for laying down general principles meant to constrain legislators is when legislators are actually being constrained. Constitutional judges also know that the best and most durable defence against charges that they have usurped the legislative function is to explain that the solution arrived at – usually declared as the only one possible – is *required* by constitutional law. From a policy perspective, leading decisions function to legitimize a court's own policy-making behaviour. At the same time, in order to avoid such 'misunderstandings' in the future, the judges may construct quite detailed prescriptions meant to guide future policy-making in the area.

It is important to emphasize, however, that it is nearly impossible for lawmakers, within a given legislative process and in advance of a leading decision, to know the exact nature of the constitutional constraints which face them. A leading decision has the effect of at least partly codifying these constraints. A succession of decisions on legislative initiatives within the same policy sector can, as with the example of penal law, lead to the virtual constitutionalization of that sector. In this way, constitutional uncertainty is gradually replaced by constitutional obligation. Important examples of constitutionalized sectors include nationalization and privatization policy in France, campaign finance in Germany and – in all four countries – regimes governing broadcasting, criminal justice, electoral law, labour relations and the making and implementation of taxation and social security policies.

The second factor is the extent to which parliamentary oppositions and subnational governments exploit review processes for their own political ends, facilitating or reinforcing the control of constitutional courts over policy outcomes. Because governments cannot avoid having their legislation referred to constitutional courts, and because decisions bind legislators without the possibility of appeal, abstract review referrals are powerful weapons of opposition. Put crudely, oppositions exploit abstract review procedures – which are virtually costless – in order to win from constitutional courts what they can never win in parliament. Constitutional courts have not discouraged such efforts: as we have seen, in France, Germany and Spain, over half of all decisions pursuant to an abstract review referral have resulted in a ruling of unconstitutionality. In fact, as I have argued elsewhere, constitutional courts and parliament are connected to one another by a kind of 'jurisprudential transmission belt' (Stone 1994). Abstract review processes provide courts with crucial opportunities to construct constitutional law, to extend jurisprudential techniques of control and (the same thing) to make policy. Constitutional jurisprudence, increasingly dense and expansive, supplies the opposition with weapons that can be used to obtain concessions from the government and its majority.

Put in a power-centric language of social science, indirect effects arc anticipatory reactions structured by constitutional politics. Dahl's formula (1957) – A has power over B to the extent that A can make B do what B would otherwise not do – can be altered to account explicitly for anticipatory reactions. Thus, A – the constitutional court – has power over B – the government and its parliamentary majority – to the extent that B anticipates A's interest and constrains its behaviour accordingly. As constitutional review has developed, A's interest has been more and more precisely articulated, in a growing corpus of policy-relevant, constitutional rules binding on legislators, and B's interest in conforming to A's interest has been, in turn, made more compelling. Governments and parliaments, above all else, want to see their laws enter into force; further, they do not want to be publicly reprimanded for having violated the constitution. The role of parliamentary oppositions, in expressing and reinforcing the commands (the interest) of the court, is crucial to such politics. Most important, oppositions facilitate anticipatory reactions by threatening referral to the court during parliamentary debate and, at times, even before that debate begins.

Anticipatory reactions can occur at each stage of the legislative process, beginning with the drafting of a bill by government ministers. Intra-governmental deliberations are formally secret, but we do know that in France, Germany and Spain every bill must be submitted to legal experts, who are responsible for, among other things, evaluating the possibility of its being referred to the court and invalidated as unconstitutional. While difficult to verify, constitutional considerations can lead governments to alter and even suppress entire bills. In France, the Socialists radically altered the compensation formula contained in the 1982 nationalization bill on the advice of the Council of State (its official legal advisor). The Council of State had suggested that the government could enhance its constitutional security by taking into account certain profits and assets, raising the cost of nationalizing by some 20 per cent (Stone 1992a, 150). The Constitutional Council later invalidated the formula as insufficient. In 1986 the right-wing Chirac Government (1986–7) undertook a revision of the laws governing French nationality and citizenship and proposed to privatize the prison system. Both reforms were dropped, not least because of worries about constitutionality (Stone 1989). Certain reforms of the first and second German Social–Liberal coalition governments (1969– 72, 1972–6) suffered similar fates (Stone 1994): the pledge to introduce compulsory profit sharing in industry was dropped (due to 'insoluble legal obstacles'); and reforms of the education system and vocational training, paralysed for years by constitutional hand-wringing, were submitted to parliament only after having been gutted of some of their most controversial elements. Both latter reforms would later be sent on to the FCC for abstract review. As a result, the FCC took substantial control over the field of education, and vetoed the vocational training law on the grounds that the government had not obtained the prior consent of the *Bundesrat* – then in the hands of the opposition.

Once a bill is submitted to parliament, open constitutional debate begins. French and German political parties employ full-time constitutional specialists, usually law professors, who advise them on how to attack or defend the constitutionality of a bill, and to draft referrals to the court. Moreover, in France any National Assembly Deputy or Senator can raise a procedural 'motion of unconstitutionality', a motion which requires parliament to debate the constitutionality of a bill. After the debate, which often revolves around the precise relevance or meaning of specific decisions of the Constitutional Council, a vote takes place; if the motion is accepted the bill is rejected as unconstitutional. Such motions are now built into the legislative process: in the period 1981–90, 238 such motions were raised leading to 116 votes in the Assembly alone (statistics in Stone 1994). Subject to strict party discipline, motions of unconstitutionality are never adopted. Their importance, however, is to warn the government, explicitly, that its bill will be referred to the Council if it does not agree to compromise and amend it.

Since 1981, dozens of French bills have been altered, by literally hundreds of amendments, adopted in response to constitutional debates within parliament. The 1982 decentralization bill is the classic example, adopted after having been rewritten with a record 500+ amendments. The 1984 law designed to dismantle the Hersant group was also radically deformed. In the end, 26 of the original 42 articles were amended, including the most important anti-trust provisions (case study in Stone 1992a, ch. 7). In these and many other cases, constitutional argument gradually overwhelmed or absorbed all other aspects of the debate. Oppositions have learned to state their partisan objections to a bill in terms of constitutional law. The majority has little choice but to respond in kind. Some of the most tumultuous parliamentary battles of the Fifth Republic have been waged in the language of constitutional law.

In Germany, a similar kind of politics exists. As Kommers puts it: 'Governments and politicians continually threaten to drag their political opponents to Karlsruhe – the location of the court. Karlsruhe's presence is deeply felt in the corridors of power, often leading politicians to negotiate their differences rather than to risk total defeat' in the court (Kommers 1994). In fact, parliamentary committees regularly invite leading constitutional experts, including former constitutional judges, to testify on constitutional aspects of current legislation and to predict future FCC decisions. German committee sessions, where most legislation is amended, are formally closed, and thus constitutional bargaining and compromise is difficult to verify and measure. We do know, however, that three of the most controversial and important reforms ever attempted – the abortion reform (1975), the University Framework Law (1976) and the industrial codetermination bill (1976) – were subject to intense constitutional scrutiny and wholesale amendment efforts (see Landfried 1984). Fear of constitutional censure is probably enhanced by a deeply embedded legalism that is said to pervade German political culture. German legislators, as nearly all students of German politics have taken pains to emphasize, are 'unusually willing, even anxious to rely on law and legal scholarship to guide their work' (literature cited in Stone 1994). So risk-averse are German politicians that the government has even been known to repeal statutes after an abstract review referral, but before the decision of the FCC (see Kommers 1994).

Some constitutional decisions are not only the final stage of one legislative process but the opening stage of another. This second process I have called 'corrective revision: the reelaboration of a censured text in conformity with constitutional jurisprudence in order to secure promulgation' (Stone 1994). They occur after full or partial invalidations. In corrective revision processes, governments and parliaments ratify legislative choices made by constitutional courts. Such processes are highly structured, because courts make their legislative choices explicit, and because oppositions (which can always refer the corrected law to the court again) function to verify the government's compliance with the court's decision. A few examples, drawn from dozens available, will suffice to illustrate the point. As noted above, in 1982 the French Constitutional Council annulled the 1982 nationalization bill, on the grounds that shareholders of companies to be nationalized would not be compensated fairly for their shares. It then went on to tell the government – in precise detail – how a *constitutional* compensation formula should have been elaborated in the first place. This new formula, which raised the costs of nationalization another 30 per cent, was simply copied – virtually word for word – into a new, revised bill. In 1986 the Chirac Government incorporated the Council's language into its privatization law and the law on media pluralism after both were struck down (Stone 1989).

In Germany, corrective revision processes have enabled the FCC to take control over a number of legislative areas, including education and campaign finance. In 1967 a German law, supported by the entire parliament, approved reimbursement of campaign expenses to all parties which had received at least 2.5 per cent of the vote. The FCC, however, annulled the law because the floor had been placed too high, but told legislators that if they lowered the floor to 0.5 per cent the reform could go forward. Legislators complied. Over the next two decades the FCC, in a series of decisions, codified constitutional rules governing the organization, management and financing of political parties. In 1989 parliament wrote many of these rules into the comprehensive Political Parties Act (Kommers 1994; Landfried 1992). The control of the FCC on outcomes in the educational sector has been so extensive that the court has been called 'a veritable ministry of education' (Kommers 1989, 303). To take just one example, Social–Liberal coalition governments at both the federal and state levels (during the period 1969–76) sought to 'democratize' university governance by, among other things, diminishing what had long been the absolute authority of full professors on governing councils and expanding that of untenured professors, staff and students. Relying on article 5 of the constitution, which proclaims that 'teaching shall be free', and downplaying rights to participation, the court annulled a 1971 law adopted by the state of Lower Saxony (the law was referred by 398 disgruntled professors in individual constitutional complaints). In ruling that full professors must always prevail within university councils, the FCC transformed the federal discussion, then in progress, into a debate about constitutional compliance. Under the watchful eye of the opposition (which supported the full professors), the FCC's jurisprudence was copied into the federal law (Katzenstein 1987; Stone 1994).

In both Germany and Spain, constitutional courts annulled legislative efforts to decriminalize abortion and then went on to tell the legislatures how they should rewrite their reforms. The courts stipulated the precise conditions under which abortion would be tolerated – if the woman's life or health was in danger, for example – and administrative procedures for verifying such conditions. These revisions were dutifully ratified by parliament. After German reunification (1989) the Social Democrats, the Greens and the Free Democrats pressed the Christian Democrat-dominated government to revisit the abortion issue, in order to honour abortion rights possessed by the former citizens of East Germany and to extend them to women in the West. In 1993 the FCC struck the bill down, largely restating its 1975 jurisprudence.

In Italy, where weak, coalition governments are rarely able to effect significant reforms, the ICC has at times, as in this case, aided the parties to rise above their own narrow interests and to legislate in the national interest (see Pizzorusso 1989). For reasons already stated, indirect effects are relatively more difficult to identify and study in Italy. The most politically significant example of something like a corrective revision process concerned the dismantling of the state's radio and television broadcast monopoly and the emergence of a mixed public-private system. Beginning in 1974, the ICC began to declare that certain aspects of this monopoly violated the constitutional principle of pluralism – the right to be exposed to a wide range of 'political, social, and cultural tendencies and currents of thought' – a corollary of freedom of expression and opinion. In a series of subsequent decisions (1981, 1985, 1986 and 1988) the ICC all but begged parliament to regulate the transition to a mixed broadcasting regime by, among other things, creating an independent regulatory agency to oversee the allocation of broadcast frequencies and to supervise compliance with anti-trust rules. Partisan bickering and parliamentary paralysis on the matter was not overcome until 1990, when a framework law was finally passed. The law conformed to the main lines of the ICC jurisprudence (Pace 1990).

Constitutional dialogues: protecting rights

Although a comprehensive discussion of the role of constitutional courts in protecting human rights is far beyond the scope of this chapter, some remarks on the policy-making impact of this role deserve emphasis. First, with the exception of the French Council, the caseloads of the German, Italian and Spanish courts are dominated by concrete review processes. In these processes, constitutional judges intervene in ongoing or concluded judicial proceedings, and thus the legislative impact of constitutional decisions is formally indirect. What the German FCC and the Spanish STC do most of the time is to process individual referrals (which can be accepted only if they involve a rights violation). Of the total number of constitutional review decisions rendered by the STC during the period 1981–90, 88 per cent (1,307 out of 1,491) have been pursuant to individual constitutional complaints. These complaints have enabled the STC to reinforce the new constitutional rights to habeas corpus, to controls on police searches and seizures and to due process in both the ordinary and military courts, and to develop a rich jurisprudence on freedom of the press, religion and conscientious objection to military service and rights to unionize and strike. Given certain deeply rooted Fascist tendencies within the military, police and judiciary, the role of the STC has been not only to protect new rights but to legitimize the new constitutional regime. In Germany, 79 per cent (3,689 out of 4,648) of all review decisions rendered in the period 1951–91 involved individual complaints, with decisions pursuant to concrete review making up the next 19 per cent (897). In Italy the ICC has received an astounding 17,756 concrete review referrals (Pizzorusso 1989).[8]

Second, while designed to restore or protect individual rights that have *already* been violated, concrete review procedures nonetheless have the capacity to generate or restructure ongoing legislative processes. The 1971 German decision on university governance was a result of the individual complaint procedure, while the Italian court's rulings on television broadcasting resulted from judicial referrals. But there are many other examples. In 1977, partly in response to the ban on capital punishment imposed by the European Convention on Human Rights, the German parliament sought to require mandatory life sentences for those convicted of murder in 'wanton cruelty'. A judge referred the new provisions to the FCC which, relying on the constitutional right to 'human dignity', declared that, because the state has a constitutional responsibility to rehabilitate criminals, mandatory life sentences could be imposed only under certain strict conditions. The ruling suspended the provisions until these conditions could be incorporated into the codes (see Kommers 1989, 332–6). The Spanish ombudsman, too, can get into the act. During the period 1983–5, the socialist government's budgets contained state subsidies for those trade unions considered to be 'the most representative', as determined by elections at the workplace level. In practice, having received more than the minimum requirement of 10 per cent of the vote (15 per cent in the regions), only four unions received such subsidies. The ombudsman attacked the 1983, 1984 and 1985 budgets as unconstitutional and the STC agreed, ruling that the system in place discriminated against the small unions. A proportional system was proposed (in which subsidies would roughly correspond to the percentage of the total vote obtained) and later adopted.

Third, as an evaluation of the politics of anticipatory reactions and corrective revision amply demonstrates, the development of constitutional rights – like the development of constitutional politics – is interactive. The protection of constitutional rights, like the making of legislation, is often a product of the interaction between constitutional courts and legislators. In legislating, governments and their majorities must not only take into consideration the dictates of existing rights jurisprudence but may also be forced to guess how the constitutional court might respond to new initiatives. Where abstract review exists, oppositions labour to extend the policy-relevance of constitutional rights, and to enforce constitutional court rulings by referring – and threatening to refer – legislation to the court. To make the same point negatively, if French parliamentary oppositions suddenly renounced referring legislation to the Constitutional Council, the construction of constitutional law would cease, and, with it, the elaboration of constitutional rights.

Constitutional review and democracy

Sometimes in concert, sometimes in rivalry, European governments, parliaments and administrators govern with constitutional judges. Restated in the language used at the beginning of this chapter, constitutional courts do not perform their 'judicial function' – settling (constitutional) disputes – without also participating in the 'political function' – law-making. This blurring of 'functions', which occurs wherever constitutional review is effective, inevitably raises the issue of the extent to which judicial law-making is compatible with democracy. Indeed, the classic mode of analysis of judicial–political interaction within constitutional review processes has focused attention on the extent to which (unelected and thus relatively 'illegitimate') judges have obstructed the legislative programmes of the (elected 'legitimate') representatives of the people. This kind of analysis can at times be appropriate, as when newly elected governments, pledged to implement significant reforms, find their way blocked by constitutional courts (e.g., Landfried 1984; Keeler and Stone 1987; Stone 1989). Although the importance of constitutional politics has greatly increased over time, overt confrontations between elected politicians and constitutional judges have nevertheless been quite rare. Why has this been so?

No systematic research on this question has yet been undertaken, but tolerance of constitutional review on the part of political elites appears to be related to a number of interrelated factors. First and most important has been the gradual acceptance of the ideology of 'constitutionalism', the notion that, in a constitutional democracy, all government acts must conform to constitutional law to be considered legitimate. Constitutionalism is today a powerful counterweight to the traditional ideology of parliamentary supremacy. Because constitutional courts have clear status as 'guardians of the constitution', and because review powers are expressly provided for by constitutional texts, the legitimacy of constitutional review has come to be associated with the legitimacy of the constitution itself. In consequence, attacks by politicians on the work of the court usually prove counter-productive. Such attacks are too easily characterized (by supporters of the court) as irresponsible attacks on the constitution, or worse, on the system of protection of individual rights. Second, the composition of constitutional courts is largely controlled by elected politicians themselves (the make-up of the court generally 'follows the electoral returns'). In fact, the political profiles of parliaments are rarely out of alignment with the profiles of constitutional courts for very long and, in fact, nearly every significant period of 'court bashing' on the part of politicians has occurred after elections yielding new governmental majorities. Third, in pluralist democratic systems, where political parties take turns governing, each party may have a more or less natural 'interest' in having fixed 'rules of the game' (constitutional law). Such rules bind all participants, providing protection against arbitrary or despotic actions of political opponents when in power. The rules are made effective to the extent to which they are policed by an outside 'referee' (the constitutional court). Viewed through this lens, constitutional review may appear inherently democratic, to the extent that it facilitates the acceptance of changes in power by those who compete for it. Further, after losing an election, former governing parties have unapologetically exploited constitutional review processes, legitimizing the review system and repudiating protests made while in power.

Constitutional Politics in the European Community

Founded as an international organization of states, the European Community (EC) can today be called a constitutional polity. The transformation of the founding treaties, the most important of which is the treaty establishing the European Economic Community (1958), into a constitution has been the singular achievement of the European Court of Justice (ECJ). This achievement has been described in great detail by legal scholars, some of whom have been (unusually) sensitive to the concerns of political science (Burley and Mattli 1993; Stein 1981; Weiler 1981, 1991). The purpose of this section is to survey, if all too briefly, the main elements of European constitutional politics at the supra-national level. After summarizing the basic features of the community system, I will turn to the role of the ECJ in constructing a judicially enforceable constitutional law out of the treaties, and the impact of that construction on national and supra-national policy-making.

The community system in brief

The heart of the EC project is the commitment by (since 1995) fifteen European states to economic integration: the establishment of a common market and the adoption of common fiscal and monetary policies. Simplifying, two sorts of integration processes are established by the treaties. The first can be called negative integration: the obligation of all member states to dismantle barriers to the free movement of goods, people, services and capital within EC territory, thus enhancing economic efficiency. It is negative because states, in order to promote economic growth, renounce their authority to regulate a range of economic transactions within their borders. The second can be called positive integration: the creation of new rules to regulate problems common to all member states. The processes were meant to go hand in hand. Successful negative integration would erase whole classes of national laws and regulations, leaving important legal 'holes'. Positive integration would fill these holes with EC laws. The kaleidoscope of disparate national laws that function to hinder trade – such as taxes, duties and rules governing health, licensing and environmental protection standards – would be replaced by a single, 'harmonized' law.

The EC treaties lay down the rules of negative integration and establish the institutional framework by which community laws are produced. Simplifying again, the Commission initiates all legislation, oversees administrative tasks and verifies compliance with EC rules on the part of the nation-states. The Council of Ministers, composed of government ministers from each nation-state, has the power to veto the Commission's draft legislation and has used that power to structure the Commission's work. The European Parliament, an elected body, has certain powers of amendment, but is not usually capable of blocking action desired by the Commission and the Council. The ECJ is the judicial organ of the community.

The ECJ is a constitutional court roughly conforming to the European model. It is composed of fifteen members, all of whom are career lawyers, judges or law professors. The governments of each of the fifteen member states nominate one judge as a consequence of the enlargement of the ECJ following the negotiations and ratifications of 1994. Like the German, Italian and Spanish constitutional courts, the ECJ settles conflicts between institutions – such as a dispute between the European Parliament and the Commission as to the parliament's powers in a given legislative process – or between an EC institution and a nation-state – such as when the Commission brings a suit against France for failure to comply with EC law. Also like the German, Italian and Spanish courts, the ECJ receives concrete review referrals from judicial authorities. When EC law is material to the settlement of a case before any national court, the presiding judge may – and in some cases must – ask the ECJ for a correct interpretation of that law. This interpretation, called a preliminary ruling, must then be applied by the court to settle the case. The procedure is designed to enable national courts to understand the nature and content of EC law, and to apply it correctly.

Constitutional dialogues in the EC

Supra-national concrete review has transformed the nature of the EC polity. First, in the 1960s and 1970s the ECJ, in spite of (at times, intense) opposition on the part of the member states, has been able to articulate and then diffuse a number of interrelated 'supremacy' doctrines (Stein 1981). According to these doctrines (which are not made express in the treaties), EC norms must prevail against conflicting national norms. As a result of this creative jurisprudence, nearly every subject of EC law – including individuals and companies – may sue EC member states for injuries caused by member states' failure to comply with their obligations under EC law. The national judge, after referring the matter to the ECJ for a preliminary ruling, is authorized to invalidate national legal norms or the acts of public authorities which are found to violate community norms. These procedures have facilitated and to some extent driven negative integration processes. Put in the language of this chapter, a continuous constitutional dialogue between national courts and the ECJ is taking place. This dialogue has been the construction and defence of a hierarchy of laws whose apex – within those areas governed by community law – is supra-national.

Second, the ECJ – again in interaction with national courts – has succeeded in incorporating a charter of rights into the constitutional framework of the EC (Dallen 1990). Beginning in the late 1960s, several national judges as well as the constitutional courts of Germany and Italy began to express reservations about accepting the ECJ's supremacy doctrines in the absence of a charter. These courts, noticing that national rights provisions would be formally subordinated to EC treaty provisions, threatened to opt out of the community's concrete referral mechanism unless such rights could be guaranteed in the new hierarchy of norms being constructed. The ECJ responded, seemingly without much reservation, by elaborating a bill of rights, derived from 'the constitutional traditions common to the member states',[9] unwritten, general principles of law[10] and the European Convention of Human Rights.[11] These constitutional rights bind the member states; that is, within the sphere of community law they can neither be ignored nor downgraded by national laws. Even those member states which do not have a bill of rights at the domestic level now possess one at the community level. Thus in Britain, the doctrine of supremacy combines with rights guarantees to *require* British courts to refuse to apply national legislation if such legislation can be shown to violate rights guaranteed by community law (Craig 1991). The EC charter of rights, still not fully formed, will continue to develop as a result of interaction between national courts and the ECJ (Lang 1991).

Finally, the ECJ's settlement of discrete, concrete review referrals can alter legislative processes and outcomes in ways comparable to the pedagogical, feedback or indirect effects discussed in the last section. A few examples will suffice (see Berlin 1992). In 1985, while the Commission was bogged down in a tortuous process of harmonizing certain value added tax rules, the ECJ, ruling on a referral of a German court, declared that the levying of a tax on the sale of imported used goods, while exempting taxes on the sale of domestic used goods, violated the EEC treaty's ban on the use of national taxes to obtain unfair trade advantages. The ECJ then went on to state that, in the absence of EC legislation on the matter: 'it is for the Court to lay down guidelines compatible with [the treaty] . . . sufficiently simple to be applied in a uniform manner [by national courts] throughout the member states.' The Commission then scrapped its working draft and pushed through legislation based on the ECJ's guidelines. In 1986 the ECJ invalidated certain pricing policies of national airlines, ruling that these policies violated competition rules residing in the treaty, if not yet on the books as EC legislation. If further suggested that the EC adopt a regime to govern airline transport and liberalize competition in the area. Two weeks later the Commission initiated legal actions against the practices of several nation states, and in 1987 the Council of Ministers approved a package of legislation, partly inspired by the ECJ's jurisprudence. At the national level, ECJ rulings declaring national laws incompatible with EC law routinely generate corrective revision processes. In these, national parliaments work to 'harmonize' the provisions of a censored law with the provisions of the ECJ's jurisprudence.

In at least one crucial case, an ECJ preliminary ruling helped to redefine the very core of what is meant by European integration. In 1979, in the now famous 'Cassis de Dijon' case, the ECJ ruled that Germany could not prohibit the sale of an imported liqueur simply because that liqueur did not conform to national standards. If the Cassis liqueur was legally produced and sold in its country of origin (France), the ECJ declared, its sale could not be blocked *anywhere* within the community. In retrospect, the ruling 'created a new balance between negative and positive integration' (Empel 1992, 4), since it showed how member states could retain their own national rules, capable of being applied to the production and sale of domestic goods within the domestic market, while prohibiting member states from using these same rules to restrain trade, by applying them to goods coming from elsewhere. Most important, the ruling provided the Commission and other pro-integrationists with a general strategy, one that could be extended to other sectors, like the provision of services. That strategy – minimal harmonization, mutual recognition of national standards – ultimately became a central pillar of the 1986 Single European Act (Alter and Meunier 1994).

Conclusion

European constitutional courts, as 'guardians of the constitution', are responsible for enforcing constitutional norms, and for punishing (by invalidating the acts of) governmental authorities that violate them. In fulfilling these duties, constitutional judges construct constitutional law, laying down rules governing the production of legal norms, institutional interaction and the proper interpretation of human rights. Viewed from a policy perspective, we see that these courts regularly participate in a wide range of governmental processes, constraining legislative behaviour, generating policy outcomes and structuring the implementation of legal rules by the judiciary and the administration. The spread of the new constitutionalism throughout Europe has had consequences both above and beyond West European nation-states. The ECJ has exploited the logic of constitutionalism in its jurisprudence on 'supremacy', enabling both the construction of a supra-national constitution and the elaboration of an argument in favour of the court's own democratic legitimacy. In post-communist Central Europe, constitutions rely heavily on constitutional courts to anchor new regimes. The courts of the Czech Republic, Hungary, Poland, Romania and Slovakia all possess a mixture of concrete and abstract review powers. Although it is too early to assess the work of these new courts, one would expect that, as (if) Central European constitutionalism matures, the main features of European constitutional politics, broadly traced in this chapter, will take shape in this region as well.

Notes

1   Austria, Germany, Spain and the communist states of Eastern Europe had possessed constitutional courts, of varying effectiveness, in the interwar years.
2   I have also substantially simplified the language commonly used to distinguish different modes of constitutional control. Constitutional courts also perform many other functions not discussed here, including: reviewing the constitutionality of international agreements, verifying compliance with electoral laws, settling disputes between national and subnational governmental entities, and so on.
3   The Spanish ombudsman also has the power to initiate abstract review.
4   The best source for such information is the symposium on judicial recruitment to constitutional courts, 'Les juges constitutionnels', *Annuaire international de justice constitutionnelle* (Aix-en-Provence: Economica, 1990), 81–227.
5   Excluding the ratification of rules pursuant to international agreements.
6   The discrepancy in these figures is due to multiple referrals of the same law, withdrawals of referred laws by governments and FCC delay in deciding cases.
7   Statistics provided by the STC and compiled by the author.
8   Most referrals are rejected. In response to this flood, the ICC has developed a dense, technical jurisprudence laying down rules governing concrete review referrals.
9   The terms of the ECJ's decision in *Nold*, a 1974 case.
10   Such as 'equality before the law' and 'non-retroactivity'.
11   The European Convention of Human Rights (1950), a comprehensive charter of fundamental rights, has now been ratified by 23 European states including the EC twelve. It is judicially enforceable in two ways. First, individuals may refer

complaints, even against their own governments, to the European Court of Human Rights (ECHR) for a ruling. Second, European courts, like the ECJ and the German FCC, now refer to the authority of the Convention and to the ECHR's decisions in disputes before them. See Stack 1992.

Bibliography

Alter, K. J. and Meunier, S. (1994). 'Judicial politics in the European Community: European integration and the pathbreaking *Cassis de Dijon* decision'. *Comparative Political Studies* 26: 535–61.

Berlin, D. (1992). 'Interactions between the lawmaker and the judiciary within the EC'. *Legal Issues of European Integration*: 17–35.

Burley, A.-M. and Mattli, W. (1993). 'Europe before the court: a political theory of legal integration'. *International Organization* 47: 41–76.

Craig, P. P. (1991). 'Sovereignty of the UK parliament after Factortame'. *Yearbook of European Law*: 221–56.

Dahl, R. (1957). 'The concept of power'. *Behavioral Science* 2: 201–15.

Dallen, R. M. (1990). 'An overview of EC protection of human rights'. *Common Market Law Review* 27: 761–90.

Di Manno, T. (1992). 'L'activité contentieuse de la Cour constitutionnelle en 1990'. *Annuaire international de justice constitutionnelle* 6: 769–96.

Empel, M. van (1992). 'The 1992 programme: interaction between legislator and judiciary'. *Legal Issues of European Integration*: 1–16.

Escarras, J.-C. (1987). 'Italie: éléments de référence'. *Annuaire international de justice constitutionnelle* 1: 475–550.

Favoreu, L. (1990). 'Constitutional review in Europe', in L. Henkin (ed.), *Constitutionalism and Rights*. New York: Columbia University Press, 38–62.

Furlong, P. (1988). 'The constitutional court in Italian politics'. *West European Politics* 11:.7–23.

Jackson, D. J. and Tate, C. N. (eds) (1990). 'Symposium: judicial review and public policy in comparative perspective'. *Policy Studies Journal*: 19.

Katzenstein, P. J. (1987). *Policy and Politics in West Germany*. Philadelphia: Temple University Press.

Keeler, J. T. S. and Stone, A. (1987). 'Judicial-political confrontation in Mitterrand's France: the emergence of the constitutional council as a major actor in the policy making process', in S. Hoffmann et al. (eds), *The Mitterrand Experiment*. New York: Oxford University Press, 161–81.

Kelsen, H. (1928). 'La garantie juridictionnelle de la constitution'. *Revue du droit public* 44: 197–257.

Kommers, D. P. (1989). *The Constitutional Jurisprudence of the Federal Republic of Germany*. Durham, NC: Duke University Press.

—— (1994). 'The federal constitutional court in the German political system'. *Comparative Political Studies* 26: 470–91.

Landfried, C. (1984). *Bundesverfassungsgericht und Gesetzgeber* (The federal constitutional court and legislation). Baden-Baden: Nomos.

—— (ed.) (1989). *Constitutional Review and Legislation*. Baden-Baden: Nomos.

—— (1992). 'Judicial policymaking in Germany: the federal constitutional court'. *West European Politics* 15: 50–67.

Lang, J. T. (1991). 'The sphere in which member states are obliged to comply with the general principles of law and community fundamental rights principles'. *Legal Issues of European Integration*: 23–35.

Pace, A. (1990). 'Constitutional protection of freedom of expression in Italy'. *Revue européenne de droit public* 2: 71–113.

Pizzorusso, A. (1989). 'Constitutional review and legislation in Italy', in C. Landfried (ed.), *Constitutional Review and Legislation*. Baden-Baden: Nomos, 109–26.

Shapiro, M. J. (1992). 'The European Court of Justice', in A. Sbragia (ed.), *Euro-Politics*. Washington, DC: Brookings Institution, 123–56.

Shapiro, M. J. and Stone, A. (1994). 'Introduction: the new constitutional politics'. *Comparative Political Studies* 26: 397–420.

—— (eds) (1994). Special issue: 'The new constitutional politics of Europe'. *Comparative Political Studies* 26.

Stack, J. F., Jr. (1992). 'Judicial policymaking and the evolving protection of human rights: the European Court of Human Rights in comparative perspective'. *West European Politics* 15: 137–55.

Stein, E. (1981). 'Lawyers, judges, and the making of a transnational constitution'. *American Journal of International Law* 75: 1–27.

Stone, A. (1989). 'In the shadow of the constitutional council: the "juridicisation" of the legislative process in France'. *West European Politics* 12: 12–34.

—— (1990). 'The birth and development of abstract review in Western Europe: constitutional courts and policy-making in Western Europe'. *Policy Studies Journal* 19: 81–95.

—— (1992a). *The Birth of Judicial Politics in France*. New York: Oxford University Press.

—— (1992b). 'Where judicial politics are legislative politics: the French Constitutional Council'. *West European Politics* 15: 29–49.

—— (1994). 'Judging socialist reform: the politics of coordinate construction in France and Germany'. *Comparative Political Studies* 26: 443–69.

Volcansek, Mary L. (ed.) (1992). 'Special issue on judicial politics in Western Europe'. *West European Politics*: 15.

—— (1994). 'Political power and judicial review in Italy'. *Comparative Political Studies* 26: 492–509.

Weiler, J. (1981). 'The community system: the dual character of supranationalism'. *Yearbook of European Law* 1: 268–306.

—— (1991). 'The transformation of Europe'. *Yale Law Journal* 100: 2403–83.

Part III

From Leader to Follower

11

Towards a European Foreign and Security Policy?

Jolyon Howorth

European Political Cooperation in Historical Context

Historically, Europe has been marked by infinite diversity and precious little unity. From the very outset there was a lack of any internal unifying principle. The Greek and the Roman bases came from the periphery, the Christian basis from Asia Minor. Successive waves of migrations and invasions resulted in Latinization, Germanization, Slavization of vast expanses of land, which were then stirred and shaken in a confused cocktail of tribal, ethnic and eventually national diversity. Before 1945 the very concept of a European identity was, to all intents and purposes, a contradiction in terms. And yet, since that date, various attempts to create a common European foreign and security policy have peppered the historical landscape. Whether informed by a confederal or inter-governmental impulsion, as in the Fouchet Plan of 1960–2 (Bloës 1970; Soutou 1992), or inspired by a federal or functionalist vision, as in the 1950–4 European Defence Community scheme (Fursdon 1980), whether restricted to Western Europe or aspiring to embrace the entire continent 'from the Atlantic to the Urals', the various plans for foreign and security policy cooperation all fell foul of Europe's seemingly intractable fissiparousness.

Although the 1950s saw the rampant nationalism of the previous two centuries straight-jacketed by the hegemonic influence of two antagonistic superpowers, each exercising effective control over its respective half of the continent (henceforth known as blocs), the various countries of Europe viewed the postwar security order in very different ways. Broadly speaking, these fall into three main groups. First, there were those Central and East European countries whose unfortunate geo-strategic situation led to their involuntary incorporation into the Soviet bloc. For Latvians, Lithuanians, Estonians, Poles, Hungarians, Czechs, Bulgarians and Romanians, opportunities for self-expression – before the late 1980s – were minimal. Had those opportunities existed, there is little doubt that the alternatives to the existing European order which each might have advocated would have been several and varied. Second, there were a number of neutral or non-aligned nations, but each of these assumed their status in rather different ways. Switzerland and Sweden have, since 1815, been 'permanently neutral', the former as a result of treaty recognition (the Congress of Vienna, confirmed at Versailles in 1919), the latter as a result of political choice. The neutrality of Finland and Austria has been more a question of geo-strategic prudence, although in the case of Austria neutral status was underwritten by international treaty, whereas in the case of Finland it derived from political common sense. Ireland's neutrality has essentially been informed by the complex relationship between that country and Great Britain and is quite different from that of any of the other neutrals. Spain, which had been neutral during the Second World War, was originally ostracized by NATO though linked through bilateral security arrangements to the United States, only recently integrating with the remainder of Europe (NATO in 1982 and the EC in 1986). Yugoslavia was one of the founders of the 'non-aligned' movement, but (as recent events have underlined) this was as much out of an effort to hold together as a federal state as it was out of any genuine attachment to neutralism. European 'neutralism' thus has almost as many different forms as it has member states (Carton 1991).

The third group of countries comprised, of course, those Western nations which, along with the United States and Canada, signed the Atlantic Treaty in 1949 and formed a military alliance in NATO: Belgium, Denmark, France, Holland, Iceland, Italy, Luxembourg, Norway, Portugal and the UK. Greece joined NATO in 1952, the Federal Republic of Germany in 1955 and Spain in 1982. Once again, the motives and intentions of these different countries (as well as their vision of Europe and the world) varied significantly. The UK saw NATO, at least in the early years, as a vehicle for the retention of a world role, underpinned by a 'special relationship' with Washington. Germany and Italy saw it as a means of holding communism at bay pending political and economic reconstruction and the emergence of a new international identity as key members of a Euro-Atlantic community. France regarded the alliance essentially as a transitional structure which would eventually be superseded by a European defence or security identity, dominated, naturally, by Paris and extending, potentially, as far East as the Ural mountains. While all West European nations identified their security interests with those of the United States and NATO, some of them (Germany, Italy, France and the Benelux countries) also began to consider their economic, industrial, commercial and broadly politico-cultural identity as belonging to a nascent West European community. Others initially excluded themselves from this emerging Euro-identity, either through illusions of grandeur (UK), or through cultural reticence (Denmark, Norway, Iceland, UK) or through their retention of anti-democratic political regimes (Portugal, Spain, Greece). The neutral countries, either through conviction (Switzerland, Sweden) or through prudence (Austria, Finland), tended to equate the EC with the 'Western bloc' and elected to stay outside.

Clearly, therefore, despite the apparent uniformity of 'world view' imposed by the Cold War, and despite the apparent demise of European nationalism as an actor on the world stage, there was, for much of the postwar period, a considerable divergence of opinion within Western Europe concerning relations with the rest of the world. This was in large part because European concerns remained predominantly internal, whereas all too little attention was paid by Europe's leaders to the way in which Europe as a whole might wish (or be obliged) to structure its relations with the other major nations or landmasses. The two principal exceptions to this rule were Charles de Gaulle and Jean Monnet, both of whom had, from 1944 onwards, a constant vision of Europe's need to emerge as a coherent, united and increasingly autonomous actor on the world stage. However, their diametrically opposed approaches to the process involved (inter-governmentalism versus federalism) did not help the European cause. Moreover, de Gaulle's uncompromising style, itself essential to the promotion of his European agenda, resulted in widespread misunderstanding of his real intentions, which were most often confused with the promotion of French nationalism. It was not until after de Gaulle had resigned and *détente* was in full swing that serious progress on what was now to be called European Political Cooperation (EPC) became possible. Starting with a proposal formulated by Georges Pompidou at the EC summit in The Hague in 1969, EPC, though initially rather limited in scope, grew constantly both in ambition and in credibility throughout the 1970s and early 1980s (Taylor 1979; Nuttall 1992). The reasons for its success are historical, political and structural. The 1970s saw, at one and the same time, the blossoming of *détente*, the erosion of the American claim to or desire for sole leadership of the West, the emergence and consolidation of the EEC as an economic and commercial giant, the economic challenge to the West – but particularly to Western Europe as a whole – of the OPEC cartel, and the advent of global interdependence. In other words, the reconfiguration of the rest of the world around a number of major poles was increasingly forcing Europe into a single mould.

Politically, several factors helped to promote the cause of EPC: the leadership of committed Europeans such as Valéry Giscard d'Estaing and Helmut Schmidt, combined with a widespread sense that success in foreign policy coordination was relatively easy to achieve, diplomatically advantageous and a welcome alternative to the technical difficulties of economic and industrial/commercial integration. At an institutional level, bureaucratic infighting between the various government departments traditionally involved in foreign affairs led almost inevitably to the preponderance of the foreign ministries which, alone, had the necessary overview to achieve coordination in external relations (Allen 1978; George 1991). Moreover, as the practice of diplomatic concertation grew through the institutional structures established after the Davignon Report of 1970,[1] it became increasingly unrealistic for ministers (and particularly for foreign ministers) to compartmentalize their agendas in order to respect the somewhat byzantine division of responsibility implicit in the text of the various treaties governing European affairs (Lodge 1989, 225–34; George 1991, 219). Increasingly, as the frequency of foreign ministerial meetings was stepped up, the practice of wide-ranging consultation became the norm.

The Single European Act (SEA) of 1986 gave further impulsion to EPC by bestowing upon its meetings a dedicated secretariat which allowed not only for increasingly coherent follow-through but also, in part because of its permanent location in Brussels, for tight coordination with the Commission itself. The early 1980s, during which the recent isolationism and diffidence of the Carter years were replaced by the crusading unpredictability and unilateralism of the Reagan presidency (from a European perspective, both approaches being equally unsatisfactory), gave further impulsion to the perceived need for the EC to speak to the world with one voice. Thus, despite a number of failures in foreign policy coordination (Afghanistan, South Africa, the boycott of the Moscow Olympics in 1980), the record of achievement was considerable. Building on the major successes of the 1970s – particularly coordination over CSCE, United Nations voting and especially the Middle East[2] – the community was able, by the late 1980s, to formulate joint policy documents on a vast range of issues covering literally every corner of the globe. In 1988 alone, no fewer than 78 joint EC resolutions were agreed, concerning 37 different foreign policy issues (Wessels 1992, 166). It is true that, for the moment, these initiatives remained at the level of texts. Europe's influence in world affairs did not take off or even become coherent overnight, but the practice of foreign policy concertation was, in and of itself, an important learning process.

Nowhere, perhaps, was this more evident than in the field of defence and security policy *stricto sensu*. Given the alarm bells sounded by the Euromissiles crisis, the Strategic Defense Initiative and the Intermediate Nuclear Forces (INF) treaty,[3] the impetus in favour of a relative autonomization of Europe's security capability developed rapidly. As usual in such matters, the initiative was Franco-German. Throughout the 1980s, Franco-German defence cooperation was marked by a multiplicity of initiatives, each one seemingly more significant than the last (Friend 1991, 67–72). In parallel, the long-moribund Western European Union was brought out of the cold storage effectively imposed upon it by the primacy of NATO and, via a series of meetings and declarations in Rome (1984), Bonn (1985), Venice (1986) and Luxembourg (April 1987), gradually led to the adoption, at The Hague on 27 October 1987, of the 'Platform on European Security Interests', which amounted, in effect, to the laying of the foundation stone for the long-heralded 'European Pillar' of the Atlantic Alliance (Western European Union 1988). The presence, in Europe's key foreign ministries, of committed Europeans in the persons of Geoffrey Howe, Hans-Dietrich Genscher, Roland Dumas and Gianni de Michelis augured well for the elaboration, in the 1990s, of an increasingly coherent and harmonious diplomatic and security entity as the pendant of what, via the impetus of the Single European Act, was becoming a concerted move towards economic and monetary union (EMU) (Owen and Dynes 1992, ch. 8). The presence in the Kremlin of Mikhail Gorbachev and the promise of lasting and genuine *détente* was an added and unexpected bonus. Everything seemed for the best in the best of all possible (Cold War) worlds. And then the Cold War came to an end.

1989 and the Challenge of the Post-Cold War World

> *Now what's going to happen to us without barbarians?*
> *They were, those people, a kind of a solution.*
> Constantin Cavafy, 'Waiting for the Barbarians' (1904)

The fall of the Berlin Wall and the *de facto* demise of the Cold War brought to an abrupt end the cosy certainties on which the previous decades of foreign and security policy concertation had been based. If, in Cavafy's image, the 'barbarians' had disappeared, how would the new world be structured? Would Washington continue to commit itself to the defence of Western Europe? Against whom would that defence be directed? What was the future (if any) for NATO? With the effective collapse of one superpower, would the world now revolve around a unipolar system, dominated in every field by the United States, or had the hour of multi-polarity finally arrived? How was the end of the Cold War to be interpreted in terms of international relations theory? Did the demise of ideologies also put paid to classical 'realist' theories of balances of power? Equally important (although barely discerned at first) was the broader commercial and industrial impact of the demise of bipolarity. With US attention turning increasingly to the Pacific, the ending of the Cold War placed firmly on the international agenda for the first time the question of the global competitiveness of rival socio-economic systems. How were trade wars to be prevented from degenerating into shooting wars? Alternative approaches to an understanding of the future direction of world history included Samuel Huntington's controversial vision of a 'Clash of

Civilizations', which rejected both ideology and economics as the fundamental source of future world conflict: 'The great divisions among humankind and the dominating source of conflict will be cultural' (Huntington 1993). In all of these new scenarios, Europe clearly stands or falls together as one coherent model of social and industrial organization.

Just as important as global issues were the regional implications of the new dawning. If a united Germany were to re-emerge as a geo-strategic giant in the centre of Europe, what impact would that have on an adolescent community which had just learnt to live with its own internal balances – political, economic, industrial and diplomatic? In particular, what would be the future for Franco-German cooperation – which had hitherto provided the motor for most community initiatives? If the Soviet Union was to remove its iron grip from the satellite states of Central and Eastern Europe, what was to be the future place of the forgotten European cousins in the new family of European nations? In what ways would any potential 'broadening' of the community be compatible with the planned 'deepening'? How would the community meet the joint and contradictory challenges of economic development and resurgent nationalist rivalries in the East? The questions were endless, and were to grow more numerous and complex with every passing year.

In April 1990, in an attempt to help the community come to grips with these questions and to stabilize its own institutions and project, President Mitterrand and Chancellor Kohl issued a joint proposal that an already planned inter-governmental conference on economic and monetary union (EMU) should meet in parallel with a second one on European political union (EPU), thus reinforcing the movement towards a Common Foreign and Security Policy (CFSP). These two conferences, which convened in Rome in December 1990, concluded their endeavours with the signature, one year later, of the Maastricht Treaty creating the European Union. Maastricht stated ambitiously that 'the Union and its member states shall define and implement a common foreign and security policy . . . covering all areas of foreign and security policy.' Earlier in 1991, before the ink was dry on the text of the treaty, a whole series of new and relatively unforeseen foreign and diplomatic crises (in addition to the still unanswered questions rehearsed above) broke onto the scene: the Gulf War and the spread of Islamic fundamentalism, the collapse of the Soviet Union and, perhaps above all, the violent disintegration of the former Yugoslavia. The suddenness and scale of these dramatic events, and the obvious lack of preparation on the part of the EC to provide immediate answers to them, inevitably led to a spate of critical and negative comment implying that the prospect of foreign and security policy harmonization in Europe had receded if not actually disappeared (Brenner 1993). In what follows, I shall aim to examine this proposition by looking as dispassionately as possible at three broad (and overlapping) areas: the crisis of identity currently afflicting Europe and its respective states and the impact of this identity crisis on the quest for a CFSP; the institutional bases of a hypothetical CFSP; and, finally, some theoretical considerations on the shifting nature of international relations as the new century approaches.

Nations, Identities and Security in Post-1989 Europe

For 45 years after the Second World War the relationship between nation-hood, identity and security was effectively dictated by the geo-strategic constraints of bipolarity. To that extent, the forms of identity which were assumed by most of the nation-states of Europe contained an element of artificiality which was usually compounded by a mismatch between their 'being' and their 'doing' (Pisani 1992; A. D. Smith 1992). Some, like Italy and Germany, concentrated massively on 'doing' and avoided, for obvious reasons, too many questions about their 'being'. Others, like Britain and Spain, prioritized a relatively atavistic form of 'being' at the expense of any purposeful 'doing', although in the case of Spain entry into the EC seemed to many to have resolved the contradiction in one simple move. The crisis of European political definition which has afflicted the entire continent since 1989 derives to a very large extent from the process of national introspection in which virtually every country has been engaged. This has taken on many forms, from soul-searching over something called 'sovereignty', as in Britain and France, via a wholesale quest for national redefinition, as in Germany, Italy and the former Czechoslovakia, to violent armed conflict, as in the Balkans and the Caucasus. But everywhere, questions about national identity have been inseparable from questions about Europe and from questions about security.

Paradoxically, the debate is probably most urgent in the one country – Britain – where it has taken place in the least overt fashion. Most commentators on contemporary British dilemmas with regard to foreign and security policy take it as read that Britain's only conceivable future is with Europe (Wallace 1992; Coker 1992). Indeed, by signing the Maastricht Treaty, the British government committed the UK to a long-term future in which the country's foreign and security policy would progressively be merged with that of the European Union. Vociferously opposed to that option was a noisy minority of 'Euro-sceptics' taking their cue from Mrs Thatcher, who were projected by the media as the last defenders of British – or, perhaps more accurately, English – identity. But in fact, the British foreign policy elite, especially the main political parties at Westminster, remains, despite occasional European rhetoric, and frequent smiles and handshakes, firmly wedded to a vision of Britain's role in the world which has very little basis in contemporary reality. That vision is also systematically promoted by important sections of the

British press. Christopher Coker has argued provocatively that Britain remains suffused with nostalgia for a 'special relationship' with the United States which amounts to the UK 'turning its back on its future and looking forward to the past'. Such an attitude, Coker insists, is not only astonishing in that it enjoys minimal reciprocation in Washington, but is also misguided in that it involves 'clinging to a power whose only reassuring thought is that it might prolong its own decline as skilfully as the British did' (Coker 1992, 413). But beyond nostalgia for the special relationship, Britain is also obsessed with 'punching above her weight' in foreign affairs, in maintaining a 'leading role' in the world which little in her current situation can justify. One prominent observer has recently asked whether such an attitude 'any longer serves the interests, or meets the wishes, of the constituent interests and regions of the UK' (Wallace 1992, 438). What, one might ask, is the British specificity of UK foreign policy which differentiates it from that of our principal partners in the Union?

Beyond a relatively corporatist desire on the part of the Foreign Office to retain control over Britain's diplomacy, and allowing for the nostalgia factor, it is difficult to see any serious justification for the UK's insistence on retaining a strictly inter-governmental framework for the development of a European CFSP. To all intents and purposes, in the world of GATT, NAFTA, APEC and the new regionalization of international relations, the UK's interests 'overseas' are increasingly difficult to distinguish from those of her European partners. That is clearly the view from Washington. One way forward might be if Whitehall elites came to believe that the best way of retaining the 'special relationship' with Washington would be for Britain actually to become what the USA has, for several decades, wanted her to be: a true European partner, and, as such, the main guarantor of continuing harmony between the two sides of the Atlantic. This, at the same time, might be the course which would continue to allow Britain to 'punch above her weight' as a key part of a coordinated European foreign and security policy geared to maximizing the interests of the newly formed Union in the coming reshuffle of the international pack of cards.

France is, of course, a similar case to that of Britain: a former colonial empire, with worldwide responsibilities, whose real impact in world affairs is increasingly limited to her role in and via Europe. The difference between the two countries is that France has long understood, in the words of President Mitterrand, that 'France in my country, Europe is my future'. To that extent, France is probably the European nation which was most successful in avoiding a major crisis of identity throughout the Cold War years. Her 'being' and her 'doing' were harmonized through her European commitment, along with her aspiration to play a leading role. The reality of the latter was almost certainly minimized by her conflictual, often arrogant diplomatic style – particularly with respect to the United States. In the post-Cold War world, France's identity crisis has been of a different type, involving adaptation to a new relationship with a much more powerful Germany. Here again, the only solution lies in intensification of the European process. All the signs are that France's foreign policy establishment is as aware of this as ever (Tiersky 1992; Vernet 1992; Bozo 1992). Indeed, it is not unlikely that both France and Britain will jointly come to identify their future role as that of committing to the European (rather than to any strictly national) cause their very considerable assets in international diplomacy.

If that were to happen, it would in and of itself facilitate the harmonization of Europe's foreign and security policy with that of the united Germany. For Germany's henceforth pivotal role in any European order derives precisely from her key position in both the European and the Atlantic communities. 'If there is any "special relationship" between the United States and a European country, it should be with Germany. In contrast to Britain, which has often used its own special relationship with the United States to weaken Europe, and in contrast to France, which has used Europe to weaken the United States, a Germany bolstered by the United States would be a cornerstone of a Europe both stronger and more supportive of American interests' (Kielinger and Otte 1993, 62). The international jury still remains undecided about the long-term diplomatic and security intentions of Germany. Many, particularly in Britain and France, but also in Eastern Europe, fear a resurgent Germany with hegemonic if not imperial aspirations over a reconstituted *Mitteleuropa* (Thatcher 1993; Valance 1990). Others, particularly Americans, see a liberal and democratic Germany providing – in a largely positive manner – a new assertive sense of direction in a Europe running out of steam (Pond 1992; Livingston 1992). Still others, particularly Germans (Kaiser 1991; Schlör 1993), but also astute connoisseurs of the German scene (Garton Ash 1993; Le Gloannec 1993), present the situation in all its contradictory complexity. Whereas previously, as Anne-Marie Le Gloannec has noted, Germany was either too strong or too weak in Europe, there is a risk in the future that she will turn out to be *both* too strong *and* too weak. Germany, we are reminded, is powerful, but cannot be expected to perform all the miracles which are currently being heaped, often by others, onto her foreign policy agenda. These include taking the lion's share of responsibility for the development not only of the Eastern European countries but also of the CIS, continuing to act as the economic and monetary driving force of the European Union, redesigning the FRG's security policy so as to take a much more proactive role in NATO and also in more strictly European security arrangements, particularly towards the Balkans, acquiring a permanent seat on the UN Security Council, helping to break the GATT log-jam and, more generally, easing the dialogue between Washington and Brussels. Germany's diplomatic agenda is nothing if not overcrowded.

Germany's overriding preoccupation in the immediate future will have to be with her Eastern neighbours. But three points should be noted here. The first is that such a concern derives more from a sense of *Zwang nach Osten* than from *Drang nach Osten*, or, as Gregory Treverton has put it, 'more the pull of perceived obligation than the push of imagined destiny' (Treverton 1992, 100). The task of creating political, social and demographic stability and, eventually, economic prosperity in Eastern Europe is one of Herculean dimensions which, to date, Germany has assumed to a degree which puts all other countries in the shade. From 1989 to 1992 Germany contributed more than \$50 billion in aid to the former Soviet Union, while the US and Japan contributed, respectively, \$9 billion and \$3 billion. Germany also contributes well over half of the EC's PHARE programme of investment in the East. And this is precisely the second point. Although Germany may be more immediately and directly interested in the outcome of this 'new *Ostpolitik*' (Drummond 1993), the remainder of the European Union countries have an equal stake in the final result. And because the German economy suffers from structural weaknesses and imbalances which make it incapable of coping alone with the scale of the problem, the European imperative becomes inescapable. A coordinated policy towards the East is indispensable, the more so in that the third point concerns the compatibility between the new *Ostpolitik* and the strengthening of the European Union itself. In the early months after the fall of the Berlin Wall, it was widely assumed that strengthening of the community was incompatible with enlargement. Today there appears to be a consensus in both halves of the continent that the broad principles behind the two projects are complementary rather than contradictory. It is only a politically stable Union, blessed with a coherent economic and industrial policy, which would be capable of generating a viable stabilization plan for the East. At the same time it is a strong and coherent Union (rather than a weak and aimless one) which the former Warsaw Pact countries wish to join.

Yet when we turn to the huge issue of the detailed relations between the EU and Central and Eastern Europe (CEE), the consensus rapidly vanishes. In the immediate aftermath of 1989 the newly emerging CEE democracies clearly held unrealistic expectations about the time-scale of any future integration into the structures of Western Europe. Indulging in their own form of identity crisis, these countries tended to make overoptimistic assumptions about the cultural proximity between themselves and Western Europe, assumptions which were at least partially conditioned by an all too natural desire rapidly to dissociate themselves from their erstwhile Eastern overlord. Their expectations were not reciprocated in the West. While Germany has always been sympathetic to rapid integration, and while the UK under Mrs Thatcher toyed with enlargement mainly as a way of avoiding any deepening trend towards West European federalism, other EC countries were alarmed at the implications of a rapid extension of the community to the East. François Mitterrand attempted to devise a holding structure, the *Confédération*, intended to offer the CEE countries a temporary framework while negotiations took place on association with and then membership of the community. However, this structure, after initially being received with enthusiasm by the CEE countries, was subsequently rejected by them as an ill-disguised 'waiting-room' with no fixed – or indeed an intolerably lengthy[4] – time-scale.

In December 1991 the so-called Visegrad countries (Poland, Hungary, the Czech Republic and Slovakia) signed the 'Europe Agreement' with the community. These association agreements 'combine an asymmetrical opening of EC markets, technical and economic cooperation and approximation of law with a framework of political dialogue [and] are designed to meet the require-ments of each individual country and to take into account democratic and economic progress, thus providing scope for a gradual development of the association' (Michalski and Wallace 1992, 136). Similar agreements were signed in 1993 with Romania and Bulgaria. While there can be little doubt that the agreements offer the CEE countries a real prospect of gradual integration into the structures of the Union (including, one day, membership), there is equally little doubt that they carry serious potential risks. First, as Michalski and Wallace have shown, the trade agreements involved carry minimal prospects of facilitating rapid economic growth in those sectors of the CEE countries which most need a boost: heavy industry, textiles and agricul-ture. Second, the grey areas and indeed overall ambivalence surrounding the objectives of the agreements themselves suggest to many in Eastern Europe that this may be yet another long-term 'waiting-room', intended more as a pacifier than as a conduit to genuine integration.[5] Thirdly, the argument goes, in the absence of a clear time-frame or even a clearly enunciated ultimate objective (such as, say, full membership of the European Union) there is a real danger that popular frustrations will run ahead of the capacity of political elites to deliver, leading to a nationalist backlash, the overthrow of reformist, pro-Western governments and reversion to some new form of populist authori-tarianism which will almost certainly fan the flames of localist, nationalist or ethnic conflict and further intensify regional instability.

Between those who argue that the Union, particularly during a recession, simply cannot afford to do much for the CEE countries without destroying its own delicate internal organism (Tsoukalis 1993), and those who plead in favour of rapid membership of the Union, at least for the Visegrad countries, in order to avoid unmanageable destabilization in the East the EU needs to develop a concerted policy which will combine essential commercial con-cessions (such as meaningful access to Western markets), clear political objec-tives (such as the short-term consolidation of a transcontinental security pact) as well as a clear timetable, and above all well-defined diplomatic and economic instruments (Pinder 1991). In this context, a combination of current German practical assistance, with the implementation of the French/European plan for a regional security pact (see below), backed by clear signals of firm political resolve on the part of all members of the Union, may just be sufficient to tip the delicate balance of Europe as a whole towards constructive optimism. The stakes for Europe are very high and the broad issue of relations with the CEE countries has been identified as the number one priority for the emerging CFSP.[6] I shall return to the issue of the institutional problems posed by this relationship in the next section of this chapter.

The problem is essentially one of identity. Most of the Central and Eastern European countries feel strongly that their primary identity lies with the family of nations grouping within the European Union. This obviously poses the question of where to draw a new 'identity line' across the continent and, of equal importance, how to interpret that line. Whatever regional partnership eventually emerges between the European Union and the CEE countries, it must not lead to the marginalization or traumatization of the former countries of the Soviet Union proper. It is unrealistic to imagine that the CIS or even Russia on its own would one day accede to membership of an enlarged EU. Moscow will remain the hub of a vast power zone which will – given appropriate economic and industrial development – have no difficulty in standing alone in the international arena. Indeed, from a strictly security angle, it seems increasingly likely that Russia will henceforth wish to exchange its former overstretched superpower status for that of a regional hegemon and that the geographical area which it defines as the 'near abroad' (basically covering the countries formerly included in the Soviet Union) will be re-garded as coming under the aegis of a type of Russian 'Monroe Doctrine' (Holoboff 1994). The biggest obstacle to the peaceful implementation of such a new order will be relations between Russia and Ukraine (Morrison 1993; Allison 1993). Assuming that such a new order can be implemented and managed peacefully (a highly perilous assumption), it should be perceived by the West not only as relatively inevitable but also as relatively healthy. While there will undoubtedly be winners and losers in such a quasi-hegemonic scheme, the degree of stability which it would confer on a region prone to fissiparousness can, in that sense, be seen in a positive light. The overt relief in Western chancelleries which greeted Boris Yeltsin's success in persuading the Serbs to withdraw their heavy artillery from Sarajevo in February 1994 illustrates the point.[7] This section has concentrated on problems of identity. Nowhere is that issue more problematic than in former Yugoslavia, which starkly illustrates both the dilemmas of and the prospects for foreign policy concertation within the European Union.

The conflict in the former Yugoslavia has consistently been cited as the prime example of the weakness of Europe's attempts to devise a CFSP. This is too hasty a judgement. While there is little cause for complacency, the evolution of the overall picture is not entirely negative. If one takes as a starting-point the situation in the summer of 1991, the picture is indeed one of total divergence, indeed disarray, among the main European capitals in terms both of their analysis of the Yugoslav situation and of their respective 'solutions'. Germany was, for a variety of largely historical and politico-cultural reasons, not unhappy to see the break-up of the old Yugoslav federation and was actively promoting, via political and diplomatic channels, the cause of Slovenian and Croatian separatism. France, on the other hand, for similar types of reasons, was pursuing a diametrically opposite approach, involving overt support for the maintenance of Yugoslavia's federal structures, implicit or even explicit sympathy for Serbia and active preparation for French military intervention to achieve that result. Britain, for its part, ever conscious of the intractable nature of the Irish situation, seemed to adopt a policy of wishful-thinking, hoping desperately that the problem would go away, and being very reluctant, if it did not, to get involved in any serious way, especially militarily (Freedman 1994). The futile attempts at conciliation on the part of a European *troika* composed of the foreign ministers of three other countries, none of which had any specific policy towards Yugoslavia, merely highlighted the nature of the problem.

The specific national approaches of the three main 'powers' proved either impracticable or misguided. France's proposal on military intervention at the European Council meeting in the autumn of 1991 was only supported by a totally sceptical Germany because of the knowledge that it would be vetoed by a totally hostile Britain.[8] Germany's unilateral recognition of Slovenia and Croatia in December 1991 (followed only weeks later by official EC recognition) was motivated essentially by an idealistic assumption that the *de facto* creation of an *inter-state* (as opposed to a *civil*) war would legitimize international intervention and bring a rapid end to hostilities. The recognition of Slovenia and Croatia inevitably led, in the spring of 1992, to the recognition of Bosnia, which in turn led to further, and more complicated, hostilities. Gradually, the European capitals came to a number of convergent if not identical conclusions. First, that no 'national' solution was possible for the Yugoslav problem. If any diplomatic, economic or even military pressure was to be brought to bear on the warring parties, it could only be effective if concerted, first at a European level and then within the context of the United Nations. Germany was forced to acknowledge that diplomatic recognition, while probably inevitable, had by no means solved the problem but merely created a rather different one. France too, even in the person of Serbia's staunchest overt ally, François Mitterrand, was eventually led to recognize that, in the overall apportionment of responsibility for the war, Belgrade was the main offender. France also shifted from being the country initially most prepared to contemplate unilateral military involvement to an official position which insisted that the only organism appropriate to authorize military operations should be the United Nations. Britain was eventually obliged to become fully involved in the Yugoslav situation not only by providing the two European negotiators (Lords Carrington and Owen) but also by convening the London Conference.

As the war dragged on and the range of available options narrowed, there was a notable convergence within the EU around a consensual approach which is something more than a mere lowest common denominator. That approach included the tactical political use of economic sanctions against Serbia and Montenegro (admittedly backed by minimal policing of the Danube and the Greek border); the imposition of political conditions for recognition of Croatia; refusal to seek a self-regulating solution through the lifting of the arms embargo; constant diplomatic pressure on the three main ex-Yugoslav capitals involved in the fighting and the relentless pursuit of a political solution through the efforts of the various mediators; concerted pressure on the United Nations to exert increasing diplomatic, political and physical pressure on the warring parties, particularly the Serbs, as well as to maximize humanitarian assistance; and considerable arm-twisting in Athens (admittedly with minimal effect). By December 1993 the umpteenth European peace offensive was a Franco-German initiative backed and negotiated by the British mediator Lord Owen. There have no doubt been isolated French, British, German and other individuals operating 'on the ground' in either a private or a semi-official capacity who have attempted, over the years, to promote what can easily be interpreted as more narrow, nation-specific interests. But in early 1994 there was virtually no distinction between the overall approach to the Yugoslav problem being advocated in London, Paris, Bonn or Brussels. Significantly, when, in February 1994, France (with German backing) succeeded in persuading the USA to cross the Rubicon and prepare for NATO air-strikes to lift the siege of Sarajevo, even the British government, which had long been totally opposed to such a move, was whipped into line by the combined diplomatic pressure of Paris and Washington. The lesson drawn from the Yugoslav experience in the various capitals of Europe is that, for an international problem of this dimension, the only possible solution is an international one, with as concerted a European input as possible. This poses the question of the institutional framework.

The Institutional Bases for a Common Foreign and Security Policy

> *The Union and its Member States shall define and implement a common foreign and security policy, governed by the provisions of the Title and covering all areas of foreign and security policy.*
>
> (Title V, Article J.1.1. of the Maastricht Treaty, December 1991)

The bold and somewhat stark assertiveness of the Maastricht text conceals a twofold institutional conundrum. First, by referring to *both* the union *and* its constituent parts, it immediately raises the issue of the division of labour between national capitals and Brussels. Second, by embracing all areas of security policy, it suggests the need for a more or less radical revision of the relationship between the EU's own 'official' security organism – Western European Union – and existing security institutions such as NATO and CSCE. The first problem is that of the potential clash between collective (European) and individual (national) interests and/or objectives. Recent examples of policy clashes pitting an individual nation both against the Commission and against the remaining eleven members of the Council are Greece's lone stand on recognition of Macedonia, France's obduracy over GATT and Germany's unilateralism over recognition of Slovenia and Croatia. When issues of such fundamental importance are involved, there is likely to be effective blockage of the entire process as long as Article J.8. (which calls for unanimity within the Council) remains in force. However, J.8. is itself the subject of two potentially contradictory qualifications. The first comes in article J.1.(4), which states that 'The Member States . . . shall refrain from any action which is contrary to the interests of the Union or likely to impair its effectiveness as a cohesive force in international relations.' Thus, considerable moral pressure will be exerted against recalcitrant nation-states in an effort to bring them into line. In practice, this is unlikely to have much effect other than to ensure that on divisive issues the community will be forced to find a form of wording which reflects the vaguest and most general lowest common denominator. The other qualification of J.8. comes in article J.3.(2), which states that 'The Council shall, when adopting the joint action and at any stage during its development, define those matters on which decisions are to be taken by a qualified majority.'[9] Some have seen this as a recipe for confrontation, involving first a quarrel over whether or not to apply qualified majority voting to a given issue, followed by a wrangle – and potential recriminations – over the vote itself (De la Gorce 1992). Realism suggests that on any issue where a state (particularly a big one) feels that matters of 'sovereignty' are concerned, the unanimity rule will be applied; in other cases, consensus is likely to prevail.

The institutional framework for CFSP decisions is charged with ambiguity in that the respective responsibilities of the Commission and the Council are left totally unspecified, although the spirit of inter-governmentalism informs the basic principles of the text. At the same time, the support structures for CFSP are increasingly being centralized in Brussels. The old EPC coordinating secretariat, in addition to being expanded from six members to 23, has now been merged with the Council of Ministers secretariat, with a staff of over two thousand. Furthermore, the political directors from the twelve foreign ministries have, since November 1993, held monthly meetings in Brussels (rather than in the capital city of the presidency, as previously). This complex Brussels-based bureaucracy, directly responsible to the national foreign ministries, will therefore inevitably have to coordinate its activities with the CFSP support structures which have been set up within the Commission itself. In December 1992, while reshuffling the portfolio of his commissioners, Jacques Delors divided 'foreign policy' (formerly overseen by a sole commissioner) into three separate briefs: political issues proper, including enlargement; international economic issues; and overseas development. Inevitably, given the difficulty of distinguishing between these areas, there were early demarcation disputes between the main commissioners involved (Hans van den Broek and Leon Brittan) and fierce 'turf' battles between the respective bureaucracies. The bewildering multiplicity of CFSP actors and the minefield of institutional demarcation disputes both call for urgent rationalization. Which organism is most likely to prevail? Under almost any scenario short of a total disintegration of the Union and wholesale renationalization, the arguments in favour of foreign and security policy concertation at the centre (and the concomitant progressive decline in the influence of individual foreign ministries) are compelling. Resolution of this issue will become increasingly urgent as CFSP procedures advance. This is all the more crucial when one begins to analyse the situation in the field of security *per se*.

The distinction between 'foreign' and 'security' policy is, in practice, increasingly meaningless. Although the traditional objective of foreign policy has been to promote the interests of a given collectivity in the universal competition for resources and influence, whereas security issues proper were felt to involve matters of vital national interest, this distinction is increasingly difficult to make. The forty-year nuclear stalemate in Europe taught state actors two important lessons. The first was that 'resources' could no longer be considered to include territorial aggrandizement. Although border disputes are likely to simmer on for some years in Central and Eastern Europe, the Paris Charter of November 1990 commits all states to recognition of Europe's existing borders. The second lesson to be learnt from the Cold War was that security is indivisible. A 'fortress Europe', hermetically sealed off from the economic and social chaos of a former Eastern bloc (or of a turbulent Maghreb) left to its own devices, would in no way be secure. 'Security' is therefore defined increasingly in terms of the promotion among neighbouring states of economic development, demographic and social stability, environmental cooperation and cultural harmony (Mathews 1989; Bluth 1993). From an institutional perspective, it is clear that, in this sense, foreign and security policy, in addition to involving the national and European actors just reviewed, will need to involve investment banks, multi-national companies, communications corporations and a host of other autonomous actors, including 'bottom-up' democratic and non-governmental organizations. In this sense, 'foreign policy' becomes little more than the external application of 'policy'.

Notwithstanding the preceding remarks, the 'institutional' question which is likely to prove more difficult to resolve than those connected with foreign policy as such has to do with security issues in general and with the new European security 'architecture' in particular. Since the end of the Cold War, the security dominance of NATO may appear to have been relativized by a profusion of new or renascent institutions: WEU, CSCE, the North Atlantic Cooperation Council (NACC) and, of course, the United Nations itself. While all these bodies undoubtedly play a role, the most important institutional question is nevertheless that of the evolving relationship between NATO and WEU, in other words between the USA and the EU. In the immediate aftermath of 1989, a temporary jostling for position took place between these different actors which implied that confrontation rather than consensus and complementarity would be the order of the day. The 'Baker Doctrine' of December 1989[10] was perceived – at least in Paris and Brussels – as a bid for continuing American hegemony over the affairs of the old continent, and the precipitate military restructuring of NATO which followed hard on the heels of Baker's initiative paid little heed to the political imperatives of identifying wth some care and precision the security objectives of the new European order (M. Smith 1992; Heisbourg 1992; Williams et al. 1993).

While the ubiquitous German foreign minister Hans-Dietrich Genscher (1974–92) performed miracles of prestidigitation in promoting, at one and the same time, the restructuring of NATO, the creation of NACC, the upgrading of WEU and the launch of the Franco-German army corps, other European actors (particularly the French) were beginning to concentrate their hopes on a renascent Western European Union. Jacques Delors in particular, in a speech to the International Institute for Strategic Studies in March 1991, trail-blazed the notion of WEU as the principal (and increasingly autonomous) military instrument of the European Community/Union (Delors 1991), thereby implicitly leaving a relatively secondary role for NATO in the affairs of Europe. The stage seemed set for a bizarre trial of strength between, on the one hand, an aspirant and ambitious, but still very embryonic and problematic, European defence entity and, on the other hand, a somewhat ambivalent and politically transitional, but nevertheless operationally efficient and militarily unchallengeable Atlantic Alliance. World events (the Gulf War, the collapse of the Soviet Union, the Yugoslav crisis) together with the advent of a new and diplomatically untried administration in Washington put an end to what was, in reality, little more than a charade. By 1993 France was to all intents and purposes cooperating actively with the restructuring of NATO (indeed increasingly taking a lead role within the alliance), Washington was stating quite openly that the Atlantic Alliance welcomed the development of a more autonomous and self-reliant WEU, and the only remaining question was: how could all this be set into an appropriate balance?

The first point to stress is that NATO and WEU are very different institutions – in kind as well as in objective. While the Brussels Treaty of 1948 which eventually gave birth to WEU contained a collective security element intended to demonstrate the determination of the West European nations to prevent the recurrence of war, two even more significant facts about the treaty should be borne in mind. The first is that its strictly defensive (i.e., military) dimensions were in effect superseded the following year by the creation of NATO – and that situation remains largely unchanged today. The second point is that the Brussels Treaty was, in reality, the first clear expression of a determination to move towards West European integration. It is in this second context that the current revitalization of WEU should be understood. For the foreseeable future, WEU is in no position either politically or militarily to rival NATO as an organization capable of power projection, major peace-keeping or peace-enforcing operations or (still less) waging war.

The fundamental significance of current WEU reorganization is political. In the context of the birth of the European Union, with its attendant political and diplomatic ambitions, it is indispensable that real progress be made towards the creation of an integrated European security entity whose primary significance would be triple: first, a political statement that, in the new world order or disorder, purely *national* defence for Western European countries is an increasingly meaningless concept; second, an empirical demonstration, via such initiatives as the Eurocorps, that a unified military force, bringing together armies which had spent the last few centuries fighting *each other*, is not only conceivable but workable (however long it takes); and third, a determination to proceed towards a new balance in transatlantic relations by progressively bringing Europe's political capacity in line with her economic capacity and, in a second stage, by bringing her military capacity in line with her political will.

A turning-point in WEU revitalization came with the Petersberg Declaration of 19 June 1992 following a meeting in Bonn of the foreign and defence ministers of the WEU member states. While nevertheless detailing arrangements for strengthening the operational capacity of WEU,[11] the vast majority of the articles in that declaration stress the political intention of WEU to assist the European Union in emerging as a credible partner in a new transatlantic relationship for peace and security across the continent. In this sense, WEU is likely to develop in parallel with the EU as an emerging twin symbol of Europe's gradual diplomatic maturation. Eventually, and inevitably, WEU – if it is to have any meaningful existence at all – will have to be subordinated to the political control of the European Union.

Meanwhile, for the foreseeable future, effective military security will continue to be provided by NATO. But the institution will have to be radically restructured in order to face up to the multiple challenges it faces. The first challenge is renascent American isolationism, a bogeyman which surfaces with predictable regularity and which was given a recent fillip by presidential candidate Clinton's overwhelming preoccupation with domestic issues, added to a widespread perception in the USA that Washington could no longer aim to be all things to all men (Tonelson 1992, 1993; Bandow 1993; Layne and Schwarz 1993). However, the urgency of international affairs in every part of the globe, added to the successful negotiation of the NAFTA and the rise of the APEC process, suggest that the historical balance-sheet of the Clinton presidency (not to mention the prospects of a second term) will depend crucially on the White House adopting a new approach in the world arena. The consensus appears to be that Clinton will give a new priority to foreign policy, but that it will be recast as essentially economic foreign policy, with military security increasingly underpinned by collective security arrangements (Halverson 1993, 1994).

As far as the European 'theatre' is concerned, this, in turn, will depend very largely on the successful conclusion of a new US–European strategic bargain. The essence of that bargain will be balance. US supremacy in NATO during the Cold War was to a large extent inevitable both for political reasons (Europe lacked unicity and – therefore – power) and for strategic reasons (nuclear deterrence depended predominantly on there being a single finger on the trigger). These reasons no longer hold in the post-Wall world. If NATO is to be transformed 'from an alliance based on collective defence against a specific threat into an alliance committed to projecting democracy, stability and crisis management in a broader strategic sense' (Asmus et al. 1993), then it can only work in a balanced structure. From a US perspective, burden-sharing has become not only the economic price Europeans must pay for the continuation of the partnership itself, but also the political condition the White House will impose for staving off 'isolationism'. From a European perspective, the very future of the new Union depends on the emergence in Brussels of a mature and responsible executive capable of dealing on an increasingly equal footing with the transatlantic cousins. That will be the major challenge of a common foreign and security policy.

As far as the institutional structures of the new NATO are concerned, the climate of mutual trust and cooperation which alone can make the new transatlantic partnership work will eventually have to translate into a genuine multi-national command framework, the rotation of Supreme Allied Commander Europe (SACEUR), and the continued evolution of fully integrated European forces such as the Eurocorps. Two significant decisions were taken at the NATO summit in January 1994: first, President Clinton's commitment to keep 100,000 troops in Europe while simultaneously encouraging the EU to develop its own security identity (the first time an American administration had positively welcomed moves towards European 'autonomy'); second, the creation of 'combined joint task forces', effectively permitting the deployment of special units under either a NATO or a WEU mandate. These policy shifts can be interpreted either as the first move in the direction of genuine 'multi-nationality', or as the first signs of American disengagement from the security problems of Europe. Indeed, the two interpretations are not necessarily incompatible. Europe now has a green light to develop its own operational security system, and it seems probable that, during a transitional period, this will gradually assume many of the responsibilities formerly underwritten by the USA. This is all the more likely in that the US plan for cooperation with the CEE countries, unveiled at the NATO summit as 'Partnership for Peace',[12] implicitly poses the fundamental dilemma for the old Atlantic Alliance. Either NATO as a bloc extends its remit somewhat further east, fully embracing the Visegrad countries and clearly excluding the CIS, thereby creating precisely the new confrontational situation it desperately hopes to avoid, or the alliance declares 'open-house' membership with the entire world as its potential clients, in which case it ceases to have any real meaning at all. Partnership for Peace was more than a fudge but much less than a credible programme. It must be interpreted in the context of the transitional arrangements mentioned earlier, the eventual outcome being a radically new security framework across the continent of Europe, in which much of the former US (NATO) role would gradually be inherited by Brussels and the WEU. NATO, as it has traditionally existed, cannot survive into the long term. Precisely what it will be replaced by remains very unclear, although it will inevitably have a much greater European impetus.[13]

Much may now depend on the European Union's first serious experiment in CFSP: the preparations for a 'Pact on Stability and Security in Europe', launched at a conference of fifty-odd nations in Paris in the spring of 1994. The brain-child of French premier Edouard Balladur, the pact scheme became official EU policy at the Brussels Council meeting in December 1993. The idea is to organize a series of bilateral security 'conferences' bringing together different combinations of Central East European countries with potential security disputes, under the benign chairmanship of a senior EU official. An exercise in preventive diplomacy, the pact idea aims to reach political settlement between potential adversaries long before any shooting starts. Embracing in the first instance the nine countries which have been designated by the EU as having a 'European vocation' (the three Baltic states, the Visegrad four, plus Romania and Bulgaria), these conferences will nevertheless involve other neighbouring countries such as Belorussia and Ukraine. The scheme specifically excludes any areas (Balkans, Caucasus) where hostilities currently rage.

The challenge is enormous, the obstacles considerable, but the method, particularly in light of Norway's successful mediation of the Israeli–PLO dispute, is considered to be the most constructive currently available. The pact scheme does not involve the creation of a new institution as such, but is presented as a politico-diplomatic process which will lead (according to optimistic estimates, as early as 1995) to a formal treaty guaranteeing the stability of the Central and Eastern European states. That treaty will then be deposited with the Conference on Security and Cooperation in Europe (CSCE), which will be entrusted with the responsibility for its implementation.

Paradoxically, eventual success for the pact method may well call further into question the credibility of CSCE itself. The importance of this rather unwieldy institution, which now embraces some 57 nations across the northern hemisphere, has declined considerably as a result of the collapse of the Soviet centre, the intractable nature of the Yugoslav crisis (precisely the type of situation CSCE was intended to 'manage') and the rise to new prominence of the United Nations. Another institution which seems to have been superseded by events is the North Atlantic Cooperation Council (NACC), a German-American creation, designed to facilitate dialogue between the former adversaries of NATO and the WTO. While dialogue is important, NACC is too clearly perceived as a holding operation pending the creation of a genuine transcontinental security structure. How it will continue to operate as the Partnership for Peace scheme is brought on stream remains unclear.

What is clear is the vital importance of new international linking systems which avoid the construction of new 'fault-lines' such as the Iron Curtain. Such linking structures can perhaps best be imagined in terms of a series of interlocking circles of security and development, ideally under the overall political aegis of the United Nations. In other words, if NATO represents a circle encompassing Western Europe and North America, and if WEU was eventually to represent a circle encompassing, *de facto*, the entire continent of Europe as far as the borders of the former Soviet Union, other security circles need to be devised to cover, for instance: Central and Eastern Europe and the CIS (perhaps a restructured CSCE); Western Europe and the Maghreb (the Conference on Security and Cooperation in the Mediterranean – CSCM), with extension to the African continent; Europe as a whole and the Middle East, in association with the US and the CIS; the CIS and Asia, etc. The model is infinitely extensible, the 'interlocking principle' ensuring that no region feels excluded from the international or regional community and thereby fundamentally threatened. The creation of the most appropriate structures within this framework is the biggest single challenge faced by the newborn European Union. In order to assist in the task, it is necessary, however, for Europe to look beyond its own confines and to see itself as part of an international community which does not share its specific cultural approaches. For several centuries, world affairs have been dominated either by European nations or by European issues (or both). That is unlikely to remain true in the twenty-first century.

The Nature of International Relations in 2000

'You are children', said the Chinaman. 'I know your Europe. I saw and felt its insane disorder.'

Paul Valéry, 'Le Yalou' (1895)

Since the late 1980s, the international relations journals have been packed with articles offering fresh thoughts on the likely direction of world affairs in the post-Cold War era. Amidst the welter of issues and ideas thus generated, two deserve some further consideration within the context of this chapter: How many different regions or 'poles' are likely to emerge in the newly reshuffled global pack? and what will be the relative influence, within and between those poles, of different types of international actors and processes? These are vital questions if we are to begin to understand Europe's potential role in the world of the twenty-first century.

Joseph Nye has detected five distinct answers to the first question (Nye 1992). He dismissed out of hand the fears of those 'realist' commentators who foresaw an anti-reformist Soviet backlash and a new Russian superpower restoring the world to bipolarity. He warned against fashionable but oversimplisitc talk of multi-polarity by stressing the enormous disparities in types of power and influence which characterize the USA, Europe, Russia, China and Japan. Similarly, he drew attention to the restrictively economistic approach of those who saw little further than the emergence of a tripolar trading system. Aficionados of unipolar hegemony were equally taken to task for failing to see that American economic influence is on the wane and that military power is increasingly inappropriate for the solution of planetary problems. Nye's own preference therefore went to what he describes as multi-level interdependence, in which the top (military) level of the layer cake is effectively unipolar, the middle (economic) level tripolar and the bottom (transnational interdependence) level multi-polar. Lawrence Freedman, for his part, foresaw an essentially tripolar world with the three main poles of 'order' increasingly having to contend, on their immediate borders, with a more or less extensive area of 'disorder' (Freedman 1992). Samuel Huntington, on the other hand, saw the main fault-lines of the new world order as cultural/civilizational, with seven or eight contending parties, but the main clash being between 'the West and the rest' (Huntington 1993). The common feature of all these theses is that a world of nation-states is a phenomenon of the past. For all sorts of reasons connected with a multiplicity of interdependent networks of communications and exchanges, the world is getting smaller while its constituent units are getting bigger. Despite the recent upsurge of tribalism in various parts of Central and Eastern Europe, the adoption of a policy of unlimited self-determination would, argues Nye, 'turn into a principle of enormous world disorder'. Assuming that such a course can be avoided, it therefore seems inevitable, whichever scenario one favours, that the world of 2000 will be structured by a very small number of powerful units or poles, one of which, in every scenario, is Europe (however defined). This is where the second question becomes important.

For if global harmony is to be achieved, it will be incumbent upon these various poles to stabilize and assist in the development of their respective peripheral zones. One point on which virtually all commentators seem agreed is that traditional Hobbesian 'realism' (in which power is equated with military might and peace depends on appropriate balances), while not entirely disappearing, will no longer be sufficient to order the world. Additional forces and actors will progressively exercise influence, whether these be the political or economic actors of Grotian 'rationalism' or the civil forces which have inherited the mantle of Kantian 'universalism' (Booth and Wheeler 1992). Europe's contribution in this context can be rich but must be wise. For Europe, in the past half century, has blazed important trails in both fields. The emphasis on democracy and the respect for human rights which have under-pinned the increasingly important activities of the Council of Europe will have a significant input into international relations. So too will the essentially humanitarian and civilian objectives of non-governmental agencies and actors which have characterized European politics over the past two decades (Kaldor 1991). Such moral ideals and humanitarian aspirations inform the theoretical contributions of the international relations literature under review here. Lawrence Freedman calls for new attention to be paid to 'vital principles' (instead of 'vital interests'). Joseph Nye stresses the growing significance of liberal approaches to justice in international relations; Booth and Wheeler discuss the prospects for a developing global civil society.

The United Nations is gradually emerging as the forum within which such new instruments of international relations are being implemented. New emphases on human rights, the rights of minorities and, most significant of all, the 'right of intervention' (first implemented on behalf of the Kurdish peoples after the Gulf War) have changed the very framework of international relations, from one in which the sovereignty of nation states was sacrosanct towards one in which the lives of individual human beings are regarded as a legitimate concern of 'the international community'. But it is precisely here that great wisdom and a considerable degree of subtlety are required. For as

Huntington points out, it is too little appreciated in Europe that 'the values that are most important in the West are least important worldwide'. Governor Chris Patten may feel a mission to democratize Hong Kong before handing the colony back to China; President François Mitterrand may lecture Francophone African heads of state on the linkage between the granting of aid and the liberalization of state institutions; European editors and intellectuals may well point sanctimonious fingers at Boris Yeltsin. But Europe must learn to accept the cultural limitations of its own 'model' of socio-political organization. It is only if it does so in a non-proselytizing spirit of genuine respect for diversity that the grander principles of international relations we have just been outlining will stand any chance of becoming international norms. And it is important for all of us that they do.

Notes

1   On the background to this report, sometimes also referred to as the 'Luxembourg Report', see Nuttall 1992, 51–5, and Lodge 1989, 228. The institutional arrangements involved semestrial meetings of the Council of Foreign Ministers and trimestrial meetings of the foreign ministries' political directors. The aim was to increase the flow of information, to coordinate views and positions and to attempt to arrive at common actions.

2   Probably the high point of this phase of EPC came when, in June 1980, the Europeans signed the Venice Declaration, which recognized, for the first time, the right of the Palestinians to self-determination and also the role the PLO could play in that process. Although this declaration was criticized by Middle East experts as lacking any political follow-up, it did constitute and breakthrough in terms of European autonomy from Washington.

3   In December 1979 NATO decided to deploy Pershing 2 and Cruise missiles in Europe in December 1983 if, prior to that date, agreement on arms control had not been reached with the USSR; in 1983 Ronald Reagan launched the 'Strategic Defense Initiative' (SDI), which aimed to protect the United States with a defensive, space-deployed shield; in December 1987 Reagan and Gorbachev signed a treaty eliminating land-based INF nuclear missiles globally. For an attempt to situate these developments in the context of an emerging European consciousness, see Jolyon Howorth, 'The Third Way', *Foreign Policy* 62 (Winter 1986–7), 114–34; repr. in Charles William Maynes (ed.), *A Decade of Foreign Policy* (Washington: Carnegie Endowment for International Peace, 1990), 26–47.

4   In an extremely unfortunate June 1991 interview with *Radio France Internationale* the day before flying to Prague to inaugurate his *Confédération*, Mitterrand said that the CEE countries could not hope to join the EC for decades.

5   Oral testimonies to the conference *Europe: Enlarged or Divided?*, Certosa di Pontignano, October 1993, by a variety of representatives of the Central and Eastern European countries.

6 Commission of the European Communities, Internal Document on *External Relations*, 20 November 1992. The proposals contained in this document were finally accepted by the extraordinary European Council meeting in Brussels on 29 October 1993. The five priority CFSP areas, all of which have a major security dimension and all of which have been the subject of growing concertation – if not actual consensus – among the member states are: 1) peace and stability in Europe; 2) the Middle East peace process; 3) transition to multi-racial democracy in South Africa; 4) a peace plan for the former Yugoslavia; 5) support for democratic reform in Russia. *Quai d'Orsay Bulletin d'Information* 200/93, p. 3. See also Charles Goldsmith, 'EC ministers list five areas of foreign policy emphasis', *Wall Street Journal Europe*, 27 October 1993.

7 NATO issued an ultimatum to the Serbs on 11 February 1994, warning of air strikes if the guns were not removed. Most commentators, while noting that 'the West' had little alternative to this policy, given repeated Serb defiance of UN resolutions, also noted that the last thing any government wanted was an escalation of the war. Relief was widespread when Moscow intervened in what seemed at the time to be a face-saving compromise for all involved.

8 For the proposal itself, see *La politique étrangère de la France*, September–October 1991, pp. 57–63. The French president and the German chancellor attended the Council in the wake of Mitterrand's state visit to Germany, where it is clear that German support for the French proposal had been extracted in exchange for French acquiescence in the integrated military structures of the proposed Eurocorps. However, neither Genscher nor Kohl had any doubts that intervention would be vetoed by John Major.

9 Article J.3.(2) states, in its second paragraph, that voting 'shall be weighted in accordance with article 148(2) of the Treaty [of Rome], and for their adoption, acts of the Council shall require at least fifty-four votes in favour, cast by at least eight members.' In the EU of 12 member states, there were a total of 76 votes available, Germany, France, the UK and Italy having ten each, Spain eight, Belgium, Holland, Greece and Portugal five each, Denmark and Ireland three and Luxemburg two. The 'blocking minority' of 30 per cent was therefore 23 votes. In discussions about the accession of new members, it was proposed that Austria and Sweden should have four each and Finland and Norway three each, thus bringing the total to 90. After vigorous and sustained opposition from the UK, it was agreed that the blocking minority should be raised from 23 to 27 in order to retain the 70 per cent–30 per cent split.

10 In what was widely considered in Europe to be a 'pre-emptive' speech, in Berlin on 12 December 1989, then Secretary of State James Baker proposed the creation of a security structure spanning the Northern hemisphere 'from Vancouver to Vladivostock', which would be implicitly underwritten by a new *Pax Americana*.

11 The Petersberg Declaration is reproduced in full in *Letter from the Assembly* (Information Letter of WEU), No. 12, July 1992, pp. 12–15. Under Section II of the Declaration, ten separate articles deal with the creation of special military units drawn from the WEU member states to be used for humanitarian and rescue missions, peace-keeping missions, and even combat ('peace-making') missions, all

of them in coordination with NATO. These activities, structured as 'Combined Joint Task Forces', are henceforth to be organized and commanded from a central WEU planning cell whose first director was Major-General Caltabiano (Italian Air Force).

12   Devised mainly in response to the pressing demands for NATO membership on the part of the Visegrad countries, *Partnership for Peace* offers such countries joint military exercises with NATO forces, recourse to article 4 of the Washington treaty, which refers to 'consultations' in the event that a member country should perceive a security threat from a neighbour, and the prospect of eventual full membership of NATO at an unspecified point in the future.

13   The recent literature on the creation of foreign and security policy mechanisms is already vast. The following are some of the most important works (excluding those already cited): A. M. Sbragia (ed.), *Euro-Politics: institutions and policymaking in the 'new' European Community* (Washington: Brookings, 1992); A. Clesse and R. Vernon (eds), *The European Community after 1992: a new role in world politics?* (Baden Baden: Nomos, 1991); M. Telò (ed.), *Towards a New Europe?* (Brussels: University of Brussels, 1992), esp. pt II, ch. 1: J. Lodge, 'The European Community Foreign and Security Policy after Maastricht: new problems and dynamics'; W. Weidenfeld and J. Jannings (eds), *Global Responsibilities: Europe in tomorrow's world* (Gütersloh: Bertelsmann, 1991); R. Rummel (ed.), *Toward Political Union: planning a common foreign and security policy in the European Community* (Baden Baden: Nomos, 1992); G. Edwards and E. Regelsberger, *Europe's Global Links* (London: Pinter, 1990); D. Buchan, *Europe: l'étrange superpuissance* (Rennes: Apogee, 1993); Y. Boyer (ed.), *Les Européens face aux défis d'une politique de sécurité commune* (Paris: CREST, 1992); P. Chaigneau, *Europe: la nouvelle donne stratégique* (Paris: Berger-Levrault, 1993); D. David, *Conflits, puissances et stratégies en Europe: le dégel d'un continent* (Brussels: Bruylant, 1992). Finally, see the series of *Chaillot Papers* on European Security produced by the Institute for Security Studies of the Western European Union (18 papers published by November 1994).

Bibliography

Allen, D. (1978). 'Foreign policy at the European level: beyond the nation-state?', in W. Wallace and W. Paterson (eds), *Foreign Policy-Making in Western Europe*. Farnborough: Saxon House.

Allison, R. (1993). *Military Forces in the Soviet Successor States*. London: IISS/Brasseys, Adelphi Paper 280.

Asmus, R. D. et al. (1993). 'Building a new NATO'. *Foreign Affairs* 72 (4).

Bandow, D. (1993). 'Avoiding war', *Foreign Policy* 89: 156–74.

Bloës, R. (1970). *Le 'Plan Fouchet' et le problème de l'Europe politique*. Bruges: Collège d'Europe.

Bluth, C. (1993). *The Future of European Security*. Colchester: University of Essex.

Booth, K. and Wheeler, N. (1992). 'Contending philosophies about security in Europe', in C. McInnes (ed.), *Security and Strategy in the New Europe*. London: Routledge.

Bozo, F. (1992). 'A French view', in R. Davy (ed.), *European Detente: a reappraisal.* London: Sage/RIIA, 54–79.

Brenner, M. J. (1993). 'EC: confidence lost'. *Foreign Policy* 91: 24–43.

Carton, A. (1991). *Les neutres, la neutralité et l'Europe.* Paris: FEDN.

Chalmers, M. (1992). *Biting the Bullet: European defence options for Britain.* London: IPPR.

Coker, C. (1992). 'Britain and the new world order: the special relationship in the 1990s'. *International Affairs* 68 (3): 407–21.

De la Gorce, P.-M. (1992). 'Vers quelle politique étrangère commune?'. *Le Monde Diplomatique* June.

Delors, J. (1991). 'European integration and security'. *Survival* 33 (2): 99–109.

Drummond, S. (1993). 'Germany: moving towards a new *Ostpolitik?*'. *The World Today* July: 132–5.

Freedman, L. (1992). 'Order and disorder in the new world'. *Foreign Affairs* 71 (1): 20–37.

—— (ed.) (1994). *Military Intervention in Europe.* London: Political Quarterly (Fifth Issue).

Friend, J. W. (1991). *The Linchpin: French–German relations, 1950–1990.* New York: Praeger.

Fursdon, E. (1980). *The European Defence Community: a history.* London: Macmillan.

Garton Ash, T. (1993). *In Europe's Name: Germany and the divided continent.* London: Jonathan Cape.

George, S. (1991). *Politics and Policy in the European Community.* Oxford: Oxford University Press.

Halverson, T. (1993). 'The Clinton administration: foreign and defence policies'. *Brassey's Defence Yearbook*: 380–96.

—— (1994). 'Disengagement by stealth: the emerging gap between America's rhetoric and the reality of future European conflicts'. *Political Quarterly* 5: 76–93.

Heisbourg, F. (1992). 'The European–US alliance: valedictory reflections on continental drift in the post-Cold War era'. *International Affairs* 68 (4): 665–78.

Holoboff, E. M. (1994). 'Russian views on military intervention: benevolent peacekeeping, Slavic Monroe Doctrine or neo-imperialism?'. *Political Quarterly* 5: 154–74.

Howorth, J. (1992). 'France and the defence of Europe: redefining continental security', in M. Maclean and J. Howorth (eds), *Europeans on Europe: transnational visions of a new continent.* London: Macmillan, 77–97.

—— (1994). 'The debate in France on military intervention in Europe'. *Political Quarterly* 5: 106–25.

Huntington, S. P. (1993). 'The clash of civilizations?'. *Foreign Affairs* 72 (3): 22–49. See also the responses to the Huntington article, *Ibid.* 72 (4): 2–27 and Huntington's reply to his critics, *Ibid.* 72 (5): 186ff.

Jouve, E. (1967). *Le Général de Gaulle et la construction de l'Europe (1940–1966).* Paris: LGDJ.

Kaiser, K. (1991). *Deutschlands Vereinigung: die internationalen Aspekte.* Bergisch-Gladbach: Bastei-Lübbe.

Kaldor, M. (1991). *Europe from Below.* London: Verso.

Kielinger, T. and Otte, M. (1993). 'Germany: the pressured power'. *Foreign Policy* 91: 62.

Larrabee, F. S. (ed.) (1989). *The Two German States and European Security*. London: Macmillan.

Layne, C. and Schwarz, B. (1993). 'American hegemony: without an enemy'. *Foreign Policy* 92: 5–23.

Le Gloannec, A.-M. (1993). *L'Allemagne après la Guerre Froide: le vainqueur entravé*. Brussels: Complexe.

Lellouche, P. (1993). 'France in search of security'. *Foreign Affairs* 72 (2).

Livingston, R. G. (1992). 'United Germany: bigger and better'. *Foreign Policy* 87: 157–74.

Lodge, J. (1989). 'European political cooperation: towards the 1990s', in J. Lodge (ed.), *The European Community and the Challenge of the Future*. London: Pinter.

Mathews, J. T. (1989). 'Redefining security'. *Foreign Affairs* 68 (2): 162–77.

Michalski, A. and Wallace, H. (1992). *The European Community: the challenge of enlargement*. London: RIIA.

Morrison, J. (1993). 'Pereyaslav and after: the Russian–Ukrainian relationship'. *International Affairs*: 69 (4).

Nye, J. S., Jr. (1992). 'What new world order?'. *Foreign Affairs* 71 (2): 84–96.

Nuttall, S. (1992). *European Political Cooperation*. Oxford: Clarendon Press.

Owen, R. and Dynes, M. (1992). *The Times Guide to the Single European Market*. London: Harper Collins.

Pinder, J. (1991). *The European Community and Eastern Europe*. London: RIIA/Pinter.

Pisani, E. (1992). 'Being and doing in concert', in M. Maclean and J. Howorth (eds), *Europeans on Europe: transnational visions of a new continent*. London: Macmillan.

Pond, E. (1992). 'Germany in the new Europe'. *Foreign Affairs* 71 (2): 114–30.

Sabin, P. A. G. (1993). 'British defence choices beyond "Options for Change"', *International Affairs* 69 (2): 267–87.

Schlör, T. (1993). *German Security Policy: an examination of the trends in German security policy in a new European and global context*. London: Brassey's IISS, Adelphi Paper 277.

Smith, A. D. (1992). 'National identity and the idea of European unity'. *International Affairs* 68 (1).

Smith, G. (1992). 'Britain in the New Europe'. *Foreign Affairs* 71 (4): 155–70.

Smith, M. (1992). 'The devil you know: the United States and a changing European Community'. *International Affairs* 68 (1): 103–20.

Soutou, G.-H. (1992). 'Le Général de Gaulle et le Plan Fouchet', Institut Charles de Gaulle (ed.), *De Gaulle en son siècle*, Vol. 5: *L'Europe*. Paris: Plon.

Taylor, P. (1979). *When Europe Speaks with One Voice: the external relations of the European Community*. London: Aldwych.

Thatcher, M. (1993). *The Downing Street Years*. London: Harper Collins.

Tiersky, R. (1992). 'France in the new Europe'. *Foreign Affairs* 71 (2): 131–46.

Tonelson, A. (1992). 'America 1st – past and present'. *Society* 29 (6).

—— (1993). 'Superpower without a sword'. *Foreign Affairs* 72 (3): 166–80.

Towle, P. (1994). 'The British debate about intervention in European conflicts'. *Political Quarterly* 5.

Treverton, G. (1992). 'The New Europe'. *Foreign Affairs* 71 (1): 100.

Tsoukalis, L. (1993). *The New European Economy: the politics and economics of integration*, 2nd edn. Oxford: Oxford University Press.

Valance, G. (1990). *France–Allemagne: le retour de Bismarck*. Paris: Flammarion.

Vernet, D. (1992). 'The dilemma of French foreign policy'. *International Affairs* 68 (4): 655–63.

Wallace, W. (1992). 'British foreign policy after the Cold War'. *International Affairs*, 68 (3): 423–42.

Western European Union (1988). *The Reactivation of WEU: statements and communiques, 1984 to 1987*. London: WEU.

Wessels, W. (1992). 'EC–Europe: an actor *sui generis* in the international system', in B. Nelson et al. (eds), *The European Community in the 1990s: economics, politics, defence*. Oxford, Berg.

Williams, P. et al. (1993). 'Atlantis lost, paradise regained? The United States and Western Europe after the Cold War'. *International Affairs* 69 (1): 1–17.

Yost, D. S. (1991). 'France in the new Europe'. *Foreign Affairs* 69 (5).

12

International Industrial Champions

Jack Hayward

Promotion of national champion firms has been a perennial state preoccupation. The first modern public economic policy, mercantilism, was developed to enable states to acquire the financial resources to wage war more effectively. Beggaring one's neighbouring enemies by prohibiting imports and subsidizing exports was supplemented with the state sponsorship of trading monopolies whose purpose was more than securing a favourable balance of trade. It was to increase state power. Pioneered by the English state in the late fourteenth and early fifteenth centuries, it has become more fully identified as a doctrine with the policies pursued by Colbert in seventeenth-century France. When Adam Smith launched his attack upon mercantilism in favour of the market economy, he singled out Colbert's combination of prohibitions and privileges as 'in its nature and essence a system of restraint and regulation' from which producers and consumers should be freed (Smith [1776] 1976, II, 663; Weber 1961, 255–7). While this attack heralded a shift from a hands-on to a hands-off state relationship to trade and industry in Britain, it was much less influential on the continent, so that the revival of new-style mercantilist policies in the twentieth century was able to draw upon a deep-seated tradition of state intervention.

Nevertheless, such state-centred policies have proved increasingly ineffective because the 'boundaries between national systems are being eroded, and a process of "assimilative repetition" of American deregulatory experience seems underway, pioneered by Britain' (Dyson 1986, 25). How exposed to foreign competition has this left European firms? A hitherto industrially dominant Europe has been faced in the second half of the twentieth century by inroads first from America in the name of free trade and then from a Japan that had built up its capacity by recourse to neo-mercantilist policies. Within this context of a triad of industrial competitors, how have the

European states and the EC responded to what were recognized as external threats?

Promoting Industrial Firms to Champion Status

It was a French journalist, with an exceptional gift for quickly appreciating the developments in train and for expressing his views in clear and arresting language, who put the industrial 'assault on Europe' firmly on the 1960s political agenda. In *The American Challenge*, Jean-Jacques Servan-Schreiber used forceful phrases about the American '*seizure of power* within the European economy' and the 'capture' of the high growth, technologically advanced industries to dramatize the predicament faced by European firms (Servan-Schreiber 1969, 22–3). However, he rejected the policy of Europrotectionism (what the French prefer to call 'community preference') against industrial annexation or satellization by American multi-national corporations. Instead he recommended that European firms – 'a few global corporations and a great number of tradition-bound small businesses' – become competitive on the world market. Because they could not do so without financial assistance, this should be provided by governments 'particularly in such areas as electronics, data processing, space research and atomic energy' (Servan-Schreiber 1969, 53, 93). Nevertheless, Servan-Schreiber had the prescience to leapfrog the 'national champion' response to the problem he highlighted, moving directly to the need for a Eurochampion strategy.

While acknowledging that 'France is the country that has shown the most determination not to become a satellite . . . her frame of reference has been entirely national . . . French firms offer only a feeble assistance to the threat of American capital', Servan-Schreiber concluded that Gaullist France provided both 'a good example of the problem and of the limits of a purely national effort at economic independence' (Servan-Schreiber 1969, 117, 121). Because both national self-sufficiency and national economic planning (and not just prognostication) were no longer viable options, the only way of preventing a takeover of the European Common Market by American firms would be to develop a common European industrial policy based upon promoting up to a hundred European firms capable of competing with the American multi-nationals and becoming leading global firms (Servan-Schreiber 1969, 125–9). Such was the diagnosis and the remedy prescribed by Servan-Schreiber in 1967, which was too imaginative at that time. By the early 1980s, when it was being actively pursued by some governments, the Eurochampion strategy was already being displaced by the acceptance by firms of international market forces and the search for extra-European alliances.

The mid-1960s was a period when the restructuring of industry by government or its agencies was fashionable. In Britain, this took the form of the Industrial Reorganization Corporation, created by the Labour Government in 1966 at a time when national economic planning enjoyed a brief popularity. In France, where it had been successfully pursued for twenty years, the Fifth Plan, covering 1966–70, anticipated the Servan-Schreiber analysis but confined itself to a national solution. It fixed as the main objective for French industry the 'reinforcement of its European and world competitive position' by creating or consolidating one or two firms or groups of international dimensions capable of sustaining foreign competition (Commissariat Général du Plan 1965, 68, cf. 69). Despite the fact that it might have been expected that the heroic language of 'national champions' would have been used in the Gaullist 1960s to express the French response to the American challenge, the assertive strategy of industrial counter-attack had not yet acquired its defensively bellicose designation.

It was from the United States that the phenomenon advocated in the French Fifth Plan earned its appellation. In their percipient 1969 study of French industrial planning, McArthur and Scott seem to be consciously coining a neologism when they refer to 'the creation of a French "champion" in each industry . . . Such a champion would represent the nation in international competition, and would probably assume the aura of a public servant, a company operating in the interests of the nation as well as its owners and managers' (McArthur and Scott 1969, 525). They went on to argue: 'If the French desire to create industrial champions can be understood as a largely defensive response to the threat of American economic domination, and if an international escalation of mergers is to be predicted as a likely consequence, one may question whether the creation of champions is really the best defensive prescription for France to follow at this time.' They admit that the French may have little choice, as their mainly US competitors 'appear as "national champions" already', although there were 'many champions' in such industries as cars, chemicals, oil and electronics (McArthur and Scott 1969, 526). However, they expressed the fear that French policy might provoke other states to create industrial champions of their own on the model of ELF-ERAP, the 'French oil champion determined to muscle its way into world markets with the backing of the State', encouraging increased industrial concentration and state regulation (McArthur and Scott 1969, 525). The stage is set for the battle between Anglo-American and continental European views of industrial strategy.

In 1974, McArthur and Scott's Harvard Business School colleague Raymond Vernon followed up a pioneering study of US multi-national corporations by editing a study of the relations between big firms and governments in Europe. He noted 'a growing tendency to use large national enterprises in an effort to solve specific problems, as if they were agencies of the state' (Vernon 1974, 3; cf. Vernon 1971). While such a public policy in small countries often amounted to influencing a single firm, even in large countries, as a result of the tendency to equate size with being technologically advanced and efficient, the number of such firms could be reduced to one or two. So, 'the idea of developing a national champion – an enterprise responsive to its national government's needs and entitled to its national government's support – began to take root' (Vernon 1974, 11; cf. 6). Where France led others followed, tending to use the same policy instruments. 'Providing capital on favoured terms was one typical device; discriminating in government procurement policies was a second; subsidizing research programmes a third. Whatever the method, it implicitly or explicitly embodied one important factor: the exercise of public power to discriminate in favour of chosen national champions' (Vernon 1974, 12). However, while these firms were, in the Servan-Schreiber manner, meant to carry the industrial flag into the dynamic fields of advanced technology, short-term, political expediency in practice distorted this principle into supporting declining traditional industries, such as coal and shipbuilding.

As well as anticipating a propensity to support lame ducks, Vernon spotted reasons for the reluctance to develop Eurochampions as advocated by Servan-Schreiber. 'As long as the buyers were largely from the public sector, the markets were cut up in watertight national units.' Even when this was not the case, firms were 'quite unwilling to merge their identity with European enterprises of another nationality', preferring alliances with a stronger American partner of a more piecemeal and improvised kind (Vernon 1974, 18; cf. 19–20). As early as 1974, Vernon predicted that

> the time may well have passed when policies can any longer be made effectively at the European level without taking into account Europe's deep interdependencies with other parts of the world . . . Anything less than a global approach to industrial policy can generate consequences that may defeat the purpose of the policy . . . Europe's pace and style in creating a European technology policy have been so slow and so inhibited that few European enterprises are likely to count upon such a policy for strong sustenance and support. Besides, the nature of modern technology often demands networks larger than Europe can provide: a network for the assembly of relevant information on design and production; and a network of market outlets sufficiently large to absorb the development costs of the product. (Vernon 1974, 23–4)

What was already apparent to an acute observer in the early 1970s – the increasing impracticality of both the national and Eurochampion strategies in an ever more globalized market – became much more evident by the 1980s.

Five factors played an important part in this process. First, the accelerating decline of traditional industries and, more recently, of defence-related industries in the context of the end of the Cold War meant that industrial patriotism exerted a declining hold on the business, bureaucratic and political decision-makers. The notion that every state should have independent control over its national 'industrial base' seemed less compelling as commercial considerations became of predominant importance. Manufacturing goods employed ever fewer people, following more slowly in the wake of the decline of the farm population in the advanced economies.

Second, the increasingly rapid pace of technological innovation undermined not only national monopolies; the new information and communications technologies have promoted network relationships between economic actors. Corporate networks have, in this context, been described as 'the institutional *form* which actors tend to use in order to maximise the profit they may derive from the new technologies or the opening of new markets' (Bressand and Nicolaidis 1990, 367). The intense international interaction, speeded up by telecommunications networks, transcends national boundaries in ways that make global strategies the norm in the matter of economic transactions. 'The importance for European companies of access to Japanese technology and to the US market – as exporters, or increasingly as investors and acquirers – implies, for instance, that Europe is not an intermediate level, half way between the nation-state and the open global environment . . . but rather one dimension in the search for stronger positioning on the global market' (Bressand and Nicolaidis 1990, 30). Because corporate networks necessitate new management methods, they are a concomitant of the diversified global firm.

Third, the increasingly elusive nature of the territorially and industrially diversified firm, often a conglomerate which has delocalized a substantial part of its production, adds a further complexity to the globalization process. Such firms are constantly changing, as they establish or acquire subsidiaries, engage in or are the victims of takeovers, establish joint ventures, make share swaps and participate in research consortia. The increasing number and size of multinational corporations, the increasing percentage of shares owned by foreign institutions and individuals, the massive expansion of cross-national investment, increasing more quickly than international trade, have combined to accentuate the complexity of corporate networks. 'Within Europe, the national champions of yesteryear – Thomson, Olivetti, Siemens, CGE or even GEC – are transforming themselves by a process of collaboration and merger into global players, with research, production and marketing capabilities on a worldwide basis' (Sharp 1990, 64).

Fourth, when not sufficiently profitable to meet their investment needs by self-financing, firms have been increasingly forced to have recourse to international capital markets because national governments and banks have been unable or unwilling to provide loans or subsidies. Far from being willing to use tax revenue to provide such support for industry, governments have adopted privatization as a way of avoiding increased public indebtedness and even financing tax cuts. More generally, there has been a pervasive sense that state interventionism, popular in the early postwar years, has failed to achieve continuous rapid growth and full employment, as well as being incapable of 'picking winners' and all too inclined to prop up losers. This view, which was not even general among businessmen, has become prevalent among senior civil servants, politicians and even many trade unionists, helping to generate support for disengagement and deregulation throughout Europe. The ignominious collapse of the state-run economies of Eastern Europe has compounded the ideological, managerial and financial motivations for the precipitate retreat from state intervention. The notion that there is a public interest, other than the sum of the interactions between private interests, has been discredited. Rather, the presumption is that whatever is good for wealth-creating firms is good for the spending nation.

Fifth, the European Community – notably through the establishment of a single market, but also in its impact upon those countries that seek to join it and those who negotiate trade agreements with it – has been a contextual influence upon the movement away from rivalry between national champions, without having been capable of achieving agreement on the promotion of Eurochampions, except in a patchy and piecemeal way. An effective European industrial policy has not emerged because the EC's complex networks and inter-governmental decision-making have not been able to fill the gap left by the retreat of national governments. The result has been that the EC is more effective at curbing national champions than in transcending them. It has eliminated tariff and quota restrictions on trade; it has interceded to prevent price fixing; it has vetted and discouraged state subsidies; it has made progress with the liberalization of public procurement. However, European industrial policy can be recognized not as an assertion of collective will but as a residuum: 'a direct harnessing by European firms of the EC institutional framework for their global ambitions . . . Companies have in fact simply broadened their portfolio of alliances to new European partners without giving up transatlantic or Pacific networking' (Bressand and Nicolaidis 1990, 38). The EC's capacity to mobilize its sense of community has not been commensurate with its creation of a common market, which is itself a tributary of the world market.

Before turning in succession to a comparison of the relationships of governments and firms by country and industry to ascertain the extent and ways in which predominantly public-sector monopoly national champions have increasingly become private-sector oligopoly international champions, let us conclude by adapting a typology suggested by Elie Cohen's distinction between three kinds of national champion. First, there are the strong firms in relation to which the government plays the marginal role appropriate to a *subsidiary, auxiliary, spectator state*. The government is reduced to being a commercial traveller, lobbyist or briber, with all the deleterious side-effects this produces. Second, there are the lame-duck firms. The government's role takes two forms. It can either ease their decline before burying them, what may be described as the *undertaker state*; or it may invite a foreign firm to take them over, as was done for automobiles in Britain by Mrs Thatcher in the instance of Nissan. In the latter case, we may wish to refer to a *regenerator state*, replacing the discredited nationalization of lame ducks, characteristic of the early postwar period but surviving in France into the early 1980s. Third, there are the 'big project' firms promoted by government in sectors designated as vital for national independence or to face international competition, particularly in 'high technology' sectors. France has distinguished itself, in particular, in this role of *entrepreneur state*, with France Télécom being an exemplar (Cohen 1985). After considering how these types of state action fit European states, we shall consider how the strategies of nationalization and privatization have been used to implement or change these ways of conceiving government–champion firm relations.

National Styles of Government–Champion Firm Relations

While it would be confusing to present in their complexity all the actors in the relationships between the relevant segments of the government and the firms selected for champion status, at the cost of neglecting looser network links it might be helpful to present a model of the three main clusters of actors involved. While this 'iron triangle' assumes different forms in particular countries and operates differently in specific industrial sectors, it helps us to identify the governmental, industrial and financial insiders whose interaction is the centrepiece of our concern (see figure 12.1).

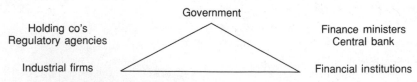

Figure 12.1   *The government–firm–finance nexus*

At the national level each cluster is highly complex, though in the case of any particular sector matters are usually much simpler. Further complexity arises from the fact that it is necessary to consider the European Community and international levels, in which additional actors are involved. However, the 'iron triangle' directs our need, in the case of each country and each sector, to identify the specific political and administrative executives, the managers of specific firms and financial institutions, who play an active part in the processes by which the measure of competitiveness and independence which both interacting states and firms can sustain are decided.

For the purpose of contrasting the emphasis which different countries place upon particular clusters of actors, we may stress the leading role given to government in the French case. The financial institutions and industrial firms were usually prepared to take their lead from the government, partly because many of them were in public ownership. Even more important were practices and norms that long predated nationalization, so that the national champion firms have been particularly identified with the interventionist state. They were accustomed to accept state guidance in terms of their objectives rather than follow market signals, and they inclined to look to public sources for finance. Even before changes since the 1980s which have shifted the initiative away from the government towards industrial firms and financial institutions, there was a wide spectrum of relationships, ranging from the government taking direct entrepreneurial action to achieve its objectives to attempts to regenerate or nurse declining or bankrupt firms back to health. Increasingly, 'national solutions' have proved impractical, so the French government has played its part in negotiating alliances with foreign firms to create international champions that preserve national interests as far as it is possible to do so. However, one must be careful to distinguish between the pretentious rhetoric of national assertion, the modest resources deployed to implement it and the limited results actually attained.

Those who have observed French industrial policy most closely and critically have pointed out that, where it succeeded in creating national champions, the main reason is that they were operating in the absence of a competitive international market. In the 1970s this applied to the electro-nuclear, space satellite and telephone successes. It was true to a lesser extent of the aircraft and petroleum industries, where in each case two national champions – Dassault and Airbus, Total and ELF – enjoyed substantial protection from foreign competition. Alongside this negative factor – the non-existence of a competitive market – there was the positive factor of a public agency, often based on a corps of engineers, which provided the non-bureaucratic administrative impetus and political support for ambitious schemes. Where these factors did not obtain – such as in machine tools or computers – successive industrial plans failed to achieve the intended results, leading to their sale to non-European competitors. The DGT or Telecommunications Division's transformation into France Télécom demonstrated the capacity of a 'missionary' state administration to become an effective public industrial enterprise and successful national champion, whereas 'today a Bull computer consists of imported components' (Cohen 1992, 390; cf. Cohen and Bauer 1985, 222–3, and chs 2 and 8).

France Télécom attempted a three-step Japanese style strategy: reconquering its domestic market; an export drive based on 'offensive protectionism'; then finally, after successfully conquering the international market, productive delocalization to reduce costs. This techno–industrial patriotism made the national champion public enterprise the chosen instrument of a state-sponsored 'big project'. Despite its early successes, notably in modernizing the French telephone system, it fell victim to the fact that 'the logic of the industrial group and of the nation state are becoming disassociated. The group works in the world market', so that the national champion strategy is bypassed (Cohen 1992, 393; cf. 120–2). The priority hitherto accorded to the national producer is replaced by that conceded to the international consumer. Under the impact of intense fragmentation of international labour, firms increasingly become 'hollow corporations', financially integrated 'pyramids of contracts between all kinds of sub-contractors' in which the firm's 'national industrial identity' becomes blurred (Cohen 1992, 391 and note).

The 'creeping liberalism' of the late 1970s became the galloping liberalism of the late 1980s. It was no longer possible for national champions to fulfil their previous functions. They could not legitimize public power, which presupposed that they at least gave the impression that the state could master the market. As a French scholar has pointed out, such pretence to industrial sovereignty involved

> a form of economic nationalism in which industrial and national interests were confused. Nowhere more than in France has the precept been exemplified that 'what is good for General Motors is good for the United States'. The loss of a market for Airbus or the Mirage 2000, the purchase of an American company by one of our national champions or the market penetration of a foreign brand is treated as a national victory or defeat. The identification of the interests of the nation and national firms is such that it precludes all thought about the dynamics of the world economy and induces a short term economic diplomacy. (Cohen 1992, 388–9; cf. Berger 1981, ch. 17, and Michalet 1974, 107, 120–5)

The socialist suspension of further nationalization in the late 1980s marked the temporary halt between the first privatization wave of 1986–7 and the second from 1993, reflecting the victory of the market over the mixed economy.

This reversal of past Gaullist and socialist policy was prompted by the fact that nationalization, far from protecting job security, had accelerated redundancy as attempts were made to rescue lame ducks and loss-making enterprises by the 'stretcher-bearer state'. It was small and medium firms that had most to offer in job creation. As for the failing national champions, Elie Cohen traces the phases through which firms move from getting into financial difficulties, which they do their best to hide, before deferring painful decisions and finally reaching bankruptcy, often absorbing substantial sums of public assistance on the way. Shipyards, steel and coal were bequeathed to the French state, without having any effective shareholders, management or future plans for survival, leaving it to the government to organize a retreat in relatively good order, at least as far as redundancies were concerned. He concludes that the government cannot retrieve lost industrial power but can play the role of merchant banks in other countries: to support entrepreneurs who have an industrial project, products, markets and risk-taking shareholders (Cohen 1989, 61, 241–2). In telecommunications, the Compagnie Générale d'Electricité (which became Alcatel-Alsthom in 1991) has been just such a success story and has formed an effective European champion alliance with GEC, winning notable success with high-speed train exports. As such, it has followed in the wake of Anglo-Dutch pioneers Shell and Unilever, preceding the abortive Franco-Swedish alliance of Renault-Volvo – neither of the latter having been able to achieve the national solutions of a French (Renault-Peugeot) or Swedish (Saab-Volvo) automobile national champion. The Volvo-Renault merger fiasco was prepared by share swaps and a joint research agreement but collapsed in December 1993 because most of the threatened Swedish management led a patriotic revolt by the shareholders. While Saab was taken over by General Motors, Volvo asserted a Swedish version of the national champion rhetoric against its French protagonists.

As industrial patriotism drew its fundamental inspiration from the need to meet the imperatives of national security, the transition from the 'arsenal logic' of producing weapons for defence to selling arms to justify the escalating costs of high technology research and development shifted the focus remorselessly from nation-state to international market. Initially, the solution chosen was concentration upon national champions.

> The French face these dilemmas: on the one hand, a credible national defense may be erected on an indigenous industrial base, but at an intolerable public cost and at the risk of destroying the international competitiveness of the French economy; on the other hand, the international competitiveness of French industry may be promoted but along lines of comparative advantage and specialisation within an evolving global division of labour that, if accepted by the French, risks sacrificing national independence, resulting in a loss of control over national defense, arms design and production, and one's home markets. [Avoidance of this awkward choice] – a policy of designated national champions – has been one of the principal means used by French planners to relax the dilemmas confronting the French economy. (Kolodziej 1987, 218)

This consensus allowed the military-industrial complex first to pursue a national champions policy in the 1960s and then, in the 1970s – as the chosen instrument of public authority – to shift increasingly in an international direction. The complex is a secretive policy community that consists of the armed services, industrial firms and the 'entrepreneur-engineer' non-warrior managers of the arms engineering corps, based upon the General Delegation for Armament within the Ministry of Defence (Kolodziej 1987, 213, 239–52, 275–83). Part of the price of this close military-bureaucratic-industrial community has been, in France and Britain, a distortion of national research and development expenditures in favour of defence. Since the end of the Cold War this defence policy community has lost much of its *raison d'être*.

An irony of the French aircraft industry has been that the national champion in civil aircraft was a public enterprise, Aérospatiale (which admittedly also produced missiles and helicopters), while the champion in fighter aircraft was the private enterprise Dassault. As long as its founder was alive, Dassault had a privileged place in the military-industrial complex. By the 1980s financial difficulties, owing to a decline in its exports, were making it less able to impose its priorities. There were two other lesser champions – the SNECMA aircraft engines public monopoly and MATRA, which shared the tactical missile market with Aérospatiale – but by the 1980s France's largest arms exporter was the French electronics champion Thomson-CSF (Kolodziej 1987, 219–31). As we shall see later, in discussing the emergence of Airbus, while France has accepted the need to cooperate in international consortia in civilian aircraft, it has clung on to an independent role for Dassault in the production of the Rafale fighter aircraft rather than joining in the European Fighter Aircraft project. Gaullist policy, most spectacularly exemplified by the production of an independent nuclear deterrent, thus survives into a world where such weapons (happily) increasingly find it difficult to win a market. However, outside this especially sensitive sector, the privatization, Europeanization and internationalization of leading French firms mark the decisive retreat of the national champion policy with which France was particularly identified. As a result, some French industrial firms have become less dependent upon government and more inclined, as in the Thomson exchange of shares with Crédit Lyonnais, to adopt the German style of associating closely with a bank.

The stern generosity with which federal Germany treated East Germany on reunification can be understood as the nationwide extension of the political economy of social consensus. There has been a price to pay. German reunification has threatened to swamp its Federal Republic predecessor's industrial practices by a weight of debt that frightens the banks and by the need for short-term subsidization that swelled the public sector borrowing requirement. These threats were doubly anathema to the Bundesbank. Nevertheless past social market economy practices are likely to continue. They involve reliance upon private sector champions, notably in the automobile, chemicals, electronics and machine tools industries such as Volkswagen, BASF, Siemens and Metallgessellschaft carrying the burden of international competition, while the publicly regulated sector – including loss-making enterprises such as Ruhrkohle and Lufthansa as well as profitable Deutsche Telekom – has been going through a slow process of deregulation.

Germany's postwar industrial policy has made a virtue of its invisibility, with government leaving it largely to the banks to restructure and refinance uncompetitive industries such as textiles and steel or to defend firms from foreign acquisition. It is this insulation from the pressures that, in countries such as France consistently and Britain episodically, led to the pursuit of an active state industrial policy, which has created problems in Germany. It could confine itself previously to assisting lame ducks in coal, shipbuilding and steel, despite EC criticism. However, the stupendous problems posed by the East German industries, with which it is trying to deal by privatization, are on such a scale that they have made this a slow and patchy process. We shall return to the effects of a switch from a closed to an open economy when we consider the effect of privatization in East-Central Europe.

Italy is an unusual case among national champions of combining a small number of family firms – Fiat for automobiles, Pirelli for rubber and tyres and Olivetti for computers – with state holding companies – the diversified conglomerate IRI and the ENI oil and chemicals combine. Despite recent attempts at internationalization, these Italian champions have been characterized by concentrating on becoming the national leader within the country at the cost of being isolated from the international market, as was pointed out by Romano Prodi (Prodi 1974, 54–5) before he was brought in to head IRI in the 1980s and again in the wake of the 1993 scandals. In the case of the two leading public enterprises, this has been compounded by their developmental function and their use for political purposes that had more to do with expediency than with industrial logic – although IRI's construction of an excellent motorway network was an infrastructural boost to Fiat.

To avoid bureaucratization of public enterprise and in the absence of financial support from private banks, holding companies assumed an even greater importance in Italy than the Austrian OIAG, the Spanish INI and INH, the Swedish Procordia or the Belgian Société Nationale d'Investissement. However, the scope for independent action that such holding companies offered was employed by public entrepreneurs such as ENI's first head in ways that left it unclear to what extent this national champion against the international oil companies was serving or using the Italian state. While Mattei had ensured before his death in 1962 that Italian industry has access to its own cheap energy, he left ENI in financial straits, and under his successors 'expansion at any cost became an end in itself, independent of content and motivation', such as its rescue of the Lanerossi textile group (Prodi 1974, 59; cf. Shonfield 1965, 184–5).

Preoccupation with avoiding dependence upon foreign firms ensured that when, in the course of an attempt by Prodi to reduce its debt burden, IRI decided in 1986 to sell off the Alfa Romeo luxury motor car firm, it deliberately did so to Fiat, rather than to Ford. When faced with a choice between strengthening a dominant domestic firm or a foreign competitor, Italy predictably chose its private national champion (Bianchi et al. 1988, 98). A much less successful attempt at a 'national solution' was that involving the 1989 sale of the Montedison chemicals group partly to ENI and partly to the Ferruzi food combine, ending in disaster for the overambitious Ferruzi family firm. The corrupt Italian politico-industrial structure collapsed in 1993 under the weight of a crushing burden of public debt and an EC-promoted international competition which made defensive protectionism decreasingly effective.

In Britain, faced by a secular problem of relative economic decline and then in the 1980s by a contraction of its industrial base, two attitudes have tended to alternate. For most of the postwar period, there has not been the resistance to foreign multi-nationals that we have noted in France and Italy. Partly because Britain has had a long history and a favourable balance of international investment and because the external 'threat' was American – perceived as less 'foreign' in Britain than in France – most government officials and politicians were not inclined to feel the need to take defensive action. There was little fear that the British government's decision-making would be constrained, while substantial benefits were assumed to accrue in terms of access to advanced technology and improvements to the balance of payments, industrial efficiency and regional development. Against this view, especially associated with Conservatives, there were periods – notably the Labour governments of Harold Wilson in the mid-1960s and 1970s – when 'picking winners' in the form of national champions through a Minister of Technology, the Industrial Reorganization Corporation (IRC) and the National Enterprise Board became the order of the day (Young and Lowe 1974; Young 1978; Grant 1982, ch. 5).

While the rhetoric about the 'commanding heights' had lost its association with nationalization, it was used to justify financial support, notably through research and development subsidies and public procurement decisions, to create internationally competitive large firms, able to protect employment and promote exports. The government-prompted merger of three British computer manufacturers into International Computers (ICL) and the creation of the British Leyland Motor Corporation (BLMC) were bold attempts to create national champions, both of which failed. Characteristically, *The Economist* enthusiastically predicted that BLMC might 'become a European General Motors' (Hodges 1974, 211; cf. chs 5 and 6).

Partly with a forlorn view to persuading de Gaulle that Britain would make a congenial EC partner, Harold Wilson asserted in 1967: 'There is no future for Europe, or for Britain, if we allow American business and American industry so to dominate the strategic growth industries of our individual countries, that they, and not we, are able to determine the pace and direction of Europe's industrial advance, that we are left in industrial terms as the hewers of wood and drawers of water' (Hodges 1974, 175). ICL first failed to win the support of Siemens in Germany, Philips in the Benelux, Olivetti in Italy or CII in France to create a Eurochampion. It then failed to preserve an independent British computer industry because 'the Labour Government had created the largest non-American manufacturer of central processing units but had not created a similar capability in software, peripherals or microcircuits' (Hodges 1974, 272; cf. 247–8, and Wilks 1983, 148–55). IBM reasserted its dominance in the 1970s, only to lose it to the Japanese competition in the 1980s. Anticipating the Thatcherism of the 1980s, John Davies, the first Director General of the Confederation of British Industry and then Conservative Minister of Trade and Industry, declared in 1970, in justification of the abolition of the IRC: 'if any of our overseas friends wanted to invest in a lucrative state enterprise in Britain, who am I to stop them?' (Hodges 1974, 292). Both the ministerial modesty and the 'friendship' help to explain why ICL was sold off in 1979.

British complacency had been encouraged by the past success in the international market of some of its large firms – including government-sponsored firms such as ICI and BP. This inclination to rest upon past laurels has been accentuated by the prestige of the City of London as a global money market. Appreciating the need to modernize the City with the 'Big Bang' reorganization and to render British industry more dynamic, the Thatcher governments of the 1980s sought to do so through a combination of privatization – which assisted firms such as British Airways to make the transition from national to international champion – and openness to foreign investment. In the latter case, Japanese firms have followed in the wake of earlier American control of the British motor industry, being invited to act as the chosen instruments of a regenerator state. At the same time the British government drastically reduced state aid to industry, and in the case of the coal industry has clearly moved from the role of an auxiliary, spectator state to that of undertaker. Having put the interests of consumers before those of producers, British Conservative governments have led the way in denationalizing the public sector and left firms to the mercies of the market, subject to some regulatory controls to protect consumers from what, in some cases, have simply converted public into private monopolies. We should note, however, that the Thatcher governments increased the share of defence expenditure, which doubled between 1974 and 1983 in manufacturing GDP from 6 to 12 per cent and in engineering GDP from 17 to 33 per cent (Ergas 1993, 7).

Shifting from a country where exposure to foreign competition has deliberately been pursued to those where, as small countries, it is a fact of economic life, the contrast between those that adopt a more passive attitude towards their dependence upon the international market, such as Switzerland, the Netherlands and Belgium and the more active Austria and Norway, is noteworthy. Netherlands industry has been traditionally dominated by a very small number of very large firms – Philips, Shell, Unilever – which put their global role before being specifically national champions, Dutch transnationals having three times as many employees outside than inside the Netherlands. When faced with the crisis of its watch industry, it was the Swiss banks rather than the Swiss government that played the major role in the rescue. By contrast, particularly in relation to North Sea Oil, 'the Norwegian government has explicitly chosen to develop national champions as a defence against Swedish – and US – based multinationals and as a way of enhancing the international competitiveness of Norwegian industry' (Katzenstein 1985, 115; cf. 70–1, 117, and Katzenstein 1984, 91, 155, 216–29). Austria, until it turned to privatization in the 1980s, had the largest public sector in non-communist Europe, so that it relied on its nationalized champions, under the umbrellas of the OIAG conglomerate and the Creditanstalt bank, to protect it from foreign competition. Their serious financial difficulties, resulting from the reluctance to adapt to economic changes in the 1970s, led to a loss of competitiveness and the general enthusiasm for privatization from the mid-1980s (W. Muller 1988, 103–6).

As far as a national champion strategy is concerned, there has been a marked contrast between Britain and France, where a major motivation of privatization was to achieve commercial autonomy – albeit in the French case with special protection through a publicly created 'inter-locking network of French-controlled holdings' – whereas in Italy and Spain a prime concern was to escape from the effects of partisan patronage (Vickers and Wright 1988, 24; cf. 12, 18–19). In Central and Eastern Europe, this use of state firms as part of the communist power structure has made privatization both an indispensable part of post-communist reorganization and a particularly awkward enterprise. The uncompetitive nature of many firms, the inflated book value of their assets, a large but uncertain legacy of liabilities and the costly need in some cases to repair environmental pollution have complicated the task of those picking over the contents of the industrial graveyard. In Germany, the Treuhandanstalt had initially to break up the old conglomerates, creating at first more firms than it was able to sell. Despite its commitment to competition enforced by the Cartel Office, preference has been given to acquisitions by West German firms even when they secure positions of market domination (Padgett 1992, 195–7, 204). Volkswagen has been particularly active, its most spectacular acquisition being the Czech automobile champion Skoda at a time when the motor car market was entering recession. Volkswagen's 31 per cent of Skoda, bought in 1991, was to be increased to 70 per cent by 1996, but the interim planned investment was curtailed in 1993.

Despite the many and varied experiments with privatization currently being made in Central and Eastern Europe, it is inevitable that large state firms will continue to dominate their industries for the foreseeable future. Apart from the reasons already mentioned, the lack of a capital market and opposition from trade unions where they are strong (Poland) have also slowed down the process. In the Czech Republic, with a stable and determined government and no effective trade union opposition, privatization has attracted substantial foreign interest, notably through a small number of large investments. In Poland, large state enterprises have been little affected because state-owned banks have supported them. As a result, privatization has initially been concentrated in very small businesses in Poland, whereas Hungary had received by 1992 $5 billion in foreign investments 'from firms such as General Electric, General Motors, Suzuki and Nestlé'. However, there have been Italian takeovers of major Polish steel and motor car enterprises. Meanwhile, in Hungary, state enterprises 'are not paying their bills, taxes, social security contributions, unemployment contributions or customs duties' (Okolicsanyi 1993, 53). Particularly in Bulgaria, privatization has been accepted for small firms but not large, overvalued, industrial state enterprises. Privatization in former communist countries differs most from Western mixed economies, as Janus Lewandowski, former Polish Minister for Privatization put it, in that it consists in 'selling property that belongs to no one, which has no value to people who have no money.'

Industrial Styles of Government–Champion Firm Relations

While each country has its peculiar way of conducting relations between governments and firms, each industry imparts its own special characteristics to these links. Specific examples will enable us to develop both a cross-sectoral and a cross-national understanding of the complexities.

Aircraft

The natural starting-point for a policy of industrial patriotism was, as we have mentioned, an armaments-centred strategy based upon an 'arsenal logic': the need to provide an independent supply of military equipment. So, we shall commence with an industry, aircraft manufacture, which started life in the national champion mode. It is all the more significant that, even in such industries, as market forces shift power from governments, the tendency for champion firms to acquire increasing independence has become clear. Furthermore, as well as becoming detached from the public policies of national governments, the very identities of the aerospace firms have become increasingly blurred through the network of international links they have developed.

The importance of defence-related research and development expenditure in postwar Britain and France has been out of all proportion to this total innovation 'spin-off'. Aircraft R & D amounted to over one-third in Britain and over a quarter in France of the total in the early 1960s. In that decade, government-sponsored mergers led to the creation of British Aerospace and Aérospatiale, using the leverage provided by military-style procurement to respond to increasing international competition. However, because no protected national market was sufficient to justify producing national commercial aircraft in Europe, an attempt was made to secure collaboration on a programme to produce Airbus which foundered on a quarrel between France and Britain over industrial leadership. Britain having withdrawn from the project (only to rejoin it a decade later after it had been successfully established), Germany denied leadership to Aérospatiale and ensured that it was in the hands of a relatively independent joint firm: Airbus Industrie (P. Muller 1995; P. Muller 1989). As well as allowing Germany to re-enter civil aviation in a major way, it ensured that control passed out of the hands of the French armaments engineers and into those of a management concerned with winning orders in the world market rather than manufacturing planes in the hope that there would also be a foreign demand for them. Concorde was a calamitous example of putting technological prowess before commercial viability, and it played its part, with the bankruptcy of Rolls Royce, in shifting public responsibility in Britain from the Ministry of Technology (which had taken over from the Ministry of Aviation) to the Department of Trade and Industry. This change by the Heath government was followed a decade later by the Thatcher government's much more far-reaching privatization of both British Aerospace and Rolls Royce (Hayward 1983).

Three countries dominate the European aeronautical industry. Britain, France and Germany each have about one-third of the turnover, with Italy having the remainder. While British and Deutsche Aerospace are both private (the latter owned by Daimler-Benz), the much smaller Italian Alenia (a subsidiary of IRI) and Spanish CASA (a partner in Airbus) are public. Partly because France was most firmly wedded to the armaments logic and because the socialists were in power from 1981 to 1986 and from 1988 to 1993, it has found making the transition to a single international champion firm the most difficult of all. It has been split between Aérospatiale (74 per cent public) and Thomson (82 per cent public), with Matra as a third civil aviation contender. Attempts to secure a military aviation marriage between Aérospatiale and Dassault have failed, but the 1992 purchase of 20 per cent of Aérospatiale shares by Crédit Lyonnais provided a German-style bank–industry link. Both Aérospatiale and Thomson were scheduled in 1993 by the Balladur government for privatization (but neither was at the top of the list). This will augment their ability to contract international alliances.

Consortia have become a feature of high technology industries, with their interlocking contractual and subcontractual ties. They threaten to dismember firms as identifiable industrial actors. The retreat of national governments has been accentuated in the 1990s by the post-Cold War defence cuts and the recession-induced reduction in public funding of expensive and risky R & D. By a combination of regulation and aid to R & D, the EC has partially replaced the role played by the national governments. While the strategic character of aerospace is open to dispute, it is no longer technological independence but the technological capacity of firms engaged in collaborative networks to produce profitable aircraft for sale over a twenty-year period that is at stake. It is in this context that the EC – under pressure from the US government – has increasingly intervened to ensure respect for the rules of competition, particularly in the matter of refundable advances made to the firms involved in Airbus, as part of the prolonged GATT negotiations. However, as the US government has continued to provide substantial R & D aid to American aerospace firms, it is not in a comfortable position to oppose EC assistance of this kind.

Electricity

A second case of transition from the protected and privileged status of national champion to the exposed but ambitious role of international champion is the electricity supply public utility. When it moved beyond local to national provision, the electricity industry not only remained frontier-bound; it was considered to be a natural monopoly. Faced with the 1973 oil shock, European countries reacted in different ways. France, where in matters of energy policy Electricité de France (EDF) has been regarded as a state within the state, was able to promote an 'all-electric' energy policy in association with a massive investment in nuclear power. It was able to replace reliance upon French technology – based on a 1960s alliance between President de Gaulle and the Atomic Energy Commissariat – with the better commercial proposition of American technology favoured by EDF and Presidents Pompidou and Giscard in the 1970s. As with ENI in Italian oil policy, one may question how far EDF was promoting French national interests or using them as a justification for the public enterprise's own expansionist schemes. Its exuberant commitment to growth led to an excess of supply over demand, particularly in the recession of the early 1990s. EDF's internationalist response has been to promote exports of electricity aggressively. It has resisted EC attempts to regulate its conduct in ways that the French government has not been able to achieve (Lucas 1979; McGowan 1995; Gravelaine and O'Dy 1978).

Whereas EDF has not as yet been seriously threatened with privatization, the Central Electricity Generating Board in Britain was a victim of more governmental interference and mismanagement prior to being split into one transmission and three generating companies. This failure to preserve its identity – unlike British Gas and British Telecom – was due to the priority accorded to promoting competition. The results have been disappointing as far as lowering the cost of electricity is concerned, while there has been forlorn resistance from those who oppose the closure of coal mines due to the switch to gas-fuelled power stations. Germany and Italy have followed neither the French nor the British pattern. In Germany, the high-cost coal mines have been protected and electro-nuclear power has been curbed by the environmental lobby. In Italy, the electricity corporation ENEL has, like EDF, accumulated an enormous debt, without the achievements that were anticipated from the investment programme.

Increased trade in electricity, with France and Belgium exporting surplus nuclear power and Italy becoming a major importer, has allowed the EC to become involved, through the promotion of an internal Energy Market at the end of the 1980s, with the aim of establishing an EC-wide electricity system. (Globalization is technically precluded.) Apart from practical problems, such as the transport of electricity from France to Portugal via Spain, there are the wider issues raised by reregulatory liberalization which have met with opposition by most European governments and by the Centre for European Public Enterprises. A public utility industry that has been the preserve of a closed community of governments and enterprises is becoming subject to the same forces of international competition, although in much less rapid and dramatic ways than telecommunications, where the modernizing challenges to statecraft and entrepreneurial skill have been especially great.

Telecommunications

Like electricity supply, telecommunications was regarded as a natural monopoly that presupposed provision by a national champion public administration or enterprise. The US-mediated impact of new technologies on the segregated European national markets, protected by public procurement policies, led to large price differentials that in turn promoted the American-style, Thatcherite response. 'Because the Thatcher government set a premium on rapid deployment, the bulk of the technology and associated equipment had to be imported from the US, Japan and Sweden. Britain, it seems, is more prepared than France and West Germany to bypass indigenous suppliers to gain access to advanced telecommunications' (Morgan and Webber 1986, 59). To implement this strategy, British Telecom (BT) was privatized in 1984, the pioneer for the subsequent privatization of the other public utilities. To guarantee 'fair competition' between BT and a second firm, Mercury, licensed in 1982, a regulatory Office of Telecommunications (Oftel) was established. How successful was Britain in exporting its ultra-liberal approach to the rest of Europe? One consequence was to promote defensive Franco–German telecommunications collaboration.

In the early 1980s France seemed to be firmly embarked in the opposite direction to Britain. The great 1970s modernizing success of the Direction Générale des Télécommunications (DGT) in transforming the French tele-phone network, when half the population was mockingly described as waiting for the telephone to be installed and the other half were waiting for the dialling tone, was a superb advertisement for state-led industrial policy. The DGT's achievement 'depended upon a strong political commitment to a huge investment programme, involving public procurement in a protected national market for basic network equipment' (Morgan and Webber 1986, 66). This favourable set of circumstances was not to persist into the 1980s. Its main electronic suppliers, CGE and Thomson, were nationalized in 1982, but in 1983, without consulting and against the opposition of the DGT, they decided to merge their telecommunications activities into CIT – Alcatel, a subsidiary of CGE. DGT's opposition was due to the fact that it saw itself as France's national champion, playing off two national suppliers, rather than being at the mercy of a monopoly. It argued that this would inhibit an alliance strategy with other European firms to face the rigours of international com-petition. Privatized in 1986, CGE (which became Alcatel-Alsthom in 1991), with the help of substantial government aid, emerged as the telecommuni-cations national champion. The DGT sought to retrieve the initiative by promoting telematics – the ambitious combination of telecommunications and computers – with a state administration, en route to becoming a state enter-prise as France Télécom in 1988, being given the key role (Morgan and Webber 1986, 62–7; Cohen 1992, 147–83). In 1993, when the right returned to power, France Télécom, having lost a battle with British Telecom to establish a worldwide joint venture 75 per cent owned by BT with MCI (the main US rival to ATT), was scheduled to become a joint stock company to allow it to link up either with Alcatel or with a German partner, Deutsche Telekom (DT).

Despite its 1989 change of name, DT has formally remained a constitution- ally guaranteed public administration. However, the Bundespost was split into three, with DT being expected to operate as a commercial enterprise. Although there has been increasing pressure for privatization, notably from the small FDP Liberal coalition partner of the CDU-CSU, this has been strongly opposed by the SPD, which can block change in parliament. The DT has also had the self-interested support of its principal supplier, Siemens, for the preservation of its network monopoly, as well as that of the German Post Office Workers' Union, which did not resist the introduction of labour-saving technology (Esser 1995). DT's main preoccupation has been the massive task of modernizing East German telecommunications. However, the EC's de- cision to prise open all the telecommunications monopolies by 1998 has led Germany to plan to begin privatizing DT in 1996, to face increased compe- tition, notably from BT, which has the advantage that many transnational corporations have their headquarters in Britain. So, Germany will have to join in domestic deregulation and cross-national collaboration, probably with France, under the threat of US, Japanese and other European competitors and under EC pressure.

Owing to the attraction of cost-sharing, winning new markets, acquiring new technology and sharing in new products, telecom firms have been especially active in developing networks of alliances both with European and especially with non-European firms. However, the EC Commission has, since its 1984 Action Programme for Telecommunications, recognized the costs of continuing national divergence. 'Different regulatory regimes, incompatible technical standards, duplicative R and D efforts and chauvinistic procurement policies all conspire to the same end, namely an uncommon market in which European firms are denied the economies of scale available to their US and Japanese competitors' (Cawson et al. 1990, 182). After consulting the major organized interests, especially the Conference of European Post and Telecom- munications Administrations and the International Telecommunications Users Group, the EC has moved to set minimum standards and secure mutual recognition of licensing and testing to reduce national protection. In 1988 the European Telecommunications Standards Institute was set up and in 1990 an EC Directive ensured that 'Equipment licensed and tested in one member state can be marketed and attached to telecommunications networks in all member states, without any further licensing or tests' (Thatcher 1995; Cawson et al. 1990, ch. 8 *passim* and Appendix 1).

European High Technology Collaboration

Pressures to adapt national champion strategies have been exerted most intensely in the rapidly changing high technology industries. Despite each nation's attempts to make the EC regulatory framework conform as closely as possible to their own, the overall effect has been progress towards competition within a single European market. As Elie Cohen has pointed out, a French attempt to transpose its Colbertist model to the EC would fail because none of its preconditions existed: 'neither integration of research policies, public procurement or the promotion of industrial champions, the discretionary intervention by government, offensive protectionism, nor a public service ideology and there is no elite ready to carry out big projects. Having disappeared from the national scene, these preconditions are nowhere near emerging on the European plane' (Cohen 1992, 383). Short of projecting an outdated French model onto the EC, is this assessment too pessimistic in its implications?

France played a leading role in the high technology collaboration of the mid-1980s, notably Eureka, which was an inter-governmental programme outside the EC Commission's purview, operating through a multiplicity of multi-national joint projects. Eureka was prompted by the Reagan Strategic Defense Initiative or 'Star Wars' programme (abandoned in 1993 by President Clinton). The need to respond to the new American challenge in the fields of information technology, telecommunications, robotics and biotechnology, among others, led to the adoption in 1985 of a Eureka Charter (Shearman 1986, 149–50, 156–7), which by mid-1987 had rallied nineteen countries and led to the signature of 108 agreements. Not surprisingly, France was most active, being then involved in sixty projects, Britain in 41 and Germany in 29. However, non-EC states such as Sweden (twenty) and Switzerland (sixteen) were also heavily involved. Thanks to the flexible way in which they were organized, these programmes often quickly reached the pre-industrial stage.

The main EC initiatives have been through the European Strategic Programme for Research and Development in Information Technology (ESPRIT), Research for Advanced Communications in Europe (RACE) and European Cooperation in the field of Scientific and Technical Research (COST). Despite the Thatcher government's slowing down of the ESPRIT programme, funding on a fifty:fifty basis between at least two member states and the EC helped to promote a variety of projects in micro-electronics, software technology and office systems, particularly involving Philips, Siemens and GEC. 'The ESPRIT programme has seen the emergence of a core of key decision-makers comprising representatives from Western Europe's 12 largest computer companies, officials from the European Commission and national civil servants, whose continued contact with each other has developed into and reinforced a relatively closed and "privatised" world that reflects a consensus on the problems to be addressed and the strategies to be adopted' (Shearman 1986, 157; cf. 158, 161, and Sandholtz 1992). The future of European industrial–governmental collaboration depends upon the emergence of more policy communities of the ESPRIT type, otherwise market forces will result in piecemeal and unpredictable improvisation. They have so far been conspicuous by their absence.

The projection of the 'mission-oriented' efforts of Britain, France and Germany onto the EC plane, from the 1950s Euratom failure to deliver its promises to the Maastricht Treaty call that member states should coordinate their research and development policies, has been criticized as likely to lead to rising costs, longer time-scales and less genuine rationalization to achieve scale economies. Instead of European ventures being an *alternative* to national ventures, they have been *additional* to them in R & D total expenditure. Far from duplication between countries being reduced, this has increased as the EC industrial mission supplements the national industrial mission. However, there has been simultaneous concentration within countries: 'the "national champion" model has become even more firmly entrenched, with firms such as GEC and BAe totally dominating their fields in the UK, Thomson and Aérospatiale in France and Siemens and Daimler Benz in Germany' (Ergas 1993, 15; cf. 13–17). What is happening is that the inability to transpose the French model onto the EC has at least initially reinforced national champions, but this does not resolve the problems posed by global competition.

Restructuring and Regulating European Champions

By the end of the 1980s a consensus view had emerged that attributed the loss of market share by European firms mainly to the lack of a unified European market. In turn, this was blamed on the survival of a variety of non-tariff barriers and state support for national champions.

> State intervention at the national level has been weakened as a result of the opening of frontiers and the constraints imposed at the European level, and this has not been compensated by similar intervention undertaken by the new (EC) central institutions . . . Europe's industrial policy consists mainly of competition policy which applies both to private enterprises and increasingly to state aids and nationalised firms. Otherwise, public intervention at the European level is mainly directed at the promotion of R and D, especially in high technology sectors, and inter-firm collaboration across national borders. This is a very mild European version of the old policy of national champions which it has partially replaced. (Tsoukalis, 1993, 335)

Between 1986 and 1990, government industrial subsidies in the four major countries of Western Europe ranged from 2 per cent in Britain, through 2.5 per cent in Germany to 3.5 per cent in France, up to 6 per cent of GDP in Italy. As long as the EC budget remains small, most aid will be from individual EC states, yet from July 1991 each government has had to notify the EC Commission in advance of aid for state-owned enterprises. How far has the substantial development of acquisitions, joint ventures and mergers changed the firms that have displaced governments as the key actors? How far has the EC succeeded national governments in the role of industrial regulator?

The substantial increase in restructuring of national champions that has taken place since the early 1980s was due to the belated recognition that (with the partial exception of Germany and, in a limited number of cases, France) European firms were losing the competitive battle with American, Japanese and newly industrializing Pacific Rim firms. Joint ventures have tended to predominate in the more technologically advanced industries such as computers, mechanical engineering and electrical and electronic engineering and disproportionately to involve cross-national and non-EC collaboration. By contrast, mergers were more often confined within a single nation and were relatively frequent in the extractive, textiles and food and drink industries (Cox and Watson 1994).

While intra-national mergers between large industrial companies continued to have pride of place in the late 1980s, they were being rapidly overhauled by intra-European mergers, with non-EC mergers still quite a long way behind. Intra-European mergers were especially popular in the chemical industry, where three German (Bayer, BASF and Hoechst) and one British (ICI) firm dominated the world market. France and Britain led the way in European acquisitions, with the USA being ahead of Germany, while Japanese acquisitions were concentrated in sectors such as motor cars.

> It is France's nationalised and newly privatised companies which have emerged as the most aggressive cross-border acquirers. Privatisation in particular released a pent-up potential for international expansion frustrated in the years spent in the state sector. Yet the relish with which French firms have taken to launching foreign bids is also a reflection of their former insularity: there is a great deal of catching up to be done, and very little time now in which to do it. (Maclean 1992, 28)

Aérospatiale has been the first victim of EC control over 'Community scale' mergers which it sought with de Havilland in 1992. France was the main target of German acquirers, while Italy and Spain were especially attractive to French firms. However, the effects of the Single Market and of deregulation have not systematically produced European champion firms, partly because the EC has not been able to agree that this should be part of its industrial policy.

While Article 130 of the Maastricht Treaty provides for an EC industrial policy, it is couched in such general terms and requires such an improbable unanimity to operate that it can be discounted for the foreseeable future. In so far as it may be effective, it is likely to reinforce the national champions because each country will insist on receiving its 'fair share' of the collaborative venture. The EC, despite tendentious diatribes to the contrary, has not sought comprehensive regulation or harmonization in its concern to remove national barriers to competition. Rather, it has concentrated upon guaranteeing minimum common standards and then leaving it to a 'competition among rules' to prevail (Woolcock and Wallace 1995). This minimalist approach is also accentuated by the fact that the EC does not have the staff or political support to enforce its rules rigorously. Nevertheless, governments which, for their own budgetary or policy reasons, wish to curtail industrial subsidies can and have used the EC as a scapegoat. In contrast with British cuts, aid remained high in Italy and increased in Germany, especially owing to reunification. Similar pressures have operated across nations in specific industries. Thus the escalating losses sustained by most European national airlines have faced governments increasingly with the problem of trying to sustain ailing national champions such as Sabena, Air France, Alitalia and Lufthansa or accepting that they need to merge. The attempt by Austrian AUA, Dutch KLM, Scandinavian SAS and Swissair to merge in the Alcazar project failed in November 1993, owing partly to the fact that two of them, KLM and Swissair, significantly, already had links with separate American airlines (Northwest and Delta respectively) which they were not willing to abandon. The choice between a European and an international market logic is painfully underlined by such conflicts of interest.

Announcements of the death of national champion firms are premature, despite their need to manoeuvre within more turbulent and unpredictable markets. Even if governments are no longer regarded as interveners of the first resort, they will still be called upon, if only as a last resort, by firms as well as others who consider that the defence of their interests requires such assistance. They will be expected to champion the national interest, both in relation to other European governments and in such international contexts as GATT. They will be relied upon to create the most favourable conditions for the firms that have become domiciled within their borders. The great strength of markets is that they do not need to be centrally organized in the way that the modern state functions. Nevertheless, if market forces are not to become socially and politically as well as economically destructive, an enforced regulatory framework is indispensable. So, despite the discredit into which state industrial activism has fallen throughout Europe, governments are still necessary to work out the compromises that must be struck between territorial and international market forces. That is the humdrum rather than the heroic challenge to the statecraft of those who manage industrial affairs.

Bibliography

Berger, S. (1981). 'Lame ducks and national champions: industrial policy in the Fifth Republic', in W. G. Andrews and S. Hoffmann (eds), *The Fifth Republic at Twenty*. Albany: SUNY Press.

Bianchi, P. et al. (1988). 'Privatisation in Italy: aims and constraints'. *West European Politics* 11 (4): 87–100.

Bressand, A. and Nicolaidis, K. (1990). 'Regional integration in a networked world economy', in W. Wallace (ed.), *The Dynamics of European Integration*. London: Pinter.

Cawson, A. et al. (1990). *Hostile Brothers: competition and closure in the European electronics industry*. Oxford: Clarendon Press.

Cohen, E. (1985). 'Le politique, l'administratif et le pouvoir industriel'. Paris: Association Française de Science Politique, Colloque, mimeo.

—— (1989). *L'Etat brancardier: politiques du déclin industriel, 1974–84*. Paris: Calmann-Lévy.

—— (1992). *Le Colbertisme 'High Tech'*. Paris: Hachette.

Cohen, E. and Bauer, M. (1985). *Les grandes manoeuvres industrielles*. Paris: Pierre Belfond.

Commissariat Général du Plan (1965). *Cinquième Plan de Développement Economique et Social, 1966–70*. Paris: Documentation Française.

Cox, A. and Watson, G. (1994). *The Restructuring of European Industry*. Winteringham: Earlsgate Press.

Dyson, K. (1986). 'West European States and the communications revolution'. *West European Politics* 9 (4): 10–55.

Ergas, H. (1993). 'Europe's policy for high technology: has anything been learnt?'. mimeo.

Esser, J. (1995). 'Challenges to the old policy style in Germany', in J. Hayward (ed.), *Industrial Enterprise and European Integration*. Oxford: Oxford University Press.

Grant, W. (1982). *The Political Economy of Industrial Policy*. London: Butterworth.

Gravelaine, F. de and O'Dy, S. (1978). *L'Etat EDF*. Paris: Alain Moreau.

Hayward, K. (1983). *Government and British Civil Aerospace*. Manchester: Manchester University Press.

Hodges, M. (1974). *Multinational Corporations and National Governments: a case study of the United Kingdom's experience, 1964–1970*. Westmead: Saxon House.

Hodges, M. and Woolcock, S. (1993). 'Atlantic capitalism versus Rhine capitalism in the EC'. *West European Politics* 16 (3): 329–44.

Katzenstein, P. (1984). *Corporatism and Change: Austria, Switzerland and the politics of industry*. Ithaca: Cornell University Press.

—— (1985). *Small States in World Markets: industrial policy in Europe*. Ithaca: Cornell University Press.

Kolodziej, E. (1987). *Making and Marketing Arms: the French experience and its implications for the international system*. Princeton: Princeton University Press.

Kurzer, P. (1991). 'The internationalisation of business and domestic class compromises'. *West European Politics* 14 (4): 1–24.

Lucas, N. J. D. (1979). *Energy in France: planning, politics and policy*. London: Europa.

McArthur, J. H. and Scott, B. R. (1969). *Industrial Planning in France*. Cambridge, MA: Harvard University Press.

McGowan, F. (1995). 'The European electricity industry and EC regulatory reform', in J. Hayward (ed.), *Industrial Enterprise and European Integration*. Oxford: Oxford University Press.

Maclean, M. (1992). 'The unfinished chrysalis: market forces and protectionist reflexes in France', in M. Maclean and J. Howorth (eds), *Europeans on Europe: transnational visions of a new continent*. London: Macmillan.

Michalet, C.-A. (1974). 'France', in R. Vernon (ed.), *Big Business and the State*. Cambridge, MA: Harvard University Press.

Morgan, K. and Webber, D. (1986). 'Divergent paths: political strategies for telecommunications in Britain, France and West Germany'. *West European Politics* 9 (4): 56–79.

Muller, P. (1989). *Airbus, l'ambition européenne: logique de marché, logique d'état*. Paris: L'Harmattan.

—— (1995). 'Aerospace companies and the state in Europe', in J. Hayward (ed.), *Industrial Enterprise and European Integration*. Oxford: Oxford University Press.

Muller, W. (1988). 'Privatising in a corporatist economy: the politics of privatisation in Austria'. *West European Politics* 11 (4): 101–16.

Okolicsanyi, K. (1993). 'Hungary', in B. Slay (ed.), *Roundtable: privatization in Eastern Europe*. Radio Free Europe Research Report, II, no. 32 [thanks to Archie Brown for this reference].

Padgett, S. (1992). 'The new German economy', in G. Smith et al. (eds), *Developments in German Politics*. London: Macmillan.

Prodi, R. (1974). 'Italy', in R. Vernon (ed.), *Big Business and the State*. Cambridge, MA: Harvard University Press.

Sandholtz, W. (1992). *High-Tech Europe: the politics of industrial cooperation*. Berkeley: University of California Press.

Servan-Schreiber, J.-J. (ed.) ([1967] 1969). *The American Challenge*. Harmondsworth: Penguin.

Sharp, M. (1990). 'Technology and the dynamics of integration', in W. Wallace (ed.), *The Dynamics of European Integration*. London: Pinter.

Shearman, C. (1986). 'European collaboration in computing and telecommunications: a policy'. *West European Politics* 9 (4): 147–62.

Shonfield, A. (1965). *Modern Capitalism*. Oxford: Oxford University Press.

Smith, A. ([1776] 1976). *An Inquiry into the Nature and Causes of the Wealth of Nations*. Oxford: Oxford University Press.

Thatcher, M. (1995). 'Regulatory reform and the internationalisation of telecommunications', in J. Hayward (ed.), *Industrial Enterprise and European Integration*. Oxford: Oxford University Press.

Tsoukalis, L. (1993). *The New European Economy*. Oxford: Oxford University Press.

Vernon, R. (1971). *Sovereignty at Bay: the multinational spread of US enterprises*. London: Longman.

—— (ed.) (1974). *Big Business and the State: changing relations in Western Europe*. Cambridge, MA: Harvard University Press.

Vickers, J. and Wright, V. (1988). 'The politics of industrial privatisation in Western Europe: an overview'. *West European Politics* 11 (4): 1–30.

Weber, M. (1961). *General Economic History*. New York: Collier Books.

Wilks, S. (1983). 'Crisis management in Britain', in K. Dyson and S. Wilks (eds), *Industrial Crisis: a comparative study of state and industry*. Oxford: Martin Robertson.

Woolcock, S. and Wallace, H. (1995). 'European Community regulation, national and transnational enterprise', in J. Hayward (ed.), *Industrial Enterprise and European Integration*. Oxford: Oxford University Press.

Young, S. (1978). 'Industrial policy in Britain, 1972–77', in J. Hayward and O. Narkiewicz (eds), *Planning in Europe*. London: Croom Helm.

Young, S. and Lowe, A. V. (1974). *Intervention in the Mixed Economy*. London: Croom Helm.

13

Redefining the Welfare State

Richard Parry

The new Europe will have to decide how much uniformity and diversity is possible in the social services and protection accorded to citizens as part of what since the Second World War has come to be known as the 'welfare state'. The term has proved an irresistible one but has never been very helpful in specifying just what turns a country from being a state into a welfare state or how much welfare is provided. Perhaps the best approach is to see it as denoting the response to political and social imperatives which in almost every system have impelled the state to take responsibility for the reproduction of the population – in terms of education, health and social care – and the replacement of the economic resources of citizens placed outside the labour market. In the 1990s a rather different political context is taking shape in this area. Policy is being driven not by political pressure for improved social standards but by the demands of international economic competitiveness. The concept of free trade is being widened to prescribe common standards for all the factors of production, with social protection as an overhead cost – necessary at a minimal level for economic efficiency but unsustainable at a level much more generous than the world norm. This is the dilemma facing the European Community as it confronts its relatively weak performance on economic growth and employment generation, and it provides the main theme of this chapter.

Conceptualizing the Welfare State

As welfare states typically involve the extension of income and service rights to those on average or low incomes, it would be natural to conceive the welfare state as a contested theme in a left–right political struggle in European nations. There is a body of thought, associated with Walter Korpi and Göran Therborn in Sweden, which takes the view that the welfare state is the fruit of working-class political action, but it has to rely on indirect and unacknowledged linkages between the structure of political forces and the observable development of policy. Korpi's study of sickness rights in eighteen countries found that 'left party government participation clearly has been an important factor during both the prewar and the postwar periods . . . variations in left voting strength do not appear to have much effect . . . [but] the effects of left votes are positive during the prewar as well as the postwar period. In addition, union density receives strong positive coefficients during the postwar period' (Korpi 1989, 323). His later work on unemployment found that left strength can produce a model of 'societal bargaining' which holds down unemployment (Korpi 1991). In summary, Korpi's research has found weak evidence that left-wing pressure stimulates welfare, but more in the nature of 'contagion from the left' (pre-emptive concessions made by the right) than direct achievement by left-wing governments.

The dominant explanations of both the origins and the current shape of welfare states emphasize consensus and inevitability rather than conflict. Most discussion of the welfare state is derived from its golden years in the mid-twentieth century when, in the title of Peter Baldwin's influential book *The Politics of Social Solidarity* (1990), support for state welfare was diffused right across the political spectrum. The apparently inexorable progress of the welfare state was indeed the main theme of the era from the early 1880s to the mid-1970s. It was only in the 1960s and 1970s that political scientists and sociologists provided the conceptual tools to understand why the welfare state had taken such a hold. Stein Rokkan was a pioneer in locating the concept in the national development of European states. He emphasized the importance of history – such as the pattern of the Protestant/Catholic divide at the Reformation – and geography – the seaward or landward orientation of trade (Rokkan and Urwin 1983). On this view, the consolidation of European nation-states in the nineteenth century was the precondition of the kinds of social formation that produced welfare states. Important themes were state education to promote a national language and culture (the key to the general ideological acceptability of public education free at the point of delivery) and social protection to deal with the effects of industrialization.

Peter Flora built upon Rokkan's work in his major *Growth to Limits* project of the 1980s; previously he had edited an important collection with Arnold Heidenheimer (Flora and Heidenheimer 1981). His thesis is that the welfare state is not so much the product of political choice as an element in the transformation of European economies and societies: 'it was born as an answer to the problems created by capitalist industrialization; it was driven by the democratic class struggle; and it followed in the footsteps of the nation state'

(Flora 1986, xii). Once the forms of welfare were established, expansion to include all of the population was a likely political result.

A key institutional form is that of the insurance fund, devised in the early days of capitalism as a necessary means for the management of risk. There is a strong mutual tradition in insurance – craft guilds or trade unions forming their own funds to tide over members who fell upon hard times. This had two implications for the state. Firstly, there was seen to be a need to regulate the funds to insure against fraud and the diversion of funds. Secondly, there was pressure to extend and subsidize the funds to incorporate workers who were difficult to organize on a mutual basis. Both these themes were acceptable to Conservative political forces, even leaving aside the more cynical motives of weaning workers away from socialism – an admitted aim of German Chancellor Bismarck when he proposed a state-supported sickness insurance in 1881, conventionally taken to mark the inauguration of the modern welfare state. The insurance fund principle remains the cornerstone of state welfare in most parts of Europe and has proved capable of mobilizing vast amounts of money while avoiding questions over the size of the state sector. In Britain it is not a principle of government social policy – the National Insurance Fund is largely a fiction – but it underpins the occupational and personal pensions industry, which covers two-thirds of the workforce and is the dominant owner on the stock market.

Flora and others were associated in the 1970s with the concept of the 'crisis of the welfare state'. This is related to sociological ideas about the sustainability of structures and their ability to absorb tensions and contradictions. It is posited that welfare becomes necessary for the consumption and investment needs of the economic system but also loses the political consent necessary to finance it. The result is the 'fiscal crisis of the state', in James O'Connor's celebrated book title (1973). The underlying strain came from the relatively faster expansion of social spending over national income in the postwar decades. The precipitating factor was the oil crisis of 1973–4, which deflated Western economies at a time when the structures of comprehensive welfare states were being completed. A potentially difficult situation, where neither tax increases nor welfare cuts were acceptable, was in fact defused quite quickly (Alber 1988). Rudolf Klein has satirized left-wing thinkers who, in his view, got it totally wrong by positing that Western welfare states would fall uniform victims to the contradictions of capitalism (Klein 1993). But at least the idea of crisis enabled social policy to make a welcome entry into the forefront of academic social science.

Gosta Esping-Andersen (1990, 1993) has to some extent merged the perspectives of Korpi and of Flora and advanced the influential idea of the 'three worlds of welfare capitalism'. One is the social democratic model, realized only in Scandinavia, under critical scrutiny even there and no longer seen as an achievable model for the rest of the world. The other two models embody an important distinction that is vital to an understanding of comparative welfare state patterns. On the one side is the liberal model, found in the United States and in Britain in recent years, with low expenditure and conservative political norms – 'lean even if not mean' in Mishra's phrase (Mishra 1990, 14). On the other are the 'corporatist-statist' countries, the major ones in Central Europe, which have generally conservative political norms reinforced by high, not low, welfare expenditure as they seek to protect the social patterns of full employment, economic harmony and traditional family structures. This protection takes the form of earnings–related benefits, universal coverage of health insurance and generous family benefits. Harold Wilensky, another pioneer of comparative analysis, found that, 'in contrast to leftism, cumulative Catholic power since World War I increases welfare effort' (Wilensky 1981, 356). He suggests that this is because Catholic power taps into 'corporatist-technocratic linkages' which are characteristic of the ancillary institutions of the Catholic Church. He also notes the convergence of cumulative Catholic power and cumulative left power in Austria, Belgium, the Netherlands and Germany since the Second World War to produce a 'not so paradoxical' corporatist and high-spending regime. This analysis has been criticized by later authors as not valid at all times, but it does emphasize the potential for welfare effort by Catholic-influenced conservative parties which have some association with organized labour.

The Reasons for Policy Diversity

This brief review of some academic approaches to the welfare state suggests that distinctions between parsimonious right-wing countries and profligate left-wing ones do not make sense. We can explore this in more detail by looking at expenditure patterns and relating them to the growth of welfare states. Since the 1970s data on the level of social expenditure and the components of change in it over time have been much improved, especially by the OECD (1988) and the EC (Commission of the European Communities 1994). This has drawn attention to the large variations in social expenditure between nations with similar socio-economic structures; in Europe, between about 20 and 40 per cent of national income, in most countries roughly half of all public expenditure. The calculus is implicitly one between cost and effectiveness, with particular interest paid to Switzerland and Japan which 'do it cheaply'. Switzerland has been able to contain welfare spending to about 20 per cent of GDP through a reliance on voluntary insurance mechanisms, but there are other 'economical' welfare states, notably Britain with its comprehensive health service and social assistance safety-net.

Table 13.1 uses the comprehensive data of the *Growth to Limits* project (which unfortunately excluded France and Spain) to provide three time-frames. There are numerous problems of comparability in all such data; the ones given in table 13.1 here exclude private expenditure (discretionary purchases by individuals such as private school fees and medical drugs) but include compulsory social insurance and transfers for which goods and services are not obtained in return, even if formal administration is by non-governmental mutual funds (such as sickness and unemployment schemes administered on behalf of employers and employees). The fluidity of the boundary between private and social provision constantly bedevils international comparisons.

In 1914 the European leaders had been the Austro-German world and Scandinavia, but by 1950 the effects of two world wars had placed British expenditure ahead of all but German and Belgian. In Britain, the report of Sir William Beveridge in 1942 into social insurance and allied services had launched the 'British revolution' of the postwar welfare state, a curious mixture of radical and conservative themes. The key was that universal coverage based upon citizenship was administratively the most efficient and corresponded best to the political structure formed during the Second World War. Compared with Scandinavia, Britain lacked the large agrarian sector that was always a complicating factor; in Sweden a universal flat-rate pension was secured in 1946 but a comprehensive health service was rejected in 1948 (Baldwin 1990). It is significant that in the Netherlands, where there were strong traditions of differentiation between social groups, the radical Beveridge-inspired approach of the van Rhijn report (1945) was shelved until the 1960s.

Between 1950 and 1965 the average European share of social expenditure in Gross Domestic Product (GDP) increased from 13 to 18 per cent, the fastest growth coming in the Netherlands and Sweden. The real take-off was in the decade 1965–75. The snapshot of 1980 generated by the *Growth to Limits* project shows how far Britain had fallen behind. The Netherlands was in the lead, with 40 per cent of its GDP accounted for by social expenditure; 26 per cent of GDP was represented by social security, which is a transfer payment spent finally by recipients, but even so this represents a large penetration of welfare into the economy and society. Sweden and Denmark had developed extensive welfare states with high public employment. Belgium and the Netherlands were notable for the generosity of the income guarantees they offered. The major nations (Germany, France and Italy) had not gone as far but still had more expenditure than Britain (reasonably comparable OECD data for France in 1981 is of social expenditure at 30 per cent of GDP, right on the average (OECD 1985, table 1)). Switzerland remains in a unique position with under 20 per cent of GDP in social expenditure. The low public

Table 13.1 *Social expenditure as a percentage of GDP*

	Total			Components, 1980					
	1950	1965	1980	social security	education	health	social services	housing	other
Netherlands	13.3	23.6	40.2	23.5	8.1	6.9	–	0.6	1.6
Sweden	11.3	18.8	37.9	15.9	7.2	8.9	5.8	–	–
Belgium	(15.0)	21.3	36.0	20.4	7.8	5.7	–	0.9	0.9
Denmark	10.4	16.0	34.7	20.3	8.2	6.8	–	0.4	–
Austria	(18.1)	20.7	33.4	18.3	7.0	3.2	–	1.3	3.6
Germany	19.2	23.3	31.0	17.1	4.9	5.7	2.5	0.8	–
Ireland	14.7	16.8	29.0	10.7	6.4	8.4	–	3.5	–
Italy	(13.4)	20.0	27.0	13.7	5.9	5.8	1.3	0.3	–
Norway	9.2	15.7	26.1	12.4	5.7	7.2	–	0.7	–
Finland	10.5	14.8	24.8	12.0	4.8	4.8	3.2	–	–
Britain	14.8	18.2	24.5	9.8	5.5	5.1	0.9	3.2	–
Switzerland	7.4	10.7	19.7	9.8	5.5	3.1	–	0.2	1.2
Average	13.1	18.3	30.4	15.4	6.4	6.0			

Note: Other dates used: Belgium 1955, Austria 1957, Italy 1954.
Source: P. Flora (ed.), *Growth to Limits*, vol. 4. Berlin: de Gruyter, 1987, appendix tables.

Table 13.2 *Social policy as a percentage of gross domestic product, 1991*

Sweden	40.2
Netherlands	38.6
Denmark	36.8
France	34.0
Norway	33.9
Austria	32.6
Belgium	31.8
Germany	30.6
United Kingdom	29.7
Finland	29.5
Italy	28.5
Ireland	26.4
Spain	25.6
Portugal	24.2
Greece	23.4 (1989)
Switzerland	20.5 (1984)

Source: education data 1989 from OECD, *Education in OECD Countries 1988/89–1989/90* (Paris 1993) table 6.1; remainder for EU countries from Commission of the European Communities, *Social Protection in Europe* (Luxembourg 1994), table 1; for other countries from OECD, *Economic Outlook* (December 1993), appendix table 21; Switzerland: OECD, *The Future of Social Protection* (Paris 1988), table 1.

expenditure on housing outside Britain and Ireland reflects continental traditions of the regulation of private renting rather than public house-building (Power 1993).

By the end of the 1980s relative growth in welfare had been halted; the European average remained at 31 per cent of GDP. Table 13.2 gathers the best available recent data from the EC and OECD for 1991 or shortly before. Of the spenders at the top of the league, the Netherlands and Belgium both retreated during the 1980s from their peaks of penetration of public social expenditure in the national economy, while Sweden and Denmark showed a marginal increase. The Netherlands fell to from 40.2 per cent in 1980 (table 13.1) to 38.6 per cent in 1988. Norway shows the biggest increase over the decade, from 26.1 to 33.9 per cent, accounted for mainly by more generous social security. The Southern European nations have continued to improve their public provision. The European Union average for spending on social protection, which excludes education, has been in the 25 to 26 per cent range since 1981, with only Belgium showing a pronounced fall (from 30.8 per cent in 1983 to 26.7 per cent in 1989 and 1991). In terms of goods and services, health expenditure shows an upward dynamic but education is tending to fall. There are also variations in the real level of GDP per head, which if taken into account would further extend the lead of the big spenders and depress the position of Britain and Italy.

How are we to explain this diversity in performance? At the macro-level, the starting-point is the breaking-down of growth and scale into its three components: the number of people falling into demographic categories where they receive benefits, the coverage of and eligibility criteria for benefits, and the generosity and value of benefits. In the approach adopted by the OECD, these are known respectively as the demographic, eligibility and transfer ratios. In addition, the relative level of inflation in social services compared with the rest of the economy needs to be taken into account. If we 'decompose' growth in this way, the real improvement in services or transfer ratio becomes somewhat less but is still evident: between 1960 and 1975 it grew at an average (OECD Europe) of 4.6 per cent a year and from 1975 to 1981 (even after the oil crisis) by 3.3 per cent. Total growth (at constant prices) was respectively 7.3 and 4.6 per cent (Gillion and Henry 1985). In the 1980s, differences between European nations widened; the value of retirement pensions rose in most countries, with demographic factors fairly constant; in contrast, the increased number of unemployed was the main factor in the growth in spending on benefits on them, with the value of benefit per person falling in most countries (Commission of the European Communities 1994, 45–9). By decomposing aggregate growth, we can detect a widening range of choices across European nations about how to manage particular benefits and services.

The political variables are the important ones in explaining this range of outcomes. Surveying health policy in France, Sweden and Switzerland, Ellen Immergut suggests that the detailed political procedures of each country determine the nature of 'veto points' in the system where change can be promoted or resisted. Interest groups are important but their power varies: 'the political impact of a particular group is contingent on strategic opportunities stemming from the logic of political decision processes' (Immergut 1992, 8). This approach can be extended to social insurance and to European Community activity in social policy. It is common in national histories to find points when coalitions of interests in a contingent set of circumstances allowed radical new policies to fall into place. Because these policies were then seen as a national political solution to social needs, they became entrenched, and the

anomalies in them, in cross-national terms, were overlooked. Detailed political analysis as found in Immergut and in Baldwin (1990) seems a better way
forward than the quantitative analysis of expenditure trends which until
recently dominated the field, and we can explore some of the themes by
looking at political processes and structures.

Political Structures of Welfare

The politics of social policy tend to be subordinate to the classical issues of
'high' politics such as the macro-economy, defence and foreign affairs. This
may seem a paradox, given that social policy bears heavily on the life-chances
of individuals. The explanation may lie in the fact that government policy in
these fields operates as an adjunct to private purchases and provision. The
model of a social insurance fund is a private mutual fund, and that of state-
delivered education, health and social care the continuing private sectors in
these fields. Especially in continental Europe, social policy has sought to
preserve the freedom of professionals and the financial autonomy of pension
funds. State penetration of welfare institutions is accordingly rather limited as
'intermediary structures' are given room for manoeuvre and protected by
political sponsors (Flora 1986, xvii). Allied to this is the general lack of
devolution of real policy discretion to local and regional government; while
the formal administration of health, education and social care is often located
there, standards and entitlements are usually set nationally.

The concept of 'subsidiarity' has been used in both a descriptive and a
prescriptive sense to define the proper bounds of state welfare activity, and has
recently been given a new lease of life in the EC's Maastricht Treaty. It is a
working-out of the idea of not entrusting to the larger scale what can be done
by the smaller. In Spicker's phrase, it means that 'solidarities are hierarchically
ordered' (Spicker 1991, 6), a line of thought deriving from Christian social
teaching, Protestant as well as Catholic. Traditionally, the concept had a
conservative connotation, for it suggested that state welfare would undermine
the solidarity and sense of mutual obligation within families, associations,
localities and religious groups. But by asserting that there were obligations to
social protection that had to be taken on by the appropriate authority, it did
promote a sense of the 'social' written into, for instance, the French, German
and Italian constitutions. It is easy to see, for instance, how the idea of a just
wage might seem to imply earnings-related benefits, and how a sense of the
moral worth of individuals might militate against building economic incentives into the social security system.

Some of these distinctions are captured in cross-national opinion survey
data on political support for the welfare state. European nations are distinctly

Table 13.3   *Public opinion of state welfare (1985 survey)*

	Britain	Germany	Italy	USA
% agreeing it is definitely the government's responsibility to . . .				
provide health care for the sick	86	54	87	36
provide a decent standard of living for old people	79	56	82	43
provide a decent standard of living for unemployed people	45	24	40	16
reduce income differences between rich and poor people	48	28	48	17

Source: P. Taylor-Gooby, 'The role of the state', in R. Jowell et al. (eds), *British Social Attitudes Survey Special International Report*. Farnborough: Gower, 1989, 41.

ahead of the United States in popular demands for the state to take responsibility for social provision. In a 1985 survey (table 13.3), Britain and Italy were also ahead of Germany on this variable. Everywhere there is a gradient of acceptability about the clienteles in need, running from health care through pensions to education to unemployment benefits, though here Germany stands out as being relatively resistant to more state spending and less discriminating between the worth of the various categories of expenditure (source as for table 13.3). This provides the background to our understanding of the diverse types of social policy system: a 'European' approach more ambitious than that of the United States but with differences of emphasis.

The structures and governance of European welfare states express the philosophy behind them. Following Esping-Andersen (1990), Ginsburg (1992), Leibfried (1993) and others, we can divide them into four broad geographical categories. In the north the Scandinavian model emphasizes completeness, universality, full employment and generous social care as rights independent of the strength of family structures; large government organizations with high public employment in social services are common here. In the heartland of Europe, the Bismarckian model serves as a support structure of pre-existing social and economic forms, with the government role an indirect one. In the south or 'Latin rim', the 1970s democracies of Spain, Portugal and Greece, and to a lesser extent Italy, display formally ambitious welfare states which lack the financial and administrative resources to deliver secure welfare to citizens. Finally, the former socialist countries to the east represent an adaptation of collectivist structures to the Bismarckian norm of the countries that are now emulated, especially Germany. Britain itself does not fit easily into any of these patterns, one explanation of its isolation within the European Community in social affairs: it is best described as an economical version of the Scandinavian pattern with a strong reliance on direct government provision. In Ginsburg's terms (1992), Britain's 'liberal collectivist' welfare state, just like the United States' 'welfare state in the corporate market economy', has a distinctive historical legacy from before the Second World War that stands apart from continental European nations, which generally took important political steps in the 1950s and beyond.

In Scandinavia there are two patterns. Norway and Finland have rather lower welfare expenditure than do Sweden and Denmark because the agrarian tradition was stronger and more resistant to universal provision; Norway has been gaining fast and had the largest increase in social spending of any Western European nation in the 1980s. Sweden has attracted interest beyond its size because of its pioneering role in promoting state welfare while preserving a benign climate for industrial capitalism. Göran Therborn has identified four pillars of this approach: '(A) a tradition of broad popular social entitlements – coming from the force of an independent peasantry – instead of segmented corporatist rights or charity concern with poverty, (B) a sharp segmentation between high personal and low corporate taxation, (C) cautious and competent state management and (D) employer–union co-operation' (Pfaller et al. 1991, 269). Even before the First World War, Sweden started to make the 'red–green' compromise with the first example of contributory retirement pensions for the whole population (1913). From 1936 to 1976 the Social Democrats were in power – though sometimes lacking an overall majority. Social policy issues were of a salience unparalleled elsewhere in Europe but all the components of an integrated welfare state were in place – flat-rate pensions at a higher level (1946), health insurance for all (1955), earnings-related pensions for all (1958 – after a referendum and a general election on the issue), comprehensive health care run by local government (1969). Most important was the acceptance of an effective income gurantee. Sweden has also been unusual in its pursuit of state-subsidized housing. Starting later than Sweden but comparable or even ahead in many respects is Denmark, which since 1973 has had an integrated health service and is the second 'best' welfare state in the EC. It is notable that neither Sweden nor Denmark has ever had compulsory unemployment insurance, though most workers are in subsidized voluntary schemes run by the trade unions.

The continental, 'Bismarckian' model originated in Germany in the 1880s when Bismarck introduced benefits for sickness (1883), industrial accidents

(1884) and invalidity and old age (1889) to, broadly speaking, the skilled working class; but it was not until 1911 that salaried workers were included, and unemployment insurance had to wait until 1927. The changes were made acceptable by the use of governing bodies of employers and employees. Much has been written about whether Germany was a true pioneer and whether the rest of Europe emulated it. It is likely that other countries had a strong enough tradition of voluntary insurance to have developed social insurance independent of any imitation of Germany. More interesting are three features of the German approach: the gradual extension of provision from the less controversial risks such as industrial accidents to the traditionally less insurable ones such as unemployment and maternity; a tradition of a 'strong state', managing and perhaps manipulating social groups to prevent social disturbance; and a related philosophical tradition (through Hegel and others) taking a more positive view of the state as a responsible social integrator than did Anglo-French liberalism. This explains why France, for all its political radicalism, approached social protection through the regulation and extension of insurance funds secured through collective bargaining; only after the Second World War were all workers covered, and there is still a strong element of private payment and insurance in health care.

In culturally divided states such as Belgium and the Netherlands, the Bismarckian model has proved an attractive means of giving linguistic or religious groups self-management of their own affairs within a general structure of entitlement. In the Netherlands from the 1960s, the right-wing parties who were continuous participants in coalition governments embraced generous benefits and social care. These culminated in 1974 in the codification of 'supplementary social provision', which in effect gave every adult an income guarantee at the level of the minimum wage. The Netherlands has particularly high spending on disability and invalidity benefit. Belgium, with its strong tradition of independent insurance funds, also adopted a subsistence minimum in 1974 as it moved from a French to a Dutch approach to welfare. These two countries showed the potential for high expenditure if earnings-related benefits, once granted to particular groups, were universalized in a wish for political incorporation; eventually the approach could not be sustained and prompted cutbacks in the 1980s.

'Southern' patterns have had a rather pejorative ring in welfare state debate, and cross-national schemas (Flora, Esping-Andersen) have often excluded them. The problem has been an unreliable administrative system which creates a discrepancy between the formal promises of services and the reality of their delivery – in Leibfried's phrase (1993, 142), an 'institutionalized promise'. As economic modernization displaces the role of traditional institutions such as the Church, the formal claims made by government are often bold, as in the introduction of national health services (by Italy in 1980 and Greece in 1983, with a comparable insurance-based system in Spain in 1978) and the setting of a level of retirement pension with a full contribution record at among the highest levels in the European Union (Commission of the European Communities 1994, table 8). In contrast, the provision of social assistance to those without an employment record, and public expenditure on education and health, fall well below the European average. The typical result is the use of patronage, the black economy, family networks and private provision to fill in the gaps. The agrarian presence in Italy, Spain, Portugal and Greece (table 13.4) tends to make unemployment a problem (particularly in Spain) and financial assistance to many of the unemployed low or non-existent. The appetite for social spending in the Latin rim is large, and the task is to reconcile it with a much lower level of economic resources than is found in Northern Europe.

The collapse of state socialism in 1989 integrated social policy in Central and Eastern Europe into comparative European debate. Many of these countries had a rudimentary social insurance system before the Second World War and in some places these funds were maintained in a vestigial way. But the general pattern was for the state to provide an income to all, mostly through a full employment labour market with under-employment, and partly through pensions to the retired and disabled financed in effect through the state budget. Farmers and the self-employed were included in a way not usually found in Western Europe and there was not seen to be any need for a safety-net of social assistance. Public subsidies kept the cost of housing, transport and fuel low, and a monopoly of state provision of health and education promoted universal access to services facilitated by low earnings of professional staff. The system proved workable at a low level of reward because the market differentials in earning power between sections of the population were suppressed.

Democratization produced a wish to conform to Bismarckian patterns. In Hungary, Poland and the Czech Republic, funds for sickness and retirement were reactivated and there was pressure from the World Bank and others to curb the generosity of indiscriminate benefits, especially to families, and introduce time-limits on the payment of benefit. The lack of any tradition of means-tested social assistance became a problem as the more marginal groups were excluded from the labour market. The withdrawal of subsidies increased the cost of living. High inflation and the lack of automatic indexation of benefits also threatened the cohesion of the systems. The health care system of the former German Democratic Republic, based on clinics with publicly employed physicians, was folded into the West German system of self-employed medical practice. Child care facilities were withdrawn. In general, the 'marketization' of social policy diminished what many regarded as the main achievement of the former socialist countries – welfare for all at a low level (Deacon 1992). For the present, health and education services have generally been maintained, but they are coming under increasing strain as government priorities focus on privatization and economic modernization and the relative earnings of staff in them decline in relation to the more entrepreneurial sectors of the economy. Property acquired during socialist rule can typically be repossessed by former owners, and even the former socialist elite can turn their connections to business opportunity, but many in mainstream jobs have experienced a clear downward shift in income and security (Ferge 1993).

The Private Contribution to Welfare

Former socialist nations have experienced in its sharpest form the substitution of privately managed insecurity for state-guaranteed security. The increasing use of private instruments is likely to happen in the rest of Europe also, as the demand for welfare cannot be satisfied through state-financed policies. This is all the more easy because there has always been a considerable use of private and voluntary mechanisms to deliver and finance welfare. This is partly a legacy of church ownership of schools and hospitals, still strong in Belgium, the Netherlands and Italy. Considerable non-state ownership of hospitals is common, particularly in Germany and France. Use of for-profit mechanisms on the lines of car insurance is unusual, although the exceptions such as industrial accident insurance in Belgium show that it can be done.

More important are the three mechanisms where private welfare can be introduced by individual choice. *Complementary* provision is used widely in pensions: an individual takes on a pension additional to the state entitlement, secured through either individual purchase or collective bargaining. Such provision sometimes becomes virtually compulsory, as in France in 1972, where earnings-related pensions negotiated at the workplace were made mandatory. But in Britain, the Netherlands, Denmark and Sweden there is a considerable presence of 'top-up' occupational and personal pensions. In health care, France and Ireland have made extensive use of voluntary private insurance to bridge the gap between the full cost and what the state will reimburse.

Substitution allows the opting-out of individuals from the state scheme if they make comparable private provision. In Britain about half the workforce are contracted-out of the State Earnings-Related Pension Scheme, and in Germany 10 per cent opt for private health insurance because of their high earnings or self-employed status – a vestige of the days when social insurance covered only part of the workforce. Finally, *competitive* provision is a matter of paying twice over – the fee-for-service private provision in addition to the taxes which give access to public provision which is not used. This has long

Table 13.4   Demographic trends in EC countries and Scandinavia

	(1) Dependency 2020	(2) Unemployment 1993	(3) Female Participation 1990	(4) Fertility 1991	(5) Births ex-marriage (%) 1991	(6) Agriculture 1990
Finland	34.8	16.6*	72.9	1.71	25.2	8.4
Germany	33.5	8.4	56.6	1.35	15.5	3.4
Sweden	33.1	9.4	81.1	2.10	48.2	3.3
France	30.6	11.7	56.6	1.77	29.7	6.1
Denmark	30.5	12.4*	78.4	1.68	46.4	5.6
Italy	29.3	10.9	44.5	1.26	6.6	9.0
Netherlands	28.9	5.0	53.0	1.61	12.0	4.8

Norway	27.9	5.9*	71.2	1.92	38.6	6.5
Greece	27.4	9.2*	43.0	1.40	2.0	24.5
Belgium	26.9	9.5	52.4	1.57	9.1	2.7
Britain	25.5	10.4	65.1	1.82	29.7	2.1
Spain	25.3	22.3	40.9	1.28	9.1	11.8
Portugal	23.9	5.7*	61.3	1.42	15.6	17.8
Ireland	18.7	19.5*	38.9	2.18	16.6	15.0
EC average	27.3	–	53.6	1.58	19.8	6.5

Sources: (1) OECD, *The Future of Social Protection* (1988), table 9 (projected population 65+ as percentage of population 15–64); (2) *The Economist* 25 September 1993, p. 151 (July/August data) or *OECD, *Economic Outlook* 53, June 1993, table 54 (estimated annual average); (3) OECD, *Historical Statistics, 1960–1990* (Paris 1992), table 2.8 (labour force as percentage of population 15–64); (4) (total period fertility rate) and (5) *Eurostat Rapid Reports* 2, 1992, table 2; (6) OECD, *Historical Statistics, 1960–1990*, table 2.9 (employment in agriculture as percentage of population 15–64).

been the case in private education, where voucher schemes redeemable at any school have never taken root. It is common in health care in systems where the nominal right to free medical services proves inadequate and physicians have the right to mix public and private work – Italy, Spain, Portugal and, to a growing extent, Britain.

The full potential of these private financing mechanisms has not yet been exploited. An obvious answer to public sector financial strains is to mobilize private finance, either by leaving bridgeable gaps between what is provided and what is desired, or by using rationing procedures that threaten the security of public provision. Bismarckian social insurance is typically inflexible in this respect, tending to include or exclude whole occupational groups and specify exact contribution and benefit ratios. The British approach has been more flexible – especially in the encouragement of personal pensions since 1988 – and may have lessons to offer in a European Community where the barriers to a free market in commercial insurance are being lifted.

The non-uniformity of welfare state development suggests that particular patterns of mobilization in the political process are more important than some general product of economic diffusion or modernization. The identification of 'types' or 'worlds' is convenient but misleading because in practice social policy has been relatively insulated from the international pressures that have forced an extrinsic orientation for most countries' security and economic policy, culminating in NATO and the EC. The question that now emerges is whether in the 1990s pressures will arise – from European integration, new social patterns and the growth in international free trade – to harmonize social policies in the same way.

The Unevenness of EC Intervention

The European Community has had only a limited impact on most aspects of social policy. For instance, it does not control access to health care, drug prices, ages of compulsory education, the level of pensions or rights to social assistance; and yet it can intervene in great detail in matters such as health and safety in the workplace, food hygiene and trade tariffs. As Leibfried points out, 'in the European Community, as well as the USA, agriculture was the first "internal" domain to be nationalised' (Leibfried 1993, 134), and takes up nearly half of the community budget while accounting for only 6.5 per cent of the workforce (table 13.4). The explanation for this unevenness can be traced to two themes in European integration. First, the community has from the start won consent to deep intervention in specific fields where political and economic interests demanded it, starting with the Coal and Steel Community in 1952 and proceeding through the Common Agricultural Policy to a common external trade tariff. Secondly, the extent of variation in social policy permissible in a common market or single internal market is not clear. In particular, non-wage burdens on employers to pay for health care or pensions may distort competitiveness in a way similar to differential subsidies to industry, but member states have not been prepared to concede uniformity.

Because of this political uncertainty EC social policy has developed on legalistic lines. Free movement of labour required the transferability of benefits, which was achieved by article 51 of the Treaty of Rome. Regulations, reinforced by a body of case law in the European Court of Justice (over 250 cases), have enforced the principles of non-discrimination (migrant workers must be treated the same as domestic ones when enrolling for schemes, and freed from the requirement to have worked or resided in a particular country for a set number of years before qualifying for the full rate of benefit) and exportation of all benefits payable from the country where title was earned to the present country of residence (e.g., when someone receiving unemployment benefit moves elsewhere in the EC to seek work, though this right is limited to three months). These rights have been extended to the families of migrants, but are confined to benefits paid as part of the contributory social insurance system and do not include discretionary social assistance. On the whole the Court has been a strong champion of citizenship rights against discrimination and has tended to ratchet upwards the somewhat ambiguous equal protection measures in the treaties (Meehan 1993).

Such measures take the form of 'co-ordination', defined by John Holloway as 'attempts to minimise the loss of rights suffered by those who move from one national system to another' (Holloway 1981, 5). In principle they can be done by bilateral arrangements between countries. The distinctive EC concept is that of 'harmonization', the implied upward convergence of best practice as an end in itself and to prevent unfair competition by countries who do not offer good social protection – so-called social dumping. In 1958 the French were in favour of such provisions for fear that the generous income maintenance secured by collective bargaining for most of their workers would disadvantage them within the common market. Other nations were opposed and the result was a compromise: vague hopes for 'approximation of provisions' (article 117) and 'close co-operation' (article 118) without the means of enforcing them.

The most fruitful opening for harmonization eventually came with article 119, calling for equal pay. Originally intended to outlaw the most obvious discrimination in pay rates, this was strengthened by a directive in 1975 to encompass work of equal value, leading to case law at the European Court – notably a series of cases brought by Gabrielle Defrenne against the Belgian airline Sabena. Another major opening came with directives of 1986 to extend equal treatment to pensions, the basis of the 'Barber vs Guardian Royal

Exchange' judgement of 17 May 1990, which outlawed lower pension payments for women than for men caused by different ages of retirement, so forcing the raising of pensions to disadvantaged women and the equalization of rules between the genders. So expensive were the implications of this that the heads of government inserted a protocol in the Maastricht Treaty to prevent the policy taking retrospective effect from before the date of the ruling. The position taken by the Court's Advocate General in May 1993 suggests that this protocol will be legally robust. The Barber ruling applies to occupational pensions only, in their capacity as part of the remuneration of workers, but the equalization of benefits and retirement ages for state pensions is also a European trend under the pressure of rising costs as well as EU norms.

The EC has had since 1977 three 'Poverty Programmes' which have gathered together information and financed small demonstration projects in the member states. Defining poverty as expenditure of less than half the national average (a relative concept not all would accept), the proportion in poverty in the EC was 15.5 per cent in both 1980 and 1985. The average masks a considerable increase in Britain (from 14.6 to 18.2 per cent of the population, which has continued since) and Italy (14.1 to 15.5 per cent) (Eurostat 1990, table 1). The Commission – through its Directorate-General V which deals with social affairs – has been active in discouraging social exclusion as a policy objective, but it lacks the policy instruments to do much about it. A Green Paper was issued by D-G V in 1993, and a White Paper in 1994, about future agendas for European social policy, emphasizing the growth of employment as a key objective (European Commission 1994).

The Single European Act of 1986 gave a new, and from the point of view of the British government unintended, impetus to harmonization by introducing two articles allowing policy to be made by a qualified majority: 100A on 'the establishment and functioning of the internal market' and 118A on 'encouraging improvements, especially in the working environment, as regards the health and safety of workers'. This provided the teeth for the Commission's 'Action Programme' of 1989, inspired by the 'Community Charter of the fundamental Social Rights of Workers', known as the 'Social Charter', a non-legal declaration adopted by all EC countries other than Britain in December 1989. At the Maastricht summit, these eleven adopted the 'Social Chapter' to allow them to use EC processes to implement the Social Charter. The 'Social Protocol' agreed by all twelve allows the United Kingdom not to take part in the deliberations and adoption of any such proposals. Two points should be noted: even within the Social Chapter, social security and collective bargaining require unanimity, and wherever possible the Commission is likely to seek to incorporate all twelve members by using existing treaty procedures as modified by the Single European Act. Hence there are still disputes with the British government on directives about maximum hours of work, which are likely to require European Court of Justice adjudication on the permissible limits of articles 100A and 118A.

This whole process has revealed a lack of consensus on the meaning of the 'social sphere' in the politics of the European Community. In the legal sense, the concept of subsidiarity has been seized upon to circumscribe the community's field of action. It culminated in article 3b of the Maastricht Treaty, which seeks to allow EC action in fields that are not its exclusive responsibility 'only if and in so far as the objectives of the proposed action cannot be sufficiently achieved by the member states and can therefore, by reason of the scale or effects of the proposed action, be better achieved by the Community.' This is more a slogan than a definition, inserted at the insistence of the British government, and is unlikely to be legally actionable or to impede moves to harmonization. It does not address the question of how far social protection is a right of citizenship that might be guaranteed at the European level.

The problem is that the presumption of the Treaty of Rome was that economic growth would be accompanied by a broadening of social rights and social protection in a manner characteristic of European history since the 1880s. The community had a particular conception of social policy – expressed in the Social Fund and Economic and Social Committee – based upon bargaining between organized labour and employers and seeking to cushion workers against the effects of economic adjustment, initially the rundown of the coal industry. It has not been comfortable with 'Thatcherite' notions about the necessity of economic change and the undesirability of national level bargaining between employers and workers.

The Impact of New Social Patterns

The welfare state relies upon patterns of social and economic behaviour that maintain a balance between contributors and beneficiaries – that the number of people paying in as taxpayers will be greater than those drawing out pensions, benefits, education and health care. In most cases the redistribution is across the life-cycle, with some periods of work and others of dependence, but in some cases individuals will require support for the whole of their lives. More importantly, at any one time there can be an imbalance between the dependent and non-dependent population, posing problems for systems funded on a 'pay-as-you-go' basis where the actual income and expenditure for the current year are more important than the level of deferred income being built up. The length of perspective necessary to see the value of social protection is usually denied to governments which have to manage budgets year to year and win elections at frequent intervals.

The result tends to be a periodical concern with worst-case scenarios in which the working-age population seems to be overwhelmed by children or the elderly. Two ratios are important. The first is the simple one of population, between those of working-age and the rest. The second is between the number of contributors to pension schemes and the number of beneficiaries. This takes account of varying ages of transition from school to work and from work to retirement, and the level of participation of females in the workforce. As economies develop, the second ratio becomes the more important.

The main variable in the demographic balance is the number of children born to each woman of child-bearing age. This has shown a dramatic decline since the 1960s to fall below the 2.1 level needed to replace the population in the long-term (table 13.4). Only Ireland is above this level, and several Southern European countries are well below a fertility rate of 1.5. Sweden has recently seen an upturn in the birth rate which may be linked to the generosity of parental benefits and the advantage of maintaining entitlement by having a further child. Another – though in fact negatively correlated – phenomenon is the high number of births outside marriage in Northern European countries. This is a sociological phenomenon – why have marriage and childbearing become less popular? – but is also a financial threat, since in about 2020 the participation of this small age-group in the labour market will coincide with the retirement of the large age-group represented by their parents, and the family structures to support the dependent population may no longer be in place. Table 13.4 shows that in that year the 65+ age group will in some countries be one-third as large as those of working age. Further projections taking account of labour force participation suggest that, by 2040, on present patterns there will be 2.37 dependents per person employed in the Netherlands, and 1.88 in Germany (against respectively 1.84 and 1.35 in 1986). Sweden, on the other hand, is projected to rise only from 0.94 to 1.05 because of the benefit of its higher birth rate and higher labour market participation (Gillion 1991, table 1). As Sweden has at present the oldest population in Europe, this illustrates the scope for addressing the dependency problem by expanding the labour force.

Responses to demographic challenges tend to vary according to whether or not the insurance is funded and uses estimates of future revenue and expenditure. In funded schemes where any deficit becomes clearly visible, as in France and the United States, corrective action through increased contributions is likely and has tended to win popular consent. In Germany there is a political culture of concern about these matters and some potential for correction by increasing the present low rate of female participation in the workforce. The Pensions Reform Act of 1992 in Germany represented a cautious first step to increasing the retirement age and making pensions less generous. But in

Southern Europe especially, the political consensus needed to deal with deficits may be lacking, and the demands for social benefits are an important reason why the disciplines required for a common European currency may not be met.

Also relevant are unconventional labour market patterns – part-time and casual work, migrant labour, short-time working supported by public funds (as in Italy and Eastern Germany) – which may undermine social insurance systems that assume a lifetime of contributions. Migrant labour can be significant: 9 per cent of the Belgian and 7 per cent of the German population are not citizens of the country, 2 per cent of German residents being citizens of Turkey; 14 per cent of Irish citizens, 8 per cent of Portuguese and 4 per cent of Greeks live elsewhere in the EC (Eurostat 1993, table 1 and figure 11). Many countries have ambitious targets of earnings replacement for retirees with a full contribution record, on average 75 per cent in the European Union, but the average pension actually received is much less. In short, social policies designed with a particular view of the labour market in mind may be ill-equipped to deal with new social patterns, and thus make welfare states seem unsustainable in the face of economic pressures.

Welfare and Economic Growth

The biggest lesson of the past twenty years is that social policy cannot operate independently of the national economy. This idea functions on at least three levels. At the financial level, it is necessary to maintain an alignment between expenditure, receipts and the expansion of the national economy. Divergences can be tolerated, especially during recession, but in political terms the pressures against deficits or the expansion of welfare spending at the expense of other categories have tended to prove decisive in recent years. At the economic level, the signals about individual behaviour sent out by the welfare system need to be compatible with the place of labour in what remain capitalist economic systems. This has checked the 'decommodification' tendency found in Scandinavian and former Eastern European welfare. This is defined by Esping-Andersen as 'the degree to which individuals, or families, can uphold a socially acceptable standard of living independently of market participation' (Esping-Andersen 1990, 37), meaning that personal incomes become detached from the market-place 'worth' of an individual's labour through high taxation and benefits to those not in work. The welfare system and the labour market cannot indefinitely send out conflicting signals about the place of work in people's lives and the appropriate labour market behaviour (e.g., age of entry into the labour market, participation by parents, how bad disability needs to be to prevent work, and the age at which it is permissible to retire from a particular occupation). At the international level, a country must trade its goods and price the labour and welfare component of them in accordance with international norms. The liberal free trade impulse of the EC has achieved a decisive philosophical victory the world over, including North America. A whole volume entitled *Can the Welfare State Compete?* was relatively sanguine on the point, distinguishing between the 'performing' competitiveness necessary to resist inflation and sell products on world markets, and the 'underlying' form which allows higher prices and rewards to workers to be sustained by quality and productivity (Pfaller et al. 1991, 6).

More recently, opinion in the EC seems to have seen the issue with greater urgency. In 1993 Jacques Delors prepared a White Paper on the poor employment record of the EC relative to other countries, and the British government was eagerly exploiting its advantage on non-wage costs (one deriving in large part from the fact that health care is financed through taxation without employers' contributions). The criteria set at Maastricht for the convergence of EC economies to a single currency were manifestly failing to be met, and a sharp recession hit most of the EC in 1992–3. No longer can external factors such as oil prices be blamed; the EC's problems seem to have a worryingly 'structural' element. In such an economic context, sociological malfunctions such as racial violence and support for protest parties fuel an atmosphere of crisis in which the whole context in which people lead their lives becomes questioned. It is then a short step to regard welfare as a force undermining the agencies of responsibility political scientists have long identified as essential to the stable functioning of the political system. This, as well as more specific problems of financing the level of welfare politicians wish to offer, has been the background to the so-called crisis of the welfare state, first apparent in the 1970s and reappearing at intervals since.

The Rhetoric of Crisis and Burden

Once we understand the relationship between social policy and economic growth, much of the recent debate about welfare becomes explicable. In the 1980s, a kind of stasis seemed to have been achieved in which tolerable levels of social expenditure are maintained by a balancing-act between rising demands and expectations on the one hand and the search for acceptable cuts on the other. It is a dispiriting process which robs welfare of its original purpose. Technically, cuts are quite easy to make in systems which have earnings-related contributions or benefits; the percentage level of either is altered, and if necessary the length of time in which benefits are paid, or for which contributions are required to have been paid, is altered. Cuts in services in kind (health and education) can be made decrementally by rationing supply or making the qualifications to receive provision more stringent.

Two cases are instructive. Germany after reunification lost the careful political and economic stability built up so well in the Federal Republic. The eastern states required the injection of large capital investment and welfare subsidies, which risked an economic overheating during a time of world recession (circumstances typical of the oil crisis in 1973). At the same time, there was pressure for new provision, notably for the inclusion of nursing-home care for the elderly and handicapped in medical insurance, and a consensus protecting the relationship of contributions and payments in the unemployment benefit funds. It proved possible to implement firm policies – such as the sharp curbs on drug prices in 1993 and the agreement in 1994 to finance nursing care by increased contributions and the removal of a public holiday – but the welfare state has come to be a source of tension rather than satisfaction in the political system.

For Sweden, the election of the Bildt government in 1991 intensified trends that had already begun to emerge – privatization, unemployment, and questioning of the high level of automatic benefits (Gould 1993, pt 3). By early 1994 unemployment was over 9 per cent (table 13.4), with 4 per cent more supported by Labour Market Board schemes. The factor precipitating action was the weakness of the currency in 1992, which prompted an all-party agreement to reduce welfare benefits. The pension age was increased (gradually) from 65 to 67; sickness benefit was removed for the first day of absence, reduced thereafter and financed solely by employers and employees; and housing subsidies were cut (Olsson and McMurphy 1993). Higher VAT allowed a reduction in the high level of employers' social security contributions, which in 1991 were at 15 per cent of GDP – the highest in the Western world (Central Statistical Office 1994). EC entry was adduced as the reason for these measures, but there was a philosophical turning away from the 'soft' nature of the Swedish welfare state towards a 'continental' approach akin to German Christian Democracy, with Carl Bildt taking on the role of Chancellor Helmut Kohl's favourite son. In these ways, the two traditional 'homes' of the welfare state, Germany and Sweden, drifted away from their old philosophical foundations under the pressure of the 1990s.

Conclusion: the Withering Welfare State?

Recent developments prompt the conclusion that the new Europe will be not so much a welfare state as a functional state, with a sufficient degree of state welfare to support a competitive, free market economic system. Expenditure will stabilize at around 30 per cent of GDP (more during economic recessions), which implies pressure on the generosity of benefits as populations age. Spending on health and social care will continue to rise while education will fall as a share of GDP. Most importantly, the boundary between public and private financing of essential welfare services will begin to blur. Co-payment, complementarity and user charges will be used to extract the maximum direct contribution. Pensions will become more of an occupational benefit on the British model and perhaps be extracted from the public sector accounts.

For European governments, the independent ideological force of state welfare will be lost in a bigger political and economic framework, especially on provision for old age. It is a sad and rather paradoxical outcome to much of the principled impetus for state welfare as a liberator of personal potential and a gift of the responsible state to those whose functioning was temporarily or permanently impaired. Capitalism is now coming as a package deal, particularly to former socialist countries and to the Scandinavian applicants for EC membership. At the moment, the welfare state is expensive but unloved. It is extraordinarily diverse, given the economic homogeneity of Europe; entitlements and transfers taken for granted in some countries are not available elsewhere.

The European Community has proved to be a rather poor integrative mechanism. It has virtually no money to spend on pure social policy (just a few initiatives in education and public health); its so-called Social Action Programmes since 1974 are more about worker participation in industry than about social rights; and the social aspects of its industrial and agricultural policy are dubious. National governments have not accorded it competence in the fields of social services and benefit transfers to individuals. The factors of production (labour, technology and capital investment) have not redistributed themselves around the community to enforce a market-driven harmonization of working conditions.

The natural political mechanism for correcting this differentiation would be transnational political parties, operating through the European Parliament and emphasizing cross-European standards in their national elections. Again, this looks no more likely than does massive movement of workers within the community in search of better economic prospects. We must expect continued economic disturbance around the EC as traditional industries strive to compete in newly liberated world markets. For its part, the welfare state may never again be able to offer the technical instruments or the philosophical impetus it provided in that happier postwar age when reconstruction rather than deconstruction was the watchword, and everything seemed possible in the delicate area where state action and individual behaviour interact in search of end-states of happiness and growth.

Bibliography

Alber, J. (1988). 'Is there a crisis of the welfare state?' *European Sociological Review* 4: 181–201.

Baldwin, P. (1990). *The Politics of Social Solidarity*. Cambridge: Cambridge University Press.

Central Statistical Office (1994). 'Taxes and social security contributions: an international comparison, 1981–1991'. *Economic Trends* February: 96.

Commission of the European Communities (1994). *Social Protection in Europe*. Luxembourg: Office for Official Publications of the European Communities.

Deacon, B. et al. (1992). *The New Eastern Europe: social policy past, present and future*. London: Sage.

Esping-Andersen, G. (1990). *The Three Worlds of Welfare Capitalism*. Cambridge: Polity Press.

—— (1993). 'The comparative macro-sociology of welfare states', in L. Moreno (ed.), *Social Exchange and Welfare Development*. Madrid: CSIC.

European Commission (1994). *European Social Policy: a way forward for the Union*. Luxembourg: Official Publications of the European Communities, COM (94) 333.

Eurostat (1990). 'Inequality and poverty in Europe, 1980–1985'. *Rapid Reports* 7.

Eurostat (1993). 'Population and citizenship in the EC, 1.1.91'. *Rapid Reports* 6.

Ferge, Z. (1993). 'Winners and losers after the collapse of state socialism', in R. Page and J. Baldock (eds), *Social Policy Review 5*. Canterbury: Social Policy Association.

Flora, P. (1986). *Growth to Limits: the Western European welfare states since World War II*, vol. 1. Berlin: de Gruyter.

Flora, P. and Heidenheimer, A. J. (eds) (1981). *The Development of Welfare States in Europe and America*. London: Transaction Books.

Flora, P. and Alber, J. (1981). 'Modernization, democratization and the development of welfare states in Western Europe', in P. Flora and A. J. Heidenheimer (eds), *The Development of Welfare States in Europe and America*. London: Transaction Books.

Gillion, C. (1991). 'Ageing populations: spreading the costs'. *Journal of European Social Policy* 1: 107–128.

Gillion, C. and Richard Henry (1985). 'Social expenditure in the United Kingdom in a comparative context', in R. Klein and M. O'Higgins (eds), *The Future of Welfare*. Oxford: Blackwell.

Ginsburg, N. (1992). *Divisions of Welfare*. London: Sage.

Gould, A. (1993). *Capitalist Welfare Systems*. London: Longman.

Holloway, J. (1981). *Social Policy Harmonisation in the European Community*. Farnborough: Gower.

Immergut, E. (1992). *Health Politics*. Cambridge: Cambridge University Press.

Klein, R. (1993). 'O'Goffe's tale – or what can we learn from the success of capitalist welfare states?' in C. Jones (ed.), *New Perspectives on the Welfare State in Europe*. London: Routledge.

Korpi, W. (1989). 'Power, politics and state autonomy in the development of social citizenship: social rights during sickness in eighteen OECD countries since 1930'. *American Sociological Review* 54: 309–28.

—— (1991). 'Political and economic explanations for unemployment: a cross-national and long-term analysis'. *British Journal of Political Science* 21: 315–48.

Leibfried, S. (1993). 'Towards a European Welfare State?' in C. Jones (ed.), *New Perspectives on the Welfare State in Europe*. London: Routledge.

Meehan, E. (1993). *Citizenship and the European Community*. London: Sage.

Mishra, R. (1990). *The Welfare State in Capitalist Society*. London: Harvester Wheatsheaf.

O'Connor, J. (1973). *The Fiscal Crisis of the State*. New York: St Martin's Press.

OECD (Organization for Economic Cooperation and Development) (1985). *Social Protection, 1960–1990*. Paris: OECD.

—— (1988). *The Future of Social Protection*. Paris: OECD.

Olsson, S. and McMurphy, S. (1993). 'Social policy in Sweden: the Swedish model in transition', in R. Page and J. Baldock (eds), *Social Policy Review 5*. Canterbury: Social Policy Association.

Pfaller, A. et al. (eds) (1991). *Can the Welfare State Compete?* London: Macmillan.

Power, A. (1993). *Hovels to High Rise: state housing in Europe since 1850*. London: Routledge.

Rokkan, S. and Urwin D. W. (1983). *Economy, Territory, Identity*. London: Sage.

Spicker, P. (1991). 'The principle of subsidiarity and the social policy of the European Community'. *Journal of European Social Policy* 1: 3–14.

Wilensky, H. L. (1981). 'Leftism, Catholicism and democratic corporatism: the role of political parties in recent welfare state development', in P. Flora and A. J. Heidenheimer (eds), *The Development of Welfare States in Europe and America*. London: Transaction Books.

14

Governing the New Europe

Jack Hayward

The claim that politics in Europe is at a turning-point is both trite and true. But we must be careful not to assume the mantle of those who, throughout the 1960s, the 1970s and much of the 1980s confidently predicted the coming crisis of capitalism and the capitalist state only to see it survive without any major challenger in the 1990s. The nature, pace and direction of major political change are often the result of events which cannot be anticipated, while anticipated developments can be thrown off course by unexpected events. Compared with such twentieth-century predictions of the way in which Europe might be expected to develop as the widely anticipated corporatist state of the 1930s or the end of ideology of the 1960s, Tocqueville's *Democracy in America* provided in the 1830s a much more accurate assessment of contemporary trends and extrapolation of their implications for Europe. In late twentieth-century Europe we have no such model that offers a glimpse of the future. Instead we have a series of challenges to old certainties. Whether these will produce radically different systems of government is beyond our capacity to anticipate.

The most significant cause of these uncertainties is the disappearance of the Iron Curtain. 1989 marked the moment at which the stalemate of East–West confrontation, which had dominated the preceding four decades, dissolved, taking with it many of the associated dichotomies – ideological, political, economic and military. It came abruptly and was the source of much self-congratulation among those who claimed the credit for their firmness in the prolonged period of deadlock that was overshadowed by the threat of nuclear war. While Europe was the potential battleground, the nations of Western Europe were dependent upon American power and support to counter-balance the threat from the Soviet Union. Since 1989, the retrospectively reassuring continuities have been displaced by the prospect of bewildering unpredictabilities.

It quickly became clear that those who had anticipated that the rejection of the polarities of the past would allow rapid pan-European convergence to take place were gravely mistaken. Western models – economic, technological, political, cultural – could not simply be transposed eastward. The end of the Cold War had not merely destabilized the countries of communist East Europe. It had also destabilized capitalist West Europe, which had been deprived of its polar opposite. Having organized itself to cope with a life and death struggle for world supremacy, the adjustments required were varied and unprecedented. We are still trying to understand the dimensions of the problems posed and to devise ways of containing those that cannot for the present be resolved.

The collapse of communism had three types of impact upon our understanding of West European political development. Firstly, it has produced or sustained *counter-trends to patterns that we had presumed would dominate*. This is especially the case with the resurgence of nationalism as the basis for a self-determining political community and the increasing penetration and subversion of attempts at state protectionism by the businesses that operate in a competitive international market economy. While the preoccupation with national interests, to preserve national culture, assert national power and promote national business, has been a permanent feature of international relations, the change from the postwar positive-sum context of uninterrupted economic expansion to the zero-sum years of stagnation, revival and recession since 1973 has exacerbated conflicts. The post-communist revival of repressed nationalism in East-Central Europe has reinforced the priority accorded to national interests in Western Europe, with paradoxical implications for European integration. The existing members of the EU have hesitated to make the institutional and policy changes necessary to sustain the integrative impetus and have adopted a defensive posture aimed to preserve the gains made from the arrival of impecunious candidates. The very capitalistic market economy, which had proved its superiority to the monopolistic command economy, seemed incapable of absorbing the East-Central European converts, both their products and their would-be migrants. The old nemesis of mass unemployment, which was thought to have been banished in both communist and non-communist Europe by different types of state intervention, had returned to encourage 'beggar my neighbour' attitudes, antithetical to both regional and global internationalism.

Secondly, the collapse of communist regimes in Central and Eastern Europe has *highlighted problems of liberal democracy*. This form of political system – which had appeared to be sweeping all before it as the only source of legitimate political authority – seemed to be losing touch with the mass public. In East-Central Europe, this appears to have occurred almost as soon as the initial period of euphoria had evaporated. The bewildering multiplicity of 'flash' parties was failing to link the insecurely established governing elites and the voters, even though the one-party system's pretence of unanimous and indefectible support had so recently and conclusively been exposed as a sham. This has often led (in Poland and Hungary, but not the Czech Republic) to a despairing recourse to redesignated and redesigned communist parties in the hope of rescuing some security of employment and livelihood from the wreckage of the past and the unfulfilled promise of the future. While class-based politics has continued its retreat in the countries of Western Europe, the disappearance of the communist regimes of East-Central Europe has not removed the incentive to vote for parties that protect the interests of the working classes, especially exposed to the winds of economic liberalization.

As well as the party proliferation that resulted from the abrupt liberalization of the political process in East-Central Europe, the rebirth of a repressed civil society has led to a proliferation of social movements which cannot be subsumed under a left–right dichotomy. The capacity of the mainstream political parties, with their associated organized interests and auxiliary associations, to integrate their supporters into clearly demarcated camps, has weakened in Western Europe, though in a less precipitate and spectacular fashion than in East-Central Europe. There, trade unions acquired the right to independence from state control, together with the freedom to organize strikes, while in West Europe their membership has often been in serious decline. This was in large measure due to increased unemployment, which meant that the interests of their members were badly in need of defence at a time when their capacity to organize successful strikes was weak.

The loss of public support for mainstream parties and the big organized interests has been reflected partly in the decline in their membership and electoral support, which has taken the form of abstention or a switch of votes to other organizations. The re-emergence of the extreme right, after decades of postwar insignificance, has been a salient feature of the late 1980s and early 1990s in many parts of Europe. These national-populist parties rely upon the voters having forgotten much and learnt little from the past. Apart from in Italy, following the 1994 elections, they have not managed to gain sufficient acceptance to become partners in a coalition government. The emergence of a variety of new social movements, particularly green and feminist movements, as well as revived regionalist movements, has prompted the major parties to compete with one another in seeking to incorporate their demands, thereby minimizing the danger of losing votes. The 1994 European elections resulted in notable successes for feminist campaigners. In the ten countries with a list voting system (apart from Ireland and the UK), the number of women given a winnable place markedly increased, although few went as far as the French Socialist Party's adoption of strict alternation – one man, one woman – in the composition of its list of candidates. While there has been some incorporation of green candidates by the mainstream parties, in their case it is their rhetoric and to a lesser extent their programme that have been selectively adopted.

Thirdly, the collapse of communism has seemed to highlight the inaccuracy of many predictions and assumptions about the course of political development in the West. Certain apparently well-established features of European political institutions have been more or less drastically modified in the emerging new Europe. It was a commonplace of political analysis that legislatures and judiciaries were doomed to humiliating domination by political, bureaucratic and technocratic executives. This was blindingly obvious in the communist countries, albeit under the control of a would-be totalitarian party. Even in West Europe, the commitment to a nominal parliamentary sovereignty and the associated rejection of the *Rechtsstaat* seemed to preclude any challenge to executive power. Nevertheless, parliaments have played a more active role in recent years. They have emerged from subservience to rightwing dictatorships in Southern Europe and from communist dictatorships in East-Central Europe. In Western and Northern Europe, parliaments have become somewhat less subordinate to governments. This has occurred not merely where coalition or minority governments mean that support cannot be presumed upon as a general rule. It has also obtained in Britain, where discipline within parliamentary parties has been more difficult to enforce, so that concessions can be negotiated and legislation amended accordingly.

There have been more far-reaching developments within the adjudication process. European judiciaries, which were traditionally denied the capacity to exercise control over the decisions of a formally sovereign parliament and an actually supreme executive, have acquired the power of review over laws and administrative acts if they are judged to have violated the constitution. Although the lead was taken by Austria and Czechoslovakia in 1920, constitutional courts with review powers really developed in non-communist Europe only after the Second World War, with Austria once again to the fore. While the encroachment upon legislative-executive supremacy in West Europe has been gradual, patchy and prudent, it has been extended with increasing judicial confidence, public support and executive tolerance or resignation. Although the creation of effective constitutional courts in the ex-communist countries had to await the change of regime, the ground had nevertheless been cautiously prepared by institutions such as the Polish Constitutional Tribunal from the early 1980s.

An endemic tension between the liberal attempt to exercise judicial constraints upon the democratic claim to an uninhibited legislative-executive sovereignty exercised by government exists throughout and beyond Europe. Constitutional courts have been probing to see just 'how far they can go too far' before provoking a legislative-executive backlash such as occurred both in France and Russia in 1993. In France, the conflict was prompted by the Constitutional Council's assertion of the priority of the constitutional right to asylum over a proposed statutory restriction. The Balladur government was able to have the last word by amending the constitution. In Russia, the clash between President Yeltsin and the President of the Constitutional Court (who sided with the parliament) ended more dramatically with the latter's resignation. Clearly, we are still a long way from the bogey of a 'government by judges'. However, the European Court of Justice, in the absence of a strong EU executive or legislative authority, has played an increasingly assertive role in giving expansive practical effect to the often opaque terms in which the European treaties are couched.

This brings us to another major source of change within Europe. It would be misleading to argue that challenges to established ideas about government in Europe have come exclusively from the influence of East-Central Europe. The chapters in this volume have shown how, even before the collapse of communism, Europeans were experiencing change in the values they attributed to government and politics, parties and party systems, the nature and structure of the welfare state and its administrative organization. The reasons for these changes have been discussed in the chapters concerned. However, one underlying home-grown cause of change, which has had wide-ranging implications for our political life, has been the expansion of the European Union, both in the size of the European citizenry it serves as well as the range of government activities it shapes. While the EU's political institutions are currently in the melting pot, in the run-up to the 1996 Intergovernmental Conference, the member states, the European Council of Ministers, Commission and Parliament are grappling with the prospects and consequences of enlargement. Having so far managed to operate without a government, there is discussion of the need to move beyond a rotating presidency every six months, but this implies a decisive institutional move from intergovernmentalism towards a more integrated political system. Just as the relative attractions of the semi-presidential and prime ministerial executive models have been attentively examined by the constitution makers of East-Central Europe, a similar choice will eventually have to be made in the EU. The exceptional French presidential style has been preferred by some ex-communist countries, but others have adopted the predominant West European arrangement of a prime minister and government accountable to parliament.

It would now be generally accepted that the interdependence of domestic and foreign policies has become so intricate that, although they may be (with difficulty) distinguished, they can seldom be separated. This is particularly evident in the field of European political economy. Attempts by national governments to 'go it alone', notably by the protection and promotion of national champion firms, have increasingly come to grief or succumbed – willingly or unwillingly – to transnational merger or takeover. The combination of international competitive pressures and the single European market has compelled collaboration or fusion. The logic driving policies of industrial patriotism was closely related to the preoccupation with national defence from times when the preparation for and the waging of war was the prime concern of governments. The urge to maximize national power and to minimize the insecurity and unpredictability deriving from co-existence with states pursuing similar objectives took pride of place. However, even in the arms manufacturing industries which most directly reflected such priorities, technological, financial and marketing imperatives have led the increasingly high-tech firms simultaneously to strengthen their links to national governments and to collaborate in joint ventures to share escalating costs and the markets required to ensure commercial viability.

In the 1990s, economic globalization and the need to collaborate for mutual defence have exerted contrasting effects in Europe. COMECON and the Warsaw Treaty Organization have disappeared. The attempts by the EU to move towards economic and monetary union and to resolve the tensions between a NATO that doubts its continuing *raison d'être* and WEU that has yet to fill the gap that would be left by an American withdrawal from Europe have so far been inconclusive. The EU's 'Eastern Policy' floats uneasily and nebulously between NATO's Partnership for Peace and the Conference on Security and Cooperation in Europe, which postpone important decisions in the hope that choices will become clearer. Furthermore, the major West European states set different store by these complementary-cum-competing inter-governmental organizations. Before Clinton's accession to the US presidency, Britain relied primarily upon NATO and France upon WEU, while Germany and Italy sought actively to support both organizations. With all countries seeking substantially to reduce their military expenditure, the day of the stage army, with many more 'hats' than personnel, seems to have arrived. Such defence on the cheap means that there are embarrassingly fewer troops available to meet the continuing calls upon them.

Whether the new Europe will become a coherent and effective entity or a diffuse mosaic, with each country selecting its commitments *à la carte*, will depend upon whether it acquires a sense of direction. The need to bargain and compromise is unavoidable, but an impetus will have to be imparted if the EU is not to acquire the unattractive characteristics of an ectoplasm. From the 1950s to the 1980s the initiatives were principally taken thanks to a partnership between France and Germany, with France as the senior partner. In the 1990s, following political reunification and the increasingly dominant role of the Bundesbank in monetary policy, Germany has emerged as the potential senior partner. However, it has not yet asserted itself sufficiently to play this role outside the economic sphere, partly because of its handicap in the military sphere, although the German Constitutional Court's July 1994 decision authorizing deployment of German forces outside the NATO area, under United Nations auspices, has begun to reduce this inhibition. The embryonic and strictly inter-governmental character of the post-Maastricht common foreign and security policy explains the EU's failure to play a decisive role in the Bosnian war, despite French and British humanitarian intervention, with the confusion being compounded by the involvement of NATO and the United Nations. Nevertheless, 'Middle Europe' is reasserting its importance, with Germany simultaneously pursuing an active East-Central European policy and a still predominant West European policy.

From the mid-1980s, there has also been a drastic redirection of the normative framework within which European economic policies have been made and carried out. Instead of the dominant role played by national governments (especially finance ministries) and public enterprises, increasingly transnational private sector banks and firms have been acknowledged as the decisive actors and their priorities have shaped public policies. Within the context of controlling inflation rather than pursuing full employment as the prime objective of macro-economic policy, power has shifted from finance ministries to increasingly autonomous central banks in the conduct of monetary policy. Financial markets have been liberalized as part of a programme of deregulation which has promoted the firm operating in the market as a free competitor.

The electorally popular wish by governments to reduce taxation and public expenditure has contributed to the urge to denationalize public enterprise. Privatization has swept Europe from West to East, as this British-initiated fashion spread via France and later Germany (through the post-unification activities of the Treuhand) to Central and East Europe, and then to Russia. Privatization has contributed not merely to the withdrawal of state control but also to the loss of national ownership, despite attempts – notably in France and Italy – to restrict the 'invasion' of foreign capital. Only in Italy has big business, in the shape of Silvio Berlusconi's Fininvest, directly obtained control over a national government, although business skills – especially when allied to control over the mass media – are now regarded as an attractive qualification for wielding political power in some European countries.

The EC's role in creating a single market, as well as reducing trade barriers, public procurement protectionism and state subsidies, has reinforced the role of globalized firms in a competitive international environment. There is resistance to following through to economic and monetary union in general and a common currency in particular because of the demanding convergence criteria that are judged to be their necessary prerequisites if governments as well as firms are to operate with maximum effectiveness. These aspirations remain difficult to achieve by inter-governmental consensus and will occupy the arena of debate within the EU in the second half of the 1990s.

Governing the constituent states of the new Europe has become more difficult as public support has weakened, while the politicians and senior civil servants have lost credibility and legitimacy. Despite their efforts to lower public expectations, they have still failed to satisfy them. The pride of place accorded to business leaders does not fill the vacuum because they constitute a self-perpetuating hard core of non-state decision-makers who cannot be held accountable and do not feel committed to any particular community, national or European. Hence national governments and the EU have to reregulate business activities to protect collective interests as the international economic environment shifts in unpredictable ways. The end of the Cold War has not merely made state boundaries uncertain but has dissolved the relatively stable polarities around which Europe's states could organize their actions. It has allowed historic diversities to re-emerge, as well as stressing the urgent need to reinforce the countervailing impulse towards European integration if the perennial objectives of political action, peace and prosperity are to be attained.

Index